A Romantic Symphony

A Romantic Symphony

The Autobiography of Howard Hanson

Compiled and edited from manuscript sources by
Vincent A. Lenti

MELIORA PRESS

An imprint of the University of Rochester Press

Copyright © 2024 Vincent Lenti

All rights reserved. Except as permitted under current legislation, no part of this work may be photocopied, stored in a retrieval system, published, performed in public, adapted, broadcast, transmitted, recorded, or reproduced in any form or by any means, without the prior permission of the copyright owner.

First published 2024

Meliora Press is an imprint of the
University of Rochester Press
668 Mt. Hope Avenue, Rochester, NY 14620, USA
www.urpress.com
and Boydell & Brewer Limited
PO Box 9, Woodbridge, Suffolk IP12 3DF, UK
www.boydellandbrewer.com

ISBN-13: 978-1-64825-103-0 (hardcover)
ISBN-13: 978-1-64825-102-3 (paperback)

Library of Congress Cataloging-in-Publication Data

Names: Hanson, Howard, 1896–1981, author. | Lenti, Vincent A., 1938– editor.
Title: A romantic symphony : the autobiography of Howard Hanson / compiled and edited from manuscript sources by Vincent A. Lenti.
Description: Rochester, NY : Meliora press, an imprint of the University of Rochester Press, 2024. | Series: Meliora press ; 39 | Includes bibliographical references and index. | Identifiers: LCCN 2024026535 (print) | LCCN 2024026536 (ebook) | ISBN 9781648251030 (hardback) | ISBN 9781648251023 (paperback) | ISBN 9781805434658 (pdf) Subjects: LCSH: Hanson, Howard, 1896–1981. | Composers—United States—Biography. | Conductors (Music)—United States—Biography. | Eastman School of Music. | LCGFT: Autobiographies.
Classification: LCC ML410.H1825 A3 2024 (print) | LCC ML410.H1825 (ebook) | DDC 780.92 [B]—dc23/eng/20240614
LC record available at https://lccn.loc.gov/2024026535
LC ebook record available at https://lccn.loc.gov/2024026536

*To the memory of Howard Hanson
Director of the Eastman School of Music 1924–64
In recognition of the leadership he provided
as an educator, conductor, and composer,
and with admiration for his lifelong dedication
to the cause of American music.*

CONTENTS

List of Figures		ix
Preface		xi
Introduction		1
1.	Bold Island	12
2.	Nebraska	16
3.	Early Years in Wahoo and Lincoln	25
4.	On the Chautauqua Circuit	30
5.	Studying in New York	35
6.	Studying at Northwestern University	44
7.	Teaching at the College of the Pacific	50
8.	Dean of the Conservatory	55
9.	Prix de Rome	64
10.	At the American Academy	76
11.	Travels in Europe and Composing in Rome	82
12.	An Invitation from Rochester	87
13.	Beginnings in Rochester and the Establishment of N.A.S.M.	100
14.	Joseph Maddy and the National Music Camp	108
15.	Finding Time for Composition	114
16.	Conductors and Orchestras	120
17.	Promoting the Cause of American Music	124
18.	Radio Broadcasts and Recordings	132
19.	Concerts at the Library of Congress	139
20.	The Lament for Beowulf and the First Two Symphonies	143
21.	Return to Rome	149

22. Conducting Concerts in Germany	153
23. A Commission to Write an Opera	157
24. The Metropolitan Opera Production of *Merry Mount*	161
25. Serious Challenges at the Eastman School	175
26. The Death of George Eastman and Rush Rhees's Retirement	181
27. Chautauqua Memories	187
28. Thoughts on Orchestral Conducting	194
29. Working for UNESCO	198
30. Working with University of Rochester Presidents	204
31. The American Society of Composers, Authors, and Publishers	210
32. Experiences with Several American Presidents	215
33. Honorary Doctorates and Other Honors	221
34. Eastman School Students	225
35. An Author and a Lecturer	229
36. An Invitation from the State Department	235
37. The Eastman Philharmonia Tour (I)	247
38. The Eastman Philharmonia Tour (II)	252
39. The Eastman Philharmonia Tour (III)	257
40. The Eastman Philharmonia Tour (IV)	263
41. The Eastman Philharmonia Tour (V)	267
42. The Eastman Philharmonia Tour (VI)	272
43. Encounters With Various Musicians	276
44. Composing During the Nineteen-Fifties	280
45. Reflection at the End of a Long Career	288
Appendix: Letters from Howard Hanson to His Parents	299
Index	323

FIGURES

Figures 1–14 follow p. 91.

1. The Swedish Evangelical Lutheran Church (Augustana Synod) in Wahoo, Nebraska.
2. The Eckstrom family (Hanson's maternal grandparents).
3. The Eckstrom family home in Omaha, Nebraska.
4. Howard Hanson's mother, Hilda Eckstrom, before her marriage.
5. Howard Hanson's father, Hans Hanson.
6. Howard Hanson's mother, Hilda Eckstrom.
7. Howard Hanson's parents.
8. Howard Hanson's parents later in life.
9. Howard Hanson at the age of four.
10. Howard Hanson at the age of eleven (July 4, 1907).
11. Howard Hanson with the Wahoo, Nebraska, singing group "The Jenny Linds."
12. The young Howard Hanson.
13. The young Howard Hanson.
14. A portrait of Howard Hanson (c.1913–15).

Figures 15–25 follow p. 167.

15. Howard Hanson playing the cello.
16. Howard Hanson at his writing desk.
17. A portrait of Howard Hanson (c.1916).
18. Howard Hanson at age twenty-one.
19. Howard Hanson with his overtone analyzer.
20. Howard Hanson with his new goatee and mustache.
21. Howard Hanson in the early 1930s.
22. Howard Hanson composing at the piano in 1934.

23. A studious Howard Hanson in 1936.
24. Howard Hanson in his office at the Eastman School of Music.
25. Howard Hanson conducting.

Figures 26–36 follow p. 238.

26. Howard Hanson with his father.
27. Howard Hanson with his mother in front of Cutler Union in Rochester, New York.
28. Howard Hanson and Margaret Nelson at their wedding.
29. Howard Hanson.
30. Howard Hanson with his mother.
31. Howard and Margaret (Peggie) Hanson.
32. Howard Hanson.
33. Howard Hanson.
34. Howard Hanson conducting the Eastman Rochester Symphony in a recording session.
35. Howard Hanson conducting.
36. Howard Hanson studying a score.

All images courtesy of the Sibley Music Library

PREFACE

In 2005, the Eastman School of Music acquired a collection of material that represented a significant addition to the school's archives and resources relating to Howard Hanson, who had served for forty years as the school's second director.[1] Prominent in this collection, now available in the Ruth T. Watanabe Special Collections of the Sibley Music Library, was material that had represented Hanson's efforts to write an autobiography. These efforts apparently began sometime after his retirement in 1964 and were presumably prompted by interest expressed by *Atlantic Monthly Press* in the possible publication of Hanson's work. By 1971, however, interest in Hanson's autobiography had waned, and the draft of this work remained essentially untouched for about the next thirty-five years.

I became aware of the Hanson manuscript shortly after its acquisition by the Eastman School of Music, being at that time involved in the research and writing of the second volume of my history of the Eastman School of Music, *Serving a Great and Noble Art: Howard Hanson and the Eastman School of Music*.[2] Since this particular volume was mainly concerned with the Hanson years, the newly acquired material was of great interest to me. Although it was uncatalogued at the time, the manuscript of Hanson's autobiography was brought to my attention by special collections librarian David Peter Coppen. Thus, I was able to access at least some material that proved very helpful in the completion of my forthcoming book.

Hanson most likely ended his efforts to write an autobiography in 1971, when *Atlantic Monthly* Press indicated that it was no longer interested in its publication. The autobiography, therefore, remained unfinished and unedited. What remains is a collection of folders containing various drafts, some handwritten, others typed. It would not be terribly inaccurate to say that the project was left in a state of disarray. As the historian of the Eastman School of Music, I decided that I would accept the challenge of putting this material into a fully indexed and readable format that could be made available to researchers and others interested in the life of Howard Hanson.

---

1 In more recent years, the title of the person holding this position has been changed to dean of the Eastman School of Music.
2 University of Rochester Press, 2009.

When Hanson ceased working on his autobiography, the work was divided into forty-five chapters, each ranging in length from about 1,500 words to over 5,000 words. The chapters had no titles, and most of them existed in multiple, undated versions. While it was comparatively easy to dismiss handwritten drafts as being earlier versions, it was sometimes nearly impossible to determine with certainty which of the other versions represented Hanson's final thoughts. Some of the chapters were concisely written, reflecting a process of editing and considerable revision. Others were much more loosely written, sometimes even without an overall coherent structure. There were occasional factual errors, as well as errors in spelling and grammar.

In general, the early chapters are the most polished and most carefully written. They deal with his youth, his studies in Nebraska, New York, and at Northwestern University. They provide interesting commentary concerning his early teaching career in California, his experiences as a winner of the Prix de Rome, and his appointment to the directorship of the Eastman School of Music. In my view, this material is of particular interest and provides the reader with far more insight into Hanson's formative years and early career than anything else previously published or otherwise available to researchers.

These earlier chapters are essentially chronological, but the later chapters tend to be more topical in nature. While some of the topics are certainly of considerable interest, there is a lack of continuity to the story he is relating. What is most striking isn't his choice of topics but rather what he has omitted. Especially absent from his narrative is any in-depth description of his experiences as director of the Eastman School of Music. He offers a few interesting comments about the school in the 1920s, discusses with perhaps unusual candor his experiences working with the various presidents of the University of Rochester, and offers a few pertinent pages concerning several of his composition students.

The only story of the Eastman School of Music told in any detail is that of the 1961–62 tour of the Eastman Philharmonia to Europe, the Middle East, and Russia, a topic for which Hanson devoted about ten thousand words divided into six chapters. He was especially proud of the Philharmonia tour, which he probably viewed as the culmination of his many years at the Eastman School. Except for this, however, Hanson is largely silent about his experiences for four decades as director of the school. One can only conclude that he was quite determined to write about himself and not about the school. This may have been partly due to a general reticence to discuss his Eastman colleagues, many of whom were still alive (and many still teaching) at the time he was drafting the story of his life and career.

Whatever his reasoning, the reader will find little institutional history in this volume. It is about Hanson, not about the school.

In addition, the reader will not find much controversy, misgivings, or even any substantial critical commentary. His alleged feud with Aaron Copland is not mentioned, nor is the mutual animosity that certainly existed between Hanson and Rochester native David Diamond. There is surprisingly little comment about the direction of musical composition, especially in the years near the end of his career. His disdain for atonality was well known to everyone, but it is not really a topic that he chooses to discuss in much detail, except perhaps indirectly in his general defense of romanticism.

Howard Hanson's autobiography might have been a very different book had he personally prepared it for publication under careful editorial guidance. Unfortunately, this was not the history of the project, and, for this reason, we are perhaps denied the benefit of his thoughts on many topics to which he could have brought valuable insight and commentary. Nonetheless, there is much of interest in his writing, and the work provides a valuable picture of a man who was so influential in music and education during his lifetime. This exercise in autobiography presents the opportunity to read about Howard Hanson and the things in his life that mattered most to him.

As mentioned, Hanson's manuscript is divided into forty-five chapters. Unfortunately, no draft of chapter 27 has been located. This is regrettable because this missing chapter was apparently concerned with his compositional activities during the 1930s. Because of this missing chapter, the chapters in this volume correspond to Hanson's own chapter arrangement from chapter 1 through chapter 26. Chapters 27 through 44 correspond to Hanson's chapters 28 through 45. In addition, this publication includes a final chapter that was not part of Hanson's original organization of his material but that he left with the various drafts of his autobiography.

In editing Hanson's manuscript, I have adopted certain guidelines. The first has been to maintain his chapter organization and to give each chapter a title that generally reflects the main topic about which he is writing. I have made appropriate corrections to spelling and grammar, and I have made what I trust is an improvement in paragraph organization. Any words that have been added to the manuscript are clearly indicated in brackets. Very little has been omitted, mainly confined to redundancies in the text.

Instances where Hanson's facts are in error have been appropriately noted in footnotes rather than corrected in the text itself. Footnotes have also been added to help identify many of the people who are mentioned by

Hanson, as he is reflecting upon the various individuals whom he encountered during his long and illustrious career. Yet, editorial additions and corrections have been limited as much as possible. The main philosophy has been to allow Howard Hanson to relate his own story in his own words.

Working on this project has provided a wonderful opportunity to reflect upon the man who was director of the Eastman School of Music when I arrived in 1956 as a freshman. He was certainly the dominant personality at the school during my student days. I had the pleasure of meeting with him on several occasions, but not being a composer meant that I never had the opportunity of studying with him.

Seven years after I had first walked into the school, Hanson offered me a position on the faculty. That offer was made rather casually in the main hall of the school, without apparent need of resumé or interview. Such was the way many faculty appointments were made in those days. Thus, I served as a new faculty member during Hanson's final academic year at the school. His retirement in 1964, however, did not bring an end to his presence at Eastman, and we came into contact with one another from time to time. Nonetheless, he was always "Dr. Hanson." It would have been quite impossible for me to call him "Howard."

As the years passed, I came to view Hanson with more objectively than I did in my student days or even in my early years as a member of the faculty. Moreover, my more recent role as historian at the Eastman School of Music has provided an ever-increasing appreciation for his role in guiding the school into a position of international prominence. He was by no means a man without faults, but his influence as an educator and as a proponent of American music was simply enormous. Therefore, his autobiography is important by adding to our understanding and appreciation of this very remarkable man.

Vincent A. Lenti
June 2023

INTRODUCTION

Howard Harold Hanson was born on October 28, 1896, in Wahoo, Nebraska, the son of Hans Hanson and Hilda Eckstrom. Hanson was of Swedish ancestry on both sides of his family. Hans Hanson, the son of a Nebraska farmer, owned a hardware, plumbing, and heating store in Wahoo. Hilda Eckstrom's father had been the foreman of Paxton & Vierling Ironworks in Omaha, Nebraska. She was very musically inclined with a fine singing voice and was Howard Hanson's earliest music teacher. The family members were all congregants at the local Swedish Evangelical Lutheran Church, and the experience of being raised in a strong Christian family remained of significant importance throughout Hanson's life.

Hanson's gift for music was apparent from an early age, and he obtained permission at the age of seven to study as a special music student at nearby Luther College. At the age of fourteen, he became a regular student at the college. Earning a diploma from Luther College, he was then permitted to register at the University School of Music in Lincoln, Nebraska, commuting there to take courses on weekends even before he had graduated from high school. He subsequently graduated as valedictorian of his high school in Wahoo, and the commencement program on May 20, 1912, included a performance by the young graduate of his newly composed *Fantasia in A Minor for Piano*. His earliest compositions probably date from his high school years, and surviving documents include a copyright that he obtained in 1913 for *To the Queen of Hearts*, a song for mezzo-soprano based on words by Shelley.

A powerful influence on Hanson was his involvement with the Chautauqua movement, the popular tent shows that brought cultural and educational programs to many small towns. His involvement with the Chautauquans, first as a pianist and cellist and later as a coach, began during summers when he was still in high school. Among those with whom he toured the Midwest was the famous American statesman and orator William Jennings Bryan, who profoundly influenced the young, impressionable musician from Wahoo.

In the fall of 1914, Hanson went to New York City to pursue more advanced musical studies. Although his original intention was to study at Columbia University, he soon enrolled at the Institute of Musical Art (later to become the Juilliard School of Music), where he studied piano with James Friskin and composition with Percy Goetschius. While in New York,

Hanson stayed with his uncle and aunt, Carl and Marion Eckstrom, who lived on Riverside Drive. The Ecktroms also owned a farm in Seymour, Connecticut, which Hanson visited on a number of occasions.

Following another summer on the Chautauqua circuit, Hanson enrolled in the fall of 1915 for degree study at Northwestern University, from which he graduated with a bachelor of music degree the following June. This was the only academic degree that Hanson ever earned. While at Northwestern, he served as an assistant teacher. The graduation concert, held on June 8, 1916, included a performance of his *Prelude and Double Concert Fugue in E Minor, Op.1*, written for two pianos and performed by the composer and Carl M. Beecher. Other works dating from his year of study at Northwestern include *Three Songs for High Voice, Op.2* and *Three Songs from Walt Whitman, Op.3*.

In the fall of 1916, when Hanson was not quite twenty years old, he accepted an appointment as a full professor at the College of the Pacific, then located in San José, California. Founded in 1851 as the University of the Pacific, it was for decades primarily an undergraduate liberal arts college. It was renamed the College of the Pacific in 1911. Among Hanson's early interests was the study of acoustics, and his continued fascination with the subject led to his invention of an "overtone analyzer." This device was the subject of an article in the September 22, 1917, issue of *Scientific America*, as well as additional articles in other journals of the time.

Three years after arriving in San José, Hanson was named dean of the Pacific Conservatory at the College of the Pacific, succeeding Warren Allen, who left to take up new duties at Stanford University. In December of the following year, he was selected by Music Teachers National Association (MTNA) to represent the entire Pacific Coast on a commission to investigate schools of music in the United States, this being perhaps his earliest involvement in the larger national issues facing college-level music education in America. At the same time, he maintained a steady flow of compositions, including the *Quintet in F Minor, Op.5*, which received its premiere at the college in 1919; the symphonic poem *Before the Dawn, Op.17*; and his ambitious *California Forest Play of 1920, Op.16* for solo voices, chorus, dancers, and orchestra. The latter work was the first composition by Hanson to receive national attention.

In May of 1921, Hanson presented a Festival of American Music at the College of the Pacific. This festival of four concerts, culminating in a program presented by the Los Angeles Philharmonic Orchestra, was a major initiative in promoting the cause of America composers, and was followed by a second festival in December of the same year. A month earlier, however, newspapers carried the important announcement that Hanson had

Introduction 3

been awarded the Prix de Rome, which would provide him with a three-year fellowship at the American Academy in Rome. Hanson's selection as the recipient of the fellowship had been made by a four-member jury and was based upon his submission of scores for *California Forest Play* and *Before the Dawn*. He was the first American composer selected by a jury established by academy.

Hanson arrived in Rome that fall and took up residence at the academy. The fellowship provided a stipend for living expenses and for travel. It was expected that students at the academy—musicians, sculptors, painters, architects—would spend half of their time in Rome and the remaining time traveling throughout Europe. Therefore, in July 1922 the music department at the academy concluded its six-month season, and Hanson departed on six months of travel to major musical centers in Europe, extending his travels to include Sweden and England. This was a particularly enriching experience for the young composer. The travels also provided opportunities to meet important European musicians, among them being the conductor Albert Coates, who would have an important role in bringing Hanson to the Eastman School of Music several years later.

The fellowship provided studio and living quarters plus funds for food, clothing, and travel. Hanson, therefore, was allowed to completely devote himself to composition while in Rome. There were no classes to attend or courses to take. Although it is frequently claimed that he studied with Respighi, his contacts with the Italian composer were informal in nature as well as being infrequent. Respighi was among many musicians who frequently visited the academy.

Sometime during the fall of 1923, Walter Damrosch, conductor of the New York Symphony Orchestra, visited the academy and asked Hanson to come to New York to conduct the first performance of his *North and West, Op.22*, which he had written the previous year. The return to America brought an unexpected invitation to come to Rochester for a private meeting with Rush Rhees, president of the University of Rochester, and George Eastman, the founder of Eastman Kodak Company, who had recently embarked on an ambitious project to establish a major music school in Rochester.

The Eastman School of Music, established as a school of the University of Rochester, had opened only two years earlier in September 1921. Rhees and Eastman were searching for a new director for the school, and Hanson's name had been suggested by Albert Coates. They asked the young American composer to submit a letter expressing his personal views and opinions concerning how to develop a professional music school within the context of a university. Hanson eagerly complied with their request.

Soon after his meeting with the two Rochester leaders, Hanson conducted the New York Symphony Orchestra in his *North and West, Op.22*, and later returned to Rochester to conduct his new Symphony No.1, Op.21 ("Nordic"), with the Rochester Philharmonic Orchestra. This impressive work had received its premiere performance in Rome the preceding year, with Hanson conducting Augusteo Symphony Orchestra.

Returning to Rome after his appearance with the Rochester Philharmonic Orchestra, he soon received a letter from Rush Rhees dated April 16, 1924, offering him the directorship of the music school. In spite of advice from various friends and professional acquaintances cautioning him to not accept such an arduous and time-consuming administrative responsibility, Hanson accepted the offer. Many people worried that the position would interfere with Hanson's compositional activities, a fear that the young composer shared to some extent. Nonetheless, he accepted Rhees's offer, and in September of 1924 he began what would eventually be a forty-year tenure at the helm of the Eastman School of Music.

The selection of Howard Hanson to be director was an audacious one. Not quite twenty-eight years old, Hanson's administrative experience was limited to his three years as dean at the College of the Pacific. The challenges in Rochester would be infinitely greater. The Eastman School of Music in 1924 was staffed primarily by European-trained musicians, and its students, who came principally from the Rochester area, were mainly working toward a diploma rather than a university degree. To develop a faculty, curriculum, and student body worthy of the facilities and endowment provided by George Eastman required a man of extraordinary vision and ability, and Howard Hanson proved to be such a man.

The new director at Eastman immediately found himself involved with the newly established National Association of Schools of Music (NASM), being invited to its first meeting in Pittsburgh on October 24, 1924. Hanson was selected as chair of its commission on curriculum, and he held this influential position until 1933. The association was concerned with the establishment of national standards for undergraduate and graduate music degrees, and Hanson's leadership of the curriculum commission placed him in a position to be perhaps the single most important person in the development of those standards. Shortly after stepping down from the leadership of the curriculum commission, Hanson became president of NASM, holding that position from 1935 to 1939.

As director of the Eastman School of Music, Hanson involved himself in strengthening the school's theory program and provided the leadership to move undergraduate studies from a European-style diploma program to a curriculum leading to a bachelor of music degree. He immediately embraced the school's existing cooperation with radio station WHAM, a venture that had been established to provide live music broadcasts from the school. In time, the broadcasts took on a more educational nature, culminating in the late 1930s with Hanson's highly imaginative series entitled Milestones in the History of Music. Eventually, regular radio broadcasts from the Eastman School of Music came to an end in the face of determined opposition from the Musicians' Protective Association of the American Federation of Labor, which insisted that only union members could take part in such activities. Nonetheless, his involvement in radio broadcasting brought serious music to countless numbers of listeners throughout the country and, not coincidentally, enhanced the reputation and prestige of the Eastman School of Music.

Hanson's passionate advocacy for American music, which had already been in evidence during his tenure at the College of the Pacific, needed little time in manifesting itself in Rochester. In December of his first year as director, Hanson proposed to Rush Rhees that the school present two concerts of music by American composers. Although only one such concert was given during the 1924–25 school year, the event marked the beginning of the annual American Composers' Concerts, which provided an important venue for music that was being unduly neglected by other performing organizations in the United States.

In May 1931, Hanson presented a Festival of American Music, which became an annual event at the Eastman School of Music through May of 1971. The first such festival took place over four days at the school and was presented in commemoration of the school's tenth anniversary. The festivals, along with the American Composers' Concerts, were arguably Hanson's most important achievement as an educator. Nearly five hundred American composers had their works performed in Rochester at a time when other opportunities for performance of these works were limited at best. In selecting works for performance, Hanson showed extreme fairness, even performing the works of several American composers with whom he had a less-than-cordial personal relationship.

Although Hanson had been concerned that the directorship of the school might curtail or interfere with his own compositional activities, his early years at Eastman saw the completion and first performance of many of his finest and most noteworthy works. His *Quartet in One Movement, Op.23*, which he had written in 1923 after receiving a commission from the Elizabeth Sprague Coolidge Foundation, was given its premiere at the Library of Congress in Washington, DC, on October 30, 1925. His *Lament for Beowulf, Op.25*, for chorus and orchestra—a work that he had begun in Rome—was completed in 1925 and received its first performance at the

Ann Arbor (Michigan) Festival on May 25, 1926, with Hanson conducting the University of Michigan Choral Union and the Chicago Symphony Orchestra. The symphonic poem *Pan and the Priest, Op.26*, was presented in London on September 28, 1926, by the Queen's Hall Orchestra under the direction of Sir Henry Wood.

Among his many professional associations, none was more important to Hanson than his friendship with Serge Koussevitzky, director of the Boston Symphony Orchestra. Koussevitzky was an enthusiastic advocate for Hanson's music. He invited Hanson to conduct his Symphony No.1, Op.21 ("Nordic"), in Boston on April 5, 1928. Soon afterward, Koussevitzky commissioned a new symphony for the occasion of the fiftieth anniversary of the Boston Symphony Orchestra. The work that Hanson produced was his Symphony No.2, Op.30 ("Romantic"), most likely the best-known and most admired of his symphonic compositions. The work received its premiere in Boston on November 28, 1930. Three years later, it was performed on March 1, 1933, by the New York Philharmonic under the direction of Arturo Toscanini. In addition, Hanson personally led performances of the symphony with the Toronto Symphony in 1935 and the Hollywood Bowl Orchestra in 1937.

The *Romantic Symphony* will always be associated with the National High School Orchestra and Band Camp in Interlochen, Michigan. Founded in 1928 by Joseph E. Maddy, the summer program at Interlochen has provided countless numbers of students with a uniquely enriching educational experience. Among those associated with Interlochen from its earliest years was Howard Hanson, and it was at Interlochen that he wrote part of the symphony. He first conducted the work there in the summer of 1931, only a year after its premiere in Boston, and he presented the theme of the work to the camp to be used as a broadcast signature and theme. Many Eastman faculty members taught at Interlochen during the summer months, and the camp became an important source of undergraduate students for the school, something that Hanson carefully nurtured.

Perhaps the most significant compositional activity for Hanson in the 1930s was in response to a request from Metropolitan Opera that he write the music for an opera. Richard L. Stokes had been commissioned to write a libretto on an American subject, and Hanson was asked to set the libretto to music. Stokes's libretto was based on Nathaniel Hawthorne's *The Maypole of Merry Mount*. Hanson's opera, entitled *Merry Mount*, was given its premiere by the Metropolitan Opera Company on Saturday afternoon, February 10, 1934. Audience response was highly enthusiastic, and the opera received fifty curtain calls, a record that still stands. New York critics generally welcomed the new work with positive reviews in the city's newspapers.

Hanson had been an exceedingly busy man during his first decade as director of the Eastman School of Music. The development and improvement of the school curriculum and faculty occupied much time, and enrollment in the school's collegiate programs grew accordingly. In spite of these responsibilities, however, he still directed his energies to other matters, including finding time to compose, exercising critical leadership in the activities of the NASM, and becoming perhaps the leading advocate in the country for music by American composers. Especially in the latter capacity, Hanson was active throughout the years as a guest conductor of important orchestras such as the New York Philharmonic, the Boston Symphony, the Philadelphia Orchestra, and the Cleveland Orchestra. In addition, he conducted in Europe in early 1933, appearing with the Berlin Philharmonic and several other German orchestras on a tour funded by the Oberlander Trust of the Carl Shultz Foundation.

Hanson's great advocacy of American music found a new outlet when he was able to negotiate an agreement with RCA Victor to produce a series of recordings of music by American composers. The first of these was released in 1939 and featured music by John Knowles Paine, Kent Kennan, George W. Carpenter, Edward MacDowell, and Charles Tomlinson Griffes. Although World War II interrupted the project, Hanson was able to record twenty-seven works by nineteen different composers over a period of about four years.

Hanson's arrangement with RCA Victor was not the only interest he showed in audio recordings. In 1934 he established a recording department at the Eastman School to provide permanence to some of the music being performed by students and faculty at the school. This surely was one of the earliest such initiatives anywhere in the country.

Hanson managed to balance all his activities with remarkable efficiency and always seemed to find time for composing. Between the years 1936 and 1938 Hanson completed his Symphony No.3, Op.33, which had been commissioned by the C.B.S. Symphony. Hanson conducted a performance of the first three movements with the C.B.S. Symphony on September 19, 1937, and the entire work was officially premiered on March 15, 1938, with the composer conducting the N.B.C. Symphony. The work was subsequently recorded by Serge Koussevitzky and the Boston Symphony Orchestra. At a later date, Hanson revised the symphony to include a choral finale, and this revision was first performed by the Rochester Philharmonic Orchestra under Hanson's direction on October 31, 1957.

Perhaps more significant was his Symphony No.4, Op.34 ("The Requiem"), written during the years 1940 through 1943 and first performed on December 3, 1943, with Hanson leading the Boston Symphony Orchestra. The work received several other important performances, including by the NBC Symphony on January 2, 1944, under the direction of Leopold Stokowski, and by the Philadelphia Orchestra on January 30, 1944, with the composer on the podium. Hanson was awarded the 1944 Pulitzer Prize for music for this important work.

At about the same time, Hanson met Margaret (Peggie) Nelson at her parents' home in Chautauqua, New York. Nearing his fiftieth year, Hanson had remained a life-long bachelor, but he fell in love with Peggie, and they were married in Chautauqua on July 24, 1946. Part of his courtship of Peggie involved dedicating to her his new *Serenade for Flute, Harp, and Strings, Op.35*. The piece received its first performance on October 25, 1945, with Georges Laurent as flute soloist with the Boston Symphony Orchestra under the direction of Serge Koussevitzky.

After the end of World War II, Hanson attempted to revive his association with RCA Victor, but he eventually turned to Columbia Records with whom he recorded three long-playing (33 rpm) records. These included performances of the MacDowell Piano Concerto with Jesús María Sanromá as soloist, and Hanson's own Piano Concerto played by the Czech pianist, Rudolph Firkusny. Hanson's concerto had been completed in 1948, and it was Firkusny who had premiered the work with the Boston Symphony on December 31, 1948. In the early 1950s, Hanson was approached by Mercury Records with a generous offer for a series of recordings of American music. It was an opportunity that he could not refuse, and in the ensuing years Mercury released over forty long-playing records in association with Hanson, creating an important recorded legacy of works by American composers.

During his long tenure as director at Eastman, Hanson had also taught composition, and in this role, he guided a generation of young American composers. Among his students were William Bergsma, Emma Lou Diemer, Kent Kennan, John LaMontaine, Peter Mennin, Ron Nelson, and H. Owen Reed. He was also a frequent speaker to various musical and educational organizations, as well as the author of numerous articles that appeared in various journals throughout his career. The great diversity of his professional activities led to many honors, including the 1945 Ditson Conductor's Award for his commitment to American music and the 1946 George Foster Peabody Award in recognition for his radio programming the preceding year. A decade earlier, he had been elected to membership in the National Institute of Arts and Letters. During his long tenure at the Eastman School of Music, he also was awarded thirty-six honorary doctorates.

At the school, Hanson was continually involved in faculty recruitment and curricular matters. Early in his career, he initiated steps that led to the awarding of a master of music degree at the school. And in 1951, he discussed with the Eastman faculty the possibilities of offering a new professional doctorate, quite distinct from the existing doctor of philosophy degree already being awarded in academic music areas such as musicology. His purpose was to offer a terminal degree for the professional musician, especially the performer. His proposal for such a degree was approved in 1952, and this decision moved the Eastman School of Music into the forefront of schools that would soon begin offering the new doctor of musical arts degree.

His compositional activities continued throughout the 1950s, including the completion of his Symphony No.5, Op.43 ("Sinfonia Sacra"), which was given its premiere on February 18, 1955, by Eugene Ormandy and the Philadelphia Orchestra. This was followed the next year by the premiere of *Elegy, Op.44*, which had been commissioned by the Koussevitzky Foundation, and written in memory of his friend, Serge Koussevitzky, who had died in 1951. The premiere was appropriately in Boston, given by the Boston Symphony Orchestra under the direction of Charles Munch.

Another work of this period was the *Song of Democracy* for mixed chorus and orchestra, written in 1956 and based on texts of Walt Whitman. This work, which proved to be very popular among choral groups throughout the country, had been commissioned by the National Education Association (NEA) for their 100th anniversary and the 50th anniversary of Music Educators' National Conference (MENC). It was given its premiere in Washington, DC, by the National Symphony Orchestra and Howard University Chorus under Hanson's direction. The audience of educators gathered for the occasion numbered 23,000.

Meanwhile at the Eastman School of Music, Hanson's young colleague Frederick Fennell had created the Eastman Wind Ensemble in 1952, an elite performing group that was smaller than existing symphonic bands because of the elimination of unnecessary doublings. Fennell reasoned that the smaller group would have fewer problems in intonation and far greater clarity of sound, and the result of his vision was a virtuoso group consisting of the best available players at the school, chosen without consideration of seniority.

Fennell's initiative was not lost on Hanson. In the fall of 1958, he assembled a group of about sixty-five orchestral players, also representing the best available instrumentalists. The new orchestra at the Eastman School of Music was named the Eastman Philharmonia, and it gave its debut performance under Hanson's leadership on October 24, 1958. In the summer of 1961, the US Department of State selected the Eastman Philharmonia to undertake an unprecedented three-month tour of the Middle East, Europe, and Russia.

The orchestra left Rochester on November 24, 1961, and returned on February 25, 1962, after having visited thirty-four cities in sixteen countries, presenting forty-nine concerts in ninety-three days. Hanson had invited Frederick Fennell to share in the conducting responsibilities, but he chose to conduct thirty-seven of the concerts, leaving only nine for his younger colleague. The men shared responsibilities for three of the performances. The Eastman Philharmonia was the first student orchestra to be invited to tour Europe during the regular concert season, and its concerts were met with great enthusiasm, especially in the Soviet Union. The orchestra's concerts in the Soviet Union took place during the height of the Cold War. Among the works frequently performed during the tour was Hanson's Symphony No.2 ("Romantic"). In many respects the Philharmonia tour represented the culmination of Hanson's career as educator, composer, conductor, and advocate for American music.

Hanson's final years as director at Eastman have often been mischaracterized as being relatively unproductive. In truth, he showed considerable initiative in several new areas, of which the establishment of the Eastman Philharmonia is but one example. In 1955, he was instrumental in establishing the school's first Collegium Musicum. His interest was to provide musical performances to correlate with the school's graduate-level music literature courses. The music performed, therefore, could range from Gregorian chant to late nineteenth-century chamber music.

A few years later, Hanson reacted with enthusiasm to a proposal to establish a church music department at the school. The department began offering graduate courses in 1959 leading to a master's or doctoral degree. Then, in 1960, Hanson published *The Harmonic Materials of Modern Music*, with the subtitle "Resources of the Tempered Scale," one of the earliest treatises on what became known as set theory. His purpose was to analyze all possible combinations of tones in the equally tempered twelve-tone scale.

Two years after the Eastman Philharmonia returned from its acclaimed tour, Hanson stepped down as director of the Eastman School of Music, being replaced in the fall of 1964 by Walter Hendl. At the time of his retirement, however, he was named director of a new Institute of American Music, which would be funded by the University of Rochester and would be dedicated to the continuation of efforts to promote American music through scholarship, performance, publication, and recordings. The annual Festival of American Music continued after his retirement until 1971.

Hanson remained active as a composer in his later years. His Symphony No.6, written in 1967, was given its premiere the following year on February 28, 1968, by the New York Philharmonic, which had commissioned the work. His final symphony, the Symphony No.7 ("Sea Symphony"), was completed in 1977, four years before his death. This work was commissioned by the National Music Camp to celebrate its fiftieth anniversary. Hanson dedicated it to his late friend, Joseph E. Maddy, and conducted the first performance in Interlochen, Michigan, on August 7, 1977. The symphony was composed for chorus and orchestra, and its three movements featured texts by Walt Whitman.

Howard Hanson died in Rochester on February 26, 1981. He is remembered as a composer with a long list of important commissions, an educator whose vision and leadership moved the Eastman School of Music to a position of international prominence, and a teacher who guided a generation of young composers. His efforts to establish standards for undergraduate and graduate music education in the United States represent one of his most lasting accomplishments. But most of all, Howard Hanson should be remembered as the leading advocate of his generation for the cause of American music. American music never had a more effective champion nor a more eloquent spokesman.

Chapter One

BOLD ISLAND

Bold Island is two miles due east, out to sea, from Deer Island, Maine. Forming an almost perfect circle in the blue Atlantic, its seventy acres rising to a rock-crusted peak 110 feet above the sea, it looks down upon its fellow islands to the west as a benevolent monarch. Its "boiling springs," which furnish fresh water to the sailing ships passing "down east," or "up to" Boston, is now protected and encompassed by concrete battlements, but the veteran fishermen around Stonington can remember when its cool, fresh water bubbled out of the rocks only inches from the salt water of the adjacent sea. Its virgin spruce, unsullied by the woodman's saw, axe, and wedge, have probably not changed since the days when Maine was a part of Massachusetts, and the great trees looked across the water to see the Maine regiment marching to the War Between the States.

Bold Island belonged to my Uncle Carl—Carl Magnus Eckstrom. He and his two brothers and four sisters—including my mother, Hilda Amanda Christina Eckstrom—had come to the United States with their parents, Per and Hanna Eckstrom, from Skåne, Sweden, settling in Omaha, Nebraska. About the same time my paternal grandfather and grandmother, Hans and Hanna Hanson, left the same Swedish province with their children—among them my father, Hans Hanson—and settled in Wahoo, Nebraska.

I have said that Bold Island belonged to my Uncle Carl, but it would be more exact to say that my uncle belonged to Bold Island, so deeply did he come under the island's spell. How the island came into his possession is in itself a "small-world" story. I had been visiting Islesford, Maine, at the home of the late Rush Rhees, then president of the University of Rochester. Returning to Boston on the side-wheeler, the "Rockland," I was approached by a real estate agent. He had in his portfolio pictures of a number of islands for sale. Would I be interested? I explained that I had no money with which to buy an island! Being a good salesman, he pressed upon me pictures of one island, named Bold, explaining that I might have friends who would be interested. On my return, I told Uncle Carl about my experience. He said that he had always wanted an island. He would become king of his own island. A few weeks later, Bold Island was duly deeded to my uncle in a formidable document which recounts in detail the passage of the island from owner to owner under the protective seal of the State of Massachusetts.

Uncle Carl was an actor, quite a good one. He had played successfully on Broadway and had been a leading man in plays with a number of famous actresses, including Grace George.[1] He had played Shakespeare with Margaret Anglin.[2] His versatility could be attested to by his success in such diverse parts as that of David in the biblical play, *The Shepherd King*, and that of the cat in Mary Roberts Rinehart's famous mystery, *The Cat and the Canary*.[3]

As a student at the American Academy of Dramatic Arts, he had been a fellow student and roommate of Cecil B. DeMille.[4] Mr. DeMille had tried to lure him to Hollywood in the early days of motion pictures, but my uncle, something of a purist and also, I am afraid, a bit lazy, spurned the celluloid circuit and stayed on Broadway. He married Marion Brooks Frothingham of Boston, of whom I was very fond. Eventually, he retired and spent the springs and summers on his farm near Seymour, Connecticut, and [on] Bold Island.

Uncle Carl was a colorful character with a puckish sense of humor. He had two favorite nephews: Richard Eckstrom, the son of his brother Dr. Edward Eckstrom, and me. When he was with Richard, Uncle Carl would spend hours extolling my virtues. When he was with me, he would spend equal time boasting of Richard's talents. It was not until many years later that the two of us, comparing notes, discovered Uncle Carl's subtle psychological technique. It is a miracle that his two favorite nephews did not come to hate one another cordially.

Uncle Carl was reasonably modest about his own accomplishments, but an inveterate boaster on the subject of his nephews' abilities. I recall going with him one noon for luncheon at his favorite club, the "Lambs," a great meeting place for men of the theatrical profession. When I was introduced to his cronies, I could tell from the looks on their faces that

---

1   Grace George (1879–1961), actress, director, and translator. She made her debut in 1894 and was instrumental in introducing American audiences to many of the plays of George Bernard Shaw.

2   Margaret Anglin (1876–1958), Canadian-born American actress. She made her debut in 1894 and became a dominant dramatic actress in productions of classic Greek tragedies.

3   Hanson is in error in attributing *The Cat and the Canary* to Mary Roberts Rhinehart. It was a stage play by John Willard (1885–1942).

4   Cecil B. DeMille (1881–1959), Academy Award-winning film director. Among his films were *The Greatest Show on Earth* (1952) and *The Ten Commandments* (1956), the former winning an Academy Award for Best Picture.

they had heard of me before and often! I assured them that they had my deepest sympathy!

Uncle Carl also had his full share of whimsy. Richard loved the island, and I, a Nebraska landlubber, loved the farm in Connecticut. In his will, Uncle Carl left the farm (which I loved) to Richard, and the island (which Richard loved) to me. There was also a bequest for a fur coat. At an earlier time, after I had conducted orchestras in the United States and Europe, he announced his firm conviction that no symphony conductor could be complete without a fur coat. I replied that I had no need for such a garment. (I now owned one thanks to the bequests in Uncle Carl's will.)

And so today, my wife and I sit on the porch of our cottage on Bold Island, looking south over the sea, wondering how we came here and pondering the mysteries of art, of the sea, the island, and of life—mysteries that are probably identical.

My wife has conferred upon me the double title of king and skipper of the fleet—one small motorboat and one rowboat. She is, of course, queen and first mate of the crew. The crew consists of two Irish terriers, Tamara Malenkaya and Peter Bolshoi, highly unsuitable names for the Irish and probably not acceptable to the kennel club (where they were never registered). But they were born while we were conducting symphony concerts in Russia for the State Department, and the names seemed appropriate.

Living is primitive on Bold Island. Water comes from the bubbling spring brought up in buckets by manpower. Plumbing is not, and light for the evening comes from the same kind of kerosene lamps that served our grandparents. The only concessions to civilization are bottled gas for cooking and heating, making ice for preprandial libations, and a marine telephone for outgoing calls only.

But the view across the waters and to the islands with their fanciful names—"Enchanted," "Single," "Shivers," "Coots," and the rests—is breathtaking in its beauty to be challenged only by the myriad of wildflowers, daisies, "paintbrushes," and the like, which make a white and gold carpet fit for a king and good for a wandering [troubadour].

The air is filled with the argumentative scolding of the gulls and soothed by the gentle song of the birds from the mainland. Under this kind of nature's tutelage, I do not believe that I shall ever be tempted to write music for the tape recorder or for the digital computer. The rapacious cormorants, the "ravens of the sea," skim the water, and a family of eleven seals on a nearby rock sun themselves and occasionally swim under the watchful eye of grandpa (or perhaps grandma) seal, who is too lazy to swim until the tide rises to make swimming a necessity.

The cottage faces south to the sea. The studio and the tool house, built with our own maladroit skills (but with patient advice, but not always consent, of our friend and mentor, Captain Roy Cook) also faces south to the sea, south toward Devil's Island, and west to Hell's Half Acre. The names of our neighboring islands sound ominous, but they are benign devils, and Hell's Acre is as idyllic a spot as the most saintly of devils could wish. And here, before one of Maine's magnificent panoramas, I sit adding one more, I am sure unnecessary, autobiography to the long list which, if laid end to end, would reach much too far.

From such a vantage point, the frustrations of a composer seem to fade away, the problems of art all seem capable of eventual solutions. The "long look" that takes the eye beyond the islands to the horizon seems to put things in proper perspective, and the magnificent rhythm of the rising and falling of the tides reassures us each day that there must be a greater plan beyond our understanding.

Chapter Two

NEBRASKA

It is a far distance from Bold Island to Carnegie Hall and the Metropolitan Opera House. It is even farther from Wahoo, Nebraska, where I was born on October 28, 1896. Wahoo is a small town and still is, [and] its Indian name is ideal for high school yells:

> Wahoo, Wahoo
> Bazip, bazoo,
> We yell hurrah
> For old Wahoo

I was a small-town boy, and I suppose still am. My father was part owner of a hardware store and plumbing and heating establishment. He was the gentlest man I have ever known, the most sympathetic. Anyone with a hard-luck story found him already listening and the softest of "touches." His fortune at his death was, for the most part, in bills payable but uncollectable.

Years later I was to make a setting of the conclusion of the Anglo-Saxon epic *Beowulf* under the title "The Lament for Beowulf." The final paragraph, in the translation by William Morris and A.J. Wyatt, goes as follows:

> The mildest of all men,
> Unto men kindest,
> To his folk the most gentlest,
> Most yearning of fame.

Whenever I conduct this work, I always think of my father, the mildest and gentlest of men.

His master tinner [i.e., tinsmith] was a real artist named Chris. He could, I am sure, have erected a Taj Mahal out of his bright shining tin. He did construct for me, after my own design, an overtone analyzer which resonated the first sixteen partials of middle C through tubes which protruded from a resonance chamber, like the guns of the *Merrimac* (or was it the *Monitor*?).

Chris's problem was alcohol, and every Saturday night would repair to the local saloon for his weekly celebration. When Chris, who was a powerful Swede, got out of control, the bartender would call my father who would promptly come to the rescue, soothe Chris's belligerence, take him home, and put him to bed. My father never seemed in the least annoyed by this inconvenience. His comment was always, "He is a very fine tinsmith."

My father loved music but had no technical knowledge. My mother, on the other hand, was a talented singer and so interested in music that, even in middle life, she was taking courses in strict counterpoint—which bored me—and supervising my piano practice. She also introduced me, as her accompanist, to the songs of Schumann, Brahms, Hugo Wolf, and Schubert (who was her favorite).

For a small town in the Midwest at the turn of the century, Wahoo was quite remarkable. Nebraska was settled less than two decades before the Civil War. It became a state only in 1867. Wahoo was in all respects a pioneer town. My paternal grandfather was a farmer when a section of prairie land could be had for the asking. Eastern Nebraska is today a delightful country with flowing brooks and thick groves of shade trees on the banks, but my father told me that, when they arrived, the land was virtually barren. Every tree had to be bought and planted. Their first home was a sodhouse on a desolate prairie, and yet at the time of my birth the land had already blossomed, and the fields were rich with corn, wheat, and barley.

According to accounts, I arrived early one stormy morning in late October. I made my appearance a little earlier than expected, very unusual for me.[1] My father was braving the storm hunting for a doctor, so that I arrived in the world through the assistance of a kind German neighbor, Mrs. Jacob Ort, who, having had many children of her own, was justifiably confident of her abilities to perform the duties of midwife in the emergency.

According to the intimate gossip of the day, I was born "under a caul."[2] This, according to my mother, was a sign of special favor. She had lost her first son a few years earlier, and she was determined that her second son should have every advantage which the protective caul and a benevolent Father could provide. No success or honor which came to me in later life ever surprised her. This was as it should be. This is what she expected. Perhaps whatever success which has come to me is due in large part to my desire to live up to my mother's expectations.

---

1   Hanson was notoriously late for appointments and social engagements, a personal trait that he readily acknowledges.
2   A caul is the membrane enclosing the fetus, part of which sometimes is found on the baby's head at birth.

The Scandinavian countries are frequently referred to as matriarchies. In both our family and the family of my material grandparents, the dominant force was that of the mother. My grandmother, too, was a woman of immense strength of character. My grandfather Eckstrom, when I knew him, was foreman in the iron works of Paxton and Vierling. He was, according to all accounts, a most able workman, but outside of the factory he was an artist. He created beautiful patterns in iron. He loved music and poetry and escaped from the pressures of mounting industrialism by playing his beloved violin.

I remember him with a long, flowing, patriarchal beard. Presiding over an iron foundry, I suppose he had to be strong, for automation was still in its infancy. I was always a little in awe of him, although he was a kindly man. On only one occasion can I recall that he scolded me, and for a very interesting reason. He had bought a player-piano, the kind that could be moved up to the piano and which literally "played" the piano with its metal "fingers" encased in rubber. He had also a library of piano "rolls," including much of the classic literature.

This modern apparatus fascinated me. I could sit at the player, determine my own tempo and dynamics, and come out with a very satisfactory performance. I would sit for hours at this contraption. Coming home from work one evening, by grandfather discovered me at the player. He was highly annoyed. "You are able to play the piano yourself. Why do you play with this damnable *apparat*? Play me some Grieg but play it yourself!" I wonder what he would think of the automation of so much of the music of today's youth!

My grandmother did her best to counteract the artistic vagaries of my grandfather, with varying degrees of success. Her concern was that her family should have light, heat, and food. Grandfather would come home with "sets" of Shakespeare, or whatever. Most of these stayed, but there came a day when a truck delivered to the door a large reed organ, which my grandfather could not play. This, in addition to the piano, player-piano, and violin, was too much. Grandmother barred the door. Small but adamant, she ordered the truckers to take it away and not come back. They meekly obeyed. The Eckstrom household was <u>not</u> to have an organ!

I never knew my paternal grandmother. She died at a comparatively early age, but not before she had brought into the world a daughter and seven stalwart sons of whom my father was the oldest. From all accounts, she was a vivacious and attractive lady. Grandfather Hanson was a handsome man with a beautiful Van Dyke beard, which I have since emulated. He was a quiet, reserved, gentle man, whom I greatly admired. I never knew him well, but when my education was in jeopardy for lack of a hundred dollars (not a small amount in those days), he quickly offered me the money. I insisted on paying him back after graduation. I am afraid that he was a little hurt at my insistence, but I was determined to make it on my own power.

Although I began to study music via the piano at the age of seven, and composition only a short time later, it was not until graduation from high school that I definitely decided upon music as a profession. Throughout my school days, I vacillated between the desire to become a Lutheran minister, an historian, a mathematician, a physicist, or a composer.

I am sure, however, that there was never any real doubt about what the eventual goal would be: that of composition. I have always been a "compulsive" composer. It has always seemed imperative that I write music, whether I wanted to or not. I think that this is important, and I have always divided composers into two groups: those who <u>had to</u> compose and those who <u>could</u> compose when they wanted to. This, I believe, is a basic distinction, even though, I must confess, the <u>compulsion</u> to compose does not necessarily guarantee the quality of the composition.

By <u>compulsion</u> I mean the almost physical necessity to write music. In my own case, I know that the expression of my musical thoughts is even a requirement for good health. If, because of pressure of other work, or even from sheer laziness, a certain period of time passes without composition, I become physically as well as mentally uneasy. When I start composing again, my "illness" disappears.

My first composition, written (as I recall) at the age of seven, was the beginning of a Fantasia in A Minor. It was a very short fantasia, a lugubrious little tune for piano, or perhaps for cello and piano. Many years later Serge Koussevitzky[3] suggested that I must be part Russian because my music had so much nostalgia! In any case, I can prove from this little piece that nostalgia began early.

Sensing my interest in a variety of professions, we embarked on a most interesting project. Whether the idea was initiated by my parents or by me, I do not remember, but we were dedicated collaborators. Beginning when I was, I suppose, about nine, we had a program every Sunday afternoon in our music room. Each program began with a short piano recital of my own compositions or improvisations and other favored composers, followed by a "lecture" in which I spoke on subjects related as a rule to religion or to history.

The audience at these events consisted of my mother and father, who sat in unbelievable patience listening to my juvenile message in words and

---

3   Serge Koussevitzky (1874–1951), Russian-born conductor of the Boston Symphony from 1924 to 1949.

music. Recounting this experience almost sixty years later sounds gruesome. The results, however, were that in later years, whether I was speaking to a class of thirty students or to an audience of twenty thousand, the experience of "speaking to" people seemed perfectly natural. It has never occurred to me to be frightened or nervous. Of the effects on my parents of this lecture series, which went on for a number of years, I cannot speak. Since they both lived to a ripe old age, the effects did not prove lethal.

As a student in elementary school and high school, I made a good record, graduating as "valedictorian" of my class. Since, however, the graduating class numbered only thirteen, the competition may not have been too severe. English, history, foreign languages, and physics aroused my greatest interest. My *bete noire* was what was called in those days "manual training." My parents felt that such a practical course, which consisted of working with wood, metals, and the like, would be a valuable broadening influence. One day, the assignment was to plane a board from one-inch thickness to a thickness of seven-eighths of an inch. The result, in my case, was not a board but a wedge. My teacher, Mr. Wicks, being himself an amateur violist, insisted that I drop the course lest my grade in manual training lower too greatly my academic standing! I am sure that, but for Mr. Wicks and his viola, I would not have been valedictorian of the Class of 1913.

Aside from my devotion to music and to academic studies, I was a normal child. I loved to play baseball, football, and particularly basketball, at which (being tall, lean and lanky) I was quite good. Although I was determined to compose, I was like most small boys in that I preferred baseball to practicing the piano. On one occasion, I recall leaving the metronome ticking away while I sneaked out to pitch for the home team. My mother, unfortunately for me and for the team, was not fooled.

Her reaction, however, was a model of good parental psychology. Instead of scolding me for not practicing the piano, she said simply, "If you do not wish to practice, there is no need for you to take piano lessons." That did it! The idea of not being able to go to Professor Peterson for my weekly piano lesson was unthinkable. From that point, I practiced assiduously. The baseball team had to get a new pitcher.

The only experience which really disturbed me, as I now recall, was with the theology of the period. My parents were both Swedish Lutherans, members of the Swedish Lutheran Evangelical Church (of the Augustana Synod). It was distinguished for its excellent music (mostly Bach chorales) and its fearsome insistence on hell and damnation. The long services with the hour-long sermon in which the pastor, from his high pulpit, thundered, "They shall be damned in eternal and everlasting damnation" (which somehow sounded even more menacing in Swedish), were often for me traumatic experiences. I could not understand how a God of love could visit such excruciating punishment upon his children far beyond even the most cruel of human parents. This never turned me from the church but did perhaps greatly influence my decision toward music rather than the ministry.

As far as problems of ethnic background were concerned, we didn't seem to have any. The population of the town seemed to be divided between Swedish Lutherans, who worshipped on the hill, and the Catholics, many of whom were Bohemians, who worshipped downtown. There were, of course, Italians and other ethnic groups of both faiths. There was, as I remember, only one Jew in Wahoo. He was a very nice man who owned a furniture store. There was no prejudice on the basis of color. There were no Negroes and no Asians. To this day, prejudice on the basis of color remains to me un-understandable.

I do recall that, at times, we were referred to as "dumb Swedes," and I am afraid that the Bohemians were sometimes known as "Bohunks" and the Italians as "Wops," but it all seemed to be in good fun. The little town was a real American melting pot, and the communal spirit was, I believe, much friendlier than I have observed it in the United States of today.

I suppose that Wahoo in the early 1900s would [now] be considered culturally underprivileged, but we didn't know it. We joined together at Luther College for performances of Handel, Mendelssohn, and even Bach. Professor Albin Peterson, Wahoo's own maestro and my beloved teacher of piano and theory, instructed me to "take up" the cello, since he had no cello in his orchestra. I immediately did so, studying cello with the violin teacher at the college. It was not until some years later that I found out that I was holding the cello bow like a violinist, the wrong way for a cellist! But I played a great deal of beautiful music and, incidentally, put myself through music school and the university by playing cello on the old Redpath Chautauqua Circuit.

I suppose that a small town puts her mark on all of her sons and daughters. We are probably more naïve and less sophisticated than the sons and daughters of Metropolis. I do not know how my famous colleagues from Wahoo felt about this, for Wahoo has had more than its share of famous sons, among them Nobel Prize winner C.W. Beadle,[4] president of the

---

4 George Wells Beadle (1903–89) shared the 1958 Nobel Prize for Physiology or Medicine with Edward Lawrie Tatum.

University of Chicago; Darryl Zanuck[5] of Hollywood; Sam Crawford[6] of the Baseball Hall of Fame; C.W. Anderson,[7] the artist; and another composer of music, Anthony Donato,[8] now professor of composition at Northwestern University. As for me, whenever I stand before a famous orchestra in a famous concert hall in the United States or Europe, I have that strange feeling that I must be someone else, a feeling best described by the immortal phrase, "Who—me?"

The lads of Metropolis probably have no sense of wonder at the unfolding of the life plan. They have seen it all before. They have at an early age rubbed elbows with the great and near-great. I recall one student of mine who referred, not immodestly but quite casually, to the great artists who came to the home of his parents to play chamber music. By contrast, I was in my teens before I heard my first symphony orchestra, at the expense of a 350-mile drive with my parents in a two-cylinder Maxwell over muddy roads to far-off Kansas City, Missouri. I remember sitting in the gallery, completely fascinated at hearing and seeing for the first time Dvorák's *New World Symphony* delivered by Sir Carl Busch[9] and the Kansas City Philharmonic. My second experience was with the Minneapolis Symphony on tour under the immaculate Emil Oberhoffer.[10] Later in life, I was to become friends with a number of great conductors, but I still remember with awe those first impressions of the knights of the baton, fabulous characters from another world, the flick of whose magic-wand resulted in the most divine music. I must admit that I still stand in awe of them, but more of this later.

---

5   Darryl Zanuck (1902–79), famous movie mogul and founder of 20th Century Fox. He received fifteen Academy Award nominations for Best Picture, winning in 1941 (*How Green Was My Valley*), 1947 (*Gentleman's Agreement*), and 1950 (*All About Eve*).

6   Sam Crawford (1880–1968), legendary outfielder for the Cincinnati Reds and the Detroit Tigers. Known as "Wahoo Sam," he was inducted into the Baseball Hall of Fame in 1957.

7   C.W. Anderson (1891–1971), American artist and writer. He studied at the Art Institute of Chicago and became noted for his drawings of horses; also wrote many popular children's books.

8   Anthony Donato (1909–90), American violinist and composer. He taught at Drake University, Iowa State Teachers College, and the University of Texas before moving to Northwestern.

9   Carl Busch (1862–1942), Danish-born American conductor. He led the Kansas City Symphony 1911–18; taught at the University of Kansas City and at the Kansas City–Horner Conservatory.

10   Emil Oberhoffer (1867–1933), Austrian-born American conductor. He studied piano at the Paris Conservatory and was the organizer and first conductor of the Minneapolis Symphony.

With all of the disadvantages of small towns, I would not exchange this heritage for any other. The very lack of easy opportunities can, in itself, be a challenge to a youngster's ingenuity. I know some of my young friends today who are bored with Beethoven, even when played by the Philadelphia, Boston, or Cleveland orchestras under such superb conductors as Eugene Ormandy,[11] Erich Leinsdorf,[12] or George Szell.[13]

A small-town boy, unsurfeited in youth, preserves, I believe, his youthful enthusiasm far into adult life, and perhaps till death. I found myself just a short time ago moved to tears by a surpassingly beautiful performance of the "Prelude and Love Death" from Wagner's *Tristan and Isolde*, by the Philadelphia Orchestra under Eugene Ormandy. (Perhaps had I been born in New York City, I still would have wept.) A small town also teaches youngsters, as they say, to "make do." My first orchestra was the Wahoo High School Orchestra. The orchestration, as I recall it, consisted of two flutes, one trombone, one bass drum, one snare drum, three violins, one viola, one cello, one double bass, and piano. Our "tour de force" was the overture to Offenbach's *Orpheus in the Underworld*, which we rendered with gusto, the score appropriately arranged by me to fit the restrictions of our ensemble. We even performed it on tour in the metropolis of Fremont, Nebraska, to what I am sure was the edification of its true music lovers.

My ingenuity as an arranger achieved its zenith when I arranged the French horns in Mozart's orchestration of Handel's *Messiah* for saxophones or trombones anointed with derby hats. I am sure that a recording of that performance, if it were available, should mean an end to the annual performances in the United States of Handel's masterpiece.

We have progressed a long way since those early days of the Wahoo orchestra, but the problems persist even in today's music education. The graduates of today's ultra-modern conservatories, with their fully complemented symphony orchestras, are no match for the exigencies of the small-town music supervisor who, even today, must still make bricks without straw.

---

11   Eugene Ormandy (1899–1985), Hungarian-born conductor and violinist. He led the Minneapolis Symphony 1931–36, and then the Philadelphia Orchestra 1936–80.

12   Erich Leinsdorf (1912–93), Austrian-born American conductor. He studied in Salzburg and Vienna; led the Rochester Philharmonic Orchestra 1947–55; subsequently conducted at the Metropolitan Opera and then was conductor of the Boston Symphony 1962–69.

13   George Szell (1897–1970), Hungarian-born conductor. He is best remembered for his long tenure as conductor of the Cleveland Symphony Orchestra 1946–70.

Many of my more sophisticated friends can find happiness only in the Philadelphia or Boston orchestras. I remember my dear friend, Serge Koussevitzky, showing me a letter from a budding young composer who wrote that his score had the opportunity of being performed by a "provincial" orchestra, but that the germination of his creation could be realized only by the Boston Symphony under Serge Koussevitzky. Dr. Koussevitzky, always sympathetic to the young composer, was concerned by the young man's plight. My own reaction was quite unprintable.

This degree of super-sophistication, or hyper-conceit, carries within itself the seeds of its own artistic destruction. The supreme technical performances of our great professional orchestras are beyond description, but there are other values sometimes superbly realized at a lower technical level. I have conducted high school orchestras and choruses which responded with a thrilling enthusiasm, which more than compensated for any minor technical deficiencies and which gave a satisfaction not always realized by our case-hardened professionals.

Chapter Three

EARLY YEARS IN WAHOO AND LINCOLN

In spite of the fact that I have spent a half century as an educator, I have never been a "methodist." The needs of the individual student, his speed of learning and degree of talent vary so greatly that it seems impossible to contrive teaching methods that are applicable to everyone. Some individuals have a built-in talent for teaching, for communicating knowledge, and stimulating intellectual curiosity in their students. Others remain indifferent teachers regardless of the number of hours of credit they amassed in psychology, history, and principles of education, and the like. I am always amused by the fact that, although I have had a part in the education of literally thousands of teachers, I could not legally teach in the public schools of New York State. I have never had a course in history and principles of education!

In my early days as a student, there were comparatively few limiting restrictions. Within reasonable bounds, the student was permitted to proceed as rapidly as his talent, energy, and learning capacity would permit. As a result of this freedom, it was possible for me to follow what today would be considered a highly unorthodox plan of education.

I attended an amazingly good high school in the small town of Wahoo, completing, as I recall, three years of Latin, three of French, three of German, three of mathematics, two of science, and four of history. There was no music "for credit" in the high school. However, I had been allowed to register as a special student in the school of music of Luther College at the age of seven. Later, I was permitted to register as a regular student in the school of music while in high school. My course of study was not limited to performance but included also music history and music theory—even the mysteries of "strict counterpoint."

My musical learning proceeded at such a rapid pace that I graduated from the school at age fourteen, before I had graduated from high school. The diploma from the school of music of Luther College permitted me to register at the University School of Music at Lincoln, Nebraska, before I had attained a high school diploma. Thus, I was able to commute to Lincoln and take special courses on weekends before high school graduation, a dispensation for which I have always been grateful.

Even the high school which, in those days, made no pretense of offering opportunities in the arts, did unexpectedly offer me invaluable experience. We had a small high school orchestra which was at various times under the direction of a teacher of French and, later on at different times, under two teachers of mathematics, both of whom were cornet players. There came a time when an arrangement was needed of a composition which was to be performed at some special occasion. I immediately volunteered for the task. The mathematics teacher generously offered me the chance to rehearse and direct the composition, which I joyously did. I followed this up with an "original" march with the intriguing title, "March of the Thirteenth." The title had to do with the date, not the number of marches! Again, I rehearsed and conducted the performance, which was highly successful.

As a result of these two minor triumphs, the mathematics teacher suggested that, since his teaching schedule was very heavy, I assume the directorship of the orchestra. My decision was hardly in doubt! I conducted not only the orchestra but [also] a gala performance of *H.M.S. Pinafore*, my first introduction to the great team of Gilbert and Sullivan. I recall, with considerable embarrassment, that I must have behaved like a young Arturo Toscanini,[1] scolding the soloists and berating the chorus for their lack of ensemble, and finally storming off the podium in high dudgeon. Why I had any friends left at the end of the dress rehearsal, I shall never know. Probably they thought that all musicians had to be temperamental, and my actions were the natural results of such artistic temperament. In any case, the performance was acclaimed as a brilliant success, and my temperament was forgiven.

My educational experiences in those early days pointed up one fact which has always seemed to me to be incontrovertible: the necessity of combining from an early age both general education and professional training in the arts. This is, I think, especially true of music. I have many friends in academic administration who, even in these enlightened times, believe that a musical education can follow the same pattern as, for example, education in law or medicine. This is utter nonsense. The training of a musician, if it is to be effective, must begin at an early age and be continued throughout life. The idea that a musician can pursue a four-year college course without opportunities for musical studies and then proceed to a professional school for music is excellent in theory but disastrous in practice.

There was one aspect of my "professional" education in those early days which was not so successful and which has plagued me ever since. My

---

1   Arturo Toscanini (1867–1957), noted Italian conductor. His autocratic and temperamental treatment of orchestras was notorious.

parents were never really poor. We had a comfortable home with plenty of the necessities and even a few minor luxuries, but at the end of each year the budget was apt to be a trifle in the red rather than black. When I began the study of the piano at the age of seven, we could not really afford a new piano, so we made do with an old upright that was available.

The old upright had a pleasant tone, but the pin-block which holds the tuning pins was decrepit and would not hold up to pitch. Therefore, the tuner, without the knowledge of my parents, tuned the piano half a tone flat, at which pitch it was possible for him to tune an "even" scale. The results on my hearing were disastrous. When I played the note "C," the sound came out "B!" When I went for my weekly piano lesson on a properly tuned piano, my ear was in a state of hopeless confusion, everything sounding a half-tone higher than I had been accustomed to during the week. I should have had the good sense to tell my parents about my predicament, but I knew that new pianos were expensive.

A few years later, my parents remedied the situation by buying a Henry F. Miller grand piano—secondhand—but the damage had already been done. When I was old enough to be fully aware of the problems involved in having what musicians might call an "ear in B," I made valiant efforts to raise my sense of pitch by a half step. I was only partially successful, and to this day, when I am fatigued, my sense of pitch is inclined to drop a half-step.

This faulty pitch sense has frequently been a source of embarrassment to me as a conductor. The orchestral musician values in a conductor, almost above everything else, a sense of pitch. A conductor without an accurate sense of pitch is, in their minds, as bad as one without a sense of tempo and rhythm. Yet, on a number of occasions, I have found myself telling an orchestral player that he was a half-tone "off" when he was right, and my ear was wrong. In this day of modern piano technicians, this sort of thing would probably not happen. I can only advise parents of musically talented children to have their pianos properly tuned.

If there is any silver lining in this specific cloud, it might be found in the fact that my own personal problem led me to study in detail the problems of so-called absolute pitch or pitch recognition. As a result, we developed at the Eastman School of Music, under the direction of the late Melville Smith,[2] and later under Allen McHose[3] and Ruth Tibbs,[4] one of

---

2   Melville Smith, a Harvard graduate and a teacher of music theory at the Eastman School of Music 1925–32.

3   Allen Irvine McHose, member of the Eastman School of Music theory faculty 1929–67 and chair of the theory department until 1962. He was the author of several theory textbooks used for the undergraduate theory program at the school.

4   Ruth Northrup Tibbs, member of the Eastman School theory department 1924–52.

the finest experimental courses in musical dictation which, I believe, this country has seen. Without my own problem, I am not sure that my interest would have been as intense.

My experience at the University School of Music in Lincoln presented problems of a different nature. I was, as I have said, fourteen at the time, and this was my first exposure to the great outside world. The University School of Music was not at that time an integral part of the University of Nebraska, but an autonomous school operating on the pattern of a foreign conservatory with emphasis almost entirely upon music. Although Lincoln was a rather small city, it was for me a metropolis, and the school of music did have a number of excellent teachers, most of whom came from that mythical region known as "the East."

I studied piano with an excellent concert pianist, Sidney Silber, and [cello] with William Steckleberg, who had been a member of the Chicago Symphony Orchestra, an organization which I was later to come to know very well. As a pianist, I did quite well. I had a natural facility at the keyboard and played major works of Bach, Beethoven, and Brahms with more technical facility than understanding. I had already become a rather unusual score reader for my age and loved to sit at the piano and give a rough-and-ready piano version of the sounds of the orchestral score, an enterprise which still fascinates me.

My problem in Lincoln was not primarily musical but rather philosophical. From my earliest days I had always assumed that the most important thing in any art was creation. I think that, even in those days, I realized the importance to music of the interpreter, but to me the composer was all-important. My reasoning was childishly simple, but I believe still accurate. Who was more important, Beethoven or the men who re-created his music? Obviously, the answer was Beethoven. Even in the area of interpretation it seemed to me that the greatest performer was the one who could bring new, fresh insights into the music, who could discover and reveal new beauties.

More than fifty years later, I still think that I was right. My very able teachers probably would not argue this basic philosophy, but in practice things were quite different. Bach, Beethoven, and Brahms were important, but they were great composers, sanctified by history. It was not necessary for any living composer to try to emulate them. In fact, even the thought of "new" music was in some way sacrilegious. I had the impression that all the great music had been written and that the museum was now full. No more was needed.

Even in the field of interpretation, the same prejudice seemed to persist. My teacher would teach me how his teacher taught him to play Beethoven. Mine not to reason why. My reaction was partially one of rebellion, but I think more one of bewilderment. This was not what I had thought music was. I had always thought of it as a glorious, free art, one calling for man's greatest creativity whether in composition or performance. As I walked along the corridors of the conservatory, I felt very lonely, like a stranger, a foreigner, someone who did not belong.

Later in life, I was to discover that this practice of artistic conformity was by no means limited to the school of music in Lincoln, Nebraska. Actually, it seems to me that, even today, it is the rule rather than the exception. Many years later as director of the Eastman School of Music, it was my duty to preside at innumerable auditions and examinations. Around me would sit the distinguished artists and teachers of the faculty. When the student performed impeccably with the "proper" tempo and dynamics, the faculty all seemed pleased—"excellent tradition." When some hapless student ventured a somewhat "personal" attitude toward the composition—a little faster, a little slower, more rubato, less rubato—the faculty with some exceptions appeared a little amused or even annoyed. On more than one occasion, I felt like saying to the young performer, "Play it your own way!" On a few occasions I did, to the delight of the student and, I'm afraid, the horror of at least some of the faculty.

In my early days as director of the Eastman School of Music, I found the same sterility of repertory that had worried me as a youngster in Lincoln. A venturesome student might, of his own choice, perform a work by a "modernist" such as Debussy, Ravel, or Scriabin. For the most part, we listened to seemingly endless repetitions of the Beethoven *Waldstein*, *Appassionata*, and the *Pathetique* Sonatas, until I almost came to hate my favorite composer.

As the years passed, I was able to arouse, in the most conservative of the faculty, a more adventurous spirit so that at times we even heard music by American composers! I am afraid, however, that in spite of all our efforts, it has been a losing battle. Established artists and teachers, with some obvious exceptions, seem to regard the realm of music as a museum whose doors are closed many years ago to new accessions.

It is over fifty years since the frustration of my student days at the University School of Music in Lincoln. I still believe that my youthful intuition was correct. I cannot believe that a new golden age of music can ever be born on the basis of this museum philosophy. This philosophy does not seem to apply to the graphic arts, but it grievously affects the art of music. The great ages of the past have all been not only periods of creativity but periods when creativity was considered of prime importance. There is much creativity in our land today, but it is not, I am afraid, considered of primary importance. Perhaps this philosophy may change. I fervently hope so.

Chapter Four

ON THE CHAUTAUQUA CIRCUIT

My trips to Lincoln were to have one unexpected result, one which was to influence greatly my future career. Miss Herold, my French teacher in high school (who was also an accomplished singer and pianist), and Mr. Beach, a violinist on the faculty of Luther College, and I formed a violin, cello, and piano trio. When we had achieved, for us, a reasonable degree of competency, we determined to try our wings in recital in Lincoln.

The recital was in a church, and (as I recall) our fee consisted of a "silver offering." I don't remember whether or not the offering covered our expenses, but this was before the days of AGMA,[1] and it didn't make much difference. However, there was in the audience a talent scout for the Chautauqua circuit, famous for his reading of "A Messenger from Mars," a fairly blood-chilling performance which might well have been a precursor of some of our modern television thrillers. I do not know why he was impressed with my performance: probably because I was young and, more importantly, because I could play the piano rather well and the cello acceptably. My cello playing would, I am sure, have appalled my good friends Gregor Piatigorsky,[2] Alfred Wallenstein,[3] and Georges Miquelle.[4] I had barely achieved the "thumb position," but what I lacked in technique I made up in tone and fervor! Pianists were, even in those days, a dime a dozen, but individuals who could play <u>both</u> piano and cello were rare, and I was offered a contract of (as I recall) thirty dollars a week plus traveling expenses to perform for thirteen weeks on the Chautauqua circuit that summer. The Chautauquans of the early part of the century are not to be confused with the famous Chautauqua Institution on the shores of Lake

---

1   Presumably a reference to the American Guild of Musical Artists.

2   Gregor Piatigorsky (1903–76), famous virtuoso cellist; taught at Curtis 1941–49, Boston University 1957–62, and the University of Southern California 1962–76.

3   Alfred Wallenstein (1898–1983), American cellist and conductor; principal cellist in the New York Philharmonic under Toscanini; music director of the Los Angeles Philharmonic 1943–56.

4   Georges Miquelle (1894–1977), French cellist; solo cellist of the Detroit Symphony 1923–54; Eastman School of Music faculty 1954–66.

Chautauqua [in New York State], with which I was later to become deeply involved. The Chautauqua circuits were tent shows which brought cultural attractions to the small towns, primarily in the Middle West. These tent shows were oases in a culturally deprived land. There was, of course, no radio or television, and the only performances possible were "live" performances by traveling musicians, actors, and lecturers.

I was well acquainted with Chautauqua programs since Wahoo had always been a good Chautauqua town. As a matter of fact, I had as a youngster learned a great deal under the Chautauqua tent. When a visiting ensemble—an "orchestra" of perhaps twenty players—would appear, I would invariably appear backstage after the performance and belabor the players with questions about their instruments. "How do you do this, how do you do that? How do you get this effect?" The players were always unbelievably patient and helpful, perhaps sensing my passionate eagerness to increase my knowledge of orchestral instruments. To tell the truth, although I have written five symphonies, I have never taken a course in orchestration! What I know has been acquired by listening and asking innumerable questions. Some of my earliest "instructors" were on the old Redpath Chautauqua circuit.

The pattern of the Chautauqua circuits was a model of logistics. The "crew" would go ahead of the performers setting up the tent and the stage for the following week. The crews were, for the most part, young fellows working their way through college by this form of summer exercise. Perhaps nostalgia has influenced my judgment, but they seemed to me to be a wonderful group of young people. They had, indeed, been carefully selected by the management. They would be a part of the community for more than a week, and the "image" of Chautauqua depended to a considerable extent upon the impression which they made upon the community.

The format of the week's programs followed a rather consistent pattern. It would consist of music, "readings," quasi-dramatic productions, and lectures on history, philosophy, religion, science, politics, in fact almost every topic. The individual programs generally began with a musical program followed by a lecture. This went on throughout the summer, two performances a day, seven days a week. Traveling was at night and early morning, but, somehow, we always seemed to be able to give fourteen performances a week—as I say, a marvel of logistics!

My first experience was with a company of four. The company consisted of Dolly MacDonald, reader and pianist; Liela Lowe, violinist; Adele Lawson, flutist; and myself appearing both as piano soloist and cellist in the violin, flute, cello, and piano quartet. We would present several ensemble numbers, some solos, and a dramatic reading. On many occasions, I would "perform" one of my own compositions, frequently preceded by an analytical and emotional explanation of the work. In retrospect, I blanch at the thought of what I may have said in my introductory remarks. I do recall a composition called "The Bell." This was supposed to be a musico-philosophical dissertation involving the sound of the bell in the life of man! After one performance, I recall that the lecturer on that particular program, Glenn Frank,[5] later to become president of the University of Wisconsin, told me that, after my explanation, he was expecting me to give the "altar call!" After all, I was only fifteen and a very dedicated young man!

The following summer, I was again on the "circuit," this time as cellist and as accompanist to an operatic singer, Madame McCloskey, at the then fantastic salary of forty-five dollars a week. She was an excellent singer, and I learned much operatic literature through accompanying her. I am sure that she was American-born and trained, but being a singer of opera, it seemed appropriate that we should call her "Madame" rather than "Mrs."

The lecturers with whom we were associated for these two summers were an exciting group. I do not remember them all, but I do recall especially Glenn Frank, who was to influence me greatly. I also recall a favorite author of those days, Opie Read;[6] a Dr. Goldsmith who was considered to have "radical" ideas on education and politics; and finally the silver-tongued orator, William Jennings Bryan,[7] whose command of the English language and magnificent sense of dramatic delivery fascinated me.

I was completely fascinated by William Jennings Bryan.[8] He was, of course, one of the great world figures of his day and had been three times the candidate of the Democratic Party for the presidency of the United States. At the time of our meeting, he was, I suppose, approaching his middle fifties. Although I was still in my teens, he was very kind to this young colleague. I drank in every silver word, and it is only natural that I should have been deeply impressed. My memory of his appearance may have been glamorized by the passage of time, but I do recall him as a man of commanding presence, with a massive head and a magnificent voice which held his audience completely under his spell.

---

5   Glenn Frank (1887–1940), assistant to the president of Northwestern University 1912–16, member of the staff of *Century* magazine 1916–25, president of the University of Wisconsin 1925–37.

6   Opie Read (1852–1939), American humorist, journalist, editor, and novelist.

7   William Jennings Bryan (1860–1925), American statesman; presidential candidate in 1896, 1900, and 1908; secretary of state under Woodrow Wilson; strong supporter of prohibition.

8   This and the following paragraph were not included in any of the drafts for this chapter. The material concerning William Jennings Bryan originates from a single, typewritten page simply entitled "Insert."

I recall that the title of his address, which I heard him give a number of times, was "The Prince of Peace." It seemed to me that I had never heard a more eloquent plea for world brotherhood. Looking back over the span of more than fifty years, his campaign against war seems curiously prophetic of another campaign which was to take place over a half-century later. Perhaps he was, after all, ahead of his time rather than behind it.[9]

Opie Read was the founder and editor of the old "Arkansas Traveler," and his lectures were punctuated with the kind of home-spun humor to be made famous by Will Rogers. He had also written a number of highly popular novels, including *A Kentucky Colonel* and *The New Mr. Howerson*. His easy, natural way with an audience, his sense of humor, and his general philosophy of life impressed me greatly.

Another of my older colleagues also impressed me, but in a different way. I have, perhaps fortunately, forgotten his name, but I do remember that he was (or had been) a minister. He had, without question, great oratorical gifts and could without difficulty play upon the emotions of his audience. I listened to him spellbound day after day, hanging upon every phrase and being profoundly moved. One day he came off the platform after he had made an impassioned plea for the spiritual life. I was on hand, as usual, to tell him how wonderful his speech had been. His reply was, "Well I certainly bored for water that time." If he had struck me in the face, I could not have been more shocked. Sincerity seemed to me at that early age to be the most important of all virtues. To have my idol admit that he had been "boring for water" hurt me deeply. A half-century later, I have still not forgotten. Perhaps he was just making a bad joke, but the effect on my young mind was devastating.

The most important influence of these older men was that of Glenn Frank. He was only eleven years older than I but was already embarked on the beginning of a successful career. He was at that time assistant to the president of Northwestern University. Later he was to become assistant editor of the *Century* magazine and, eventually, president of the University of Wisconsin. He represented the opposite extreme in temperament from the elderly Opie Read. He was incisive, factual, with a keen, steel-trap mind.

I was trying my hand at some writing, primarily about musical subjects, and he very generously offered to [critique] my writing. To this day, I remember his advice, which was to cut everything to the absolute essentials;

---

9 Hanson was a brilliant public speaker, which prompted many observers to suggest that he might have become a preacher or a politician. Being exposed at a relatively early age to the rhetorical skills of William Jennings Bryan was obviously an important influence in Hanson's own development as a public speaker.

eliminate all unessential adjectives and adverbs, cut all the phrases which can be eliminated without destroying the content of the paragraph. I do not always follow his advice successfully, but even today, when writing an article or a speech, I wonder what Glenn Frank would think. He insisted that, at some time in my studies, I must secure an academic degree, and the fact that I eventually headed for Northwestern University was almost entirely because of his influence.

As I look back on those early days and realize the tremendous impact on my life of men like Glenn Frank, Opie Read, and William Jennings Bryan, I wonder if the young people of today may not be missing a great deal. Today, in spite of labor-saving devices, we all seem so busy. There seems to be so little time to talk to people. Perhaps because of my own good fortune, I have tried in later life to spend as much time as I could with students who came to me with problems. I know that, to my wonderful secretaries Mabel Snell, Mary Louise Creegan, and Janice Naccarella, and many others, I must have been a problem.[10] A student would come in for a "five-minute" appointment, and an hour later I would still be talking with him, drawing out his problems and trying to be as helpful to him as my unofficial counselors had been to me. Automation cannot accomplish everything. There is still no substitute for Mark Hopkins[11] on one end of the log and the student on the other.

---

10 Hanson's difficulty in keeping on schedule became enough of a problem to eventually cause his secretaries, especially Mary Louise Creegan, to severely limit the ability of Eastman School faculty members to make an appointment to see him. Of this development, he seemed completely unaware.

11 Mark Hopkins (1802–87), American educator and theologian. He served as president of Williams College 1836–72 and was regarded as one of the ablest college presidents of his time. It was President James A. Garfield who reportedly defined a university as "Mark Hopkins at one end of a log and a student on the other."

Chapter Five

STUDYING IN NEW YORK

Upon graduation from high school, I was called into the office of the superintendent of the Wahoo schools, Mr. C.W. Searson. I approached the sanctum sanctorum of the superintendent's office with considerable misgiving. I had been a "good" student. My record had been very satisfactory, and I could not understand why I should be summoned into [his] presence.

I need not have worried. The superintendent simply wanted to know of my plans for the future. Considerably relieved, I told him that I had saved almost enough money from the Chautauqua circuit to enable me to go to New York for further study. "What did I intend to study?" I replied that I wished to continue the study of music. He was obviously both puzzled and disenchanted. His final remark lingers in my memory: "You do not have to become a musician. You have brains!"

Now I realize how kind it was that a busy superintendent of schools would want to take the time to discuss with me my personal future. I am afraid, however, that at that time my only reaction was one of chagrin that he should believe that the arts should be indulged in only by those who had no brains for anything else. This conception of the artist or the musician as an egocentric who cannot possibly do anything else persists, I am afraid, to this day. Perhaps it is because of our Puritan background. Irving Lowens,[1] in his excellent book on music and musicians in early America, remarks that there was a place for music in the Puritan cosmos but that the place was a small one. I am afraid that this is still true today.

The reason for this prejudice is difficult to understand. All of the studies which I have seen tend to show that there is a high degree of correlation between high musical talent and intelligence. We have had at the Eastman School countless musicians who have had equally high talents in the sciences, languages, mathematics, and the like. Many indeed have

---

1   Irving Lowens (1916–83), American music critic and musicologist. He was music critic for the *Washington Star* 1953–77, music reference librarian at the Library of Congress 1962–66, and dean at the Peabody Conservatory of Music 1977–82. The book to which Hanson is referring is *Music and Musicians in Early America* (1964).

transferred to other professions because of the greater financial security which they offer. In the great majority of cases, they have been as successful in their new professions as I am sure they would have been if they had remained in music.

In any case, I was not to be dissuaded from my first ambition, and the following fall found me on my way to New York City. My uncle Carl had generously offered to give me a home in New York for the period of my studies. He was a friend of Cornelius Rybner,[2] the composer, who was at that time head of the Music Department of Columbia University. Professor Rybner was an authority in the field of orchestration, a friend of Richard Strauss, and by all accounts an excellent teacher. I approached Dr. Rybner, received his encouragement, and proceeded to knock on Columbia's doors.

On the basis of my academic record in high school, I was duly admitted and sent to my advisor. That worthy gentleman proved to be a professor of Greek. He examined my records as a Latin student in high school and insisted that I major in Latin and Greek. I told him that I wished to study composition with Professor Rybner, but he brushed this aside as being unimportant. I meekly registered for the courses he recommended, which included no music. I then slipped out the side door with my registration in hand and was not heard from again until many years later when Columbia University awarded me the honorary doctor of music degree. And so, after all, I finally did become an alumnus of that famous university. I doubt if the authorities ever knew that at one time, many years ago, I had knocked at the front door!

My next stop was the Institute of Musical Art, later to become the undergraduate division of the Juilliard School of Music. [It] was presided over by Dr. Frank Damrosch[3] and the brilliant and unforgettable executive secretary, Emma Jeannette Brazier. But my registration problems were not yet over. I wished to concentrate on composition. Dr. Damrosch, however, had other ideas. Perhaps he believed that all the good music had already been written, or that an American composer was an anachronism. His remarks, which like Superintendent Searson's still linger in my memory, were: "You have the ability to become a concert pianist. Why should you waste your time in futile efforts at composition?" For the benefit of any critics who may read this book, I must, in self-defense, add that at the time

---

    2   Peter Martin Cornelius Rübner [Rybner] (1853–1929), Danish-born pianist, composer, and musicologist.

    3   Frank Damrosch (1859–1937), conductor and educator. He was chorus-master at the Metropolitan Opera and supervisor of music in the New York City public schools; founded the Institute of Musical Art in 1905.

of his remarks he had <u>not</u> heard any of my compositions. Perhaps that I came from Wahoo, Nebraska, was proof enough. Certainly, a gifted composer could not come from Nebraska.

The distinguished theoretician, Percy Goetschius,[4] one of the great figures in American music education, came to my rescue by admitting me to his advanced class in contrapuntal composition. I did, however, placate Dr. Damrosch by continuing my piano study with a great teacher, James Friskin,[5] who labored diligently on my behalf. He has always been a scholar as well as a pianist, and my approach to the classics must have been a source of concern, although he will not admit it today. I do recall performances of a Beethoven sonata in which I had "filled out" some bass harmonies to provide what I considered to be greater sonority. His patient remark was, "And now shall we play it again, this time the way Beethoven wrote it?"

In addition to his great musical talents, Mr. Friskin had a remarkable memory. Almost forty years later, when he was a member of the faculty of the Juilliard School and head of the Piano Department of the Chautauqua Summer School, we renewed our acquaintance. He asked me if I remembered what I had played on my graduation program at the Institute of Musical Art forty years ago. I had a vague recollection of having played a Beethoven sonata, some Bach, and something by Chopin. He countered my hazy memory by giving me in detail my entire program, naming the opus number of the sonata, the key of the Bach prelude and fugue, and the title and opus number of the Chopin composition!

As though this was not enough, he recalled that he had suggested a different Chopin Ballade, but that I had been highly critical of the form of the work which he had suggested! He graciously added the remark, "I have thought of your objections many times since, and, you know, I believe that you were right." I was, I must say, somewhat overcome at this account of the brashness of my youth. Such recollections were, however, not without value. Whenever in later life I was inclined to be upset by the positive opinions of some of my youthful students, it was helpful to be able to recall some of my own youthful indiscretions.

The old Institute of Musical Art was a very good school, perhaps the best of [its] period. It was before the days of the great professional schools

---

4   Percy Goetschius (1853–1943), highly influential American theorist, composer, and teacher. He joined the faculty of the newly opened Institute of Musical Art in 1905; author of many theory textbooks.

5   James Friskin (1886–1943), Scottish-born pianist and teacher. He studied at the Royal College of Music and joined the faculty at the Institute of Musical Art in 1914; especially known for his performance of Bach.

of Curtis, Eastman, and Juilliard (in alphabetical order!). It was also before the day of the schools of music and fine arts, which were to burgeon in many of our important state universities. The choice of the student who wished to secure a well-grounded technical training in music was limited to a relatively few institutions, mostly independent schools of music, not parts of a university or college. The most important schools of music of the time included the New England Conservatory, the Peabody Conservatory of Baltimore, Cincinnati Conservatory, the Chicago Musical College, the American Conservatory in Chicago, and a few others. Few private universities had full-fledged schools of music, the most important being, in my opinion, Northwestern University of Evanston, Illinois.

The Institute of Musical Art was a thoroughly professional school with a superb faculty and high technical standards. String players could study with members of the famous Kneisel Quartet,[6] pianists with men like Clarence Adler,[7] Edwin Hughes,[8] Harold Bauer,[9] or James Friskin. We all heard lectures by the famous critic W.J. Henderson,[10] the historian Waldo Selden Pratt,[11] the theorist and music educator Thomas Trapper, and others of equal renown.

Aside from the general lectures, the classes in all technical courses were small. My class with Dr. Goetschius consisted of four students. Dr. Goetschius sat at the piano with his students grouped two at his left and two at his right. Being a methodical man, he would begin the first class with the two students on his left. For the second class, he would begin with the two students on his right. Since he examined our work in the greatest

---

6   The Kneisel Quartet was established by Franz Kneisel (1865–1926) in Boston in 1885 and existed until 1917. He was generally recognized as the leading string quartet in the United States at the time.

7   Clarence Adler (1886–1969), American pianist, composer, and arranger. He studied at the Cincinnati Conservatory and later with Leopold Godowsky in Europe.

8   Edwin Hughes (1884–1965), American pianist and teacher. He studied with Joseffy and Leschetizky; taught at the Institute of Musical Art 1918–23; special editor of piano music for G. Schirmer 1920–26.

9   Harold Bauer (1873–1951), English-born pianist. He began his professional career as a violinist, but later made his reputation as one of the world's most distinguished concert pianists; he became the leading piano teacher at the Manhattan School of Music.

10   William James Henderson (1855–1937), American critic and writer. He wrote for the *New York Times* 1883–1902 and the *New York Sun* 1902–37; biographer of Richard Wagner.

11   Waldo Selden Pratt (1857–1939), American musician and author.

detail, he would frequently discuss the work of only two students in the hour, leaving the work of the remaining two for the next appointment.

I was consistently neglecting my piano practice for my composition exercises. One fateful week, I decided that I had "coasted" on my piano lessons as far as I dared. Since my next appointment with Dr. Goetschius fell on the day on which he started on the <u>other</u> side of the piano, I decided that I would skip the assignment and concentrate on my piano studies, which were greatly in need of attention. It was not to be. When the appointed day arrived, Dr. Goetschius looked about his small class, not without a gleam of suspicion in his eyes, fingered his brown beard reflectively, and said today we shall <u>again</u> begin at the right side of the piano. "It is wise," he said, "even in music not to be always consistent." I was number one on the right side. I stammered that I had not had sufficient time to complete the assignment. He gave me a stern but friendly lecture on the general subject of responsibility. I was both chagrined and penitent. My feelings were somewhat assuaged when it was discovered that my partner had also not completed his assignment. Dr. Goetschius sighed, shrugged his shoulders, and said, "Very well, let us begin on the <u>left</u>." Both of these assignments had been completed!

My composition "exercise" for graduation was a prelude and double fugue for two pianos, which I performed with the assistance of one of my fellow students, the brilliant pianist and composer, Charles Vardell.[12] I was careful to write the fugue in conservative, academic style, but in the prelude I allowed myself to experiment with "modern" devices. Dr. Goetschius's criticism was characteristic: "My boy, the fugue is superb, but the prelude is <u>terrible</u>!"

One day, almost thirty years after I had left his classes, I received a letter from Dr. Goetschius, written in his fine, small, meticulous hand. My fourth symphony had just been awarded the Pulitzer Prize and had been broadcast over one of the radio networks. In the letter, Dr. Goetschius congratulated me on my symphony, but at the end of the letter added, "But, young man, I must warn you against these modern devices!" He was then in his eighties, and I was in my fiftieth year, but to him I was still his responsibility. I am sure that there are many such teachers today, but with the present size of the student population I wonder if such close student-teacher relationship can much longer endure.

---

12   Charles Vardell (1893–1962), American pianist and composer. He studied at Princeton University and the Institute of Musical Art, later earning a PhD from the Eastman School of Music. Vardell was head of the piano department at Salem College and then served as dean of the School of Music 1928–51.

The third man who greatly interested me was Franklin Robinson,[13] who was in charge of the courses in aural harmony. The purpose of these courses was to develop what one might call the "inner ear," the ability to take down from dictation the music which was played, and also to develop the technique of looking at a piece of music and inwardly "hearing" how it would sound in performance, a prime requisite for a composer. Because of my hearing problem, already referred to, the course was difficult for me. My "absolute pitch" was better than my "relative pitch," but not entirely reliable since on occasions my ear would be a half-tone "off."

In order to escape the difficulty, I went to Dr. Damrosch and asked for the privilege of substituting another course. Dr. Damrosch was adamant. I complete the course. His judgment was so wise. I did complete the course successfully, and in doing so not only overcame to a considerable extent my basic problem but [also] increased my determination to become as familiar as possible with other aural problems which might handicap my future students.

Franklin Robinson was a wonderful teacher, both colorful and dynamic, and possessing a keenly analytical mind. He was deeply concerned with what he called, in his Eastern accent, "harmonic *lawr*," the theory that harmonic progressions had a will of their own, and that these tendencies should be understood by composers and performers. It was not, of course, a particularly new theory, but in Mr. Robinson's hands it took on new meaning. He became one of my youthful idols. I knew that he always left the school at a certain hour and walked up Claremont Avenue on his way home. Quite by accident, I seemed always to be wandering around the doorway just as he appeared after his classes. I always happened to be going in the same direction he was going, and so we would walk along together, discussing every conceivable topic of art, aesthetics, and philosophy, frequently far above my head. But I was a dedicated listener, and he was a superb talker, and so I gained even more from him on our walks together. He was very gracious and interested in my youthful opinions, although I am sure he must have been amused by our regular "accidental" meetings.

The fourth of my great teachers was a very young man, probably at that time a postgraduate student, George Wedge,[14] who was later to

---

13 Franklin W. Robinson (1875–1946), American theorist and author.

14 George Wedge (1890–1964), American organist and music teacher. He studied at the Institute of Musical Art, taught at New York University 1920–27, then became dean of the Institute of Musical Art and also of the Juilliard School of Music 1938–46; author of many books on ear-training, harmony, and more.

become one of the country's foremost theorists. His task was to develop the pianists' technique in sight reading through reading eight-hand arrangements at two pianos. I was a natural sight reader and as a result I was generally chosen to pilot my three colleagues through vast quantities of arrangements of symphonic literature. Since I had in my short lifetime few opportunities to hear live orchestral performances, a great part of orchestral literature first came to me in these classes.

Today it seems to me that this type of training has disappeared in many of our schools to be replaced by a rather deadly course, generally called "keyboard harmony." This replacement has probably produced more unalleviated boredom than any course in the curriculum, with the possible exception of certain "methods courses" in education. Fortunately, I never had to take these courses!

I wonder if we have progressed very far from the old days of the institute with its small classes and the intimate relationship between teacher and student. There was no need for IBM machines to process grades. Each student was an individual. Perhaps the proof of the pudding is that its graduates were to constitute in later life a veritable "Who's Who" of the musical profession. My student colleagues numbered, among many others, the distinguished violinist Jacques Gordon[15] (later to develop the famous Gordon String Quartet), and still later to become an artist member of the Eastman faculty. There was also the violinist Sascha Jacobsen,[16] the composer and violinist Samual Gardner,[17] and such outstanding orchestral players as William Kincaid,[18] one of the great flutists of the century and for many years until his retirement, solo flutist of the Philadelphia Orchestra. He sat next to me in Franklin Robinson's classes, and his ear was more accurate than mine. Years later, when I conducted the Philadelphia Orchestra, I never argued with William Kincaid about a wrong note in a modern work!

My happiest experience at the institute was only slightly connected with music. Miss Brazier had decided that, in celebration of something or other, we should present a performance of Shakespeare's *A Midsummer Night's Dream*, with incidental music of Mendelssohn. I was awarded

---

15 Jacques Gordon (1897–1948), Russian-born violinist and chamber music player. He was appointed concertmaster of the Chicago Symphony Orchestra at the age of twenty-four and founded the Gordon String Quartet in the same year.

16 Sascha Jacobsen (1895–1971), American violinist and teacher. He studied at the Institute of Musical Art with Franz Kneisel and later taught at Juilliard.

17 Samuel Gardner (1891–1984), American violinist and composer.

18 William Kincaid (1895–1967), eminent American flutist. He was principal flutist in the Philadelphia Orchestra 1921–60 and a teacher at Curtis.

the part of Theseus, Duke of Athens. Miss Brazier, who directed the performance, labored valiantly with what she called my atrocious Nebraska accent. Finally, it was partially conquered, and I appeared not exactly on Broadway but at least just a little off Broadway. With the orchestra under Dr. Damrosch in the pit (even in those days a splendid student ensemble), I trod the boards as the proud nobleman. It was not the "lead," but it amply sufficed. Ever since those days, I have always wanted to conduct Mendelssohn's beautiful music to some other person's Theseus, but the opportunity never arose. Perhaps it will still come.

Emma Jeanette Brazier was a remarkable woman. Her title was, I believe, the modest one of secretary, but, although Dr. Damrosch was the director of the institute, Miss Brazier actually ran the school. She was secretary, dean of students, counselor, disciplinarian, and in charge of anything that needed to be done. She ran the institute with an iron hand, a discipline which can hardly be imagined today. The rules and regulations were reasonable, but once having been made, they were to be enforced.

There was one rule which brought me into her office with reasonable frequency. The institute offered many recitals by its distinguished faculty, to which admission was by student identification cards only. I was constantly forgetting my card, and since the ushers were obdurate, it meant many trips to Miss Brazier's office. One day there was a recital which I wanted very much to attend. I had once again forgotten my card. Back I went to Miss Brazier. "Miss Brazier," I said, "I am an absent-minded young artist who has once again misplaced his student card." Miss Brazier looked up from her desk. "Oh, it's you again! Howard, you would lose your head if it were not screwed on." Whereupon she smiled at me quite benignly and presented me with still another card. I suspect that on occasion I lost my card purposely so that I would have an excuse to talk with her. She probably suspected the same thing.

The most thrilling experience was my first acquaintance with Arturo Toscanini from a seat high in the top balcony of the Metropolitan Opera House. As far as I can recall, I had never seen an opera before. The Metropolitan did not play in Wahoo. So that my first introduction to this fascinating but frustrating form of art was by way of Mussorgsky's magnificent *Boris Goudonov*. The conductor was Maestro Toscanini himself, and the protagonist of the Czar Boris was the great Chaliapin.[19] What an introduction to opera for an impressionable sixteen-year-old! I can still hear in memory the crashing chords of the opening of the coronation scene, and see in imagination the imperious baton of the maestro. It was almost too exciting

---

19   Feodor Chaliapin (1873–1938), the most famous Russian opera singer of the twentieth century.

to bear. I felt as though I would take off and fly, spirit separating itself from the too-frail flesh! It is not surprising that almost twenty years later, when it was my turn to write an opera for the Metropolitan, that *Merry Mount* should reflect the tremendous impact of my first operatic experience. Later I was to meet Maestro Toscanini in very different circumstances, but that is another story.

This account of my student days at the Institute of Musical Art would not be complete without some mention of student life in those ancient days. The simplest description would be to say that there wasn't any. As was the common practice in the music schools of the time, the institute had no dormitories, the students fending for themselves as best they could. There was little if any social life and little of what we would today call "school spirit." I don't believe that most of us missed it. We were, almost without exception, very "serious" students, completely absorbed in our work and in ourselves.

I was more fortunate than most of my fellows. Because of my limited financial resources, my youth, and most of all because of Uncle Carl's interest in the development of my talent, he insisted that I live with him and his family. He owned a large apartment on Riverside Drive, overlooking the beautiful Hudson River and only a few blocks from the institute. His family consisted of his wife and his mother-in-law, Mary Frothingame, a patrician lady of regal mien, who watched over my development with as much care as though I had been her own grandson.

Chapter Six

STUDYING AT NORTHWESTERN UNIVERSITY

The following year I knocked at the door of another American university, Northwestern University in Evanston, Illinois. The previous summer I had spent a third and final summer with the Redpath Chautauqua, this time as company "coach." I was located in Kansas City, Missouri, the home office of the Redpath-Horner Chautauqua circuit. My duties were assembling and training ensembles, both for the "Lyceum" and Chautauqua circuits. It was an arduous task for a youngster, since the musicians whom I was coaching were, for the most part, at least ten years older than I.

My immediate superior was a fascinating individual, Thurlow Lieurance,[1] famous as the composer of the popular song "By the Waters of Minnetonka." His musical training had not been of the academic variety, but he was a real "pro" with a fund of knowledge of the practical problems of training ensembles, "putting across" a performance, and other perhaps mundane but important techniques. In spite of the fact that I learned a great deal from him, my summer in Kansas City was not a particularly happy one. I missed the excitement of the "circuit," the daily travels from place to place, and the stimulation of the audiences. I was, in addition, desperately homesick.

The silver lining in the homesick cloud was my acquaintance with Charles F. Horner, the head of the Chautauqua-Horner circuit. Mr. Horner was—and is—a remarkable man, an amazing combination of an able businessman and an idealist. In later life I was to become closely associated with another man who combined these two qualities, George Eastman. Charles Horner was not in temperament at all similar to George Eastman, but I realize today that a combination of similar ingredients went to make up the characters of both men.

Mr. Horner was a quiet, self-effacing, and modest man, but with tremendous organizing ability and a dedication to the importance of the arts, and particularly music. In addition to supervising his Chautauqua and Lyceum circuits, he founded the Kansas City–Horner Conservatory, many

---

1   Thurlow Lieurance (1878–1963), American composer. He had a strong interest in Native Indian culture and transcribed many Indian songs.

years later to become the school of music of the University of Kansas City. And [he] was largely instrumental in keeping alive the Kansas City Philharmonic Orchestra, which today is included among the nation's major symphony orchestras. He was interested in both local and national politics and was, at one time, appointed to an important national government post by Franklin Delano Roosevelt.

He followed my youthful career with much interest. Knowing that I was pretty much on my own financially, he offered to send me to Europe for further musical training at his expense. The advice of Glenn Frank, that I needed a broader general education, still weighed heavily on my mind, and I determined instead to continue my studies at Northwestern.

Northwestern University was one of the few important universities which, in those days, numbered an excellent school of music among its professional schools and offered the possibility of general academic studies combined with advanced technical training in music. It offered two courses of study: a four-year curriculum leading to a diploma and a five-year course leading to the Mus. Bac. [i.e., bachelor of music] degree. The degree had been awarded only once in the history of the university, to Carl M. Beecher, who was later to become dean of the School of Music.[2]

The requirements for the degree seemed rather formidable, and the fact that it had been awarded only once previously was not encouraging. However, with that confidence of youth which age must envy, I applied for admission to candidacy and was accepted. Although my technical training had been rather extensive, I was low in academic credits. It seemed wise, therefore, to devote most of my time to nonmusical subjects: English, French, German, mathematics, and physics. I enjoyed them all, but my absorption in one branch of physics almost proved my academic undoing.

In my high school course in physics, I had been fascinated with the mysteries of acoustics. When we began exploring this branch of physics in college, my interest was redoubled. The resources of Northwestern's physics laboratory were, of course, infinitely greater than the meager equipment at Wahoo High School. I, therefore, asked the professor to allow me to do additional experimentation on my own.

I don't believe that he regarded acoustics as a very important branch of physics, but he did grant me the necessary permission. I spent too much time in the laboratory, neglecting my studies in the other areas of the subject. When we came to the final examination, there were no questions in my favorite field, the questions being concerned primarily with the theory

---

2   Hanson is in error when claiming that Beecher was the only recipient of the bachelor of music degree at the time. Beecher received the degree in 1920, along with Mark Ernest Wessel.

of the expansion of gases and the like. I could not have been less interested. The whole subject of the expansion of gases left me cold. I did manage to receive a barely passing grade, but my reputation as a budding physicist was irreparably tarnished.

I did, however, continue in the acoustics laboratory, doing such exciting things as preparing an instrument tuned in quarter tones and analyzing the influence of the presence or absence of overtones on the quality [of] musical tones. All went well until I found that the professor would not authorize academic credit for my "fooling around" in the acoustics laboratory. Architectural acoustics might be important, but acoustics which had anything to do with music could hardly be taken seriously!

I had counted heavily on this credit, and the withholding of credit in physics might easily hold up my graduation. I was already carrying a much heavier course load than was normally permitted, and I knew that I would not be allowed to add still another course. There was only one thing to do: devise some method of getting double credit for some course for which I was already registered! I had taken in high school considerable work in German beyond the requirements for graduation. In those days "advanced credit"—frowned on today—was still a possibility. I, therefore, applied to the German department and was told that, if I could successfully pass a third-year course in German, I might receive academic credit for both second and third-year German.

This seemed like academic manna from heaven, and I enrolled in Professor von Bernsdorf's course in German poetry. The professor liked to have his students read aloud passages from the great German poets. This I enjoyed. I loved the poems of Schiller, Heine, and Goethe, and could recall some of them from memory. Professor von Bernsdorf and I got along famously. At the end of the year, however, I suddenly realized a new and dangerous problem: the final examination. A number of years had elapsed since my high school German. I realized that, although I could read and recite in German, my knowledge of German grammar had slipped away.

Because of my heavy load of academic studies, in addition to my work at the music school, there was no time to "bone up" on German grammar. It looked as though I would not only lose my double-credit in German but that I might forfeit all of it. The day of the final class before examinations dawned. The day of academic doom was almost upon me.

Professor von Bernsdorf addressed the final class; "There are a number of students who have done such excellent work in this course that I see no reason for wasting their time in a final examination. I shall now read the names of all students excused from the examination: Herr Hanson . . ." My protecting angel had not deserted me. I received an "A" in the course.

And so, a few weeks later at commencement, I stood up in solitary splendor and received the second Mus. Bac. degree ever awarded by the university. The following year, the authorities decided that a five-year curriculum was excessive for a bachelor's degree. In the future, a master's degree would be awarded for the five-year course, and a new four-year curriculum would be instituted leading to the bachelor's degree in music. To this day, I do not know whether I possess an earned bachelor's or master's degree!

Eight years later, I was to receive my second and final earned degree, the coveted FAAR of the American Academy in Rome. In 1925 Northwestern University honored me with my first Mus. Doc. degree, *honoris causa*. I never received an earned doctorate. The doctor of philosophy degree was not awarded in music except in the field of musicology. I, therefore, never became an honest doctor. Perhaps it might be possible to trade someday eighteen honorary MusDocs., four LLDs, three doctors of humane letters, and two doctors of literature for one PhD. This would at long last make of me an honest academician!

Although most of my work was in nonmusical subjects, I did spend a good deal of time in the school of music. I was studying vocal composition with the dean of the school, the famous Peter Christian Lutkin,[3] and orchestral composition with the equally distinguished Arne Oldberg.[4] I was also playing cello in the university orchestra in return for my tuition. In addition, I was teaching an experimental course in aural dictation, testing some of the theories of my idol, Franklin Robinson. For this I received the magnificent sum of $100. The money was not important. I would gladly have taught the course for nothing. Fortunately, the university did not know this, and the hundred dollars was a welcome addition to my very lean purse.

On the side, I managed to complete a quintet for piano and strings, the first movement of a piano concerto, and my thesis: a *magnum opus*

---

3   Peter Christian Lutkin (1858–1931), American pianist and educator. He taught at Northwestern University 1879–81; then studied with Leschetizky and Moszkowski in Europe; later rejoined the Northwestern University faculty in 1891 and became dean of the music school in 1895.

4   Arne Oldberg (1874–1962), pianist and composer. He studied with Leschetizky and Joseph Rheinberger in Europe; joined the Northwestern faculty in 1897, was appointed professor in 1899, and taught until his retirement in 1941.

called Symphonic Prelude in C Minor, which was [to be] performed by the orchestra at the graduation program. It would be a pleasure to report that the work was duly performed and made a profound impression on audience and critics. It was not so. My guardian angel, having had his full share of troubles getting me through my various predicaments, must have taken a short vacation. The composition, instead of becoming my *magnum opus*, turned out to be a frightening mixture of Grieg and Wagner, with the "falling seventh" (characteristic of Grieg) intertwined with the chromatic modulations of Wagner—plus a section in "modern Hanson" style. It was really pretty bad, and I cannot blame the authorities for substituting an earlier and better work of mine, which was performed with some success.

In addition to the privilege of knowing and working with Dean Lutkin and Professor Oldberg, I made another friendship which was to be even more important, that of the great conductor of the Chicago Symphony Orchestra, Frederick Stock.[5] He has been gone for many years, but he remains in my memory as one of the great men of music whom I have had the honor to know. Frederick Stock was a thorough professional. He had "come up" through the orchestra, having been a violist in the Chicago Symphony under Theodore Thomas. Being himself an orchestra musician, his principal aim was to make the orchestra "sound." His concern was not with histrionics or with conducting tricks, but with the music itself. He had only one idiosyncracy that I can recall, a "cork-screw" beat which reminds me of Wilhelm Furtwangler.[6]

His lack of affectation was beautifully illustrated when he took the orchestra on an Eastern tour. It was already becoming the fad to conduct from memory, "without a score." In one concert it was observed that he seemed to be turning the pages of the score rather casually. At the end of the concert, the orchestral librarian noted that the score was upside down. He was conducting from memory, but he saw no reason for indicating this to the audience. Since those days, I have been present when a young conductor in rehearsal will imperiously demand that the conductor's stand be removed, as though its presence was an insult to his memory. How very different from the "old man," as Dr. Stock was affectionately called by the members of his orchestra.

---

5   Frederick Stock (1872–1942), German-born conductor. He took over leadership of the Chicago Symphony upon the death of Theodore Thomas in 1905 and conducted the orchestra for thirty-seven years.

6   Wilhelm Furtwangler (1866–1954), famous German conductor. He led the Leipzig Gewandhaus Orchestra and the Berlin Philharmonic starting in 1922; later music director of the Vienna Philharmonic, the Salzburg Festival, and the Bayreuth Festival.

Frederick Stock, although entirely different in temperament, resembled the late Serge Koussevitzky in that he, too, was concerned with the entire musical scene. He was the father-confessor of young composers, artists, and orchestral players. One amusing incident which I observed illustrates his personal concern for his colleagues. The orchestral librarian was an elderly musician, a retired trumpet player from the orchestra. Librarian salaries were not extravagantly high, and the elderly gentleman would sometimes find himself in need of additional cash. Dr. Stock would solve this problem very neatly by writing an extra fourth trumpet part into a Wagnerian score, which the librarian would then play in rehearsals and concert. Since these additional services, according to union regulations, called for additional compensation, the state of the old gentleman's finances could be gauged by the number of extra fourth trumpet parts in the library of the Chicago Symphony Orchestra.

In my student days, Frederick Stock was never too busy to look at my scores and give me sage advice. Even more important in later years, he played many of my compositions with his magnificent orchestra. It was my privilege many years later to present him for an honorary degree at the commencement ceremonies of the University of Rochester. His comment to me was, "We have played the second movement of your *Nordic* Symphony so often in Chicago that we now consider it a part of the 'pops' repertory!"

One other meeting before I left Northwestern was to have an important influence on my future career. James Lawrence Seaton, president of the College of the Pacific (the institution later to be made famous by the football coach Alonza Stagg[7]) came to the university looking for a professor of theory and composition. The dean replied that he had a promising young graduate, who seemed to have unusual pedagogic ability but that he was only nineteen, probably too young for a professorship. President Seaton asked to see me. At the end of the interview, his comment was, "You are very young, but I have observed that this is a fault which age always corrects." And so, at the age of nineteen, I became a full professor at the College of the Pacific.

---

7   Alonzo Stagg (1862–1965), legendary American sports leader. He was inducted into the College Football Hall of fame in 1951, both as a player and as a coach. He was also inducted into the Basketball Hall of Fame in 1959 and is credited with the development of basketball as a five-player sport.

Chapter Seven

TEACHING AT THE COLLEGE OF THE PACIFIC

My first-year contract with the College of the Pacific, then located in San José, California, called for a salary of $1,000 for nine months. It stipulated that I was to teach theory and composition, history of music, piano, cello, and conduct the college orchestra. For 1916 this salary was not as small as it seems today. There was no such thing as an income tax on salaries under $3,000, and the dollar had much greater traveling capabilities.

I dearly loved teaching theory, and all my students immediately became composers of sorts, some indeed quite talented. The dean of the conservatory, Warren Allen,[1] an accomplished organist and musicologist, taught history of music, and a splendid Bohemian cellist by the name of Jan Kalas[2] taught cello, so that I was spared the necessity of spreading myself over so much territory. I did teach piano to the best of my ability, but for the most part found it very boring. I am ashamed to say that my happiest hours as a piano teacher came when a student, for some reason, missed a lesson! Such golden hours I could use for my own composition.

I had one young student by the name of Kelly, the son of the brilliant playwright.[3] Young Kelly hated the piano and had no talent whatever for the instrument. In spite of this, we became good friends. We both suffered together and finally discovered an honorable solution to our mutual problem. We would get over the "lesson" as expeditiously and efficiently as possible, after which we would spend the rest of the hour discussing the finer

---

1 Warren Allen (1885–1964), American organist and educator. As related in chapter 8, Allen subsequently went to Stanford University where he later served as chair of the division of music and professor of music and education.

2 Jan Kalas had been a member of the Chicago Symphony Orchestra from 1893 to 1901, prior to his appointment to the faculty at the College of the Pacific.

3 It is not clear to whom Hanson is referring. The only important playwright of the time with the name Kelly was George Kelly (1887–1974). But Kelly was a life-long bachelor and had no son.

points of baseball. After all, being a fellow townsman of the great Sam Crawford made me something of an authority. Young Kelly's parents never understood why their son made so little progress in piano but seemed to have become a savant on the subject of baseball!

In spite of my lack of enthusiasm for piano teaching, I must say in all modesty that I was a terrific teacher of theoretical subjects and was able, by my own enthusiasm, to instill a considerable degree of excitement even among my less creative students.

Believing that composition might be attempted as a "group experience," I tried the experiment of writing a piano sonata in class. We discussed the appropriate thematic material, with the members of the class all making their suggestions. We then discussed the appropriate harmonic or contrapuntal presentations and agreed on some composite solution. The sonata was eventually completed and actually performed in concert to the delight of the class and the mystification of the audience.

One of the students in the class was a Japanese boy by the name of Giichi Ishikawa. When a phrase of distinctly oriental flavor appeared in the sonata, we knew that Giichi had, for the moment, had his inning! Giichi was somewhat of a problem and for an unusual reason. He was too polite. He was so polite that when I rose from the piano stool to get a manuscript or a pencil, Giichi immediately arose and remained standing. When I sat down, he sat down. When I stood up, he stood up. I could not move a chair or open a door without Giichi's personal assistance. His courtesy slowed me up a little, but I still remember him with affection.

In any case, some slowing down would have been good, for I seemed to be possessed by an almost frenetic energy. Although I taught about thirty-five hours a week, I seemed to find plenty of time to compose, conduct, and engage in all kinds of experimental projects, from acoustical to psychological. To paraphrase Stephen Leacock, I mounted my horse and rode off in all directions.[4]

In spite of my unfortunate experience with the study of physics at Northwestern, I continued my interest in acoustics and spent long hours in the evenings in the laboratory. Here I developed my "overtone analyzer" and other experimental techniques. One of these I recall with affection because it was so much fun to do. I would take the wire wrappings from a broken "C" cello string, attach the two ends—one to a steel post and the other over a pulley. Then I would attach sufficient weight to the wire to

---

4   Hanson is paraphrasing the words of Canadian writer and humorist Stephen Butler Leacock (1869–1944) who wrote, "He flung himself on his horse and rode off madly in all directions," in his book, *Gertrude the Governess* (1911).

create a pitch of sixty vibrations a second, or multiples thereof. By running a sixty-cycle current through the wire, I could, by adjusting the weights, cause the wire to vibrate as a whole or in segments, illustrating the various harmonics of the string.

Since this type of wire had high resistance to the conduction of electricity, the vibrating wire would soon heat to a brilliant white. When the heat increased beyond a certain point, the "nodal" points of the string which were not vibrating would melt, giving off a spectacular little ball of fire. I am sure the experiment had no practical value, but none of my students who witnessed the experiment would ever forget the theory of vibrating strings! I believe the illustration was original with me. At least, I had never seen it before, nor have I seen it since. Somewhere in my files, I have a copy of an old *Scientific America* with pictures of the budding acoustician in his laboratory!

The old College of the Pacific in San José is now a flourishing university in Stockton, but in my day it was a small, struggling liberal arts college with an associated conservatory of fine arts. The entire student body did not, as I recall, number more than five or six hundred students, of whom almost half were in the conservatory. It was here that I became convinced of the advantages of a small college. There was a rapport between students, faculty, and administration which would, I am sure, be envied by today's colleges and universities. Everyone knew everyone. The problems of one student (personal, financial, or academic) were the problems of all. The result was an "esprit de corps" which I have never witnessed before or since.

When the football team played, nearly everyone—faculty, students, and administration—were in the stands. We rarely won a game, but our optimism survived all statistics. I recall one day when, through some strange concatenation of events (or of schedules), our team played the great University of California, a giant even in those days. We were all in the bleachers rooting for our alma mater. I do not remember what the score was—probably 84 to 0. The score could be determined by the formula "M over T," "M" representing total minutes of play and "T" representing the time it took the California team to run the length of the field, but our valiant rooting section kept up an incessant chant urging our players on to "victory." I am sure that the whole thing was silly, but, as I look back, there was something touching and almost beautiful about such unreasoning loyalty.

In contradistinction to our football team, our Conservatory of Fine Arts was a very good one, certainly one of the best on the Pacific coast. It consisted of three departments—music, visual arts, and drama—all strong departments with able faculties.

Dean Allen allowed me to have *carte blanche* in developing a Department of Theory and Composition, and my experience in setting up experimental courses in these subjects was to be of incomparable value to me when, later on, I was to have an opportunity to do the same thing on a much larger scale at the Eastman School. I also taught a course in acoustics for the Physics Department of the college, a course which, I am sure, was far from orthodox!

I had hardly begun my teaching career when the question of military service raised its head. I had received a classification of "1A-Limited Service," which did not sound very promising. However, once again my guardian angel was watching, and I was assigned to "special service," my job being to train a band for the SATC (Students Army Training Corps). It was not much of a contribution to national defense, but it did permit me to continue my teaching.

I look back on my army career with a mixture of tears and laughter. The students who applied for training were, to put it mildly, a mixed group of musical talents and equipped with a mixed bag of instruments which would have frightened a more experienced director. However, I started in and did what I could with whatever was available. Since many of our "bandsmen" had only very limited training, I began with a group of marches all in the key of B-flat, the easiest key for a beginning band.

All went reasonably well until one fateful day when the company commander told me that the band had been "requisitioned" to play for a liberty bond drive. I protested that the band was so new that it could play only in the key of B-flat. This made no impression on the officer, who told me that we would have to do the best we could. We practiced like mad, and on the appointed day marched in military splendor to the auditorium.

Here we found assembled a large audience, including a number of military and civilian top brass. I raised my baton, and we were on our way—in the key of B-flat. Our efforts met with rousing applause, and we came finally to our final march—in B-flat. The applause was tumultuous. The commanding officer motioned for us to play some encores. We didn't have any. We had played our entire repertoire, but by this time I had learned my lesson: never [to argue] with a commanding officer. We began at the beginning and played all of our marches over again—in B-flat. No one seemed to notice the repetition, and we finished in a blaze of glory—still in the key of B-flat.

We were complimented by the master-of-ceremonies for our splendid contribution to the war effort, after which we marched back to the college playing our same marches—in B-flat. I still cringe when I remember the army recruiting posters showing a little boy on his father's lap saying, "Daddy, what did you do in the Great War?" My answer could only be, "I played in B-flat."

In my years at the College of the Pacific, I developed great admiration and respect for President John Lawrence Seaton.[5] As president of a small denominational college (Methodist) situated almost in the shadow of Leland Stanford, Santa Clara, and the University of California, he was constantly faced with financial difficulties which he conquered by sheer devotion and determination.

Being an eight-hour-a-day man himself, he inspired a similar devotion in his faculty. This was almost to prove my undoing. I was teaching about thirty-five hours a week, spending whatever additional time I could in the physics lab, and devoting my evenings (and a large part of the nights) to composition. I was slightly over six feet tall, weighed one hundred forty-five pounds, and looked as though I could be blown away by a stiff breeze.

One day, President Seaton called me to his office, sat me down in a chair, and read me a long lecture on the importance of health. He counseled me on my workload and insisted that, in the future, I devote more time to rest and relaxation. As I left his office he said, "Oh, Howard, by the way, the Methodist Conference is meeting here two weeks from next Sunday. Could you give us a performance of Handel's *Messiah*?" Gone was my "rest and relaxation." We prepared and performed the *Messiah*, or a part of it, at the appointed time. The difficult task we did easily, the impossible took a little longer.

A short time later the famous, or I should say infamous, influenza epidemic hit the West Coast and our little college with stunning force. In my fatigued state, I was fair game for the bug, and my career as a teacher, composer, and bandsman in B-flat was temporarily canceled. But a plainsman from Nebraska does not give up easily, and a few weeks later I was back in the fray, ready for my next challenge, which was soon to appear on the horizon.

---

5   John Lawrence Seaton later served from 1924 to 1945 as president of Albion College in Michigan.

Chapter Eight

DEAN OF THE CONSERVATORY

It was a day in the spring of 1919. I was summoned to the office of President Seaton. Dean Warren Allen had been offered the post of organist and choirmaster at Leland Stanford University and had accepted. The deanship of our conservatory was, therefore, vacant. The president asked me if I would be willing to become the new dean.

I was both touched and flattered. I was only twenty-two, very young and very green, too young to take on the responsibilities of a flourishing conservatory. However, I agreed, immediately and enthusiastically. The challenge of being responsible for the curricula of a conservatory of fine arts did not frighten me in the least. I knew exactly what I wanted to do.

The departments of visual arts and of drama were already in capable hands, the head of the latter being the highly gifted DeMarcus Brown.[1] I determined to leave these departments strictly in the hands of their capable chairmen—a decision which I recommend to all university presidents—and concentrate on increasing the prestige and effectiveness of the school of music.

It had always seemed to me that the core of any music school should be its department of theory. This is the department which teaches (or should teach) basic musicianship. The problems of teaching piano, voice, violin, and the like vary, but all good performers should be, at least in theory, good musicians.[2] My reasoning was deceptively simple. If a school of music had an inferior voice department, it had an inferior voice department. If it had a poor theory department, it was a bad school. To some extent I still believe that this thesis is basically true.

I, therefore, proceeded to build a theory department which was to end all theory departments! All of our students must study not only basic theory, but counterpoint, orchestration, and composition. Every student, regardless of his talent, must become to some degree a composer.

Many years later, my wife and I revisited the College of the Pacific, now the University of the Pacific, on the occasion of its one hundredth

---

 1   DeMarcus Brown was later the highly successful director of the Pacific Theater from 1924 to 1968.
 2   Hanson does not appear to be deliberately punning "theory."

birthday. On examining the catalog of the conservatory, I noticed to my horror that the curriculum leading to the bachelor of music degree still called for the same top-heavy requirements in theory that I had inaugurated over thirty years before. I am sure that, had the music students known that I was responsible for their horrific theory requirements, they would have demanded the return of the honorary doctorate which that university had just conferred upon me.

Although I have some reservations on the heavy theoretical curriculum to which I subjected the innocent music students of the College of the Pacific almost fifty years ago, I still believe that the basic philosophy is correct. Regardless of his talent and technical proficiency, the artist must, first and last, be a distinguished musician. Under my regime at the Eastman School of Music, many years after my early experience at the College of the Pacific, this basic philosophy of music education was preserved. For this reason, the Eastman School has sometimes been labeled by its critics a "theory school." This has never been true, but I am proud to say that the Eastman graduate, wherever he may be, is with few exceptions an excellent musician. Of this I am very proud.

Aside from my absorption in the new task of directing the conservatory, composition remained my principal interest. Probably because I have always been a romantic, the colors of the orchestra fascinated me. I had already written a few short orchestral works, and I now labored diligently to acquire a mastery of the art of orchestration. In realizing my ambition to learn the art of the orchestral composer, I was greatly assisted by two men: Walter Henry Rothwell,[3] conductor of the Los Angeles Philharmonic Orchestra, and even more, Alfred Hertz,[4] music director of the San Francisco Symphony.

In my early days at Pacific, I had written two orchestral works with the highly emotional titles of *Before the Dawn* and *Exaltation*, and a third work, the name of which I have forgotten. I had never heard any of them, since they were too difficult to be performed by our student orchestra. Knowing that many young composers had the same problem (the lack of opportunity of hearing their own works), I determined to inaugurate a festival of American music. Learning that the Los Angeles Philharmonic Orchestra was planning a spring tour, I wrote to the orchestra's musical director, Mr. Rothwell, suggesting such a festival of chamber, choral, and orchestral

---

[3] Walter Henry Rothwell (1872–1927), London-born conductor. He was educated in Vienna and later was assistant to Gustav Mahler; appointed the first conductor of the Los Angeles Philharmonic.

[4] Alfred Hertz (1872–1942), German-born conductor. He conducted the San Francisco Symphony from 1915 to 1930.

music, with the Los Angeles Philharmonic Orchestra presenting the final concert of orchestral music.

Mr. Rothwell's response was hardly enthusiastic. His interest in American music was minimal. Although he had been born in London, his training was entirely German, and he had been an assistant to Gustav Mahler at the Frankfurt Opera. It must be remembered also that this was the period of the almost complete domination of America by German music and musicians. There had been some revolt against this domination during the First World War, but it was short-lived. The very idea of a festival of American music seemed fantastic.

Personally, I was not unknown to Mr. Rothwell. [He] therefore countered with the gracious suggestion that I conduct one of my new works with the orchestra on tour. I was, of course, delighted, but it was not what I wanted. I wanted an <u>entire</u> orchestral program of American music. The correspondence between us was voluminous, but I finally won half a victory. Mr. Rothwell agreed to conduct three movements of the Second (Indian) Suite of Edward MacDowell and, at my suggestion, the Overture *Comes Autumn Time* of Leo Sowerby. [He] insisted that the remainder of the program should consist of Rimsky-Korsakoff's *Caprice Espagnole* and the *Les Préludes* and A-Major Piano Concerto of Franz Liszt.

And so, the final program of our first festival of American music introduced Rimsky-Korsakoff and Liszt as American composers! The rest of the battle, however, I won, for the remainder of the concerts presented choral works by Rossiter Cole,[5] my former teacher Peter Christian Lutkin, and the young American composer Wesley LaViolette,[6] as well as chamber music by Daniel Gregory Mason[7] and another of my former teachers, Arne Oldberg. There was, in addition, an entire solo program of American compositions.

According to the program, I seemed to be everywhere, preparing the chorus and orchestra, playing piano in the chamber music concert, and accompanying the recital soloists. The concerts extended from May 22nd to the 26th. At the end of the festival, I was exhausted, but I had at least inaugurated an almost-completely American music festival.

---

5   Rossiter Cole (1866–1952), American teacher and composer. He studied in Berlin, taught in various universities, and composed over one hundred works.

6   Wesley LaViolette (1894–1978), American composer and educator. He later taught at DePaul University, where George Perle was among his students.

7   Daniel Gregory Mason (1873–1953), American composer. He studied with John Knowles Paine, George Chadwick, and Percy Goetschius; taught at Columbia University 1905–42.

The greatest thrill of the festival was the opportunity to conduct the superb Los Angeles Philharmonic Orchestra.[8] The Los Angeles Philharmonic in those days had an "angel" in the person of William Clark[9], the millionaire philanthropist and music lover. Mr. Clark was determined to make the Los Angeles Philharmonic the greatest orchestra in the United States or, if possible, in the world. In attaining his ambition, money was no object. If the best oboe player was solo oboist in the Boston Symphony, the order was to seduce him to California, not only through climate but through money. As a result, the orchestra in those halcyon days was, I believe, one of the great orchestras of all time.

The opportunity of conducting this great ensemble in one of my own compositions was irresistible. I do not remember any details of the rehearsals or performance except a generally beatific feeling that I was in heaven, or at least in one of its suburbs. I had never had a lesson in conducting. Conducting was not "taught" in the United States in those days. This did not bother me in the slightest. I had cut my conducting teeth on the Wahoo High School Orchestra and later on the College Orchestra of Pacific. I had wheedled advice from every conductor, great or small, with whom I had come in contact. My methods were, undoubtedly, rough and ready. I handled the baton more like a rapier than a baton, with an intensity which must have been either amusing or frightening. However, the men of this marvelous orchestra, many of whom had played with the great masters of Europe, gave the young fledgling the most complete cooperation, for which I have always been eternally grateful. As a result, the performance was a success. The piece had, to use the musician's language, "come off," and I had found that the orchestral composition sounded in the orchestra the way I had heard it in my inner ear—only better! I now felt confidence in carrying on my ambition to be an orchestral composer.

My next opportunity came through that grand old man of the opera and symphony, Alfred Hertz. Mr. Hertz had been for many years the principal conductor of German opera at the Metropolitan. I had heard him in my student days in New York in magnificent performances of Wagner. In the meantime, he had resigned from the Met and had come to San Francisco to take over the direction of its excellent symphony. He was a big man with a completely bald head and a huge black beard. He walked with a pronounced limp, and when he strode to the podium he looked like some avenging angel—or devil—about to commit mayhem on the

---

    8   The piece Hanson conducted was *Before the Dawn*.
    9   William Andrews Clark (1877–1934) was also a collector of rare books and manuscripts. His collection, known as the William Andrews Clark Memorial Library, was bequeathed to the University of California at Los Angeles.

orchestra. In addition, he had a beat which began above his head and flashed out across the orchestra like a scimitar. As a matter of fact, he was, contrary to his looks, a jovial man with a wonderful sense of humor and an infectious laugh which was perilously close to a giggle.

He was very kind to me, looked at my scores, and eventually invited me to conduct one of my compositions with his orchestra. The San Francisco Orchestra gave me the same kind of whole-hearted collaboration which I had previously received from the Los Angeles Philharmonic. Once again, the score "came off," and I was further encouraged to proceed with my ambition. Before my first rehearsal, Mr. Herz called me into his room. "Mein boy," he said, "I haff vun piece of advice. If you are to be a guest conductor, you must be good." He paused for a moment, and then said with that characteristic giggle, "Aber, not *too* good."

I have thought of that advice thousands of times in later years when I have appeared as guest conductor of dozens of symphony orchestras. Some orchestras are devotedly loyal to their conductors. Others are not. The relationship of an orchestra to its conductor is a phenomenon worthy of the attention of the most gifted social scientist. The discipline of an orchestra is still, in many cases, a throwback to the Dark Ages. Whether this relationship is necessary or not, I have never been sure. In any case, the attitude of an orchestra to its regular conductor who has—or did have in the past—the power of artistic life or death over his players frequently produced an overpowering tension. I recall one instance in which I was a guest conductor of an American orchestra. After the rehearsal, the concertmaster came to me with the cryptic statement, "We like you. For you we play!" The regular conductor was an excellent conductor, but I was a new face, and perhaps a more relaxed personality, hence the statement, "For you we play."

Alfred Hertz belonged [to] the rather small group of conductors who were loved by their orchestras. He was a superb musician and highly respected, but undoubtedly the human quality which endeared him to his men was his puckish sense of humor. I recall meeting him after a performance of Mendelssohn's *Elijah* at Leland Stanford University. The baritone soloist was the famous Louis Graveure.[10] In the well-known aria, "It is enough," there was some disagreement on tempo. Mr. Hertz felt that Graveure's tempo was much too fast. Recounting the incident after the concert, Mr. Hertz remarked to me, "At the rehearsal I followed him, but at the concert I vass a mill-shtone around his neck!"

---

10   Louis Graveure (1888–1965), famous English baritone. His real name was Wilfred Douthitt, and he studied with Clara Novello-Davies; he became a popular concert artist and also taught in various music schools.

On another occasion, he was returning a score to the home of a young composer who was also a good friend. The composer was not at home. Mr. Hertz left the score with the composer's wife with the injunction: "Please be very careful with it. I vould not vant it to be shtolen again."

Mr. Hertz could also take a joke on himself. One amusing example occurred at an early morning rehearsal of the orchestra. Mr. Hertz sometimes arrived a few minutes late for these rehearsals. According to the regulations of the Musicians' Union, rehearsals are supposed to begin on time and end on time. One morning when the hour for rehearsal had arrived and Mr. Hertz had not, the orchestra decided to play a joke on the "old man." At the stroke of ten, the concertmaster, Mishel Piastro (who later was to become a well-known conductor),[11] signaled from his desk for the orchestra to begin the *Meistersinger* overture. A few moments later, Mr. Hertz entered the hall, accompanied by his wife, Lilli, who watched over Mr. Hertz's life like a guardian angel. Hearing the sounds of Wagner coming from the hall, she rushed to the stage and saw the orchestra performing minus its conductor. Dismayed, she ran back to her husband shouting, "Alfred, Alfred, come qvick, the orchestra is playing mitout you!" Geniality and a sense of humor are, I fear, at something of a premium today. Perhaps, at least partially, for this reason I look back on conductors like Alfred Hertz, Frederick Stock, Walter Damrosch, and Rudolph Ganz[12] with nostalgic appreciation.

About this time, there came an invitation which was to have the most profound effect on my career. Each year there occurred in the redwood forest in the Santa Cruz mountains a "Forest Play." The libretto, written by a young San José attorney, Don Richards, was a long and rather effective poem in praise of nature, the giant sequoias, and the majesty of the forest. It called for soloists, chorus, ballet, and orchestra. I was asked to write the score.

Undertaking a work of these dimensions in connection with my arduous teaching and administrative schedule presented formidable difficulties. However, I had by this time developed a discipline which was to become invaluable in the years ahead. This was the faculty of dividing my mind into compartments and not allowing one compartment to intrude

---

11   Mishel Piastro (1891–1970), violinist and conductor. He was concertmaster of the San Francisco Orchestra 1920–25; concertmaster of the New York Philharmonic 1931–43; assistant conductor under Sir John Barbirolli; conductor of the radio orchestra, the Longines Symphonette.

12   Rudolph Ganz (1877–1972), Swiss-born pianist, conductor, and composer. He conducted the St. Louis Symphony 1921–27; later taught at Chicago Musical College, serving there as president 1934–58.

upon another. When I began composing, I would shut off the teaching and administrative compartments, bolt the door, and for the next few hours think of nothing but composition.

Up to this time, I had written no music for chorus or for ballet, and no composition in a quasi-dramatic form. In addition, I had been invited to conduct the performances. The opportunity to engage in a major undertaking of this caliber was too tempting, and I immediately accepted. I labored long hours into the night after my conservatory duties were over and eventually, after the burning of much midnight oil, came through with the completed score.

The score had barely been completed when the blow came in the form of a court injunction against the performance of the "Forest Play." It seems that the libretto score which I had just completed setting to music was not a new libretto but the same libretto which had been the basis for a previous "Forest Play" by another composer. In other words, there were now two different settings of the same libretto. Even had I known of this previous work, I doubt if I would have considered it important. I knew that there had been over the years many settings of the same poem by different composers. There could be no possible charge of plagiarism, because if there had been another setting of the libretto, I had never seen it or heard it.

But American copyright laws constitute a fearful and complex maze, understood only by a small number of lawyers with great experience in the field. There was, therefore, a distinct possibility that a judge without knowledge of copyright [law] might indeed uphold the complaint. It was much too late to write and set to music another libretto, and the setting of new words to the music which I had written would be an almost hopeless task. There was nothing that could be done except to wait for the court's decision.

Eventually it came, only a few days before orchestral rehearsals were scheduled to begin. The judge's decision was that many songs had been written to the same poems by different composers and that it was perfectly proper for a composer, with the permission of the author, to make a new setting of a libretto.

Rehearsals of the soloists, chorus, ballet, and orchestra began in San Francisco, and for the first time in my life I found myself faced with the task of coordinating a professional orchestra in the pit with the musical and dramatic action on the stage. There is nothing more thrilling, and I can readily understand how difficult it must be for an opera conductor to leave the glamour of the operatic stage for the more sedate fare of a symphony conductor.

The night of the first performance finally came. Great floodlights from high up in the huge redwoods shone down upon the grassy stage, bathing the woods in an eerie glow which seemed to come from another world. The scene was to begin with a short orchestral prelude, followed by the entrance of the ballet. Mother Nature decreed, however, that the first protagonists in the opening scene were not to be the dancers. The quiet opening of the prelude had barely begun when a cunning little white rabbit appeared under the lights, stopped for a moment, surveyed the audience solemnly, and then walked with great dignity off the sylvan stage. The huge audience sitting on the slopes of the natural amphitheatre was charmed beyond belief and broke into enthusiastic applause. Certainly no stage direction could have been more perfect. The audience did not know that the stage direction was not ours. Mother Nature had most beneficially intervened, and the "Forest Play" was a success almost before it had begun!

I cannot leave this general subject without expressing my appreciation of the encouragement of two notable pianists, Rudolph Ganz and Percy Grainger,[13] both of whom strongly urged me to continue writing for the piano as well as for the orchestra. I had already written a number of suites for the piano, and both gentlemen assured me that they would perform my compositions on their concert programs if I would continue. They were both good as their word, and a number of my short piano pieces found their way to the programs of these two artists, as well as those of the gifted Madame Sturkow-Ryder who programmed even some of my early student compositions.

In addition, Mr. Ganz introduced me to the publishing firm of the Composers' Press, later absorbed by the Carl Fischer Company of New York City. To secure a contract for the publication of works by a young and unknown composer has always been difficult but, on the recommendation of [Rudolph] Ganz and Percy Grainger, I did receive a contract for the publication of some of my early works, including the *Clog Dance*, which I still hear frequently on programs of young pianists.

I have perhaps given the impression that my life, at least up to this time, had been completely and solely absorbed in work. It is true that, as a student at Northwestern, I have been a complete "grind." Although the College of Liberal Arts had dormitories for its students, there were none for students registered in the School of Music. We lived around the town of Evanston, wherever we could find suitable lodgings at a price we could afford. Some of us, including my roommate, the composer

---

13 Percy Grainger (1882–1961), Australian-born pianist and composer. He met Edvard Grieg in 1906 and became a famous performer and advocate for that composer's piano concerto.

Wesley LaViolette, lived above a local bank and ate at one of those "marble-topped" cafeterias, where we escaped the monotony of the menu by the liberal use of ketchup. To this day, I associate my student days at Northwestern with ketchup.

I do not recall that I ever attended a football game, a basketball game, or a track meet. My own diversion was to go to the local public library, which had a small music library and music room. Here I found a full vocal score of Debussy's *Pelleas et Melisande*, a very "modern" work for its day, and would pore over it for every available free minute. At Pacific, although my schedule was one that would have been prohibited by the Society for the Prevention of Cruelty to College Professors, I had a wonderful time. I had numerous friends among both students and faculty, dated the young ladies, and fell into and out of love with the greatest facility.

My one luxury was a second-hand automobile sold to me by one of my students, Gene Dorais. Gene was an excellent pianist, a fine "jazz" player, and (strange as it may seem) an able auto mechanic. The car which he sold me could only be described as ecumenical. It had, as I recall, a Ford engine, a Chevrolet radiator, and various other parts without relation to race, creed, or source of origin. It ran about half the time, and I am sure that I spent as much time under the car as in it. I became adept at siphoning gas from the gasoline tank for transposition to the cylinder head. I also developed an intimate acquaintance with the carburetor and the "timer." It generally took a half-hour to get it started, but once started it ran beautifully. It was a rakish little machine, without a top or windshield, and in appearance something like a diminutive racer. Needless to say, it was very popular with all my students.

It was during these years that I made my first acquaintance with the beautiful country surrounding San José—from the Russian River Country to the north to the Santa Cruz mountains and the breathtaking coast of Carmel to the south. It was in Big Sur, south of Carmel, where I had my first and only experience as a hunter. Up to that time, my prowess had been confined to knocking tin cans off fenceposts with a twenty-two rifle in the country around Wahoo. I forget who was my host, but I remember being out in that (at that time) wild country with a heavy-gauge gun looking for my first deer. In a short time, he appeared to me, and I got him directly in my sights. He stood there motionless. I started to pull the trigger, but I couldn't. He was so beautiful. How could anyone wilfully destroy such beauty. He turned and seemed to look at me, and then bounded away. My hunting companions were not intrigued. I was not invited again!

Chapter Nine

PRIX DE ROME

It seems presumptuous to think that the Lord of the Universe, who keeps the planets in their course, who supervises the galaxies of the heavens, should watch over the lives of mere mortals on the small planet of Earth. And yet there does seem to be in truth a destiny which shapes our ends. We can, all of us I am sure, testify to seemingly unimportant events which had a profound effect on our later life, strange coincidences which did, indeed, shape our destiny.

About this time, there came to our faculty a young voice student, Mimi Montgomery, whom I had engaged to fill a vacancy in the voice department. She had recently read about the newly established Prix de Rome in composition at the American Academy in Rome. A national competition for the Prix de Rome had, in the opinion of the jury, not brought forth a suitable candidate. It was, therefore, determined to set a second competition. Miss Montgomery strongly urged me to enter this competition.

I was not particularly interested. I was very happy at Pacific. I enjoyed my teaching and my administrative job. I was very fond of my students, and I had reason to believe that they were fond of me. As a composer in those days on the Pacific coast, I had little competition. I was, indeed, the proverbial large frog in the small puddle, and I was quite satisfied.

Miss Montgomery insisted on pointing out to me that this was my problem. There was not enough competition. It was too easy for me to become complaisant and self-satisfied. I could never hope to fulfill my full potential without a greater challenge. I listened to her remarks with something less than enthusiasm. Finally, goaded by her insistence, I agreed to enter the Prix de Rome competition.

I wrapped up the score to the *Forest Play*, which had had a considerable success, added the orchestral score of *Before the Dawn* for good measure, and took them over to the college office to be sent to the competition. Returning to my office, I was again assailed with doubts. Why should I leave a position in which I was happy, students and friends whom I loved, opportunities which were certain and secure, to go for three years to a foreign land?

I decided to go back to the office, retrieve the scores, and forget the whole thing. It was a Saturday morning, and the office closed at noon. I arrived about two minutes after the hour to find the door locked and the staff departed for the weekend. A few minutes after nine on Monday morning, I again returned to the office to reclaim my scores. The mailman, however, had arrived a trifle early on that particular morning, and my scores were now irretrievably in the hands of Uncle Sam.[1]

A few weeks later, I received a letter, postmarked New York, from the United States office of the American Academy in Rome. The letter announced that I had been declared the first winner of the Prix de Rome in composition and directed me to proceed to Rome at the earliest opportunity. Upon the concatenation of such seemingly unimportant coincidences do our destinies seem to depend. One cannot help wondering.

The jury set up by the academy to award the Rome Prize was a most distinguished one. Walter Damrosch,[2] music director of the New York Symphony Orchestra was its chairman. The other members included the famous American composer, John Alden Carpenter;[3] two New York critics, Richard Aldrich[4] of the *New York Times* and W.J. Henderson[5] of the *New York Sun*; Professor Walter Spaulding of the Music Department of Harvard; and the novelist, Owen Wister.[6]

The reaction of the press to the award was highly favorable. The fact that the Rome Prize had been awarded to a young, unknown California composer, born in a small town on the Nebraska plains, seemed a sign of the growth of a culture not limited to the more sophisticated East. There was only one skeptical voice, that of Paul Rosenfeld, who wrote (as I recall) for the *Dial*. Mr. Rosenfeld remarked that the Rome Prize had been

---

1   The United States Post Office.
2   Walter Damrosch (1862–1950), German-born American conductor. He led the New York Symphony 1903–27, then became counsel for the National Broadcasting Company.
3   John Alden Carpenter (1876–1951), American composer. He was educated at Harvard and later studied in England with Elgar; composed many works including several ballets.
4   Richard Aldrich (1863–1937), American music critic. He was educated at Harvard and served as critic at the *New York Times* 1902–23.
5   William James Henderson (1855–1937), American critic and write. He wrote for the *New York Times* 1883–1902 and the *New York Sun* 1902–37; biographer of Richard Wagner.
6   Owen Wister (1860–1938), American writer. He initially aspired to a career in music, but then turned his talents to writing. He is often referred to as the "father" of Western fiction and his best-known work is *The Virginian*.

awarded to a young Nebraskan for a composition with the title *Before the Dawn* or *Before Damrosch*, an unnecessarily snide remark since Mr. Rosenfeld had, I am sure, never heard any of my music.

By this time, President Seaton had left Pacific to become president of Albion College. He was succeeded by the brilliant historian Tully Knoles, who had been a professor of history at the University of Southern California. Presides Knoles was as understanding as President Seaton would have been and generously agreed to release me from my obligations at the conservatory. It was fall, and school was already in session, so that the sudden transition presented serious problems.

The situation was made easier because of the presence on the faculty of Charles M. Dennis, who had been a classmate of mine at Northwestern. His field was music education. He was an able teacher and an efficient administrator who was to become, in later years, director of music in the public schools of San Francisco and president of Music Educators National Conference. He agreed to take over the position of acting dean in my absence. I left my beloved theory department in the hands of one of my brilliant students, Jules Moullet, and a few weeks later was on my way to Rome, with a stopover in Wahoo, Nebraska, to say goodbye to my parents.

My passage was booked on the *Taormina*, a small Italian steamer plying between New York City and Naples. I had never before been on an ocean-going vessel, and the *Taormina* seemed to me to be a huge floating palace. Actually, it was a small boat of a few thousand tons. Years later, my Uncle Carl, who saw me off on my voyage, told me that the boat was so small that he wondered if it could ever arrive safely at its destination! We did have a rough voyage and were considerably tossed about, but for me it was an exciting experience, and I was thrilled at the way in which the great waves tossed about this (in my opinion) "leviathan" of the sea.[7]

After about ten days, we arrived in Naples and proceeded by train to Rome where, for the first time, I saw the Accademia Americana. The Accademia was situated high on the Gianicolo, the highest hill overlooking the Eternal City, memorialized by the third movement of Ottorino Respighi's *Pines of Rome*. It consisted of an imposing main building with the "cortile" and three "villas," one of which was the famous Villa Aurelia, a magnificent palazzo reputed to have been built by King Victor Emmanuel I for one of his favorites.

---

7 Hanson's Uncle Carl had ample reason to be concerned about the voyage. The *Taormina*, like its sister ships, *Ancona* and *Verona*, was a small vessel that was essentially designed to transport emigrants from Italy to North America.

With my usual good fortune, I was assigned a studio on the top floor of the Villa Aurelia. The studio had a terrace, higher than the dome of St. Peter's, from which one could look down not only on St. Peter's and the Vatican but [also] across the Tiber to the old Castel Sant'Angelo, made famous in operatic history by the last act of Puccini's *La Tosca*.[8]

The studio contained a beautiful Austrian Bösendorfer grand piano and a huge drawing board upon which to write. Around the villa were beautiful gardens, and on clean, warm evenings the nightingales provided a serenade more beautiful than any dared hope to be able to write. The story goes that the nightingale's song used in the Respighi *Pines of Rome* was recorded in these gardens. I never had the opportunity of speaking with any of the nightingales personally, so I cannot verify the story, but it is not at all unlikely. In any case, the scene in the third movement of Respighi's masterpiece was laid on this very location.

It is difficult to imagine a more inspiring spot in which to write music, and whenever I hear or conduct the *Pines* and arrive at this particular movement, the nostalgia is almost unbearable. It is a temptation to linger over its beauties and postpone as long as possible the militaristic finale of the *Appian Way* and the march of the Roman legions.

My studio, as I have said, was high above the other academy buildings, and on warm evenings, with the windows open, the sounds from my studio would be wafted over the Roman countryside. I liked especially to play orchestral scores at the piano (most particularly my own) *con passione* and *fortissimo*. The story, which is still legend about the academy, is that one evening a stranger, walking by the Villa Aurelia with Felix Lamond,[9] heard tremendous sounds coming from high within the villa. The stranger asked Mr. Lamond, "What in the world is that?" To which Mr. Lamond is said to have replied, "Oh, that is Hanson playing Hanson!"

Aside from its physical beauty, the Accademia had many unusual qualities which differentiated it from the formal graduate school which would be its closest counterpart. It consisted of two divisions, the division of the arts and the division of classical studies. The latter was devoted to classical studies and archeology. The former included painting, sculpture,

---

8   Hanson's memory is not accurate. Castel Sant'Angelo is not across the Tiber. It is located on the same side of the river as St. Peter's and the Accademia Americana.

9   Felix Lamond (1863–1940), English organist, choirmaster, and scholar. He came to the US and became a citizen in 1892, lectured on music literature at Columbia University, and was organist and choirmaster at Trinity Chapel; music critic for the *New York Herald* 1909–15; professor of music at the American Academy 1920–40.

architecture, and musical composition. The fellows of the academy in the creative arts included three painters, three sculptors, four architects (one in landscape architecture), and two composers, a "student body" totaling twelve. The term of appointment in those days was for three years. Each year, therefore, saw the "graduation" of one fellow and the appointment of a new fellow on the basis of national competition. In addition to the regularly appointed fellows at the academy, there were always a number of visiting fellows in residence. These were graduate students holding traveling fellowships from a number of America's most important universities.

I was fortunate in having as my fellow composer-in-residence the distinguished American composer Leo Sowerby.[10] As I have already stated, the original competition for the Prix de Rome had been unsuccessful in producing a candidate who satisfied the academy jury. In order not to delay the opening of the music department, the academy authorized the special appointment of a composer for a two-year term outside of the competition. Leo Sowerby, although still a very young man, had already achieved an international reputation as a composer. He had the honor of being, in fact, the first fellow in composition at the American Academy, although I was the first *winner* of the Rome Prize in musical competition.

I had always admired Sowerby. He was, even in those early days, a superb craftsman with a technique far beyond my own. We played our new compositions for each other, and I am sure that I learned much more from him than he learned from me.

I was working on my first symphony, the *Nordic*, at the time, and I was having difficulties with the climactic points in the first movement, of which there were a great many (perhaps too many!). They seemed to want to rise too frequently to the same pitch in each climax. He pointed out to me that music was like the configuration of mountain peaks that no two peaks were of the same height, and that music should follow nature's example. I set to work at revising the symphony according to his suggestions, with highly beneficial results.

The title of my first symphony, however, proved unfortunate. I called it the *Nordic* because of the Scandinavian background of my parents. In the summer I had visited Sweden, including the province of Skåne, where my mother and father were born. I was deeply impressed, not only with the countryside itself, but by the folksongs which I heard and the folk dances which I saw.

---

10   Leo Sowerby (1895–1968), American composer and church musician. He won the Pulitzer Prize in 1946; organist and choir master at St. James Church 1927–62.

The symphony became a kind of tribute to my parents and the land of their birth. The final movement, in fact, contains both a theme which sounds like a Swedish folk song (but isn't) and an actual folk song which dates back to the Middle Ages. The following decade was to give to the title *Nordic* very different connotations. Any such racial implication was, of course, farthest from my mind.[11]

By routine academic standards, I suppose the academy would seem a strange institution. There were no classes or seminars, and actually no teachers in the accepted sense. The academy was presided over by the distinguished classicist and archeologist, Gorham Stevens,[12] and the composition department was headed by the English musician, Felix Lamond. These gentlemen were always available for consultation and advice, as was also true in the other arts, but each fellow was, in fact, on his own. He could produce what he wanted when he wanted to. There was complete freedom. The only crime was if one did not produce something. I am sure that such a procedure would be effective only in the most advanced graduate schools, but at the academy the principle worked well.

In addition to Leo Sowerby, my other composer colleagues during my three-year tenure were Randall Thompson,[13] who came to the academy during my second year, and Wintter Watts,[14] who followed Thompson. Randall Thompson, who was later to achieve distinction (particularly in the field of choral music), was a meticulous craftsman with a highly refined sense of musical aesthetics. A product of Harvard College, his preoccupation with each note that he wrote was in sharp contrast to my own highly emotional and not always well-disciplined manner of composing. I once accused him of dipping each note in Listerine before setting it in the score (which was not a fair criticism), but his highly disciplined manner of writing was an excellent influence on my too-impulsive methods, and, as in the case of Sowerby, I also learned much from him.

Wintter Watts was the enigma of the academy. A man of great sensitivity, he was chiefly interested in writing songs and had written some very

---

11 Hanson is referring to the claims of "Nordic" racial superiority made by Hitler and the Nazi Party in Germany.

12 Gorham P. Stevens (1876–1963), American archeologist. He studied at MIT and Ecole des Beaux Arts in Paris; acting director of the American Academy 1913–17, director 1917–32.

13 Randall Thompson (1899–1984), American composer. He was professor and choir director at Wellesley College; later taught at Curtis and at Harvard. He was particularly well-known for his choral works.

14 Wintter Watts (1884–1962), American composer. He studied at the Institute of Musical Art in New York, lived for some time in Europe after leaving the American Academy, and then returned to the US in 1931.

beautiful ones. If Americans should ever become interested in the music of their own composers, the songs of Wintter Watts may well take their place among the world's great vocal literature. Rome and Italy completely absorbed him, with the result that he did practically no work.

The Academy had really only one regulation: that its fellows must have something to show at the end of each year. For the composers, this involved the presentation of some work in the orchestral concert given at the end of each year by members of the Augusteo Orchestra. At the end of the year, Wintter had nothing to present except some songs, which I suspect were of a previous vintage. I urged him to hurry and orchestrate these songs so he would have something to show for his first year. He was not particularly interested in the orchestra, nor was he really at home in the orchestral medium. However, by dint of much pushing, the two of us got the songs orchestrated for the presentation.

It was my third year at the academy, and the following August I left for the United States. Not having me to urge him on, Wintter again relapsed into nonproductivity. I have often wondered, if I had been able to continue to serve as a gadfly, [whether he would] have written an opera, for his lyrical talent was quite enchanting. I think that it was at the end of his second year that he suddenly departed, never to return to the academy.

My place at the academy was taken by George Herbert Elwell,[15] who was in later life to earn fame not only as a composer but as the erudite and distinguished critic of the *Cleveland Plain Dealer*. In addition to writing some excellent orchestral works, Herbert made one incidental contribution to the academy. Up to that time, only single men were allowed to become fellows of the academy, nor were they permitted to marry during their tenure. On a trip to Paris, Elwell had fallen in love with and married a charming French girl. This was in defiance of the most sacred rules of the academy, and his status was in the gravest jeopardy. Eventually, however, love conquered all, and the breaking of the rule on celibacy furnished a cast-iron precedent for those who wished to follow. The regulation was finally rescinded.

I also learned a great deal from my fellows in the other arts, particularly from the sculptors whose methods of dealing with the primitive clay seemed to reflect some of my problems in dealing with the intangible

---

15 George Herbert Elwell (1898–1974), American composer, teacher, critic. He was among the first Americans to study with Nadia Boulanger; taught at Cleveland Institute of Music 1928–45, then at Oberlin plus summer session teaching at the Eastman School of Music.

world of sound. Chief among them were Alvin Meyer,[16] Gaetano Cecere,[17] Edmund Amateis,[18] and Lawrence Stevens,[19] in whose studios I was a frequent visitor. With Alvin Meyer I formed a particularly close friendship which has lasted through the years. In the work of Meyer and Stevens, I had an opportunity of observing how greatly creative talents can differ. Meyer was small of stature and slightly built. His *forte* was the creation of exquisite pieces of sculpture, small delicate figures, fountains, pottery, and the like. He was fascinated with primitive designs—Egyptian and Oriental rather than with the sculpture of Greece and Rome—and his work reflected these sensitive and exotic qualities.

Stevens, on the other hand, was a powerfully built man who would have been an addition to any football team. His passion was for massive sculpture, huge figures, great charging horses, tremendous power and motion. As in music, so in sculpture the work of the artist reflected traits and attitudes hidden deep within his own personality.

Another artist who influenced my thinking was one of America's great sculptors, Paul Manship.[20] He had been a fellow of the academy in the past and was a frequent visitor. His clear conception of his own purpose as an artist, combined with a sure technical equipment and his individual style was an example to us all.

Next to the composers and sculptors came the influence of the painters. I knew best Salvatore Lascari,[21] a master craftsman whose work revealed a fantastic mastery of the technique of his art. In an era where the young painters were already beginning to say, "Anyone can draw," and when portraits which looked anything like the model were frowned on as being "photographic," I suppose Lascari must have felt very much alone. I do not believe that any camera, no matter how perfect, could ever produce

---

16 Alvin Meyer (1892–1972), American sculptor. He studied at the Pennsylvania Academy of Fine Arts and the Maryland Academy of Art; the Chicago Board of Trade Building (1930) incorporates his sculptural work.

17 Gaetano Cecere (1894–1985), American sculptor. He studied at the National Academy of Design and at the Beaux Arts Institute of Design.

18 Edmund Amateis (1897–1981), American artist. He was especially known for his architectural sculpture.

19 Lawrence Stevens (1896–1972), American artist. He was known for his sculpture, painting, and printmaking.

20 Paul Manship (1885–1966), American artist. He was among the first American artists to be influenced by Egyptian, Assyrian, and preclassical Greek art.

21 Salvatore Lascari (1884–1967), Italian-born American artist. He was known for his architectural themes and for his portraits.

a Lascari portrait. At the other end of the spectrum was Frank Schwarz,[22] a complete rebel who was against every technique devised, including his own. Somewhere in the middle was Carlo Ciampaglia,[23] who in the Second World War became a designer of battleships! The architects had less influence upon me, although they included such men as James Kellum Smith,[24] Henri Marceau[25], and James Chilman,[26] all of whom achieved distinction in various branches of their profession. Smith was to become president of the famous architectural firm of McKim, Mead, and White. Marceau eventually became director of the great Philadelphia Museum, and Chilman became professor at Rice Institute and the director of its distinguished museum.

Among the visiting fellows with whom I formed firm friendships was Jack Skinner, architect on a traveling fellowship from Harvard University. Some of the architects whom I had met seemed to me to be primarily interested in classical architectural history rather than in creation, but Skinner was a truly creative architect. A number of beautiful buildings which he later designed in the United States were to prove his creative ability.

He, together with Alvin Meyer, taught me the importance of forming my own likes and dislikes in those arts in which I had no technical competence. In those days, I liked baroque music, baroque painting, and even baroque architecture. Baroque music has since become very much "in," but baroque painting—and especially baroque architecture—were very much "out." The expression of any enthusiasm for baroque structures with their broken arches and fat, cupid-like angels, was looked upon as a form of aesthetic malaise.[27]

---

22 Frank Schwarz (1894–1951), American artist. He was known for his oil and fresco painting.

23 Carlo Ciampaglia (1891–1975), Italian-born American mural painter and interior designer. He was highly regarded for his decorative skills.

24 James Kellum Smith (1893–1963), American painter. He was a graduate of Amherst, became president of the American Academy in 1937, and was a longtime member of the distinguished architectural firm of McKim, Mead & White.

25 Henri Marceau (1896–1969), American artist. He taught at the University of Pennsylvania. He was associated with Philadelphia Museum of Art, first as assistant director, then associate director, and ultimately director.

26 James Chilman (1891–1972), American artist. He was professor of fine arts at Rice Institute (now Rice University); first director of the Museum of Fine Arts in Houston; he was host of the popular radio show, "Art Is Fun."

27 Hanson's comments on baroque art seem to reflect lingering criticism from nineteenth-century art historians. Such criticism, however, would seem to have been terribly misplaced in the Rome of Bernini and Borromini, those

I have never understood the snobbishness and intolerance of so many purported art and music lovers. I see no reason why one should not appreciate both Bach and Rachmaninoff, Gershwin and Palestrina, modern jazz and fifteenth-century music. Above all, I cannot understand the intolerance of those professionals who believe that there exists only one authentic form of aesthetic expression: theirs!

Such matters were the subject of endless debate in the dining room of the academy, a large room with a great common table similar to the commons of an English university. One thing which impressed me [about these debates] was their intensity. To these men, the problems of the creator, in whatever art form, were all important. Nations might rise or fall, civilizations might flourish or decay, but to these men the important thing was man's creative spirit. Such an atmosphere is, I suppose, rare anywhere. It seemed to me to be even rarer in the United States, where even in the university the conversation was apt to be primarily concerned with sports. To me the debates around the breakfast or dinner table were both exciting and stimulating, and I look back on them with great appreciation.

One of the debates which went on continuously and without resolution had to do with the artist, his place in society, his relation to the public, his creative philosophy. I recall that the Fellows divided themselves rather evenly between what we call the "socialists" and the "rough-necks." The "rough-neck" party, to which I belonged, charged the "socialites" with attempting to advance their status in the arts by knowing the "right people," by catering to the artistic establishment. The "rough-necks" were the rebels who decried the influence of Society (with a capital "S"), accused the "socialites" of snobbishness, although we were, I am afraid, equally snobbish and self-righteous in the proclamation of our independence.

The architects, in the main, seemed to belong to the "socialists," as did some of the composers. The painters and sculptors, for the most part, were "rough-necks." Both sides were, of course, both right and wrong. Most of us in later life found that the artist must live and work in society—with both a small and a capital "S"—but he must not be absorbed by it. The radical of yesterday frequently became the conservative of today. The radical of today may, in turn, become the strictest of conformists to the avant-garde tradition! Fifty years later, the answer remains unresolved.

One of the practices of the architects of the academy, prescribed I believe by the authorities, was to examine firsthand the architectural monuments which they were studying. I went along on some of these fact-finding expeditions, and, as a result, found myself with Meyer and Skinner

---

incomparable masters of the Roman Baroque whose influence is present in practically every piazza and on every street in the Eternal City.

on the dome of Santa Maria della Salute in Venice. Readers who have been to Venice will remember this graceful structure, towering high above the canal. Unfortunately for me, I have had a horror of heights ever since my boyhood days when, on a dare and against all regulation, I climbed to the top of the water tower in Wahoo.

All went well until it came time to hold the end of the tape measure to the edge of the dome. Looking down to the waters of the canal far below, I was paralyzed. I had sufficient presence of mind to look resolutely back to the top of the dome rather than down to the water, and eventually got back safely. I did not, however, go on any further architectural climbing exhibitions. Jack Skinner had the perfect answer. Said he, "The best way to study architecture in Italy is to seat yourself comfortably in a *trattoria* with a good bottle of red wine, and watch the architecture go by." I found the advice excellent and much safer.

We did later climb to the top of the great Cathedral of Milan, a perfectly safe climb. The cathedral is, of course, a magnificent example of Gothic architecture. I was, however, especially impressed with something which I saw at the top of my climb. On the very top of the building are a host of sculptured angels, relatively small figures, some of great beauty and delicacy. They could hardly be seen from the ground, far below, and yet they had been wrought with as much care as though they were to be on exhibition in a gallery.

I do not suppose that history records who the sculptors were. In those days, the overwhelming importance of the human ego had apparently not yet developed. They were creating in the spirit of devotion to God and to beauty. Whether anyone knew who had created them was of less importance. The artist today, with his emphasis on the supreme "I," might perhaps learn something from his early counterparts.

One of [the] architectural studies had results which almost touched off an international incident. Victor Hafner had undertaken an "on-the-spot" study of the dome of Saint Peter's. In his investigations he discovered what he considered to be large cracks in the dome's construction. Being himself a not particularly reticent person, he was not at all secretive about his "discovery." The gossip about the condition of the dome spread rapidly, calling forth agonized denials from the Roman authorities, protests to the academy administration, and (I believe) to the American Embassy. Later Hafner proudly reported that, as a result of his architectural "sleuthing," certain steps were taken to ensure the complete safety of the dome. In any event, the entire academy breathed easier when this incident was safely over.

This was not our only encounter with the Roman authorities. The fellows of the academy got along well with the Italians. Most of them acquired a reasonable competence in the Italian language and developed a real affection for this genial and happy people. We were somewhat less fond of the young fascists, many of whom were arrogant and overbearing.

On one occasion, my friend Lawrence Stevens was standing innocently on the curb watching a parade. When the Italian flag passed, he dutifully removed his hat, but when the fascist banner passed he put it back on again. Several young *fascisti*, observing this insult, set upon him. But, as I have said before, Stevens was a powerful man accustomed to working with great blocks of marble, and he fought back with vigor and determination. The young fascisti emerged considerably the worse for wear, and Stevens reappeared at the academy bloody but unbowed.

There were protests from the police, diplomatic presentations to the academy administration, but the academy supported Stevens's right to remain "hatted" during the passage of the emblem of a political party. The fascists were not yet in complete control of the government, and, furthermore, in the United States it was not necessary for us to remove our hats in the presence of either the elephant or the donkey!

Chapter Ten

AT THE AMERICAN ACADEMY

At the end of my first year at the academy, another invaluable experience came my way. Felix Lamond was a firm believer in the thesis that a young composer for the orchestra cannot evaluate the results of his composition until he hears it in [a] living performance. To realize this aim, he determined to engage the musicians of the famous Augusteo Orchestra[1] and present for the public a concert of works by the composers of the academy.

Since I was the only one at the academy with any conducting experience, Mr. Lamond asked me if I would undertake the assignment. My own professional experience at that time was limited to my few appearances with the orchestras of Los Angeles and San Francisco but beginning in my student days I had developed a considerable technique in score-reading, and I loved rehearsing new orchestral works. Needless to say, I accepted with alacrity.

My first problem was age. I was still in my mid-twenties and looked even younger. The musicians of the Augusteo were, for the most part, old "pros," and I was concerned that they might not be thrilled to find themselves under the direction of a young American. The solution seemed simple. I would grow a goatee, which was within my hirsute possibilities. My choice of a goatee was also, I am sure, historically motivated. My paternal grandfather, as I have said, had a beautiful goatee. Two of my revered teachers, Dr. Percy Goetschius and Dean Peter Lutkin had goatees, as well as President Tully Knoles. The choice seemed clearly indicated. I doubt if my newly acquired adornment fooled anyone, but it made me feel more at ease as I stood for the first time before that distinguished orchestra.

The first program, as I recall, consisted of a delightful overture, *Pierrot and Cothurnus*, by Randall Thompson (which he himself conducted), a brilliant concerto for two pianos and orchestra by Leo Sowerby, and my own Symphony No.1, the *Nordic*. In spite of my youth and relative inexperience—especially in comparison with the masters of the baton under

---

   1   The Augusteo Orchestra was founded in 1908 and is now known as the Orchestra dell' Accademia Nazionale di Santa Cecilia.

whom the orchestra was accustomed to play—the musicians treated me with the greatest consideration, and the concert came off smoothly.

Although the concert was a success, one of my contributions did not meet with official favor. For reasons of protocol, it was suggested that we open the program with the Italian anthem followed by the *Star-Spangled Banner*. The problem was that no orchestral arrangement of our national anthem was available. I set about immediately to remedy this lack by creating my own arrangement. It was my desire to produce a version of symphonic proportions, somewhat different from the usual "stock" orchestrations. Therefore, I began the anthem with four French horns *soli*, introducing a few modes dissonances on the way. After the concert, our Ambassador Chil was heard to remark, "It was a fine concert, but what in the world was that piece they played following the Italian anthem?" Such is the reward for creative ingenuity!

Another concert appearance which I recall with amusement concerned no less a personality than King Victor Emanuel. It was the king's custom to pay occasional visits to the academy, and in honor of one of his visits it was Mr. Lamond's wish to present a short recital. . . . Sowerby presented some of his chamber music, and my assignment was to produce a piano suite for the occasion. I hastily resurrected some piano sketches, dedicated them to his majesty, and performed them with considerable bravura. In presenting the dedication, my friends tell me that I clicked my heels in true imperial fashion before I sat down to play. My piano-playing was well-received, but my heel-clicking dedication was somewhat of a sensation. After all, I had little experience with kings in Wahoo, Nebraska, and the gesture seemed appropriate.

As I have said before, in those early days my conducting was of the violent variety. I used the stick more as a rapier than a baton and flailed my way through the scores with tremendous energy. My energy almost cost me a tympani player. I was rehearsing my own symphony. In the first movement, there is a long concluding passage where the tympani has a repeated *ostinato* figure played *fortissimo*. Just before the final chord, the orchestra is silent, except for the tympanist who has a final repetition of this figure played *allargando* and *fff* (as loud as possible).

It seemed impossible for me to get the effect that I wanted. I implored the tympanist in my best Italian, *fortississimo come possibile* (as loud as possible). The tympanist, anxious to oblige, struck the first tympanum a mighty blow. But he was a powerful man, and the blow broke the drum head. He was also a short man, and the impact of the blow through the broken head almost precipitated him into the kettle. The orchestra, seeing what had happened, broke into gales of laughter. I had finally secured my fortississimo. But the ice was completely broken, as well as the tympanum head, and after the experience I conducted a shade more quietly.

In retrospect, it now seems to me that I have always been out of step with the age in which I was living. In my early days, the idol among conductors was Artur Nikisch,[2] famous for his small, conservative beat. My beat, on the other hand, whipped the air in terms of feet if not yards. Now that the years have passed, and I have developed a much quieter manner of conducting, the style has changed to modern conducting, which seemed so natural to me almost fifty years ago.

In composition, too, as the "style" has changed from romanticism (whatever that may mean) to the antiseptic music of the present day, I find myself even more passionately dedicated to the philosophy of music as the most powerful form of emotional expression. But, I suppose, it really does not matter. The artist, be he composer or performer, must do what he must, must fight for the principles which to him seem right and worth fighting for. The only crime is to be unfaithful to one's own convictions.

The academy concerts, both chamber and orchestra, also had the effect of bringing us in direct touch with Italian musicians, and particularly composers. Ottorino Respighi[3] was a frequent visitor and occasionally took a personal part in the presentation of his own beautiful songs. Madame Respighi was a sensitive singer, and, with the maestro at the piano, the effect was quite magical.

Respighi himself was a delightful person. Although he was not a tall man, he had a massive, leonine head, looking very much like the portraits of Beethoven, a fact of which I do not believe he was completely unconscious. I have read in a number of places that I was a pupil of Respighi. This is not really true, since I never had formal instruction from the maestro. He was kind enough to listen to some of my works and to give me the benefit of his vast knowledge of the orchestra. (He had been a pupil of that master of orchestration, Rimsky-Korsakoff.) Most helpful was the chance to study his scores and to hear them in rehearsal and performance, the best way for any young composer to acquire a mastery of the orchestral medium. (As an aside, I might observe that once in a meeting of a number

---

    2   Arthur Nikisch (1855–1922), Hungarian-born conductor. He was considered to be an outstanding interpreter of German symphonic music; led the Gewandhausorchester Leipzig and the Berlin Philharmonic from 1895 until his death in 1922.

    3   Ottorino Respighi (1879–1936), Italian composer. He studied in Bologna and then with Rimsky-Korsakoff during several visits to Russia; best known for his colorful and brilliant orchestral pieces.

of distinguished composers, the question of the art of orchestration came up for discussion. Not one of us had ever taken a "course" in the subject!)

I shall never forget my first impression of Respighi's *Pines of Rome* by the orchestra of the Augusteo under the direction of Bernardino Molinari.[4] I think that it was the [premiere] performance. Even today, after both hearing and conducting many performances, the impact of the work remains powerful. It is difficult to imagine the tremendous excitement of hearing it for the first time. Molinari brought out all its qualities, the childlike gaiety of the first movement, the archaic solemnity of the second, the bittersweet quality of the *Gianicolo*, and the almost brutally martial quality of the finale. Indeed, in retrospect, it almost seems that the pines of the Appian Way were to forecast the dominance of fascism and the rise of the Second World War.

This, I am sure, was far from Respighi's mind. He was a quiet and gentle man, kindly and sensitive. I sometimes think that music often reflects the age and prognosticates the future quite without the intention of the composer. Respighi was thinking of the legions of ancient, Imperial Rome, marching in triumph along the *Via Appia*. To many Italians, the work must have been associated with the New Italy, *Il Duce*, the *Mare Nostrum*, and the *Gloria d'Italia*.[5] Perhaps it meant this to Molinari, who conducted it with passionate devotion.

Other occasional visitors to the academy included the brilliant Alfredo Casella[6] and Malipiero,[7] the gifted Castelnuovo-Tedesco[8] and the gentle Santoliquido.[9] In spite of his brilliance, Casella was never my favorite. He was a superior scholar with a penetrating mind, a virtuoso pianist, and a superb linguist, changing from Italian to French or English and, I would guess, to German with equal fluency. In fact, he always seemed to me more

---

4   Bernardino Molinari (1880–1952), Italian conductor. He was the director of the Augusteo Orchestra and the Orchestra dell' Accademia Nazionale di Santa Cecilia 1912–44.

5   This refers to Benito Mussolini and the slogans of Italian Fascism.

6   Alfredo Casella (1883–1947), Italian pianist, composer, and teacher. He studied in Paris with Louis Diémer, and then taught in Rome and Siena.

7   Gian Francesco Malipiero (1882–1973), Italian composer, musicologist, and teacher. He taught in Parma 1921–24, then in Venice 1939–52; edited the complete works of Monteverdi.

8   Mario Castelnuovo-Tedesco (1895–1968), Italian composer. He wrote concertos for Segovia and Heifetz; left Italy in 1939 because of rising anti-Semitism and became an important composer of music for Hollywood films.

9   Francesco Santoliquido (1883–1971), Italian composer. He studied in Rome and wrote in many genres; influenced by Wagner and Debussy. Hanson appears unaware that Santoliquido later authored several pro-fascist articles.

French than Italian, and when there was a choice of Italian or French, he always seemed to prefer the latter.[10] It was almost as though he was not particularly proud of being an Italian, though it is entirely possible that I misinterpreted his preference.

I recall hearing the first performance of his *Altre Notte* with the orchestra of the Augusteo, again under Bernardino Molinari. It was at that time considered an "advanced" work, very modern in style. After a few minutes had passed, a part of the audience, offended by the dissonance of the work, began hissing. As the hissing grew louder in volume, the music-lovers who wanted to have an opportunity of hearing the work without this competitive hissing began to hiss the hissers. The combination of the pro-hissers and the anti-hissers virtually overwhelmed the sound of the orchestra. As I recall, Molinari finally gave up and stopped the orchestra. I have often thought that American audiences are too docile, and that they might, at times, be more emphatic both in their approval and disapproval—but after the performance not during it!

The concerts of the Augusteo were exciting. In the first place, the hall was ideal for orchestral performances. It was built above the tomb of Augustus Caesar, giving rise to the name Augusteo. It was, as I recall, circular in shape with most of the audience seated around and above the orchestra. I have always thought that the proper way to build a concert hall would be to place the orchestra in a spacious circular well and place the audience in concentric circles above and around the orchestra. The Augusteo was the closest approach to such a plan that I have ever seen, and the sound seemed to me to be unusually rich and resonant. In Mussolini's campaign to restore the glories of Rome's ancient monuments, the hall was torn down so that the tomb of the emperor might be revealed. I can understand Il Duce's historical ambitions, but it seemed a shame to lose such a concert hall.

The programs of the Augusteo orchestra were also unusually stimulating. Molinari served as musical director, but each season brought a parade of conductors, including many famous composers conducting their own works. I recall seeing and hearing Sibelius, Ravel, Richard Strauss, as well as many less famous composers in performances of their own compositions.

Strauss was, of course, a superb conductor with a small, precise beat. Neither Ravel nor Sibelius were very effective conductors, but it was exciting to watch them in performances of their own works. I recall watching Strauss conduct one of his tone poems, I believe it was *Heldenleben*.

---

10   Casella was born in Turin, located in northwestern Italy adjacent to France. The local dialect and culture reflected a pronounced French influence.

Before the rehearsal began, the cellos and basses were frantically practicing their parts to give the famous maestro the best possible performance of his work. When Strauss came to the most difficult passage, he stopped the orchestra and said something like this: "Gentlemen, do not worry too much about the notes. I just want the general effect." He got it!

In addition to the composer-conductors, there were guest conductors from Germany, Switzerland, France, Czechoslovakia, England—I suppose, indeed, from almost every country with a symphonic tradition. One conductor whom I admired greatly and who was to have a profound effect upon my future career was the Englishman, Albert Coates.[11] Among all the guest conductors, he was one of the most popular. His programs were never hackneyed but always contained some new work of special interest. Here I made my first acquaintance with the exciting suite, *The Planets*, by Gustav Holst, whom I was to meet later in London. Here also I had my first experience with the massive symphonies of Alexander Scriabin, which Coates performed magnificently.

He was a big man with a powerful beat and an almost hypnotic effect upon the orchestra. I am sure that he was not as meticulous in his rehearsals as were many of his colleagues, but the effects which he obtained from the orchestra in works such as Scriabin's *Poème de l'Extase*, were tremendous, almost overpowering in their intensity. Albert Coates was, at this time, spending about half of the season in Rochester, New York, where he was (with Eugene Goossens) co-director of the newly formed Rochester Philharmonic Orchestra. His relationship [with] George Eastman and the Rochester orchestra was to greatly affect my future.

---

11   Albert Coates (1882–1953), Russian-born English conductor. He studied with Nikisch in Leipzig and introduced many new works by composers such as Vaughan Williams, Bax, Scriabin, and Holst.

Chapter Eleven

TRAVELS IN EUROPE AND COMPOSING IN ROME

One of the very pleasant duties of the fellows of the academy was to do a certain amount of traveling during each calendar year. Although such traveling was not, strictly speaking, mandatory, all of us were glad to have the opportunity of seeing as much of Europe as possible. As travelers, we operated on strictly third-class budgets. Our stipends were, as I recall, $1,000 per year for three years. Our studios and living quarters were furnished without cost. The sum of three thousand dollars had to take care of food, clothing, incidental expenses, and all expenses of travel, including the transportation from the United States to Italy and return.

Meyer and I solved our transportation problem by traveling peasant-fashion through Florence, Pisa, the [Tuscan] hill country, Perugia, Milan, and Venice in railroad carriages redolent of red wine and garlic to which we rapidly became accustomed. Since this form of transportation was very cheap, we were able to treat ourselves to a wonderful week of swimming in *Lago di Como,* certainly one of the world's most beautiful lakes, after which we used the cheapest mode of transportation, hiking, to get us to Switzerland. On the way, to prove we were red-blooded Americans, we climbed the Dormadossola for good measure.

We were charmed by the mountains and lakes of Switzerland and by the charming countryside, but we hurried on to hear Mozart in Salzburg and opera in Munich. We visited the ancient cities of Heidelberg, Oberammagau, and Rothenburg, and then headed for Berlin.

The First World War was already several years past, but its effects in both Germany and Austria were all too apparent. We were in Vienna during the days of the bread riots and left as quickly as we could with the feeling that we were, by our presence, contributing to the starvation of those unhappy citizens. The effects of the war in Berlin were less spectacular but just as grim. The terrible inflation of the early 1920s was moving to its ultimate conclusion.

It was our practice, in order to preserve our slim resources, to change one dollar at a time for German marks. One day the exchange would be, for example, at the rate of 10,000 marks for an American dollar. The following day, the exchange may have risen to 50,000 marks per dollar and, a short time later, to 100,000 marks. The effect on the German economy was, of course, catastrophic, and the plight of the lower and middle classes, who might see their life savings wiped out overnight, was frightening.

I am afraid that many tourists, including Americans, were quite oblivious to the plight of the German people and were delighted at the miracle of being able to spend an evening (which might include a sumptuous dinner with the finest wines, followed by a box at the opera) for a total expenditure of a couple of American dollars. Every American suddenly became in effect a millionaire, and I am afraid none of us were sufficiently sensitive to understand fully the *Gethsemane* which the Germans were experiencing. I hold no brief for Kaiser Wilhelm nor for Bismarckian ambitions,[1] but it has always seemed to me that the horrors of World War II conceivably might have been avoided if we had all been a little more perceptive.

After Germany, I left my friends and proceeded to Sweden to visit the land of my parents and to seek inspiration for my *Nordic* symphony. I suppose that we all have a latent nostalgia for the land of our forefathers, even though it is not our land. This feeling was very strong in me, and as I walked through the fields of Skåne (remarkably like my own fields of Nebraska) and along the beautiful lakes of central Sweden, it seemed to me that I had indeed come back to deep roots, to sources which went back to an infinite past. After all, the Swedes of Wahoo were still very close to their former homeland. I recall that, in the Swedish Evangelical Lutheran Church in which I grew up, all of the morning services were in Swedish but, as a concession to the young folks, one evening service per month was in English. Returning to Wahoo a few years later, the ratio had been reversed to one service in Swedish and all the others in English. On my last visit, the services in Swedish had completely vanished.

After completing the *Nordic*, I tried to give my impressions of the duality within me by writing what I called a "symbolic poem," *North and West*, which attempted to portray the influence of both the country of my parents and the Nebraska plain of my birth. The score was a rather massive one, calling for not only a large orchestra but [also] a wordless chorus of men's and women's voices. The score was more modern, more experimental, and less lyrical than the symphony. I was never completely satisfied with the working out of the material, and it went through several metamorphoses before attaining its final form as a concerto for organ, harp, and strings.

---

1   Hanson is referring to the expansionist policies of Otto von Bismarck (1815–89), who served as the first chancellor of the German Empire.

I devoted the following summer to finishing the symphony, working at it continuously through a part of the hot Roman summer. I had met the previous winter some members of a most charming Scottish family, the McKays, who were visiting Rome, and after completing the symphony accepted their invitation to visit them at their home near Oban on the west coast of Scotland. The combination of the warmth of their gracious hospitality and the coolness of the climate of western Scotland after the heat of Rome revived my somewhat flagging energies. It also encouraged me to begin still another composition venture, which was to prove more successful than the previous attempt.

I had found in the academy library a copy of the Anglo-Saxon epic *Beowulf*. I was very much intrigued with the story itself and the word-sound of the Anglo-Saxon. Since it was not practical to attempt to set the original, I looked about for a translation and, with the help of friends, came across the translation by Morris and Wyatt. I was no Anglo-Saxon scholar, but it did seem to me that this particular translation preserved to a remarkable degree the word-sound of the original. Scotland was, of course, not the home of the epic, but the Scottish climate, with the mist on the moors and the swirling fog coming off the west ocean, seemed to be ideal for communing with the spirit of the poem. I determined to make a setting of the final section, which recounts the death of the hero after his final battle, the mourning of his people, and the setting of the funeral pyre above the northern seas. I gave to it the title, *The Lament for Beowulf*.

Bidding goodbye to my delightful hosts, I took my copy of the translation and the ideas which had come to me in my walks along the moors and hastened back to Rome. I had already done considerable work on a symphonic poem for orchestra with viola obbligato, which I called *Lux Aeterna*, and, since it was scheduled for performance at the final concert at the Academy, it had to be finished before I could work on *Beowulf*. A music historian writing on American composers remarked with a note of beneficent condescension that all of my compositions seemed to be concerned with something which was related to my own personal emotions, in other words not "absolute" music. I have no quarrel with the gentleman except perhaps to say that, in my opinion, very little of the great music of the past has really been "absolute." Most of the great symphonies have reflected to a considerable degree the temperament and the mood of their creators. It has been left to the age of the digital computer to develop "absolute" music, music which is strictly antiseptic, far removed from the fragility of human emotions.[2]

---

2   The Eastman School of Music established an electronic music studio in 1967, three years after Hanson's retirement.

In any case, if it is criminal to be influenced by one's emotional reactions to differing situations, I must plead guilty. *Lux Aeterna* is a case in point. Coming to Rome, I was deeply impressed with its religious symbolism, embodied not only by the sight of the great basilicas but equally (for me) in their sound, the sound of their myriads of bells. In my studio, high above the city, I could hear not only the bells of St. Peter's but also the smaller bells of the churches of Rome and the high-pitched bells of the churches in Trastevere. On the most important of holy days, these bells might be joined by the greatest of them all, the "great bell" of San Pietro in Vaticano.

One Sunday morning, as I was listening to the combined rhythms of bells, there came back to me with great vividness a forgotten scene of my childhood. It was an early Easter morning service in our Lutheran church in Wahoo. The Lutheran service at its best has great dignity with its great chorales and its simple but impressive liturgy. At the end of the service, the large doors were thrown open, and the bright, golden sunlight flooded the church, lighting up even the altar itself. Here was, in truth, the "light eternal," the Easter message, the eternal hope, brought by the light of the sun and now by the sound of the bells of Rome. And so, I wrote my *Lux Aeterna*. After all these years, I still consider it one of my "good" works.

It is, I believe, a common assumption that an artist, whether he be painter, sculptor, writer, or composer, can never be an objective judge of his own work. With this, I cannot agree. I doubt if a creative artist is an adequate judge of his most recent work, but after a passage of time, I believe that an objective judgment is quite possible. Indeed, after the passage of several decades, one can look back on an early work either with the mental comment, "Why in the world did I write *that*?" or, in happier situations, "The young fellow did have talent!" I still regard *Lux Aeterna* as a "good work" and the *Lament for Beowulf* as one of my best efforts.

I was to have one fling at "absolute," nonprogrammatic music before I left Rome. During my final year at the academy, I received a letter offering me a commission of a thousand dollars to write a string quartet for the famous Coolidge Festival. Mrs. Elizabeth Shurtleff Coolidge[3] had been, for my years, a generous patroness of chamber music, and a host of distinguished composers from all over the work had written compositions for her. In 1924 she established the Coolidge Foundation in the Library of Congress and transferred her festivals to Washington. My quartet was to be commissioned as one of the works to be performed at this initial Library of Congress Festival.

---

3   She is more commonly known as Elizabeth Sprague Coolidge. Shurtleff was her husband's middle name, but she later ceased using it in favor of her own maiden name.

The thousand-dollar commission was equivalent to an entire year's stipend at the academy, and the commission added considerably to my short rations, as well as being a great honor for a young American. It was also my first major attempt in the difficult field of chamber music, my only previous attempt having been a student work, a quintet for piano and strings.

In spite of my determination to write "absolute," nonprogrammatic music, my emotions again interfered. I had fallen deeply in love with the charming young lady whose parents I had visited in Scotland. The feeling, unfortunately, was much stronger on my part than on hers. I was greatly depressed and poured my emotions into the quartet. The effects on the quartet were not entirely salutary. The violence of the emotions strained the legitimate bounds of string quartet writing, so that in the climaxes one feels that there should be at least twenty violins instead of one! I have heard it played by a number of famous quartets, including the Persinger Quartet (which gave the first performance), the Gordon Quartet, the Juilliard, and the Eastman Quartet, and in certain cases by an adroit manipulation of dynamics, it has sounded like a string quartet and not like an abortive work for full string orchestra. It contains, I believe, some of the best music I have ever written, but (to paraphrase an old musical phrase) it is written against the string quartet not for it.

As in the case of my relationship with Ottorino Respighi, I have often been impressed by the kindness of some of the masters towards an aspiring young composer. One instance which lingers in my memory concerns the late Sir Edward Elgar, whose *Enigma* variations remain one of my favorite orchestral works. Sir Edward, through that mysterious "grapevine" that seems to connect all musicians, had heard that a young American was working on his first symphony in Rome. He immediately sent word to me that he had written his first symphony in Rome and that he wished to extend to me his very best wishes for mine!

I had the opportunity later of meeting a number of British composers, including Arthur Bliss, Arnold Bax, Sir William Walton, and (above all for me) Gustav Holst. I had dinner with Holst, as I recall, on his birthday, and our conversation was concerned largely with the master's positive aversion to the music of Wagner. The aversion seemed to amount almost to a personal hatred. Knowing the difficulty which confronted the late nineteenth-century composers in freeing themselves from the powerful Wagnerian influence, his dislike for Wagner became quite understandable. Having myself been under the influence of Jan Sibelius, I can sympathize, although my affection for Sibelius has never diminished. When, in an article about me for the *Christian Science Monitor*, the distinguished historian Nicholas Slonimsky labeled his article, "The American Sibelius," I did not know whether to feel complimented or insulted.

Chapter Twelve

AN INVITATION FROM ROCHESTER

One day the academy received a famous visitor from the United States, the noted Walter Damrosch, musical director of the New York Symphony Orchestra, a trustee of the academy and chairman of its examining jury for the Rome Prize in musical composition. Having been partially responsible for my appointment to the academy, he was much interested in seeing what I had accomplished in my first two years of residence. Aside from his interest in the academy, he belonged to the estimable group of conductors who believed that composers—even young, living ones—were important.

He examined my scores and seemed particularly interested in *North and West*, with its unusual instrumentation. He had also heard from the academy favorable reports on my conducting of the academy orchestral concerts. As a result, he asked me if I would care to make a trip back to the United States to conduct the first performance of *North and West* with the New York Symphony Orchestra. The invitation did not have to be pressed. The idea of conducting the New York Symphony in one of my own compositions was enormously exciting, and I was curious to see how one of my works would stand the formidable test of the New York audience and critics.

There was an even more important reason for my [wish] to return. I had recently received word of the serious illness of my father. My parents both urged me not to return and interrupt my work, but this was difficult advice to follow. My father and I had always been very close, and his illness was constantly on my mind. The Damrosch invitation seemed heaven-sent. And so, at the appropriate time, I embarked for New York and Wahoo on a boat somewhat larger than the tiny *Taormina*.

The old New York Symphony was a great orchestra, boasting among its membership men like Georges Barrere, the famous French flutist; the Russian French horn [player,], Arcady Yegudkin; violinist Rene Poullain; the concertmaster Gustav Tinlot; and the first cellist Paul Kéfer. [Yegudkin, Tinlot, and Kéfer] were later to join me on the Eastman school faculty.

The audience reaction was friendly, the critical reaction mixed but generally favorable. I was delighted that the veteran critic, W.J. Henderson, gave the academy as well as the composer a pat on the back by writing, "One evidence of the service given to music by the academy disclosed itself in the character of the work. It was not a Leipzig Conservatory composition. It was free from the scholastic formulae established by German classicists. . . . He has heard and assimilated the works of Pizzetti, Malipiero, and even Stravinsky. But he is no mere imitator."

In reading Mr. Henderson's remarks, it must be remembered that the late nineteenth- century American composers (including even Edward MacDowell) were considered to be too greatly under the influence of German music, hence the reference to the fact that I was no "Leipzig Conservatory composer."

Following the New York concert, I hurried on to Wahoo to find out at firsthand the condition of my father. I discovered that he was a victim of polycythemia, a disease of the blood about which there was not, at that time, much medical knowledge. His condition was critical, and the surgeon recommended the immediate amputation of one leg, to which my father had consented.

The reunion would have been a very sad one, except for my father's amazing courage and cheerfulness. He insisted that he was getting along beautifully, and he promised me that he would outlive his surgeon (which he proceeded to do!). At the same time, he insisted that I must return to Rome and finish my term at the academy. I left home with a heavy heart, wondering if I would ever see my father again.

Arriving in New York, I found awaiting me a letter from my good friend Albert Coates, inviting me to Rochester to conduct the first American performance of my first symphony with Rochester Philharmonic Orchestra, and so, a few days later, I made my first acquaintance with the city in which I was to spend the greater part of my adult life. I found the orchestra in splendid form, reflecting Albert Coates's tremendous enthusiasm and dynamic leadership. The orchestra gave me splendid support, and the performance was a complete success with both audience and critics. Harvey Southgate, with whom in later years I was to form a close friendship, wrote, "The importance of the occasion grew as it became apparent that here was a work of real symphonic proportions, created in the mold of a lofty imagination, and one whose first American performance will mark a musical date." Even the dean of Rochester critics, A.J. Warner, who was later to become my devoted enemy, wrote, "It is singularly sincere, direct music, and there is contained in its pages a somber beauty as well as the suggestion of surging and strife." The reviews of Stewart Sabin in the *Democrat and Chronicle* and of William P. Costello in the *Evening Journal* were equally favorable.

An even more important aspect of my visit to Rochester was the opportunity of meeting Rush Rhees, president of the University of Rochester, and George Eastman. Mr. Eastman [had] embarked upon a gigantic dual project, involving both music education and the support of a symphony orchestra. He had built for Rochester not only a great building to house a school of music but also a chamber music hall and a large and beautiful theater for both motion picture and symphony performances and had presented the complex to the University of Rochester.

In forming the Eastman School of Music, Mr. Eastman had taken over a local music school, the Institute of Musical Art, founded in 1913 by Alf Klingenberg and Herman Dossenbach, and had appointed Mr. Klingenberg as director. I never met Mr. Klingenberg, but I gather that he was an excellent musician.[1] He was a Norwegian brought up in the European traditions of musical education, and the philosophy of a music school as a part of a university apparently did not have his sympathy. In any case, after two years as director, he resigned and returned to Norway,[2] and the American pianist, Raymond Wilson, already a member of the faculty, was appointed acting director.

After my concert with the Rochester Philharmonic, President Rhees and Mr. Eastman invited me for a conference.[3] Both men were most impressive, although in very different ways. Dr. Rhees was a man of great dignity, short of stature and slightly rotund, every inch a university president. He possessed a command of the English language which I have never seen surpassed, and it was a delight to hear him discuss any subject. Mr. Eastman was not, I suppose, much taller than Rush Rhees, but his sparser built at that time gave him an appearance of greater height. He said very little, except to interject from time to time short and pertinent questions, but listened attentively to everything that was said. His sudden and terse questions were somewhat terrifying but also most stimulating.

President Rhees was anxious to set up within the university a professional school of music which would attract talented young musicians who could, at the same time, secure a general as well as a professional education. This had always seemed to me preferable to the plan of the European conservatory, with its complete devotion to technical and professional training. We discussed the problems of such an educational organization in considerable detail. At the end of the discussion, I was asked to draw

---

1   Klingenberg and his wife visited Rochester in 1934, and the first meeting of that visit was with Howard Hanson. He was quoted in Rochester newspapers as being very impressed with the Eastman School's young director. It is strange that Hanson does not recall that meeting.

2   Alf Klingenberg's resignation was requested by George Eastman.

3   Hanson's recollection of the specific chronology of events is strangely flawed. He was invited to come to Rochester to meet Rhees and Eastman in early January 1924. His performance with the Rochester Philharmonic occurred two months later on March 19. Therefore, his conversation with Rhees and Eastman took place before rather than after the Philharmonic concert.

up a plan for the organization of a professional undergraduate school of music within the framework of a university and present it to President Rhees. This I agreed to do, and within a few days my recommendations were in his hands.

Much as I admired George Eastman and Rush Rhees and appreciated the opportunity of serving as a consultant in developing plans for the Eastman School of Music, my first impression of Rochester was not particularly favorable. I had enjoyed working with the Rochester Philharmonic and had been thrilled by the warm reception of the Rochester audience, but there [was] something about the city which depressed me. To this day, I have never been able to define or to analyze that impression. The social structure of the city (what little I was able to observe in a short time) puzzled me. There seemed, in the first place, to exist a basic philosophy that being born in Rochester was in itself a high distinction. It was almost like "back-bay Boston." I was constantly being presented to someone "who comes from one of our oldest Rochester families." Many of them were charming and cultivated people, but it did not seem to me that their cultivation and charm were the direct result of being born in Rochester!

Then, too, the reaction of the citizenry to George Eastman was most perplexing. Mr. Eastman was not himself a member of the Rochester-born social hierarchy. In spite of his generous and unselfish gifts to the city, he seemed to be considered almost an interloper, an outsider who was trying to foist a musical culture upon a somewhat reluctant city. Mr. Eastman seemed to be unaware of this. He had, so far as I could observe, no "social" ambitions and was completely devoid of cultural pretense. He disclaimed any knowledge of music, but it was obvious to any but the most obtuse that his love of music was very deep and very genuine. Indeed, he needed music the way other men need food and drink. Above all, he was completely frank in his likes and dislikes. He loved Wagner and disliked Bach (a preference not likely to endear him to the elite) and he gloried in transcriptions of Wagner for organ and string quartet, made for him by his gifted organist, Harold Gleason. The fact that the most erudite of his Rochester friends preferred Bach, at least in theory, disturbed him not in the least.

At the same time, I am sure he was also much feared. As founder and head of the great Eastman Kodak Company, a millionaire and philanthropist, he wielded tremendous power. Such power is bound, I suppose, to breed a host of sycophants, among them musicians who wished to use his interest in music to their own selfish advantage. Mr. Eastman, of all of the men I have known, was the least subject to sycophancy. The musicians who neglected their responsibilities, hoping to impose on Mr. Eastman's lack of technical knowledge about music, generally discovered their mistake too late!

In any case, after delivering my report to President Rhees, I went back to Rome and promptly lost myself in composition. *Lux Aeterna* had to be completed for performance in Rome in the late spring, the string quartet was scheduled for performance at the Coolidge Festival in the Library of Congress in the autumn, and the ideas for *The Lament for Beowulf* had been germinating for some time. Albert Coates had asked me for the first performance of *Beowulf* at the Leeds Festival in England in the fall, but the pressure of completing three major works was too much, and it was not completed in time for the English premiere. Mr. Coates graciously substituted *Lux Aeterna* on the Leeds Festival program. The score [of *Beowulf*] bears a dedication to the Leeds Festival, but after my failure to deliver the work on time, it has never to my knowledge been performed at that famous festival.

About this time, President Rhees paid a visit to the academy. The story, as it was told to me many years later by Raymond N. Ball, chairman of the board of trustees of the university, was that Mr. Eastman liked everything about [me] except my youthful goatee. He had nothing against beards, but he wondered if the goatee might cover a weak chin! According to later accounts, President Rhees visited the academy and talked with my fellow academician, Randall Thompson. Randall reported that there was no need to worry about my chin; that I had been elected *massier* of the academy (a position comparable to that of president of student government) and that my nickname was Mussolini!

President Rhees apparently took Randall Thompson's reassurance back to Mr. Eastman, and shortly thereafter I received a cable offering me the directorship of the Eastman School of Music. I hesitated a long time in coming to a decision. The academy authorities, in particular Felix Lamond, did their best to persuade me to decline. They were convinced of my creative ability and were sure that the arduous task of administering an important professional school of music would ultimately stifle my composition talents. I debated the problem with my friends (and with myself) at great length. Could an important administrative position be successfully combined with creative work? I owed a great deal to the academy, and the advice to decline the appointment weighed heavily on my mind. On the other hand, the serious illness of my father demanded that I assume the financial responsibilities for my own family. I realized also that the directorship of the Eastman School would give me unparalleled opportunities to contribute to the cause of musical education in the university and [to] the American composer. I wired President Rhees my acceptance. I still believe it was a wise decision.

Figure 1. The Swedish Evangelical Lutheran Church (Augustana Synod) in Wahoo, Nebraska.

Figure 2. The Eckstrom family (Hanson's maternal grandparents).

Figure 3. The Eckstrom family home in Omaha, Nebraska.

Figure 4. Howard Hanson's mother, Hilda Eckstrom, before her marriage.

Figure 5. Howard Hanson's father, Hans Hanson.

Figure 6. Howard Hanson's mother, Hilda Eckstrom.

Figure 7. Howard Hanson's parents.

Figure 8. Howard Hanson's parents later in life.

Figure 9. Howard Hanson at the age of four.

Figure 10. Howard Hanson at the age of eleven (July 4, 1907).

Figure 11. Howard Hanson with the Wahoo, Nebraska, singing group "The Jenny Linds."

Figure 12. The young Howard Hanson.

Figure 13. The young Howard Hanson.

Figure 14. A portrait of Howard Hanson (c.1913–15).

Chapter Thirteen

BEGINNINGS IN ROCHESTER AND THE ESTABLISHMENT OF N.A.S.M.

In the summer of 1924, before leaving for the United States and my new position in Rochester, I decided to find out as much as I could of music education in Europe by visiting some of the typical European schools of music, such as the [conservatories] of Paris and of Brussels, and the Hochschule für Musik in Berlin. I was again impressed with the complete dichotomy of the European concept of music education. In Berlin, for example, if one wished to study musical performance, composition, or pedagogy, one enrolled in the Hochschule. If one wished to study *Musikwissenschaft* (which we have translated, I think badly, as "musicology"), aesthetics, acoustics, and the like, one attended the university.

There seemed to me to be two objections to this point of view, although it seemed presumptuous for a young American to challenge (even in his own mind) the educational philosophy of these famous institutions. The first was the irrational dissecting of an art, the separation of interests which should be mutually complementary, the separation of scholarship from both composition and performance, the separation of musical aesthetics and philosophy from practical theoretical problems.

The second objection, in my mind, was the rigid separation of professional from general education. I could see no reason why the training of the Hochschule could not be combined to some degree at least with the education of the university. It was, of course, possible that something might be lost in attempting to combine the two, but the advantages seemed to outweigh the disadvantages. The pioneering experiments of universities like Northwestern (and my own experience at Pacific) convinced me that the philosophy of education in music being followed in an increasing number of American universities and college conservatories had genuine merit. I returned to the United States with the ambition to create a music school which would be fully professional but which should also take into consideration the students' need for education outside [the] area of purely professional training.

I was to have forty exciting years in which to attempt to create the school of my dreams. My return to the United States, however, was to prove more exciting than I had anticipated. The previous trip on the *Conte Verde* had broken all weather records, but the return trip on the *S.S. Arabic* was to prove the climax. A few days before reaching New York, we were involved in the worst storm that I have ever witnessed. Huge waves broke over the ship so that it seemed almost impossible that it could survive. There was only one redeeming feature. The storm gave me my one chance to be a hero!

The New York *American* reported, "In the forward lounge at the time were seated a group consisting of Charles Dickens, coach of the Argentine-Chile Olympic team; his five-year-old son, Charles Jr.; and Mr. and Mrs. M.E. Baldwin of No.1140 Fifth Avenue; and about fifteen other persons, mostly women. The ship gave a terrific lurch as the tremendous wave hit it. In through half a dozen broken port holes came a great rush of water. Every article of furniture, including tables, desks, chairs, and a piano, together with the passengers and stewards went against the port side in one screaming, hysterical mass. Out of the twenty-one people in the room, Mr. Baldwin said at least fifteen were injured. Dickens, clinging tightly to his five-year-old boy, was caught by the great inrush of water and swept out of the great double door on the port side. The two, limp, were flung against a rail and covered by two feet of water. Howard Hanson, the composer, dove through the debris and yanked the child to safety, just as another wave came through the open passage from the starboard side. A second later, and the child would have been swept into the sea."[1]

My one concern in all the excitement was that this violent reintroduction to the United States did not forecast an equally stormy career in Rochester! I think I had some reason to be concerned. The climate of Rochester was highly conservative. Furthermore, the Rochester public was, I am sure, expecting some much more glamorous figure to head its famous new music school. Mr. Eastman had already attempted to induce Jan Sibelius to come to Rochester to head the composition department.[2] Sibelius, wisely I think, declined to leave his beloved homeland, and the noted Norwegian composer, Christian Sinding, came in his place. Sinding remained for only a year, to be followed by the Finnish composer, Selim

---

    1   In several drafts of chapter 12, Hanson included a similar story involving his voyage to New York to conduct the New York Symphony. While the earlier voyage may also have been a difficult journey, it is likely that Hanson's account of his bravery refers to this voyage and not the earlier one.
    2   There are many written accounts, including biographies and the respected *Grove's Dictionary of Music and Musicians*, that claim Sibelius was offered the directorship of the school. This is not accurate. Hanson is quite correct in stating that Sibelius was asked to teach composition.

Palmgren. It must, therefore, have seemed doubly strange that a young American from a town with the unlikely name of Wahoo, Nebraska, who had not yet attained his twenty-eighth birthday, should be selected for the directorship. Rochesterians were probably thinking in terms of someone like Richard Strauss, or perhaps Arturo Toscanini.

As I look back on those early days, I am continually amazed at the courage of Rush Rhees and George Eastman in entrusting a post of this importance to a young man, and one virtually unknown except for the Prix de Rome. I am also somewhat taken aback by my own temerity in accepting the assignment. Had I known the demanding nature of the position, I am not sure that my courage would have been sufficient.

The problems were very real. The faculty was largely of foreign birth and training. My ideals of musical education were, I am sure, quite different from theirs, and they could not be blamed for wondering whether the young man could fulfill the responsibilities pressed upon him.

The student body was small and, with some exceptions, not very good. Mr. Palmgren had, as I recall, only one student, a young lady who had written a few songs and piano pieces. He was a charming man and a gifted composer, but I am sure that he was overcome with boredom. He would frequently be "taken ill" at the time of his one "class" and would leave his studio and go to the movies, indicating that his illness was apparently not serious.

All of the classes in history and theory were taught by a wonderful old gentleman named George Barlow Penny, whose passion was numerology and who puzzled the students with the presentation of diagrams in various colors depicting the history of "musicke." Few of the famous teachers had students worthy of their teaching, and to build a student body worthy of the faculty was an immediate and pressing problem.

In only one department did this problem not exist: the opera department. Vladimir Rosing had persuaded Mr. Eastman of the wisdom of creating an opera department which would, in turn, develop a professional opera company. From Mr. Eastman's point of view, this was an excellent idea. His plan in building the Eastman Theatre was to create an organization in which a motion picture theater could be used to support a symphony orchestra.

The inspiration for this idea came from Mr. Rothafel and his famous "Roxy" Theatre in New York City. The [new] orchestra [in Rochester], an excellent body of about sixty-five players, could be used for overtures, stage productions, and the accompaniment of the feature motion pictures. It could also be used as the nucleus of a philharmonic orchestra in presenting a series of symphony concerts.

The opera department, as an adjunct of both the Eastman School and the Eastman Theatre, could be used not only for the performance of opera but also for the presentation of opera scenes in connection with the motion pictures. To develop an opera department capable of undertaking such an assignment, nationwide auditions of young singers were held. Students who were accepted received free tuition and an annual stipend of a thousand dollars, a rather generous "scholarship" for those days. As a result, the opera department was composed of a large group of very talented singers, many already on their way to artistic maturity.[3]

Aside from the opera department, which was a prime example of "forced growth," the student body was in pretty much of an embryonic state. We had a student orchestra of about thirty players, with faculty members "sitting in" to give us a complete instrumentation. The entire student body, exclusive of the opera department, had a total of only 230 students, 138 of whom were candidates for the "certificate" and 92 who were candidates for the bachelor of music degree. In the certificate course, there was only one academic requirement (one year of French), the reason for which I do not to this day understand!

My ambition to create a full-fledged university school of music with emphasis both on professional and general studies was to meet with difficulties. The students felt that, since they were attending a music school, they should study only musical subjects. The faculty, most of whom were the products of European "conservatories," fully sympathized with the students' point of view. Nor did I receive much support from the College of Arts and Science. The college had begun as a small liberal arts campus consisting of a group of old buildings which had served the college for many years. The faculty of the arts college looked on the new music school, with its magnificent new buildings and its ample endowment, with not a little envy.

It was clear that my efforts to combine general with professional education were to encounter many obstacles. In the first place, many of the faculty of the arts college sent to give courses at the school of music were not particularly anxious to do so. It was equally apparent that the lack of enthusiasm on the part of the college faculty was well-matched by a similar lack of enthusiasm on the part of many of the students. It seemed as

---

    3   Vladimir Rosing came to the Eastman School of Music to teach opera in 1923. The Rochester American Opera Company, a professional company whose members were Eastman students who had displayed special talent, was formed in November 1924. George Eastman withdrew financial support for the opera company in 1927.

though a long period of mutual indoctrination would be necessary before the desired results could be obtained.

The solution, it seemed to me, was to try to secure an academic faculty whose members had a genuine interest in the arts, at least not an aversion to music. As long as we had a peripatetic academic faculty whose members dashed to the school, threw their collective hats and coats on the rack, taught their classes, and rushed away as quickly as possible, the development of any sustained interest in academic subjects seemed virtually impossible. Finally, after a number of years, I was able to persuade President Rhees to allow the Eastman School to develop its own academic faculty. This plan was met with something less than enthusiasm by the college, which was concerned with "standards" of instruction of academic subjects in a music school.

The plan, once in operation, proved a great success. The faculty was selected from instructors in the various disciplines who were themselves amateur musicians, or at least very interested in music. They were also sufficiently sensitive to the problems of a performing musician to realize that a student who was playing a solo recital in the evening might be inclined to "cut" a class the afternoon of the day of the performance.

Charles Cook Riker, a teacher of English who was also an excellent pianist and chamber music player, assisted me in assembling such a faculty. The effect on the music students was nothing short of miraculous. When they discovered that the school possessed an academic faculty whose members were interested in the musical ambitions of the student, who actually attended recitals, and who were concerned with the overall development of the individual, their attitude was completely changed. Previously, I had spent long hours persuading the student that the study of English, of foreign languages, the social sciences, and the like was important. Now suddenly the students began coming to me and asking for permission to take extra courses which were of particular interest.

The arts college faculty was not yet completely convinced of the wisdom of my plan, but the college for men had moved to a new campus several miles from the school of music, and faculty members were having enough problems commuting between the campus of the men's college and that of the women's college [which had remained downtown].[4] The final proof of the pudding came, I believe, when the French classes of the Eastman School under the tutelage of a devoted teacher, Anne Theodora Cummins, won all of the top French prizes within the university.

---

4   The University of Rochester maintained separate colleges for men and women until 1955.

Apparently, the academic standards of Eastman were keeping pace with its musical standards.

The second problem, the development of an excellent department of theory for all music students, posed fewer problems. We were able to persuade Melville Smith, later to become director of the Longy School in Boston, to take over the direction of courses in basic theory. His views were very similar to mine, and, within a short time, we had established a theoretical discipline which, I believe, had few equals and no superiors. Smith was followed by Allen McHose, the author of a number of widely used texts, and in turn by another excellent teacher, Donald White, when McHose became the school's associate director.

There was still a third problem, more difficult [to solve] than either of the other two. The academic degree in music, the bachelor of music, had gradually over the years been falling into disrepute. There was no national accrediting organization to set standards for the degree. As a result, the attainment of the Mus. Bac. degree in the United States was rapidly losing any meaning. In some institutions, it might be earned in as little as one year after high school. In others, it might require as many as five years of post–high school study. The bachelor of arts degree did not promise any solution, since this degree was firmly in the hands of faculties whose conception of music study was, in many cases, limited to the study of music history and theory, with little or no interest in the problems of musical performance.

The only solution, therefore, seemed to be the setting up of an accrediting organization to bring some order out of the chaos into which the bachelor of music had fallen. The moving spirit in this decision was Burnet Corwin Tuttle, at that time director of the famous Cincinnati Conservatory. Kenneth Bradley of the Bush-Temple Conservatory of Chicago became president of the newly formed National Association of Schools of Music, and I became chairman of the commission on curriculum, which also served as the committee on membership.

In February of 1925, with a grant from the Carnegie Foundation, I invited the heads of the most important music schools of the country to meet at the Eastman School to consider the problems involved. The meeting proved to be a "who's who" of professional music education in the United States. I do not have the complete list, but they included such men as the distinguished American composer and president of the New England Conservatory, George Whitefield Chadwick; Frank Damrosch, director of New York's Institute of Musical Art; Harold Randolph of the Peabody Conservatory of Baltimore; Earl Moore of the University School of Music of Michigan; the composer and critic Felix Borowski, president of the Chicago Musical College; John R. Hattstaedt, president of the American Conservatory of Chicago; Grace Spofford of the Curtis Institute in Philadelphia; Gilbert Coombs, director of the Coombs Broadstreet Conservatory; Kenneth Bradley of the Bush Conservatory; William McPhail, director of the McPhail Conservatory of Music in Minneapolis; Dean Harold Butler of the School of Music of Syracuse University; W. Grant Egbert of the Ithaca Conservatory; Earl Rosenbery of the Horner Institute of Kansas City; Kate Chittenden, director of the American Institute of Applied Musical Arts of New York City; Frederick Cowles, director of the Louisville Conservatory; Louise Westervelt of the Columbia School of Music of Chicago; Dallmeyer Russell, director of the Pittsburgh Institute of Music; Karl Faelton of Boston; and Burnet Tuthill of Cincinnati.

It will be noted that the majority of schools represented were private schools not associated with any college or university. Most of their directors or presidents were supreme individualists. Their interest in any form of control or regulation was minimal. They were, however, convinced that the standards of the professional music schools of the United States were being seriously questioned by academic authorities, and our choice in saving the validity of a music degree was whether we should hang together or hang separately! I recall particularly an impassioned speech by Walter Damrosch, in which he inveighed bitterly against the intrusion of colleges, universities, and academic authorities in general, in artistic affairs. The debate has gone on ever since in both artistic and academic circles without resolution. In the case of the music schools, however, the die had been cast, and the National Association of Schools of Music, which was to become one of the important professional accrediting agencies of the United States, had successfully passed through its baptism of fire.

Much work remained to be done.[5] The association was small, consisting of only a couple of dozen schools. Many of the private schools, which constituted the majority of the members, had little or no endowment and were looked [upon] with some suspicion by colleges and universities which were already members of powerful accrediting organizations, such as the North Central Association. Many of the presidents and directors of the independent conservatories looked with equal suspicion on the mechanics of accreditment with its "credit hours," academic requirements, strict regulations for admissions to degree courses, and the like. In general, however, they worked diligently to bring their institutions up to the standards for accreditment, frequently at considerable financial sacrifice.

---

5   The material from this paragraph to the end of the chapter was located separately in the archives. Since it pertains to the subject Hanson is discussing, it has been appended to the draft of this particular chapter.

Many of the conservative colleges and universities declined to join our new association, although we had strong support from universities such as Yale, Michigan, Illinois, Syracuse, Kansas, the University of Southern California, and others. After almost fifty years, the Music Department of Harvard is still not a member, a kind of "let them eat cake" philosophy!

Dean Harold Butler of Syracuse University and Dean Earl V. Moore of the University of Michigan were among the early presidents who labored diligently for the success of the association. Burnett Tuthill was the first executive secretary, serving in that capacity for many years. The fact that the association today consists of [so many] member schools and is now recognized as the official accrediting agency in professional music education is a tribute to the effective work of the early pioneers.

I began my duties with the organization as chairman of its commission on curricula and membership and later [served] for twenty years as its president. When the association decided to enter the field of graduate work, I became the first chairman of its graduate commission, serving until my retirement from the directorship of the Eastman School in 1964.

I still vividly recall a national association meeting on a stormy winter's day in Minneapolis, when we announced the beginning of graduate accreditation within the association. I explained that we would proceed to examine the institutions granting graduate degrees with all possible speed, and that no institution could be accredited at the graduate level until its examination had been satisfactorily completed. There was an uproar which could be heard in [nearby] St. Paul, many directors insisting that all schools should be examined at once. I explained that this was physically quite impossible but that no official list of accredited institutions would be issued until all examinations were complete. My recommendations were finally approved, but it was a great fight while it lasted!

In spite of my conviction that accrediting agencies do make an important contribution to the maintenance of educational standards, I must admit that I have considerable sympathy for the dissenters. Associations of this kind can become unbearably "stuffy" and conformist. Having discovered some educational philosophies which seem to be sound and effective, it is a temptation to force all institutions into the same mold.

"Standards" can become educational straitjackets, inhibiting experimentation and change. On certain occasions, to the astonishment (and at times dismay) of my colleagues, I have supported the right of the dissidents to go their own way, even if it meant the infraction of certain of the sacred pronouncements of the commission on curricula. The balance between a safe and sane conformity and imaginative experimentation is always a delicate one, but it must be preserved.

Chapter Fourteen

JOSEPH MADDY AND THE NATIONAL MUSIC CAMP

One of my most pressing tasks as the director of the newly created Eastman School of Music was to develop a student body. We had a distinguished faculty. We had the most modern buildings and equipment. We had, for those days, a substantial endowment, and, even more important, George Eastman standing by to give us additional support for any expansion which seemed appropriate.

Our student body, with the exception of the opera department, was largely local. There were, of course, individual talents, but the student body as a whole was both small and provincial. There were, for example, not enough competent instrumentalists to form even an acceptable "little symphony." There was no chorus and few gifted soloists.

It is true that the school from the beginning had a large and excellent preparatory department[1] presided over by Raymond Wilson, the assistant director and himself an able pianist and pedagogue. This department made important contributions to the cultural life of the city, as literally thousands of Rochester youngsters received the advantage of superior training from excellent teachers. From this standpoint, at least, Mr. Eastman's desire that the Eastman School and [Eastman] Theatre be—to use his own phrase—"for the enrichment of community life" was already realized.[2] As a professional school, however, we had hardly begun to function.

In the area of performance, the logical place to begin seemed to be the development of a first-rate orchestral department. An orchestra, after all, opens up not only the whole vast field of orchestral music and chamber music, but [also] serves as the essential accompanying force for solo

---

[1] The school's preparatory department offered noncredit lessons and classes for children and adults in the Greater Rochester area. It was later renamed the Community Education Division to reflect the growing number of registered adult students, and more recently it has been renamed the Eastman Community Music School.

[2] The words "For the Enrichment of Community Life" are inscribed high above the entrance to the Eastman Theatre. However, this phrase was selected by Rush Rhees, not by George Eastman.

performance of concertos, choral music, and opera. The obvious place to look for gifted instrumentalists was in the American high schools, for the growth of superior instruction in instrumental music—a movement which was soon to make the United States preeminent in this field—had already begun.

I was fortunate at this point to come to know Joseph E. Maddy,[3] who may quite properly take his place in history as the father of instrumental music in the American public schools. Dr. Maddy was not only an excellent musician, a superb teacher, and a first-rate organizer. He was also, fortunately, something of a showman and a brilliant propagandist for the cause of instrumental music.

On of his projects was to organize, under the aegis of the Music Educators' National Conference, a "National High School Orchestra," where gifted players from all over the United States came together for rehearsals and a gala concert. The effect of such a concert on the audience was little short of overwhelming. The effect upon the youngsters themselves was even more important.

Communities would vie with each other for the honor of having the greatest possible number of their talented young players in the National Orchestra. To be accepted in the orchestra was considered a great honor, and the National High School Orchestra became a kind of high school musical Olympics.

In 1928, I was invited by Dr. Maddy to be one of the conductors of a great orchestra, which was to be assembled in Chicago. The other two conductors were Frederick Stock, music director of the Chicago Symphony, and Dr. Maddy. I do not recall the size of the orchestra, but it was huge, perhaps between two and three hundred players. I do remember that the instrumentation included twelve harps placed (as was proper) on the top risers, and naturally prompting many remarks that we were, at last, in heaven!

The important thing, however, was not the size of the orchestra, impressive as it was, but the quality of the performance. For these young players constituted the cream of the country's musical crop, the most gifted instrumentalists from the States of the Union.

Some of these young people went on to become professional musicians, leaders in the country's musical life. Many others entered other professions, but I am sure that everyone received inspiration which would remain with them throughout their lives.

---

3   Joseph E. Maddy (1891–1966), American music educator. He was educated at Wichita College of Music, taught in Rochester, NY, and Richmond, Indiana; founder of the National Music Camp at Interlochen; faculty member at the University of Michigan.

A short time ago, I was attending commencement ceremonies at Denison University. On the platform next to me was a distinguished professor from a neighboring institution, a candidate for an honorary doctorate. When we were introduced, he said, "Oh, but I have met you before. I played cello under your direction in the National High School Orchestra in Chicago in 1928. I was on the second stand, Frank Miller was the solo cellist." Frank Miller later became first cellist of the Chicago Symphony, a brilliant soloist and later a conductor. My commencement partner became chairman of the Department of Philosophy and Religion at Oberlin College. But he still plays the cello!

As far as I know, there are no statistics as to the careers chosen by these talented young people. I would guess that only a small percentage entered the musical profession. I am sure, however, that the remainder added greatly to the sum total of America's musical culture, for they had all enjoyed the most important of music experiences, the joy of participation.

If participation in this experience was an unforgettable thrill for the young people in the National High School Orchestra, it was, I can testify, equally thrilling for the conductors. In my lifetime, I have been guest conductor of every major symphony orchestra in the United States, with the exception of the orchestras of Pittsburgh and Houston, as well as a number of famous European orchestras. There can be obviously no comparison between the technical competence of the great professional symphony orchestras and an orchestra of high school youngsters. And yet, if you like young people, there is a thrill in conducting such an orchestra which is quite different from any other experience. They do not perhaps always play all of the notes with complete accuracy, but there is a quality of inspiration which can only be described as spiritual.

It transcends technique. It soars above physical barriers. Playing under an inspiring conductor, they can literally play "better than they know how." A music critic once asked me how it was possible for young people to play difficult music so beautifully. To which my response was, "They have not found out how difficult it is."

After the concert, I went backstage to talk with the students and ran into (almost literally) Oscar Sonneck,[4] one of America's most brilliant musical scholars, for a number of years chief of the music division of the Library of Congress. As we talked, I noticed that there were tears in his eyes. "Oscar, what is wrong?" I asked. To which the eminent musicologist replied, "I can't help it. It was so beautiful." Beautiful it was, and inspiring.

---

4   Oscar Sonneck (1873–1928), American librarian, author, editor, and musicologist. He was head of the music division at the Library of Congress 1902–17; also editor of *The Musical Quarterly*.

I can only wish that more young musicians could have such an experience. I can wish, too, that some of our more sophisticated symphony conductors might find for themselves how thrilling the music of youth can be.

It was natural that the success of the National High School Orchestra should prompt the ambition to establish a summer camp where a similar experience could be offered high school musicians, not for a few days but for an entire summer. The fruition of this hope was the establishment the following summer of the National High School Music Camp at Interlochen, Michigan.

In establishing the camp, the motivating force, the inspiration, and the organizing genius was, again, Dr. Joseph Maddy. He did, however, have the assistance of a number of individuals for whom the idea had enormous appeal. Chief among these were Thaddeus P. Giddings,[5] director of music for the city of Minneapolis; C.M. Tremaine, founder of National Music Week; Judith Waller, Frank Dunham, and a number of conductors and music educators who had observed firsthand the possibilities of Dr. Maddy's dream.

In all my experience as an educator and musician, I have never seen another team like that of Giddings and Maddy. Dr. Maddy was a dreamer, a visionary, but at the same time a man of volcanic energy and (in the best sense) a "salesman of ideas," the likes of whom I have never met. His ideas came so fast that it was almost impossible for his speech to keep up with them. As a result, his speech had an almost breathless quality.

Thaddeus Giddings, on the other hand, was a schoolmaster of the old school, a disciplinarian before whose eagle eye the brashest young student might quail. The camp, which might easily have become an undisciplined home for temperamental young geniuses, had a regimen the likes of which could not be found today. The motto was, "early to bed, early to rise," and [a] schedule so full that it was difficult for any youngster to find time for mischief.

The rehearsals began on time (the morning rehearsal at the heathenish hour of 8:20 a.m.) and ended on time. When the conductor was on the podium, there must be complete silence, and woe be to the young player who violated the rule. Any student, no matter how talented, who violated "T.P's" rules was on the train bound for home before he realized what had

---

5 Thaddeus Giddings (1868–1954), American music educator. He studied at the University of Minnesota; supervisor of music for Minneapolis public schools 1910–42; instructor of public school music at the University of Minnesota 1915–28; instructor of public school music at McPhail College of Music 1923–42.

happened. I am sure that such a discipline would not work today, but it would be fun to see it tried.

The third member of the trio, C.M. Tremaine, had the awesome task of trying to keep the camp within shouting distance of financial solvency. He was a man of small stature, delicate build, and mild manner. His appearance belied his nature, for he had a tenacity and a determination to see the job through, without which the camp could hardly have survived.

A trio such as this proved unbeatable in the end, but the early days of the National Music Camp, although artistically and educationally successful, were financially most precarious. I was always reminded of a remark made by the president of a struggling university in the midst of the Depression. When I asked him how the university could possibly have gotten along in those difficult times, his answer was, "We lived on the interest from our indebtedness."

This would aptly describe the National Music Camp in its early days. We were always only one step ahead of the sheriff. Indeed, I remember one year when the bankers of Traverse City threatened to foreclose the camp because of its financial condition. Dr. Maddy told them to go ahead. He reminded them, however, that the camp, in spite of its beautiful surroundings, was useful only for a purpose similar to that for which it was being used. He called their attention to the thousands of dollars spent each summer by students of the camp and their parents and families in the stores of Traverse City. The bankers thought again, and the National Music Camp was, at least for the moment, saved.

The camp also had the fierce loyalty of its students and faculty, the kind of loyalty which seems to thrive on adversity. It also had the devotion of a number of distinguished conductors who believed in the camp and its ideals. It was Dr. Maddy's desire to have, as conductors for the national orchestra and chorus, men of outstanding ability and reputation. It was impossible to pay them the kind of salaries which they would normally expect.

This fortunately proved no obstacle. A number of conductors of reputation gave their services without compensation. As I recall, many of us paid our own expenses in order to see Dr. Maddy's dream realized. Among these men were such distinguished conductors as Walter Damrosch, Frederick Stock, Ossip Gabrilowitsch,[6] Eugene Goossens,[7] [and] Frederick

---

6   Ossip Gabrilowitsch (1878–1936), Russian-born American pianist and conductor. He studied in St. Peterburg with Anton Rubinstein and in Vienna with Theodore Leschetizky; founding director of the Detroit Symphony.

7   Eugene Goossens (1893–1962), English conductor and composer. He led the Rochester Philharmonic Orchestra 1923–31 and Cincinnati Symphony

Fennell.[8] Seldom in history have high school students had the privilege of working with such a group of eminent men.

Today the National Music Camp is internationally famous, with the support of many foundations and at least one generous "angel," the philanthropist Clement Stone.[9] The campus contains beautiful new classrooms, auditoriums, and dormitories. The most distinguished artists are on its advisory committee. There are some of us, however, who have a wistful feeling for the old days when Dr. Maddy's dream was fighting for its life and when we had at least a small part in keeping that dream alive.

My own connection with the camp covered a period of over thirty years, and one composition of mine will always be associated with it. During the early days, I was engaged in the composition of my Second (or *Romantic*) Symphony, which had been commissioned by the Boston Symphony Orchestra. One late evening, after the rehearsals of the day had been completed, I wandered back to the rustic shell where all of the concerts in those days were given. It was a beautiful evening with the moonlight filtering through the great pines and lighting both the land and the lake. I sat down at the piano and, in the silence of the deserted amphitheater, began to improvise. I had wanted this symphony to be a symphony of and for youth. I wanted to express in music the nostalgia which is as much a part of youth as of age.

As I was improvising, a melody came to me which seemed to express that youthful nostalgia. It became the "slow section" of the first movement of the symphony. That it was, indeed, a theme of youth seemed to be borne out by the fact that the young people of Interlochen, when they first heard it, adopted it as "their theme." Every broadcast and every concert began and ended with this melody, until it became known as the "Interlochen Theme." The title is quite justifiable, for without Interlochen it might never have been written.

1931–46; he spent nine years in Australia, including conducting the Sydney Symphony and directing the New South Wales State Conservatorium of Music.

8   Frederick Fennell (1914–2004), American conductor. He attended the Eastman School of Music, earning bachelor's (1937) and master's (1939). He also founded the Eastman Wind Ensemble and was later principal guest conductor at Interlochen Arts Academy.

9   Clement Stone (1902–2002), American businessman, author, and philanthropist.

Chapter Fifteen

FINDING TIME FOR COMPOSITION

My major personal challenge, after taking time to analyze the problems of my new job, was to attempt to discover how my administrative responsibilities could be combined with my own creative work as a composer. The solution of the marriage between the administrative and the creative was imperative. I have always been a "compulsive" composer. I write because I have to. Whenever I stop composing beyond a certain period of time, I become frustrated and unhappy.

I have always divided composers into two categories: those who write because they have to and those who write because they want to. I hasten to add that I make no claim to the superiority of the first category. I do say that composers in the "compulsive" category, unless they are so fortunate as to be able to devote all of their time to composition, must find some way to compromise these two imperatives: the necessity of making a living and the need to create music.

In my case, the problem was especially difficult. I had accepted a highly responsible and difficult administrative position against the advice of most of my colleagues at the American Academy in Rome, including, most importantly, my friend and mentor, Felix Lamond. The augurs for the success of the marriage of administration and musical creation were not too propitious. One of my colleagues, a distinguished composer, had taken a position as the director of a well-known school of music. After accepting the position, he was invited to meet his board of directors. They informed him that, although they knew that he was a composer, they wanted him to understand that he must do his composition "on his own time." In other words, no composition on company time!

I was infinitely more fortunate because of the sympathetic understanding of President Rhees and George Eastman, both of whom insisted that my desire to compose should be realized. This assistance extended even to the appointment of an assistant to help me with the preparation of orchestral scores and parts, those time-consuming tasks which fall to the lot of most young composers.[1]

---

    1   In the era before computers and programs such as *Finale* and *Sibelius*, scores and parts were handwritten. The Eastman School even required for

In spite of all of this generous assistance, the task was not an easy one. Mr. Eastman had erected a highly complex organization, as he put it, "for the enrichment of community life," embracing a school of music, a theater, a symphony orchestra, and a division of opera and ballet, to serve both the school and theater.

The entire complex, although presented by Mr. Eastman as a gift to the University of Rochester, was governed by its own board. The board consisted of four members: George Eastman, President Rhees, George Todd (a longtime friend of Mr. Eastman), and me. This board of four was subdivided into two units: a board of three (Mr. Eastman, President Rhees, and George Todd) to govern the theater, and a board of three (Mr. Eastman, President Rhees, and me) to have jurisdiction over the Eastman School of Music. Compared with today's super-organization, Mr. Eastman's design was deceptively simple. I must say that when Mr. Eastman did not approve of a proposal for either the school or the theater, the vote of the board was apt to be unanimously in the negative.

I am sure that all of us, including even President Rhees, stood in awe of George Eastman. I must say, however, that he was one of the fairest men I have ever known. I have known a number of philanthropists in the arts who, regardless of their competence or lack of it, have kept a controlling hand on the disbursing of their largesse. In the case of George Eastman, this was not true. On numerous occasions, when decisions on policy needed to be made, I would go to him with alternate proposals. Without exception, his reply would be, "You decide. You're the expert."

In addition to his loyalty to those in whom he had confidence, he had a sense of humor of which all of his colleagues were, perhaps, unaware. It was his custom to have two musicales each week, to which his friends were invited on some sort of rotation system. The music was provided by his own string quartet and by the distinguished American organist, Harold Gleason, who was with him for many years.

At the end of a long and strenuous day at the music school, the last thing that I needed was another evening of music. On a previous occasion, because I have been for many years an inveterate cigar smoker, Mr. Eastman had shown me where he kept his choice "Coronas" and urged me to "help myself" whenever I wanted to smoke.

On this particular evening, rather than listening to the string quartet and organ in the music room, I repaired to the living room, helped myself to a cigar and a magazine, and seated myself in a comfortable chair in front of the fireplace. In the distance, I could hear the pleasant sound of music, far enough away to be comfortable but not obtrusive.

---

their composition majors a course in musical calligraphy.

As I was enjoying this idyllic state, I sensed that someone had entered the room. I looked up and saw the figure of George Eastman advancing toward me. "What are you doing in here?" asked Mr. Eastman. "Mr. Eastman," I replied, "You know I hate music." "I know you hate music," said Mr. Eastman, "but I brought you here to educate you!" It was to prove an exciting but strenuous education, an eighteen-hour-a-day job. The recruitment of faculty was important. Even more important was the recruitment of a student body of a caliber worthy of a distinguished faculty.

Also, although I was not technically charged with the responsibility of the theater, I found that I was spending almost as much time consulting on theater problems as I was working on the problems of the school. The manager of the Eastman Theatre, Eric T. Clarke, was a man of great sensitivity, imagination, and originality. Under his direction, the theater did indeed serve Mr. Eastman's motto, "[for] the enrichment of community life."

The financial problems were, however, tremendous. Perhaps, if Rochester had been a much larger city, Mr. Eastman's dream of supporting a major symphony orchestra through the operation of a first-rate motion picture theater might have been realized.[2] As it was, the problems of the hardboiled motion picture business, with its "block-booking" and other idiosyncracies, pressed upon our young idealistic plans with devastating force. The final blow came with the advent of sound movies. Who wanted to listen to a symphony orchestra, when one could see a picture screen which could actually *talk*?

If any further discouragement [was] needed, it came in the form of the Great Depression. While the Eastman School was operating "in the black," the theater was building up accumulated deficits in the millions of dollars.[3] It was apparent that Mr. Eastman's dream was, at least for the time being, incapable of realization. The theater was leased by the university to a commercial motion picture corporation, which itself later went into bankruptcy.[4]

---

2   George Eastman's master plan presupposed that playing in the theater orchestra that accompanied the movie shows would provide full-time employment to orchestral musicians who could also form the nucleus of the symphony orchestra. His plan also envisioned the theater operating at a surplus, which would then be directed toward the operation of the school.

3   This is most probably an exaggeration.

4   It was announced on December 15, 1928, that the Eastman Theatre would be leased to Paramount Pictures Corporation for a period of ten years. The harsh economic realities of the ensuing years resulted in the discontinuation of regular movie shows on April 2, 1931, and the following year Paramount was relieved by the university of its obligations under the lease that they had signed less than four years earlier.

All was lost except, paradoxically, the philharmonic orchestra which the theater was erected to support. By this time, the citizens of Rochester had become conscious of the importance of their orchestra. Through the organizing genius of Arthur M. See, financial secretary of the Eastman School, and with the help of the Eastman School and George Eastman himself, the Rochester Civic Music Association was formed to perpetuate the symphony. In spite of the Depression, through the cooperation of Rochesterians and the musicians themselves, the orchestra was saved. It remains today one of the country's major orchestras. Perhaps Mr. Eastman's dream was a success after all, even though not in the manner he had planned.

During those strenuous years, with the problems of a new, young music school directly on my hands, and indirectly with the problems of the theater and of the orchestra bearing down upon all of us, I became a midnight composer. If one cannot compose in the daytime, one must compose at night.

In any case, and regardless of the obstacles, the years from 1924 to 1932 saw the completion of the choral work *The Lament for Beowulf*, which had been sketched in Rome; a symphonic poem, *Pan and the Priest*; a concerto for organ and large orchestra based on *North and West*; *Heroic Elegy* for chorus and orchestra, written for the Beethoven Centennial of 1927; and my second symphony, the *Romantic*, commissioned by the Boston Symphony Orchestra for its fiftieth anniversary.

Pan and the Priest was something of a test of my ability to work creatively in my new environment, to combine the arts of creation and administration. The *Lament for Beowulf*, which I still consider one of my best works, had been conceived and completely sketched during my idyllic years in Rome. *Pan and the Priest*, however, was a product of the new environment.

The work, in spite of its programmatic title, has no story, which caused no little confusion to the program annotator in London where the work had its first performance under Sir Henry Wood.[5] At Sir Henry's request, I sent him the score and parts for the world premiere. A short time later, I received a cable from London, "Please send immediately program notes explaining story of *Pan and the Priest*." I cabled back, "No story or program except that indicated in the title." A few days later, I received a second cablegram which read, "Imperative to have story of *Pan and the Priest* immediately!"

---

5   Henry Wood (1869–1944), English conductor. He was associated for more than a half century with the famous Promenade Concerts (now the BBC Proms).

The truth of the matter was that there really was no story involved. I had merely used the title to indicate two facets of man's spiritual nature, the mysticism of the priest and the sensuous qualities of the creative artist in his search for his conception of beauty. In later years, various program annotators wrote their own stories. It was, however, their story, not mine!

It spite of the lack of "story," the London performance was apparently an immediate success, with the great English critic, Ernest Newman,[6] concluding his highly favorable review with the sentence, "The work is certainly the best that America has sent us for some time."

The first New York performance, by the New York Philharmonic under Willem Mengelberg, also met with considerable success, not only with the public but [also] with a number of New York's most influential critics. Certainly, a generous portion of credit for its success should go to the dynamic conducting of the famous Dutch maestro,

He has been gone for a good many years, but I am sure that none of us who heard him will ever forget him. He was short of stature, of stocky build, and with a thatch of flaming red hair. His conducting temperament was as flaming as his hair and gave to his interpretations a dramatic quality rarely surpassed by any other conductor of his time.

He was also a meticulous craftsman, and I can recall his famous lectures to the orchestra on the relationship of the dotted eighth note to the sixteenth in the *Semiramide* overture of Rossini. I recall having the temerity at one time to ask him why he felt it necessary to rehearse in such detail an overture which the orchestra knew so well. Instead of being annoyed, he looked at me with a mischievous twinkle and said, "Young man, you do not understand. The audience also knows this work very well!"

At this time in the history of the New York Philharmonic, Mr. Mengelberg was sharing the philharmonic season with Arturo Toscanini. This was unfortunate for everyone concerned. Both men were musical giants with powerful personalities and temperaments to match. It was natural that both the musicians and the public should "choose up sides." One had to be either a Mengelberg man or a Toscanini man. In the ensuing battle, the adherents of Maestro Toscanini eventually conquered, and Willem Mengelberg returned to his native Amsterdam, never (so far as I recall) to return to the United States. His departure left us much the poorer. The philharmonic had had two great conductors. Now it had but one.

Mr. Mengelberg must have enjoyed conducting *Pan* because he played it not only in New York but [also] on tour in Boston, New Haven, Holyoke, [and] Philadelphia, although he very graciously invited me to conduct the

---

6   Ernest Newman (1868–1959), English critic and musicologist. He was a music critic at the *Sunday Times* in London, 1920–59.

Philadelphia performance as a part of a program for the Sesquicentennial Exposition of that city.

The review which pleased me most came from Lawrence Gilman[7] whom I admired, one of the most articulate of all American critics. He wrote, in part, "This is music of brawn and sinew and ruddy skin. It strides with energy and lifted head; it is large-molded, full-throated. As the music evokes him, this might be some Titan Pan, flaunting his pagan eudaemonism in the giant shadows of the California redwoods and scarcely being dwarfed by them."

Another criticism, which I value highly for an entirely different reason, was written by Harold A. Strickland of the *Brooklyn Times*. It deserves a place in that marvelous book of my valued friend, Nicolas Slonimsky,[8] *The Lexicon of Musical Invective*. "To this reviewer, the result of Mr. Hanson's delirious outpourings appeared to be an orgy of dissonances with clashing cymbals, rampant tympany, and untuned strings. Add to this woodwinds that are raucous and brass that comes in fortissimo at the least excuse, and we have Mr. Hanson's poem. Casella, Taylor, yes even Stravinsky and Gershwin, we can stand if the dose is not too much, but in the name of Brahms deliver us from any more Hanson." Which proves, I suppose, that all of us at one time were "modernists."

---

7   Lawrence Gilman (1878–1939), American author and music critic. He worked for the *New York Herald* 1896–98, *Harpers Weekly* 1901–13, *North American Review* 1915–23, and the *Herald Tribune* 1925–39.

8   Nicolas Slonimsky (1894–1995), American author, conductor, critic, lexicographer. As a young man, he was associated with the Rochester American Opera Company.

Chapter Sixteen

CONDUCTORS AND ORCHESTRAS

The success of *Pan and the Priest* had encouraged me greatly. I had been deeply concerned about the possibility of combining a creative with an administrative life, and the writing of a new work in the new environment of Rochester convinced me that such an adjustment might indeed succeed.

In the meantime, the compositions from my sojourn in Rome seemed to be taking their place in the concert repertory. Eugene Goossens, the brilliant young British conductor who share the podium of the Rochester Philharmonic with Albert Coates, had performed several of my works in Rochester and had repeated *Lux Aeterna* in New York City as guest conductor of the New York Symphony.

The experience of hearing my orchestral works under Eugene Goossens's direction was especially rewarding. He was, himself, a gifted composer, a conductor of enormous technical skills, and a musician of impeccable taste. In addition, he had that most valuable of conductorial gifts, a "perfect" ear. I recall vividly numerous occasions when he would discover in a standard orchestral work wrong notes which had remained undiscovered by other conductors who had used the same orchestral material.

On one occasion, he used his phenomenal hearing to play an innocent joke on the members of the orchestra. He was rehearsing George Antheil's *Ballet Mechanique*, which, I recall, was scored for a huge orchestra, including a player-piano and at least one live pianist. In the midst of a particularly cacophonous passage, where it seemed utterly impossible to distinguish one note form another, Mr. Goossens stopped the orchestra and said to the pianist, "F-sharp, please, not F-natural." The orchestra broke into roars of laughter, whereupon Mr. Goossens asked the pianist, "Did you not play F-natural instead of F-sharp?" "Yes, I did. I'm sorry." The attitude of the orchestra changed from laughter to one of amazement. Here at last was the perfect ear, superior even to that of the great Toscanini.

After the rehearsal, I asked my friend how he could possibly, in that welter of sound, pick out one little wrong note in the piano. He looked at me and replied with complete candor, "I looked down and *saw* that she was playing F-natural." I never told the story. It was too wonderful a spoof on the orchestral musician to be destroyed. It has since occurred to me that perhaps the joke was on me. Perhaps he *did* hear the wrong note. With his ear, I would not be too surprised.

In the meantime, my youthful works were moving about the country. Frederick Stock, whom I had greatly admired when I was a student at Northwestern University, invited me to conduct *Pan and the Priest* with his great orchestra. Nicolai Sokoloff[1] invited me to Cleveland. At the invitation of my dear friend, Rudolph Ganz, I conducted his St. Louis Symphony. Walter Henry Rothwell asked me to conduct *Lux Aeterna* with the Los Angeles Philharmonic orchestra. I conducted the *Nordic* Symphony in Cincinnati, Kansas City, and in San Francisco, where the friend and mentor of my earlier days, Alfred Hertz, remained as conductor of the [orchestra].

Of all these exciting experiences, my association with the Los Angeles Philharmonic was one of the most thrilling. The Los Angeles Philharmonic is a great orchestra today, but in the twenties, when great orchestras were less common, it was unique in its virtuosity. A just portion of the credit should go to its musical director, Walter Henry Rothwell, an excellent musician and orchestral drillmaster. But the orchestra had an even greater asset, an angel in the person of Mr. William A. Clark, Jr., a wealthy and generous patron, equalled only, I suppose, by Boston's Higginson[2] and the New York Symphony's Flagler.[3]

As I have said before, it was Mr. Clark's ambition to make the Los Angeles Philharmonic the greatest orchestra in the United States, or perhaps the world.[4] He spared no expense to bring this about. The Eastern orchestras were raided for some of their best players, and the combined lure of climate and, for those days, high salaries brought to Los Angeles players from some of the world's greatest orchestras. At the end of each season, Mr. Clark would ascertain the amount of the deficit and write a check for whatever number of hundred thousand dollars was required.

---

1   Nicolai Sokoloff (1886–1955), Russian-born American conductor. He was the founding director of the Cleveland Orchestra, which he led 1918–32; he later conducted the Seattle Symphony 1938–40.

2   Henry Lee Higginson (1834–1919), American banker and philanthropist. He founded the Boston Symphony Orchestra in 1881.

3   Henry (Harry) Harkness Flagler (1880–1952), president of the Symphony Society of New York 1914–28. He continued as president when the Symphony Society of New York merged with the New York Philharmonic, serving in that capacity until 1934.

4   Hanson is elaborating on material that he previously included in chapter 8.

His contributions to this generous form of deficit financing, I have been told, amounted eventually to several million dollars.

The problem is, of course, that even the most philanthropic of angels do not live forever, and the orchestra was to experience difficult days. In the meantime, the orchestra continued in a rosy, or perhaps I should say golden, glow.

I was privileged to conduct not only in the regular season's concerts but also in the famous Hollywood Bowl. These were the great days when the emphasis was more on music than on Hollywood. The presiding genius was a remarkable woman, Artie Mason Carter,[5] whose passion for music embraced the new as well as the old. Included in her philosophy was a firm belief in the importance of the composer, the living composer as well as the masters of the past. As a result, many new works of living composers were included in a repertory of more than unusual interest.

The Bowl in those days was much simpler and more primitive. The wooden benches, not too comfortable, took advantage of the natural contour of the Bowl. The shell was of a rustic simplicity but of excellent acoustics. There was, as I recall, no amplification in those early days. The natural sound of the orchestra fell gratefully on the ears of the thousands who flocked to hear music, both old and new. They may have been physically uncomfortable, but they were aesthetically happy!

Today, the Hollywood Bowl is magnificent in its iron and concrete, its modern stage, and brilliant lighting. I wonder if the sense of adventure, of musical pioneering, of the Artie Mason Carter days will ever return. I somehow doubt it, for those were truly the days of "Symphonies Under the Stars." Later, both the orchestra and the Bowl were to meet difficult times. The death of Clark, followed by the full impact of the Depression, created severe financial problems. So serious did they become that the governing body of the Bowl decided it was no longer feasible to finance the summer concerts. The orchestra decided that, rather than cancel the summer series, they would continue the concerts on a cooperative basis, the musicians themselves assuming financial responsibility. This adventure in management led to some unusual experiences, one of which I recall with considerable amusement.

The relation of an orchestral conductor to the members of the orchestra poses problems which could be analyzed only by an authority on sociology, psychology, and psychiatry, who was also a symphony

---

5   Artie Mason Carter (1881–1967), civic and cultural leader. She conceived the "Symphony Under the Stars" programs in 1922 in an effort to keep the Los Angeles Philharmonic working during the summer months, which led to the famous Hollywood Bowl concerts.

conductor with experience as an orchestral player.[6] The conductor on the podium to a considerable degree must be a musical dictator. The orchestra begins when he begins. They conclude (hopefully) when he does. He dictates tempo, dynamics, interpretation, indeed almost everything which goes into the concoction of the musical dish to be served. [The conductor's] degree of authority makes that of a top sergeant in the army pale in comparison.

It is understandable, therefore, that many conductors develop a dictatorial complex on (and sometimes as well as off) the podium. I have known some conductors who related to the members of their orchestras as colleagues. Eugene Goossens belonged to this category. His requests to the orchestra were generally couched in sentences such as, "Gentlemen, would you be so kind as to repeat the section beginning at letter B?"

I think that most orchestral musicians who played under Fritz Reiner[7] would agree that Mr. Reiner did *not* belong to this category. He was a superb musician, a conductor's conductor, with an impeccable technique of the baton which was the envy of his colleagues. The admiration in which his musicianship was held by the men of his orchestra was not always accompanied by an equal portion of affection. He was, in other words, sometimes brusque in his directions to his players.

One week I found myself conducting the orchestra in the Bowl in company with three distinguished conductors: Ernest Bloch,[8] Walter Henry Rothwell, and Fritz Reiner. Being a great admirer of Mr. Reiner's conductorial skill, I asked him if I might attend his first rehearsal, to which he readily assented. Early in the rehearsal, something happened which was not to his liking. He put down his baton [and] glared at one of the offending flute players. "Mr. Plowe," he began in steely tones, [but] suddenly a change came over his face. He smiled benignly and finished the sentence, "Mr. Plowe, would you be so kind as to play your solo passage a little more *forte?*" He had suddenly remembered that Mr. Plowe was the chairman of the orchestral committee charged with engaging guest conductors! The rehearsal continued in an atmosphere of the greatest amity.

---

6   Again, Hanson is elaborating on a subject he previously explored in chapter 8.

7   Fritz Reiner (1888–1963), Hungarian-born American conductor. He led the Cincinnati Orchestra 1922–31; taught at Curtis, where his students included Leonard Bernstein, Lukas Foss, and Walter Hendl; and led the Pittsburgh Symphony 1938–48, and Chicago Symphony 1953–63.

8   Ernest Bloch (1880–1959), Swiss-born American composer. He was the first director of the Cleveland Institute of Music 1925–30, then director of the San Francisco Conservatory 1925–30.

Chapter Seventeen

PROMOTING THE CAUSE OF AMERICAN MUSIC

I have related some of my early experiences as a composer-conductor, not in order to try to build up a "history of achievements," but to indicate that at least one young American could have no reasonable complaint as to his treatment by his colleagues, the critics, and the musical public. Certainly, to quote the psalmist, my lines had "fallen in pleasant places."[1] During the first year of my return to the United States, however, I discovered that the lot of the American composer was not necessarily a uniformly happy one. On my trips around the country, I met many young composers. I heard numerous stories of manuscripts submitted and returned unopened. I met many young composers of undeniable gifts who had never heard one note of their orchestral music in living performances.

The composer faces one problem which is indigenous to no other art except perhaps the art of the theater. For the composer, it is imperative that he have the opportunity of hearing what he has written. Without this experience, his whole career as a creative artist is jeopardized. In the case of the dramatist, it is at least possible to read a play without the accompanying dramatic action, unsatisfactory though such a performance may be. In music there is literally no substitute for performance.

I desired, therefore, to attempt to set up at the Eastman School a "laboratory" for young composers, where gifted young men might come and hear their works performed by a competent professional orchestra and under circumstances where compositions could be played without consideration of the box-office. It was my hope also to invite critics of national importance to be members of our audience and to receive the benefit of their criticism.

Both President Rhees and Mr. Eastman approved the idea, and I set about the task of finding foundation support for the financing of the project. Everyone to whom I spoke, including a number of New York City's

---

1 Psalm 16:6, which reads in the King James Version: "The lines are fallen unto me in pleasant places; yea, I have a goodly heritage."

most influential critics, were enthusiastic about the plan and fully agreed that it could be of enormous help to the American composer.

Raising the necessary funds was a different matter. I had the expressed interest and encouragement of one foundation. We had a number of meetings, all of which were most friendly and all equally abortive. The answer was always that my plan was excellent but needed "further consideration."

Returning to Rochester from one of these meetings, I met George Eastman. He inquired how things were going. I replied that I was delighted with the progress of the school, but that my pet project for the American composer had yet to get off the ground. I then told him of my unsuccessful attempts to get a firm commitment of funds with which to begin the experiment. Mr. Eastman's reply was typical of the man. "Howard," he said, "You are not stupid! Why don't you ask me for the money?" I did, and the American Composers' Concerts have gone on without interruption for over forty years.

The first "laboratory concert" was presented by the Rochester Philharmonic in the Eastman Theatre on May Day of 1925, a suitable date for a revolutionary experiment.[2] Seven young composers were represented at this first concert, a number of whom were to become among America's most important composers: Aaron Copland, Quincy Porter, Bernard Rogers, George McKay, Adolph Weiss, Mark Silver, and Donald Tweedy. The program had been selected from a total of fifty-four submitted manuscripts by a jury consisting of Ernest Bloch, Albert Coates, and me.

A number of distinguished critics, including Olin Downes[3] from the *New York Times*, Francis D. Perkins of the *New York Herald Tribune*, and Winthrop P. Tryon of the *Christian Science Monitor*, attended the concert and praised both the concert and the idea behind the project.

Aaron Copland, speaking to the press for the composers, remarked that the value of hearing a competent performance of one's orchestral music could be appreciated only by a composer; that without such an opportunity the composer must realize his work only through aural imagination. Will the composer's inventions, both in ideas and in tone combinations, be what he intends? This can be known only when the music is performed. Thus did the young composer, who was in later years

---

2   The first of May has marked the date of many different holidays, but it was especially noted as International Workers Day. Especially in Soviet Russia, May Day was celebrated as a day of international proletarian solidarity in opposition to the exploitation of capitalism.

3   Olin Downes (1886–1955), highly influential music critic. He worked for the *Boston Post* 1906–24 and the *New York Times* 1924–55. He also championed the cause of new music.

to become (next to George Gershwin) the best-known of American's twentieth-century composers, recapitulate in his succinct style the entire philosophy upon which the American Composers' Concerts were based.

Copland's music cannot easily be classified. It is frequently kaleidoscopic. It can be nostalgic as in *Quiet City* and parts of *Appalachian Spring*, rowdy and rollicking as in excerpts from *Billy the Kid*, jazzy and puckish as in the *Music for the Theater*, or enigmatic as in the *Piano Variations*.

The second concert of the series did indeed "discover" a young man who was to become one of America's most famous composers, Roy Harris. The young composer submitted an *Andante for Orchestra*, his first work for that medium. The work exhibited such an individual gift that it was rapidly taken up by other conductors. Its success, I am sure, contributed to his development as one of America's most important symphonists.

The music of Roy Harris offers problems of a quite different nature. His *Andante for Orchestra*, of which we gave the first performance in the season of 1926–27, is an excellent example. Roy almost invariably paints on a large canvas. His purpose is, to him, very clear, but the translation from notes to sound frequently poses problems. He has, for example, the habit of writing into the score some word, such as *sonore*, which indicates exactly the kind of sound he desires. He may, however, score the passage in a manner which requires the complete cooperation of every musician to secure the desired result. The conductor must, therefore, use all of his ingenuity in balancing the dynamics of the orchestra. Otherwise, the result will not "come off."

I recall one rehearsal when we could not get the exact sound from the tympany which Mr. Harris wished. We tried again and again, but without success. The excellent timpanist, William Street,[4] who has students playing in dozens of symphonies around the country, was gradually becoming more "edgy." Finally, Roy came on the stage to show Mr. Street how to play it! The confrontation almost resulted in a boxing match, and it took all of my diplomacy to resolve the matter. However, we did finally work out the passage to the composer's satisfaction.

Another problem is that composers are not always exact in the marking of the scores. On one occasion, we were rehearsing Virgil Thomson's *Symphony [on a Hymn Tune]* in preparation for a recording session. Mr. Thomson was present at the final rehearsal at my request to give us his criticisms and suggestions. All went well until we came to a passage for three trumpets. Virgil cried out from the hall, "Trumpets, louder. I can't

---

[4] William Street (1895–1973) taught percussion at the Eastman School of Music 1927–67.

hear you." Whereupon the first trumpeter, Sidney Mear,[5] replied quietly but with some acidity, "Mr. Thomson, the parts are marked *pianissimo*— very softly." To which Mr. Thomson replied, "Don't pay any attention to that." Everyone laughed, and the rehearsal proceeded amicably and to the satisfaction of the composer.

On another occasion, we were rehearsing Wallingford Riegger's Third Symphony, again in preparation for recording. I had studied the rather difficult score carefully, and we had rehearsed meticulously, but I was bothered by the tempo of the first movement. It did not seem to "go" at the indicated tempo. This was all the more puzzling, since the tempi had all been carefully indicated by exact markings, the exact speed at which each beat should be played. In spite of this, I decided at this one point to trust my instinct rather than the metronome and rehearsed it at my own speed. I did, however, insist that the composer come to the final rehearsal for a check on my interpretation.

Wallingford Riegger was one of the kindest composers who ever lived, a gentle and lovable man with whom it was a pleasure to work. He listened to the entire work and, at the end, expressed himself as completely delighted with the results. After the rehearsal, I asked him whether he was satisfied with the tempo of the opening. He replied that my tempo was "perfect," exactly as he wished it. "Wally," I said, "I am playing the opening passage twice as fast as you have indicated!" Either the composer or, perhaps the printer, had indicated a metronome marking for an eight note instead of for a quarter not, exactly one half as fast as it should have been.

Composers sometimes seem to delight in writing orchestral parts which task the players' ability to (or beyond) capacity. One evening at a party in New York City, I met Roger Sessions. We had recently recorded his orchestral suite from *The Black Maskers*, in my opinion, one of our best recordings. He graciously expressed his delight both with the performance and the recording. After we had talked a while, he suddenly said to me, "Your first bassoonist seemed to have no problem at all with the high C in his solo. "Not at all," I replied. He looked a little puzzled. "Roger," I went on, "You seem a little disappointed. Did you want him to have trouble with it?"

In the ensuing years, the American Composers' Concerts offered performances of approximately 2,000 works by over 700 American composers. This list is too long for inclusion, but it may be of interest to note that almost every winner of the Pulitzer Prize in musical composition had received [in Rochester] a first performance of at least one of his works.

---

5   Sidney Mear (b.1919), teacher of trumpet at the Eastman School of Music 1949–80.

I especially enjoyed meeting some of the older American masters who came to Rochester to hear their works, men like George Whitefield Chadwick, Edward Burlingame Hill, Daniel Gregory Mason, Arthur Shepherd, Edgar Stillman-Kelley, and others. They were without exception gracious and generous in their praise of what we were trying to do for American music.

I recall with especial pleasure a program devoted to the works of George Whitefield Chadwick, the grand old gentleman, at that time president of the New England Conservatory, was present as our guest. After one of the rehearsals, we took Mr. Chadwick around the buildings of the Eastman School, still shining new. His biblical remark I still cherish. Said he, after viewing the architectural magnificence of the new school, "I would rather be a doorkeeper in the House of Eastman than president of the New England Conservatory!" I am sure that he was exaggerating.

I recall with affection the visit of Dr. Stillman-Kelley in the season of 1935–36, to hear his monumental *New England Symphony*. He was accompanied by his wife, who was a dynamic figure in the pioneering work of developing an appreciation of symphonic music in the United States. Stillman-Kelley was a delightful man with a wonderful sense of humor. One day he was showing me the score of his suite based on Swift's *Gulliver's Travels*. When we arrived at the movement [depicting] the Lilliputians, he called my attention to the orchestration. "You will notice that I have included two piccolos in the score. After all, the Lilliputians were very little people!"

It is difficult even for me to realize that the American Composers' Concerts program at the Eastman School has gone on for almost a half-century. We began with our first American Composers' Concert in 1925, added an annual Festival of American Music in 1930, and "reading symposia" in 1948. The festivals have covered the gamut from chamber music, orchestral music, chorus and orchestra, and music for wind ensemble, to ballets and operas. In their preparation, I have had the assistance of a number of dedicated conductors and directors. Orchestral concerts have been under the direction of Dr. Paul White,[6] Clyde Roller,[7] Frederick Fennell, Willis Page, and [me]; the Wind Ensemble under Dr. Fennell and Dr.

---

6   Paul White (1895–1973), a member of the Eastman School of Music faculty 1932–70. He taught violin and conducting, as well as being one of the school's orchestral conductors.

7   A. Clyde Roller (1914–2005), orchestra and wind ensemble conductor at the Eastman School of Music 1962–65.

Donald Hunsberger;[8] the chorus under Dr. Herman Genhart[9] and Milford Fargo;[10] chamber music under John Celentano[11] and Georges Miquelle. Ballets were choreographed by Thelma Biracree and Olive McCue,[12] and the operas were under the direction of Emmanuel Balaban,[13] Nicholas Konraty,[14] and Leonard Treash.[15]

The repertory has come from works by young composers, from well-known contemporary composers, and from American masters of the past.[16] The latter include most if not all of the American composers who have made musical history: Ernst Bloch, Charles Wakefield Cadman, John Alden Carpenter, George Whitefield Chadwick, Eric De Lamater, Arthur Farwell, Arthur Foote, George Gershwin, Henry Gilbert, Charles Tomlinson Griffes, Henry Hadley, Victor Herbert, Edward Burlingame Hill, Charles Ives, Charles Martin Loeffler, Edward MacDowell, Daniel Gregory Mason, John Knowles Paine, Horatio Parker, Johann Peter, Lawrence Powell,[17] Ernest Schelling, Arthur Shepherd, Charles Sanford Skilton,

---

8   Donald Hunsberger (b.1932), conductor of the Eastman Wind Ensemble 1965–2002. He joined the Eastman faculty in 1962.

9   Herman Genhart (1899–1976), member of the Eastman School faculty 1925–65. He taught opera and conducting, and was the conductor of the Eastman School Chorus.

10   Milford Fargo (1928–86), a member of the Eastman School of Music music education department faculty 1957–86. He also served as conductor of the Eastman School Chorus 1967–69, as well as being the founding conductor of the Eastman Chorale.

11   John Celentano (1912–2009), a member of the Eastman School of Music faculty 1946–80. He served for many years as the director of chamber music studies at the school.

12   Thelma Biracree and Olive McCue had been members of the Eastman Theatre Ballet in the 1920s. After the ballet corps was disbanded, Hanson allowed them to maintain private teaching studios at the Eastman School of Music in Annex I on Swan Street.

13   Emanuel Balaban (1895–1973), teacher of opera at the Eastman School of Music 1925–44.

14   Nicholas Konraty (1891–1972), voice teacher at the Eastman School of Music 1929–57.

15   Leonard Treash (1909–96), director of the opera department at the Eastman School of Music 1947–76.

16   The listing of composers in this and subsequent paragraphs might have been better placed as an appendix. However, Hanson was obviously very proud of his achievement in presenting works by so many American composers, and his listing of their names presents an opportunity to more fully appreciate his accomplishment. In his manuscript, he offered only their surnames.

17   It is unclear whether Hanson is referring to Lawrence Powell or John Powell.

John Philip Sousa, Edgar Stillman-Kelley, Geroge Templeton Strong, Deems Taylor, Edgard Varèse, Karl Weigl, and Kurt Weill.[18]

The list also includes contemporary masters such as Samuel Barber, Robert Russell Bennett, Harold Brown, Elloitt Carter, Norman Cazden, Aaron Copland, Henry Cowell, Paul Creston, Mabel Daniels, Norman Dello Joio, Nathaniel Dett, Richard Donovan, Herbert Elwell, Ross Lee Finney, Vittorio Giannini, Don Gillis, Morton Gould, Ferde Grofé, Louis Gruenberg, Edmund Haines, Roy Harris, Charles Haubiel, Herman Haufrecht, Walter Helfer, Everett Helm, Wells Hivley, Alan Hovhaness, Mary Howe, Frederick Jacobi, Philip James, Werner Janssen, Werner Josten, Harrison Kerr, Beatrice Laufer, Wesley LaViolette, Dai-Keong Lee, Benjamin Lees, Eric Leidzen, Normand Lockwood, Otto Luening, Leopold Mannes, Robert McBride, Karl McDonald, Carl McKinley, Colin McPhee, Gian-Carlo Menotti, Douglas Moore, Harold Morris, Spencer Norton, Vincent Persichetti, Walter Piston, Quincy Porter, Wallingford Riegger, George Rochberg, Ned Rorem, Orrego Salas, Lazare Saminsky, Robert Sanders, Gunther Schuller, William Schuman, Alan Shulman, Elie Siegmeister, Leo Sowerby, Tomothy Spelman, Alexander Steinert, Halsey Stevens, William Grant Still, Albert Stoessel, Lamar Stringfield, Edwin Stringham, Randall Thompson, Virgil Thomson, Harold Triggs, Burnet Tuthill, David Van Vactor, Constant Vauclain, William Verrall, John Vincent, Bernard Wagenaar, Joseph Wagner, Adolph Weiss, Alan Willman, and Emerson Whithorne.

The composers on the faculty—including Wayne Barlow, Thomas Canning, Robert Gauldin, Louis Mennini, Burrill Phillips, Bernard Rogers, Edward Royce, Gustave Soderland, Melville Smith, Donald Tweedy, and Paul White—strongly supported the program. We, too, profited from the opportunity of hearing our own works, and I acknowledge my personal debt to the concerts.

It is natural that the emphasis on composition in the Eastman School should attract to the school a large number of talented young composers. As a result, the list of composition alumni includes the names of many of the most gifted of today's younger composers. Several have been awarded the Pulitzer Prize. A large number have won the Prix de Rome. Others have won important awards, such as the George Gershwin Memorial Award, the New York Philharmonic Award, the awards of the National Institute of Arts and Letters and the National Academy, the Edward Benjamin awards, and many others.

---

18   Karl Weigl and Kurt Weill were Austrian and German respectively, but both became naturalized American citizens. Hanson would appear to be overreaching by including them in a listing of "American masters of the past."

Pulitzer Prize winners include Gail Kubik, John LaMontaine, and Robert Ward. Winners of the Prix de Rome include the names of Jack Beeson, Will Bottje, David Diamond, Vincent Frohne, Kenneth Gaburo, Herbert Inch, Hunter Johnson, Ulysses Kay, Kent Kennan, Robert Palmer, Richard Willis, and Frederick Woltmann.

American Academy of Arts and Letters awards went to William Bergsma, Peter Mennin, Robert Palmer, and Robert Ward. Koussevitzky Awards [went] to William Bergsma, David Diamond, Earl George, Peter Mennin, Louis Mennini, [and] Robert Palmer. Three graduates won awards or commissions from the New York Philharmonic: Homer Keller, Gardner Read, and Peter Mennin. And two graduates, Ulysses Kay and Peter Mennin, were winners of the George Gershwin Memorial Award, and Robert Palmer of the Dimitri Mitropolous Award.

Thomas Beversdorf, Willard Elliot, [and] William Parks Grant won awards from the National Federation of Music Clubs, and Anthony Donato from the Society for the Publication of American Music. Finally, Edward Benjamin recording awards went to Michael Mailman, Ron Nelson, Robert Gauldin, Robert Stemp, William Pursell. Other recording contracts [were given] to Kent Kennan, John LaMontaine, Ronald Lo Presti, Lyndol Mitchell, Owen Reed, Peter Mennin, Louis Mennini, Burrill Phillips, and Wayne Barlow.

Chapter Eighteen

RADIO BROADCASTS AND RECORDINGS

My connection with Interlochen and with music in American high schools was to have a profound effect not only on me but on the Eastman School as well. Serving as a guest conductor summer after summer, I came to know hundreds of gifted young students and, in many cases, their teachers. I came to know also that group of dedicated individuals known as music supervisors, and to have a high respect for their devotion to music and to music education.

From these experiences came dozens of invitations to conduct, not only performances by the successors of the National Youth Orchestra in Chicago but [also] concerts by state symphonies, regional orchestras, and youth orchestras. Here was a student body of the greatest potential, and I became the Eastman School's super-salesman. As a result, the reputation and prestige of the Eastman [School] was growing rapidly, and many of the talented youngsters from Interlochen and the various national youth orchestras came to Eastman to continue their professional studies. In a few years, the student orchestra at Eastman had developed from the fledgling orchestra of the early days to an orchestra of over one hundred players of almost professional caliber.

The orchestra was so proficient that Dr. Walter Damrosch, at that time musical advisor to the National Broadcasting Company, invited the Eastman School Symphony Orchestra to give a series of weekly broadcasts over the NBC network.[1] A weekly symphonic concert of an hour's duration over a national network was an enormous challenge to a young student orchestra, but they met it successfully.

Those were, of course, the golden days of radio broadcasting. Television had not yet begun its questionable influence on serious orchestral music, and radio was the accepted medium for the broadcasting of good music. Rochester alone, through Stromberg-Carlson's station WHAM (under the enlightened directorship of William Fay), originated as many as three national radio symphony programs each week broadcast from coast to coast.

---

    1   Broadcasting of live concerts from the Eastman School of Music began in July 1922 prior to Hanson's appointment as director.

One of the series of which I was particularly proud was called *Milestones in the History of Music*.² The series was organized by Dr. Harold Gleason and Professor Charles Riker and presented a "living history" of music from Gregorian chant and Renaissance music to the works of living composers. The series made, I am told, a considerable impact on the whole field of educational broadcasting and had a very distinguished audience. For example, Eugene Ormandy, music director of the Philadelphia Orchestra, told me that he was a regular listener to our broadcasts. This radio acquaintance was later to broaden into a warm personal friendship, one for which I have always been grateful.

With the coming of television, tape recording, and the perfection of electronic equipment in general, the world of music has undergone radical change. This mechanization of music has brought many advantages, but it has also, I believe, been accompanied by changes [that are] less advantageous. Through electronic recording, it is possible to build a library of great music, a possibility not always realized by recording companies. At the same time, the tendency to tape live performances to be broadcast or telecast at a later time or date has brought a certain quality of nonreality. Most of us would admit, I believe, that no symphonic experience is greater than the sound of a great orchestra "alive" in a symphony hall blessed with good acoustics. It engenders a certain excitement, anticipation, even uncertainty because one is not sure how it will turn out. Perhaps the presiding maestro will give the greatest performance of his career. Perhaps, however, he may have a momentary lapse of memory, bring in the brass section one measure too soon, [and] have a terrible time gluing the performance together again!

To some extent, I find less sense of adventure in a taped orchestral concert, less excitement. One knows that this is not actually a live performance, but that it took place weeks or even months before. The announcer or program commentator may provide some sense of immediacy, but the feeling, at least to me, is quite different when you know that the concert is taking place at the same time you are hearing it.

The capturing of this sense of "presence" is even more difficult in listening to recordings. Curiously enough, one of the many problems of modern-day records is that they are *too* perfect, By repeating difficult passages, cutting and splicing tape, it is possible to almost entirely eliminate human error, with the result that the whole performance may have a kind of dehydrated and antiseptic smell. At the same time, I must express my admiration for the "good music" stations which broadcast tremendous

---

2   This series of broadcast concerts began in the fall of 1938 and continued for another two seasons.

repertory of great music hour after hour throughout the entire day and, in many cases, through the night as well. They constitute invaluable oases in the arid wasteland of commercial radio broadcasting.

As early as 1926, we undertook a publication project in cooperation with the music publishing firm of Carl Fischer, Inc., of New York City, the first work to be published being the *Soliloquy for Flute and String Orchestra* by Bernard Rogers. In the beginning, we planned the publications as a series of awards for works selected by a jury from the new works [we were performing.][3]

The awards started out auspiciously with the first award going to William Grant Still for his interesting and original *Darker America*. Later awards, however, caused us to doubt the wisdom of our policy. It was all too possible that an award-winning work, no matter how competent the jury, might prove a financial disaster from the standpoint of publication. I recall one orchestral work which we published as an "award" at great expense, of which no copies were ever sold! We decided, therefore, to discard the "award" idea and publish works on the basis of practical demand.

This policy proved much more successful but also presented problems. The most gifted composers were already beginning to come into their own. Many of them had their own arrangements with their own publishers, and as a result their manuscripts were not available. A further difficulty arose with the arrival of the Depression. Our publication budget, already very modest, was cut in half, and the entire project was in jeopardy. It was at this time that I decided to turn over approximately one-half of the copyrights of my own works to the Eastman School. The royalties on these works, both from publication and performance already totaled a sizeable amount, and the income helped the [publication] program to continue.

In 1930, the American Composers' Concerts were expanded to include an annual spring Festival of American Music. In the meantime, [the Eastman School] had begun to build [its] own library of recordings of American music, first on the old aluminum disks, then those on acetate, and finally modern tape recordings. It was natural, therefore, in 1939 to undertake the dissemination of some of this music through recordings which would be commercially available to the general public.

My first experience with the art-science of recording [was] as an observer in the early twenties, when my friend Albert Coates invited me to attend a recording session which he was conducting with one of the

---

3   This paragraph and the three that follow (plus some other material later in the chapter) was not included in Hanson's draft of chapter 15. It exists as separate pages without a clear reference as to where it belongs in the narrative. However, the material seems pertinent and important to chapter 15, and has been inserted at this point in the text.

London orchestras. The room seemed to be filled with microphones and cornucopias which looked like the horns of an old-fashioned phonograph. I especially recall the tuba player, sitting high up on a platform at the rear of the orchestra and blowing his tuba into one of these huge "amplifiers." I remember wondering how it was physically possible to compress all these sounds on one small disk of wax.

My first personal experience in recording came many years later. Our American Composers' concerts and festivals were becoming widely recognized, and the Victor Company agreed to record some of the music performed at these concerts. Fortunately, the director of artists and repertory [at Victor] was an excellent musician, Charles O'Connell, himself a conductor. Charles was deeply interested in American music and anxious to develop a library of recorded American music.

I was delighted to become associated with Charles O'Connell and the Victor Company. In those days, to be a member of the select group referred to as "Victor Red Seal" recording artists was a rare distinction. We decided to issue a series of albums of American orchestral music and selected for the first album the Overture to *Oedipus Tryannus* by America's first symphonist, John Knowles Paine; *Jubilee* by the veteran George Whitfield Chadwick; a portion of the *Indian Suite* by Edward MacDowell, America's most famous composer; *The White Peacock* by Charles Tomlinson Griffes, whose untimely death at the age of thirty-four robbed the United States of one of its exciting young talents; Leo Sowerby's overture *Comes Autumn Time*; William Grant Still's "Scherzo" from his *Afro-American Symphony;* Charles Vardell's *Joe Clark Steps Out*, based on the old American folksong; Kent Kennan's *Night Soliloquy*; and my *Romantic* Symphony.

The orchestra, which was called the Eastman-Rochester Symphony, was composed of members of the Rochester Civic Orchestra (a purely professional group) augmented by members of the Eastman School faculty and advanced students. The orchestra played well and our initial offering was unusually well-received.

Recording in those early days was a much more hazardous undertaking than in the modern days of tape. The master recording was made on a so-called wax disk. The disk [was] recorded at the rate of seventy-eight revolutions per minute, and it was possible to get four minutes and forty seconds of music on each disk. There was, of course, no way in which a mistake could be corrected. If someone played a wrong note, or if a player sneezed, coughed, or dropped a pair of cymbals, the only remedy was to do the entire recording over again.

This could at times become nerve-wracking both to the conductor and to the players. One incident remains indelibly engraved in my memory. We were recording the second movement of my first symphony, the *Nordic*. At the end of the movement there is a solo passage for the French horn which centers [on] a written high G in the instrument. It is completely exposed and, even more important, must be played softly. The solo horn, an excellent player, was tired after a long session, and when he came to the final high G, he "blooped." We went back to the beginning of the movement and tried it again. Luck was not with us. He "blooped" again. We tried it a third time from the beginning. It was no use. The solo horn player was becoming increasingly nervous, and the sound which came out on the high G was something that should not go on any respectable recording.

By this time, the entire orchestra was panicky. I, too, was almost ready to call it a day, almost but not quite! I told the orchestra that it was really not important. We could record it some other time. But could we all calm down and try it just once more? Everything went smoothly, and we approached the previously fatal high G. The solo horn went to attack the high note but, for a moment, no sound came. And then, following this breathless pause which certainly lasted no more than a fraction of a second, came the most beautiful high G which has ever come from a French horn.

The movement is in a very quiet and nostalgic mood, and the slight pause before the beginning of the phrase sounded like a sigh. It was more beautiful than I had written it. The recording [session] ended without incident, and the old Victor 78 recording remains one of the most beautiful we have ever made.

Some years later, my young friend and colleague Frederick Fennell, later to become famous as the director of the Eastman Wind Ensemble, told me this amusing story. He was conducting the *Nordic* with an all-state orchestra on the West Coast. When he came to the passage at the end of the second movement, the young solo horn made a slight pause before the final high G. Dr. Fennell asked him why he made the slight pause, since it was not indicated in the part. The young man replied solemnly, "Dr. Fennell, this is tradition!" He had, quite obviously, been studying our recording. I often wonder how much "tradition" is the result of similar accidents.

After recording a very respectable library of American music under the supervision of Mr. O'Connell, recording disaster struck us in two forms. The recording engineers perfected the so-called 33 1/3 LP, or long-playing record. It was no longer necessary to record only four minutes and forty seconds of a symphony on a record, and then turn over the record for the next four minutes and forty seconds. Instead of using five sides for a movement of a symphony, the entire movement could be recorded on one side of a long-playing record. As a result, the entire production of 78 rpm records quickly became obsolete.

The second disaster was the resignation of Charles O'Connell from the Victor Company. Rumor had it that he had written a book, *The Other*

Side of the Record,[4] which had offended some individuals high in the councils of the Victor Company. To this I cannot, of course, testify. I do know that he left, and we lost a great and powerful friend.

The combination of the obsolescence of our entire catalogue because of the new LP records and the sudden resignation of Charles O'Connell was a body blow. Those left in charge showed no interest in American music unless it could "sell big" and make money.

Later we moved to Columbia Records where we met, at that time, much the same conditions. We finally moved again to Mercury Records, for which we recorded what I believe is a highly important library of serious American music. This company has recently been absorbed by a European company, and the fate of the American recording program remains in doubt.

The recording of a viable and quasi-permanent library of American music posed almost insurmountable difficulties, partially because the American recording industry has never developed as a mature entity with an adequate conception of its responsibilities to the music of its [own] country. In spite of these [difficulties], we have finally developed a significant library of recorded American music through Mercury Records. That this library is important, both to the music student and to the music lover is, I believe, obvious. How long it can be maintained in this age of extreme commercialism in the recording industry is a serious question.

Our recording difficulties point up the problems of the industry, problems which have kept the industry from becoming the tremendous aid to the development of American music which it might have been. These problems are complex, but at least a partial explanation is possible.[5] First, the American orchestral musician has practically priced himself out of a viable market. Recording today is so enormously expensive that the price of unselfish idealism is very high, perhaps impossibly high except for a great foundation.

The result is that it is not practically possible for a recording company to do much more than to record the most famous repertory with the most famous orchestras under the most famous conductors. The outcome is, quite logically, the recording and re-recording over and over again of the same comparatively small orchestral repertory. At one time there were, as I recall, forty-two different recordings of a famous Tchaikovsky work. At the same time, there was not one recording of an orchestral work by Edward

---

    4   Charles O'Connell. *The Other Side of the Record*. New York, 1947, Alfred Knopf.

    5   Hanson's comments concerning the recording industry reflect problems he observed more than forty years ago. The recording industry today faces a host of new challenges.

MacDowell. I remember distinctly that, at the time of our first recording of MacDowell, his orchestral works were completely absent from the recorded repertory.

I am particularly proud of the fact that our recording of Edward Mac-Dowell's masterpiece, the *Indian Suite*, was the first orchestral recording of the American master in the Schwann Long-Playing record catalogue. Our recording of MacDowell's famous second piano concerto was also a "first" on long-playing records. Even the justly famous Charles Ives, acclaimed by all modernists, was relatively unknown to record collectors until we recorded his Third Symphony and his *Three Places in New England*.

Second, the recording industry has an obsolescence problem which is not paralleled, so far as I know, in any other form of publishing. A book printed in 1930 is, I would suppose, as readable today as the day it was published. A record "printed" in 1930 has no practical value unless it has for some reason become a collector's item.

Third, the recording companies have shown little interest in the history of the art. It would be invaluable if such recordings as the magnificent performances of the Strauss tone poems by Willem Mengelberg[6] would be re-pressed in the LP format. The same thing would apply to the Beethoven symphonies recorded by Wilhelm Furtwängler and many others. The fantastic recordings of the Boston Symphony under the great Serge Koussevitzky have practically disappeared, and yet his recording of a work such as the *Poème de l'Extase* of Scriabin (to mention only one) would open the eyes and ears of music lovers who never had the opportunity of hearing the work under his direction.

A short time ago, one of the major companies re-pressed a "collectors" album containing some of the most famous arias of the great American baritone, Lawrence Tibbett.[7] Among other accomplishments, Mr. Tibbett was noted for his singing of a group of arias by American composers during the golden days of the Gatti-Cassaza[8] regime at the Metropolitan, and a number of these arias by American composers were included. In the re-release, all of the American arias had been carefully deleted! I suppose this made room for another aria by Verdi. The American recording companies are not bothered by nationalism!

---

6   Willem Mengelberg (1871–1951), Dutch conductor. He led the Concertgebouw Orchestra 1895–1945, and the New York Philharmonic 1922–28.

7   Lawrence Tibbett (1896–1960), American opera singer. He sang at the Metropolitan Opera 1923–50 and was considered one of the most outstanding baritones of his time.

8   Giulio Gatti-Cassaza (1869–1940), Italian opera manager. He managed La Scala Opera in Milan 1898–1908 and the Metropolitan Opera in New York 1908–35.

Chapter Nineteen

CONCERTS AT THE LIBRARY OF CONGRESS

My first real introduction to the rarefied atmosphere of chamber music and chamber music players came in the fall of 1925. Mrs. Elizabeth Sprague Coolidge, who probably did more for the development of chamber music in the United States than any other patron of the arts, had for many years presented annual festivals of chamber music in the Berkshires. This year she decided to move the festivals to the Library of Congress in Washington, in an auditorium built for this purpose. An important part of these festivals was the encouragement of the contemporary composer through both prizes and commissions. For some reason, I was asked to write a string quartet for the occasion. Other composers commissioned were the distinguished Charles Martin Loeffler of Boston and Frederick Stock of Chicago.

I was as surprised as I was pleased to receive the invitation. My experience in the field of chamber music was slight. In my student days, I had written a quintet for strings and piano. I had also written the first movement of a concerto for piano which I re-wrote in Rome as a *Concerto da Camera* for piano and string quartet. The latter work had been performed in Rome and in New York under the direction of my good friend Albert Stoessel,[1] where it had a modest success. It was hardly adequate preparation for the formidable task of writing a string quartet for a festival of international importance.

The *Concerto da Camera* was a quite proper work in classic form and dutifully containing a fugal section. The string quartet was an entirely different matter. It was a "protest work," violent in character, with only occasional moments of repose, extremely difficult and making almost inhuman demands on the players. I was fortunate in having as interpreters the Persinger Quartet, at that time resident in San Francisco. They labored with the greatest devotion. They must have liked it for, after the first Washington performance, they played it extensively on tour.

---

1   Albert Stoessel (1894–1943), American composer, conductor, and violinist. He was head of the music department at New York University 1923–30, director of opera and orchestra at Juilliard starting in 1931, and music director at Chautauqua 1929–43.

The critics in Washington, New York, and elsewhere were in unanimous agreement that it was a very "modern" composition. I am sure the audience must have felt the same way. I don't know how Mrs. Coolidge felt about it. She beamed upon me most pleasantly, but I am not sure how much she actually heard. Her approaching deafness required her to use a hearing aid, and some of her close friends reported that, when music became too "modern," she solved the problem by turning down the volume.

She was quite a remarkable woman. In the first place, her love of music was completely genuine. In addition, she was a composer in her own right with strong feelings about the importance of the living composer. She was an impressive woman physically, of tall and commanding presence. Her entrance into a room, like a ship under full sail followed by an entourage of hopeful composers, made one think of what must have been comparable scenes of the court of an earlier Elizabeth.

There was at least one distinguished visitor who did not like my quartet. This was the great Scotsman, Sir Donald Francis Tovey.[2] Sir Donald was certainly one of the greatest musical scholars (if not the greatest). He was the author of numerous articles and reference works, and a man of encyclopedic knowledge. He was also a composer of numerous works, especially in the field of chamber music, and my youthful, uninhibited impetuosity must have fallen harshly on his ears. I believe that it was Rebecca Clarke Friskin,[3] the wife of my piano professor at the Institute and herself a gifted composer, who told me that Sir Donald's tremendous memory stood between him and his own creative development. (I have always believed that it is dangerous for a composer to be too intelligent!)

In any case, after the program on which my quartet had been performed, I joined a group of musicians discussing the concert. Sir Donald was engaged in conversation with the noted American composer, Mrs. H. H. A. Beach, one of whose compositions had been played. Seeing me approach, he turned abruptly to Mrs. Beach and said, in a voice which all could hear, "I am grateful that *some* composers can still write melodies!"

Since that initial performance, the quartet has had many brilliant performances by such quartets as the Gordon Quartet, the Eastman Quartet, the Juilliard Quartet, and other ensembles, but perhaps because of its difficulties and its general ungraciousness toward the strings, it has never

---

2   Donald Francis Tovey (1875–1940), eminent English composer, editor, essayist, musicologist, and pianist.

3   Rebecca Clarke (1886–1979), English composer and violist. She was the sister of Eric Clarke, who was manager of the Eastman Theatre in Rochester during the 1920s.

taken a permanent place in chamber music repertoire. Perhaps Sir Donald was correct!

In future years I was to venture only rarely into the field of pure chamber music, although I did write a number of works for string orchestra and solo instruments. The most important of the chamber works was also a Coolidge premiere at the Library of Congress under the aegis of Dr. Harold Spivacke, chief of the music division. It was a setting of four psalms for baritone and a string sextet consisting of two violins, two violas, and two cellos. One of the two cellos is in the form of a solo obligato, which introduces the first psalm and serves as a connecting link between the psalms which follow.

It was first performed by the Musical Art Quartet with the assistance of Walter Trampler,[4] violinist, and Benar Heifetz,[5] cellist, and with the gifted young baritone of the Metropolitan Opera, Gene Boucher,[6] as soloist. Unlike the early quartet, the psalms proved completely idiomatic both for the voice and for the string instruments, and [the psalms] met with the enthusiastic approval of musicians and audience. A later quintette (for string quartet and solo viola), to which I shall refer later because of the curious circumstances of its conception, had an almost equally successful premiere at the Library [of Congress] a few years later.

One experience in the Library of Congress concerts which brings back happy and also amusing memories concerned a concert in a festival of the music of Bach and Handel. For this event, I was invited to bring from Rochester a small orchestra selected from the Rochester Philharmonic Orchestra. The soloists were to be the eminent organist, Carl Weinrich,[7] and the famous tenor, John McCormack.[8] I was surprised at

---

4   Walter Trampler (1915–96), important viola teacher and performer. He was a founding member of the Chamber Music Society of Lincoln Center and violist in the Yale Quartet.

5   Benar Heifetz (1899–19?), Russian-born cellist. He was principal cellist in the Philadelphia Orchestra and had a notable career as a chamber music player with the Albeneri Trio, the Guilet Quartet, and the Kolisch Quartet.

6   Gene Boucher (19?–94), Metropolitan Opera baritone. Born in the Philippines, he was raised in the US and sang twenty seasons with the Metropolitan Opera.

7   Carl Weinrich (1904–91), American organist. He taught at Westminster College 1934–40, Wellesley College 1936–46, and Columbia University 1942–52, and was director of music at the University Chapel at Princeton University 1943–73.

8   John McCormack (1884–1945), famous Irish tenor. He was the most celebrated lyric tenor of his time, with a long career in opera and on the concert stage.

the invitation. My conducting experience, although growing steadily, had been concerned primarily with new music. I had made no claims to being either a Bach or Handel scholar, although the latter has always been one of my favorite composers. For this reason, I had no concern about the accompaniment of the Handel organ concerto. I was somewhat less sure of my ability to handle both Bach and John McCormack.

I must admit that, as I raised my baton to accompany the golden-voiced Irishman, I was subjected to a nervousness which I tried not to show. Just as we were about to begin, the tenor turned to me and, in that wonderful Irish accent, whispered into my ear, "I've been singing Mother Machree for years and here I am now singing Bach. I'm scared as hell!" My own nervousness departed magically!

Many years later, the thought occurred to me that perhaps he was not nervous at all, but was merely trying to reassure a young conductor that everyone gets nervous occasionally. In any case, he proved a magnificent musician as well as singer, and it was a joy to accompany him.

Since this experience early in my career, I have accompanied a good many artists, pianists, cellists, violinists, as well as singers ranging from young artists presenting their graduation "concerto programs" at Eastman to soloists of international fame. I have also witnessed the accompaniments furnished [to] various artists by famous conductors. There seem to be two basic philosophies of orchestral accompaniment, poles apart. The first is the theory that the "maestro" is always in command, and that the artist must accommodate to some extent to the interpretation of the conductor. The other is that the soloist is the one most concerned, and that the conductor should be literally an "accompanist." This has probably caused more friction on the operatic stage than in the concert hall.

Certainly, in the performance of the Beethoven Violin Concerto, the interpretation should hopefully be a happy synthesis of the meeting of three minds—the composer, the soloist, and the conductor. At the same time, there can be only one conductor of the orchestra at a time, and when the maestro insists on superimposing his interpretation on that of the artist, the poor artist is put in an impossible position. For this reason, I have always believed that in a concerto the conductor should be willing, subject to technical limitations, to serve as a good, cooperative accompanist. This applies only occasionally to opera where many different singers are involved (frequently in ensemble), and the opera must be produced in an integrated interpretation. Here I believe the man in the pit must be in charge.

Of course, there are exceptions to all rules. I recall an incident where an inexperienced conductor became hopelessly lost and the professional orchestra ignored the conductor and dutifully followed the soloist to a triumphant conclusion!

Chapter Twenty

THE *LAMENT FOR BEOWULF* AND THE FIRST TWO SYMPHONIES

May of 1926 saw the beginning of a long and certainly for me most rewarding relationship with the famous Ann Arbor May Festival, with its music director, Earl V. Moore, dean of the University of Michigan School of Music, and its impresario, Charles Sink. Dean Moore showed a strong interest in my *Lament for Beowulf*. I was most happy to accept [his] suggestion for a first performance by the Ann Arbor May Festival chorus and the Chicago Symphony Orchestra. Dean Moore graciously invited me to conduct the world premiere, and on May 21, 1926, the *Lament for Beowulf* made its initial appearance.

Few new works have been born under such a beneficent start. The chorus had been beautifully trained by Dean Moore, the Chicago Symphony under Frederick Stock was at its best, the audience was enthusiastic, and even the visiting critics were unanimous in their approbation. In later years, through the interest of Dean Moore, three more of my works were to have premieres at the Ann Arbor Festival, the *Heroic Elegy* written for the Beethoven Centennial in 1927, and a concert version of [my] opera *Merry Mount* in 1933.

Beowulf was immediately taken up by many different choral groups and remains even today one of my most frequently performed choral compositions. Early performances were given at the Worcester Festival in Massachusetts and by the Cleveland Symphony at the invitation of Vladimir Sokoloff, a most sympathetic friend of the American composer. The chorus for this performance was made up of the combined choirs of the First Methodist Church and the Glenville (Cleveland) High School. They had been trained by a superlative chorus master, Griffith J. Jones. They knew the music quite literally "by heart," singing the difficult score from memory. The result was a quite spectacular performance which I will never forget.

The critical reaction was most interesting and confirmed my constant wonder at how it is possible for two critics to get such diverse impressions from the same performance of the same work. The distinguished American composer, Arthur Shepherd, at that time music critic of the *Cleveland Press*, wrote: "Hats off to Howard Hanson! With his *Lament for Beowulf*, he has achieved a masterpiece. Granitic in its tragic import, the poem is evocative of heroic rhythms, of keen and searching vocal stress. Granitic, too, in harmony; fibrous in polyphony; somber and heroically expressive in the tonal investiture hewed out in manful strength and integrity by this gifted descendant of hardy Norseman."

Archie Bell[1] of the *Cleveland News* felt differently. "The composer came from Rochester to conduct his number; and so far as this particular listener is concerned, he can take his manuscript back to Rochester, keep it there, and I will promise to remain away from Rochester. This condition of things seems particularly unfortunate because Hanson is a fine musician, capable of accomplishing things of less pother and of more genuine value. There are grinding, smashing, blowing of trumpets, scraping, banging, blasting. We are becoming used to some of these noises in modern music, and perhaps they are right in their place; but never did they seem to be more weird, monotonous, and meaningless than in this composition." He must not have liked it! But it is difficult to believe that both critics were writing about the same piece.

The year 1929 marked my first meeting with the Boston Symphony Orchestra and its great conductor Serge Koussevitzky, who was to have a greater influence on my musical life than any other living musician. He had invited me to Boston to present the first performance in Boston of my first symphony, the *Nordic*. It was my first opportunity to know this truly remarkable man, for whom I soon developed a tremendous admiration and affection.

The reception of the *Nordic* by the audiences in Symphony Hall was warm and appreciative. The critics, except for the *Christian Science Monitor* and the *Boston Traveler*, were at best lukewarm, although they did testify to the enthusiastic audiences. Philip Hale, the veteran critics of the *Boston Herald*, termed the symphony "yeasty." I gathered that this was not intended as a compliment. No yeast for Boston! I was somewhat encouraged to see that he did not care too much for Richard Strauss's *Death and Transfiguration* either. He complained "that the death of the sufferer is long delayed."

During my rehearsals of the symphony, Dr. Koussevitzky would sit in the hall listening attentively. He would constantly urge me to take more time, rehearse more carefully, work for greater accuracy and greater expressiveness. It was a superb conducting lesson and one from which I profited greatly.

---

1   Archie Bell (1877–1943), American music critic and author. He worked for various newspapers in Cleveland but retired due to ill health in the mid-1930s.

During one intermission, I went back into the auditorium where he was sitting to ask for his suggestions. With him was a handsome man with an impressive beard, beautifully trimmed. It was the famous Alsatian American composer, Charles Martin Loeffler, who had come to attend my rehearsal. I was flattered by his interest and expressed my appreciation. His reply was delightfully modest, "I think that we older fellows can learn something from you young fellows." His enthusiasm and interest in everything that was going on in the field of composition was amazing. He told me that at that time he was studying the ways in which jazz composers were using the saxophone. In later life, I had the chance to conduct and record a number of his orchestral works, including the magnificent *Pagan Poem*, but to my regret I never saw him again.

Regardless of Philip Hale, Dr. Koussevitzky liked the *Nordic*. He agreed with the audience! And so I received from him a short time later an invitation to compose a symphony for the fiftieth anniversary of the Boston Symphony Orchestra. This was to be my second symphony, the *Romantic*. As I have said, I began writing the *Romantic* under the pines of Interlochen and the inspiration of my association with those wonderful young people. Perhaps it was this spirit of youth [in] Interlochen which had something to do with the character of the symphony, for it became, indeed, a symphony of youth.

The first performance of the *Romantic* took place in Boston on November 28, 1930, under Serge Koussevitzky's direction. At his request, I had written some program notes explaining my reasons for labeling the symphony "romantic." In those notes I wrote that this meant a "definite and acknowledged embracing of the romantic phase." I went on to say that "I recognize, of course, that romanticism is at present the poor stepchild, without the social standing of her older sister, neo-classicism. Nevertheless, I embrace her all the more fervently, believing that romanticism will find in this country rich soil for a new, young, and vigorous growth. It is my attempt to create a work, young in spirit, romantic in temperament, and simple and direct in expression."

The reaction of the audience was most favorable, and the reaction of the critics was, for the most part, an improvement over that of the *Nordic*. Even Philip Hale, while objecting to the "sturm und drang" episodes, referred to the effectiveness of the "gently romantic" passages. For me, the most rewarding experience was the opportunity of watching Serge Koussevitzky rehearse and conduct my new work. I had already, in my short career, met and worked with a number of famous conductors. I had met a few conductors who showed little interest in composition as a living art, who seemingly were quite willing to go along indefinitely [with] the repertory which had come down to them from the past. However, there were many who felt keenly their duty to contemporary music and the living composer, who felt that such a concern was the unquestionable responsibility of all who held a position of musical leadership. It had been my good fortune to have met a large number of the latter.

In the case of Serge Koussevitzky, however, it was more than a sense of obligation. It was a burning passion, almost a religious belief. This philosophy was not one which he developed on coming to these shores. It had motivated his entire conducting career in Europe, where he presented for the first time innumerable new works of living composers—Russian, French, German—anyone indeed who, in Dr. Koussevitzky's opinion, had a musical message worth presenting.

On coming to the United States, he offered to the American composer the same courageous devotion which had characterized his musicmaking in Europe. Under his direction, Boston and the Boston Symphony Orchestra became a mecca for the American composer, both young and old. The number of prominent American composers who owe him a deep debt of gratitude is legion. Many of them were young and comparatively unknown when he championed their compositions, but his insistence that their works be heard had much to do with their ultimate success. I am proud to have my name included on the list.

Serge Koussevitzky had an additional quality which endeared him to most of us. Having decided to perform a new work, he brought to the composition a dedication which many conductors reserve only for the masterpieces of the past. I have heard it said at times that a work under Koussevitzky sounded like Koussevitzky rather than the composer who wrote it. With this I disagree. It is true that every great conductor (and Koussevitzky was one of the greatest) does to some degree put the [imprint] of his personality on every work that he conducts. In his case, however, the search was always for the meaning of the music, for "what lies behind the notes," as he used to put it.

It is no more possible for a great conductor to interpret a composition without leaving the mark of his personality on the performance than it would be for a great actor to read his lines without introducing his own personal diction, tempo, and inflections. I had an opportunity of observing at first hand a striking illustration of differences in interpretation based on the temperament and personality of the conductor.

Within a comparative short space of time, I heard three performances of my second symphony. The first was under Serge Koussevitzky, the second under Arturo Toscanini, and the third under Fritz Reiner. Each performance was superb but bore little resemblance to the other two. Under Toscanini the fanfare of the final movement marched with the same implacable, relentless rhythm with which he conducted the march of the Roman legions in Respighi's masterpiece, the *Pines of Rome*. Reiner secured the greatest contrast by taking the two outside movements somewhat faster, and the inside movement somewhat more slowly. Koussevitzky conducted it *con amore*, as though he had written it himself. So convinced was I of his interpretation that I later somewhat altered my own interpretation of my own work.

Some of my friends who have seen Serge Koussevitzky conduct from the auditorium of Symphony Hall in Boston or Carnegie Hall in New York have referred to him as a tall, slender, handsome man. Slender and handsome he was, but not tall! We have a picture of him taken with his wife at Koussevitzky's summer home, Serenak, in Lenox, Massachusetts, and they are both about the same height.

However, on the podium such was the impressiveness of his manner that he seemed six feet tall. His gestures had a grace, a power, and a communicative quality which are difficult to describe. Behind his beat there was a dynamic energy and a complete dedication to the music. At the end of a rehearsal, he would be completely exhausted with the great veins of his forehead standing out like taut cords. There could be no question as to the depth of his commitment.

The performance of the *Romantic* by Toscanini provided one of the best of the numerous Toscanini stories. Before his performance of the symphony by the New York Philharmonic, the maestro kindly invited me to attend the final rehearsal. I was impressed with his rehearsal technique and delighted with his interpretation. After the rehearsal, maestro Toscanini beckoned me to the conductor's stand and asked me what I would like changed. I replied that I had no suggestions, that I was delighted with the performance. His reply was, "Non mi faccia complimenti" ("Don't make me compliments"), and demanded that I tell him what changes I wanted.

When I replied again that I had no suggestions to offer, he looked at me with disapproval. Suddenly he said, "Young man, three bars after letter A in the first movement, you conduct it too fast." I replied, "Maestro, how do you know how I conduct it?" Came the reply, "Last year you conducted this symphony in Berlin with the Berlin Philharmonic. It was broadcast and I was sitting before the radio in Milan with the score. Three bars after letter A, you conduct it too fast. Remember, young man, to always conduct the composition the way the composer wrote it!" It took me several minutes to remember that *I* was the composer!

Another conductor to whom I owe a great deal was the venerable Walter Damrosch, for so many years music director and conductor of the New York Symphony Orchestra. As I have already said, he was the chairman of the American Academy jury which awarded me the first competitive Prix de Rome, although I had [not] met him at that time. His later invitation to me to premiere *North and West* gave me my first introduction to New York City, an important milestone in my professional career. Our friendship continued until his death.

Walter Damrosch was not, from the purely technical standpoint, perhaps the most spectacular conductor of his generation. He was, however, one of the greatest educators among the conductors, deeply concerned with the sociological position of music in the lives of people. His "Young People's Concerts," presented for many years over the radio, were a model for all of the "music appreciation" concerts to follow. He, like Koussevitzky and Stock, had a lovely appreciation of the importance of the composer in society, and was a staunch protagonist of the American composer. He was not, however, too happy about the "avant-garde" music, beginning to raise its head in public.

Sometime after my return from Rome, I was invited to become a member of the Rome jury to select fellows for the American Academy. The meeting of this jury was quite fascinating. Dr. Damrosch and I were the only members of the jury adept at reading orchestral scores at the piano. As a result, the two of us at each jury meeting would seat ourselves at the piano and read through the multitude of scores submitted in the Prix de Rome contest.

One day I received a message from Mrs. Damrosch. Could I come to lunch? "The doctor has a suggestion which he wishes to discuss with you." I was quite curious as to his suggestion, and arrived promptly at the appointed time. Mrs. Damrosch met me at the door and explained that Dr. Damrosch was engaged in planting some new trees but that he would be with us in a moment. In a few minutes he returned, and we had a delightful luncheon accompanied by stimulating conversation for which the Damrosch family was famous.

During the luncheon, nothing was said about Dr. Damrosch's suggestion, and I was becoming more and more curious. Finally, after we had drunk our demitasse, Dr. Damrosch addressed me. "Howard," he said, "we have been together on the academy jury for several years. We have read many new scores together. I have a suggestion. Let us offer a series of awards of one thousand dollars to young composers on the condition that they write *no music* for an entire year!"

It was half jest, but also half in earnest. We discussed the proposal in mock seriousness. Finally, Dr. Damrosch excused himself, and Mrs. Damrosch accompanied me to the door. As I left, I could hear from the upper floor Dr. Damrosch playing the orchestral score of the "Ring des Nibelungen" of Wagner with a technique and a passion which belied his age.

Chapter Twenty-One

RETURN TO ROME

Attending the first performance of my second symphony in Boston presented a serious logistic problem. I had accepted an invitation to conduct the Augusteo Orchestra of Rome on December 10, and had booked passage from New York on the *Saturnia*. The *Saturnia* was scheduled to leave New York on the afternoon of November 28, arriving in Naples one day before my first orchestral rehearsal.

Then came the news that Dr. Koussevitzky had programmed the premiere of my symphony for November 28 in Boston. It was too late to change the date either of the Boston or of the Rome concert. It appeared that it would be necessary for me to miss the first performance of my symphony or cancel the appearance with the Augusteo. I could not imagine not being present at the christening of my symphonic child, especially under the direction of Serge Koussevitzky. It was equally difficult to give up the opportunity of returning to my beloved Rome.

Fortunately, the choice was not necessary. Cables were dispatched from Washington to the Italian government telling of my predicament. Once again, luck was on my side. It seems that there was a cargo in Boston waiting to be dispatched to Naples. The *Saturnia* was re-routed to Naples by way of Boston. And so, the morning following the Boston premiere, I embarked from Boston, arriving in Rome a few hours before my first rehearsal.

It was a joy to return to Rome and to the American Academy. It was a joy also to have the privilege of conducting the great orchestra of the Augusteo in its own famous hall. I had conducted this orchestra in special concerts at the academy when I was a resident fellow, but this was my first chance to conduct the orchestra in its regular concert series.

Having conducted a number of the famous orchestras of the United States since leaving Rome, I found the orchestra of the Augusteo more relaxed, less "tight" in discipline, and on the whole less "virtuoso" than its American counterparts, I had, as I recall, six rehearsals of three hours each. In the United States, I would not have known how to use so much time in rehearsing one program. In Rome, however, because of the relaxed atmosphere and the leisurely intermissions (two per rehearsal), I found that I could use the time profitably.

Perhaps one reason for the relaxed atmosphere was the fact that the orchestra's permanent conductor, the fiery Bernardino Molinari, was in the United States appearing as guest conductor of some of our American orchestras. The players probably could stand a more relaxed atmosphere! In spite of this, the players gave me splendid cooperation. After my three years in Rome, they considered me at least part Italian. One Italian critic attributed my melodic gift to the fact that I had spent three years under the beneficent Italian sun!

The program, as I review it today, seems a rather curious one. It consisted of works by Sibelius, Mendelssohn, and Wagner, in addition to a new work by the young American composer Alexander Steinert (at that time a fellow of the American Academy in Rome) and my second symphony.

Years later, in going over old papers and clippings, I found an interesting article written by Theodore Fitch,[1] the American composer and educator, who had come with me to Rome to attend the concert. He wrote, in an article for an American magazine:

> In accordance with the true continental custom, most of the audience stood up before the concert, peering around to see who was there. There was no small flurry of attention when the American ambassador and his wife entered our box. Besides Mr. and Mrs. Garrett and other members of the embassy, my hostess, Mrs. Felix Lamond, the wife of the director of music for the American Academy, pointed out many notables in the audience. To see the descendants of some of the old Roman families brought to mind episodes of the Italian Renaissance. But of more interest to me was a short heavy-set man of middle age who was seated just the other side of the royal box from us. Unless one knew him, it would be hard to suspect that he was the man who had composed the *Pines of Rome*.
>
> During most of the program he sat quietly attentive. However, in the third movement of Dr. Hanson's *Romantic* symphony, at the point where the pizzicato passage in the strings sets the stage for the crashing horn fanfares, his face became tense and pale, and he leaned forward in his seat. When the climax came and the secondary theme of the first movement returned on the top of the mighty billows of sound, he looked like one transported.
>
> When I again noticed Respighi, he was on his feet applauding vigorously the return of Dr. Hanson after the performance of the symphony.

In addition to the famous Italian composer, the audience included another eminent personage whose presence gave me a few bad moments.

---

1   Theodore Fitch (1900–76), American composer and writer. He taught composition and theory at the Eastman School of Music 1928–32.

The concert was just about to begin when I was informed that the Queen Mother, a great lover of music, had entered the royal box. It was, therefore, necessary that the orchestra play the *Marcia Reale* in her honor. The problem was that I did not know the *Marcia Reale*! There is no special difficulty in conducting a march, but it is essential to know how [the] march ends. Otherwise, it is possible for the conductor to continue conducting after the orchestra stops, an embarrassing experience! I consulted hurriedly with the concertmaster. He told me that he would look up just before the final cadence. I would then [know when to conclude my conducting.] I watched him devotedly [as we neared] the end of the march. At the appointed time, he gave me the signal. At the next measure, I concluded with a flourish. His cue had been perfect. We all finished together, and the day was saved![2]

I would have loved to have been able to linger in Rome. It has always been my favorite European city, and I could spend hours wandering about its picturesque streets, its busy [piazzas], and its ancient monuments, but time was pressing. I had been elected the previous year to the presidency of the Music Teachers National Association and was scheduled to speak at the banquet of its annual convention in St. Louis. As it was, I was tardy in arriving. Rudolph Ganz was the toastmaster of the banquet, and the audience was delighted to hear him introduce me (with that puckish sense of humor) as "the late Dr. Hanson."

Returning to Rochester, I was happy to find Bernardino Molinari, whose orchestra I had just conducted in Rome, appearing as guest conductor of the Rochester Philharmonic Orchestra. He was, as I have said before, a small man of fiery temperament and somewhat short in temper. This combination furnished me with one of most valued orchestral stories. Maestro Molinari, when I entered the Eastman Theatre, was rehearsing with great concentration and not too much patience. His command of the English language was negligible, and his communication with the orchestra was carried on with the aid of the English horn player, a Signor Bottesini.

At one point in the rehearsal, Maestro Molinari, for some reason not clear to me, became furious with the players. As I recall the incident, he began a tirade in Italian of the utmost ferocity which lasted several minutes but which must have seemed an eternity to the players. He then proceeded to break his baton and throw the pieces on the floor. After this, he tore off his collar and threw it on the podium, at the same time carefully removing a gold collar button and putting [it] in his pocket. The

---

2   Hanson's manuscript continues here with a description of the Augusteo. This material has been omitted since it duplicates his comments in chapter 10.

orchestra sat completely bewildered, not knowing what could have caused the emotional outbreak. Signore Bottesini rose from his chair and interpreted the maestro's [words]. Said Signor Bottesini, "The Maestro says, please a little more *piano*."

In spite of (or perhaps because of) his temperament, he was an exciting conductor, and I doubt if his performances of Respighi have ever been equalled. His success in the United States was enormous. I had the impression that he was even more successful in the United States than he was in his native Rome.

Part of his problems at home were, I am sure, political. Rumor had it that his musicianship was much admired by Benito Mussolini, who gave him virtual *carte blanche* in Rome's musical life. With the fall of fascism and the violent death of its leader, Molinari's star also went into a decline from which it never recovered.

Chapter Twenty-Two

CONDUCTING CONCERTS IN GERMANY

Sometime early in the year 1932, I received an exciting invitation from the Oberlander Trust. The trust was a division of the Carl Schurz Foundation, dedicated to the purpose of promoting cultural relations between the United States and Germany. It was Mr. Oberlander's hope that the interchange of contemporary music of the two countries might serve as one means of promoting greater understanding.

I had always been interested in the possibilities of music as a means of communication across language barriers and readily agreed to accept the appointment. Later, I received a formal invitation from the German government to present a series of concerts of contemporary American music with some of the German orchestras. Late in December, accompanied by Mr. [and Mrs.] Richard L. Stokes, I set off for Germany. Richard Stokes was the librettist of [my] opera *Merry Mount*, which had just been commissioned by the Metropolitan Opera Company.

The concerts scheduled for my short tour included concerts with the Berlin Philharmonic (*the* ranking orchestra of Germany), the Reichs-Rundfunk (radio) Orchestra of Berlin, and the symphony orchestras of Leipzig and Stuttgart. For the programs, I had selected works which seemed to present a reasonably accurate cross-section of the American music which was being [performed] by our own orchestras. These included works by Daniel Gregory Mason (at that time the dean of American symphonists), the late and greatly talented Charles Tomlinson Griffes, John Powell, Leo Sowerby, William Grant Still, Robert Russell Bennett, Bernard Rogers, Herbert Elwell, Randall Thompson, [in addition to] my *Romantic* Symphony.

The reaction of the audiences and of the orchestra musicians was most cordial. The scherzo movement of William Grant Still"s *Afro-American Symphony*, with its "jazzy" rhythms, [was] such a hit with the Berlin audience that it had to be repeated. Critical acclaim of the music itself was something less than unanimous, especially in Berlin. The distinguished musicologist Dr. Hugo Leichtentritt commended my selection of American works. Herbert Peyser,[1] the well-known New York critic writing from Berlin, noted

---

1   Herbert Peyser (1886–1953), American author and critic. He wrote for *Musical Quarterly* in the 1920s and was also foreign critic for the *New York Times*.

that "American music had one of the most successful innings that it has ever had," but that "some of the gentlemen of the press could not understand how the names of Varese, Ruggles, Cowell, Ives, and Sessions could possibly be omitted from a representative American program. He added that "it was the skilled and vital conducting of Dr. Hanson, however, which came in for general commendation and gained the composer the wholehearted affection of the philharmonic players."

Conducting the Berlin Philharmonic was, for this young American, a thrill. Presided over in those days by Wilhelm Furtwängler, it was a superb orchestra of the greatest integrity. The old philharmonic concert hall was in itself an inspiration. There were, as I recall, five or six levels of orchestral players, so that the conductor seemed to be conducting from the bottom of a kind of acoustical well. The sound, as I recall, was indescribably rich and vibrant. The hall was one of the casualties of the Second World War and now lives only in the memories of those who played or listened there.

Mr. Furtwängler received me most graciously, and on the occasion of one of his concerts invited me to attend as his guest. The symphony of the evening was to be the Tchaikovsky Sixth. He seemed somewhat apologetic about including this symphony on his program, remarking that the Berlin audience was really too sophisticated for Tchaikovsky. I listened to the performance with the greatest interest. His interpretation, as I recall, was too *langweilig* ([i.e., boring)] for my taste, but it was most expressive. At the conclusion, the Berlin audience went wild with excitement, shouting its approval and giving Mr. Furtwängler a standing ovation.

In the green room, after the concert, I could not resist remarking to Mr. Furtwängler that the Berlin audience did not seem to me "too sophisticated" for Tchaikovsky! The public reaction to Tchaikovsky seems to be the same in New York, Moscow, and Berlin.

In those days, there was still little conception in Germany of the status of music and musical performance in the United States. I recall one amusing experience, which is vouched for by my friend, Dr. Harold Spivacke, now the distinguished chief of the music division of the Library of Congress, but at that time a young student of *Musikwissenschaft* ([i.e., musicology)] at the University of Berlin. After one of my rehearsals with the Berlin Philharmonic, I was approached by the conductor of the student orchestra of the Berlin Hochschule für Musik. He thought that the student orchestra would be interested in the opportunity of playing under a young American conductor and invited me to attend one of their rehearsals.

I was delighted to accept and went to Hochschule at the appointed time. The conductor introduced me to the orchestra and asked me what I would like to conduct. I, in turn, asked him what the orchestra was studying. He replied that they were rehearsing the first symphony of Brahms. I suggested that I rehearse the first movement of the symphony, to which the conductor responded, "Kennen sie Brahms in Amerika?" ("Is Brahms known in America?") I said that we had heard of Brahms even in America! Dr. Spivacke insists that I declined the score and proceeded to rehearse Brahms from memory. I don't remember whether I did or not. I hope Dr. Spivacke's version is correct. It makes for a better story!

Almost thirty years later, I was to take the Eastman Philharmonic, an orchestra of the Eastman School's most gifted players, to Europe, the Near East, and Russia as part of the State Department's cultural exchange program. After a performance of the orchestra in Berlin, a critic on one of the important West Berlin newspapers, wrote that, after hearing the brilliant performance of the young Americans, Germany should reexamine its own methods of music education. So does the passage of time affect all things.

The orchestra of the historic Gewandhaus in Leipzig proved highly competent, and the hall one of great beauty. My principal recollection, however, was the conductor's podium, which I was informed was that used by the fabulous Artur Nikisch. According to accounts, Artur Nikisch was a slight man with a small and immaculate beat. The podium was small in size and "fenced in" with an iron railing. I was tall and strenuous, using the baton, as one critic remarked, as though it were a rapier. Confining my conducting to the physical limitations of the Nikisch podium imposed serious problems, but the privilege of conducting from the podium of the famed maestro of the past made the discomfort worthwhile.

Proceeding from Leipzig to Stuttgart, I was impressed with the gracious hospitality of that delightful city, and once again delighted with the ability of the German musicians to cope with the new American scores. The atmosphere was friendly, relaxed, and thoroughly delightful.

My only worry was the fact that the concert was to be broadcast throughout Germany, and I was not sure of the "timing" of the program, including the radio announcements. The radio announcer was to present himself a few minutes before the concert for consultation on the announcements and, particularly on the pronunciation of the English titles on the program. The broadcast was to begin at eight o'clock. I arrived promptly at 7:30 for the consultation with our announcer. No announcer appeared. At 7:45 no announcer. At 7:50 there was still no announcer. Finally at five minutes before the scheduled beginning of the broadcast, the announcer strolled in and began leisurely asking me details of the program.

Accustomed to the split-second timing of the radio programs of the United States, I was rapidly approaching a state of panic. I pointed to the clock and told him that there was no time for further questions, that if we did not begin immediately, the program would run beyond the scheduled time. He looked at me in some surprise and said, "This is no problem but I would hope that we would not run more than fifteen minutes behind schedule." How relaxed can you get!

Returning to Berlin for a final concert, I proceeded to my hotel the *Kaiserhof.* In the plaza in front of the hotel, I met a crowd of thousands of Germans obviously in a state of great excitement. Approaching the desk, I told the clerk with my nonnegotiable American sense of humor, that I deeply appreciated the tremendous crowds welcoming my return to Berlin. He replied politely, but without a trace of a smile, that he was sorry. The crowds were not assembled to greet me. Mr. Hitler had just been elected chancellor of the Reich.

During my previous stay at the *Kaiserhof,* I had seen Adolf Hitler from a distance on several occasions. He was living in the hotel at the time and was apt to appear in the afternoons with members of his staff. He seemed to be a quiet little man. Any gesticulating or vehement conversation seemed to come from his staff officers rather than from him.

That evening, however, I heard his speech from the balcony of the Reichstag to, I suppose, a hundred thousand brown-shirts who had been parading in the plaza. The passion of his speech and the terrifying "Heil Hitler" from the huge crowd was like nothing I had ever experienced. Here were obviously inflamed passions which boded no good for the peace of the world.

I was both fascinated and horrified but decided to stay through the ceremony. When it was over, I asked one of the hotel attendants if he thought Mr. Hitler would return to the hotel at the conclusion of his speech. The attendant thought that in all probability he would. I waited in the hotel lobby, curious to get another look at this frightening little man. At least an hour passed, the crowds began to disperse, and I decided that my vigil was in vain. I heard the elevator door open and decided that it was time to go to bed. Making up my mind to catch the elevator before it made its next ascent, I ran toward it. As I passed the revolving door of the entrance to the hotel, Hitler entered with members of his storm troopers. I tried to stop but I was moving too fast. I literally ran into him. I stammered my apologies in German. He responded, "Bitte schön." The troopers looked at me with suspicion, and I got out of there as fast as I could. It occurred to me later that never before had I taken such a good chance of being shot.

Chapter Twenty-Three

A COMMISSION TO WRITE AN OPERA

Before leaving for Rome [to conduct the Augusteo Orchestra], I had received an interesting letter for Otto Kahn, the philanthropist and chairman of the board of the Metropolitan Opera Company. Richard L. Stokes, music critic of the *New York Evening World*, had been commissioned by the Metropolitan [Opera Company] to write a libretto on an American subject, the score to be written by an American composer.

Mr. Stokes chose as his subject the conflict between the Puritans and the Cavaliers in the settling of New England. The [libretto] receives its initial inspiration from Nathaniel Hawthorne's *The Maypole of Merry Mount*, but the dramatic plot was the result of Stokes's own fertile and creative imagination. The following condensation of the story appeared at the time of the opera's premiere:

Merry Mount depicts outwardly the conflict between Puritan and Cavalier colonists in New England, and inwardly the struggle between religion and carnal love in the breast of a fanatical Puritan clergyman. At the outset Wrestling Bradford, religious leader of a Puritan village, publicly rebukes two prisoners held in the stocks, one as a freethinker, the other as an immoral woman.

The preacher confides to Praise-God Tewke, elder of the congregation, that he is tortured by hellish dreams in which a beautiful temptress appears to him. The elder suggests that he is "over-ripe for marriage" and proposes holy union with his daughter, Plentiful Tewke. Bradford agrees and he and the maiden subsequently plight their troth, dividing between them a broken ring, according to the custom.

In the scene comes a mountebank, Jack Prence, who plays games with the children of the village on the Sabbath. He is seized and is being whipped at the post when Lady Marigold Sandys and other members of the group of Cavaliers, to which Prence belongs, enter. She strikes Bradford across the face with a riding crop, in defense of the mountebank.

Bradford recognizes her as the creature of his dreams and is instrumental in stopping the fighting that ensues between the Puritans and the Cavalier band. A truce is declared for the Sabbath, but when Bradford learns from Lady Marigold that she is about to wed Sir Gower Lackland, one of the Cavaliers, he decides upon immediate attack.

The second act shows the scene about a Maypole which the Cavaliers have set up near the sea. There are old English dances and a pageant in which Sir Gower plays the King and Lady Marigold the Queen of the festivities. The Puritans arrive in force and break up the celebration, chopping down the Maypole and seizing the Cavaliers.

The commander of their Trainband angrily drives away some Indian spectators, while Bradford accompanies the soldiers who have seized Lady Marigold.

The scene shifts to a forest, where Bradford tells his prisoner of his love for her. She resists him, and Sir Gower, escaping from his guards, comes to her assistance. He is killed by a soldier in the fight that follows. Lady Marigold, over his body, pledges herself to follow him into eternity.

The exhausted Bradford prays for divine guidance, then goes to sleep upon a rock. The hellish visions return and take the form of a distorted reenactment of the Maypole festivities, with Sir Gower as King and Marigold as Queen of a rout of evil spirits. Bradford, unable to resist the beauty of Marigold, signs the devil's book, and Sir Gower transfers to his head the King's crown.

The last act opens with the battle cries of the revengeful Indians, who have set the village on fire. The congregation assembles sorrowfully amid the flaming ruins of their homes. Bradford appears and horrifies his fellow Puritans by renouncing his faith and throwing away his Bible.

Into this throng comes the distraught Marigold, still wearing the flimsy attire of the Maypole pageant. Bradford declares her a witch. She tells her sorry story and repeats her pledge to Sir Gower, to follow him into eternity. Bradford seizes her and drags her with him to death in the flames.

The next problem for the Metropolitan, having secured a powerful and exciting libretto, was to find an American composer to provide the score. The story of the manner of that selection, as told to me later by Richard Stokes, was as follows: Mr. Kahn decided to ask three New York critics—Lawrence Gilman, Richard Stokes himself, and (as I recall) Olin Downes—to send him the name of the American composer whose music would seem to best fit the dramatic and emotional needs of the libretto. According to the story, in due time Mr. Kahn received the three letters. Upon opening them, he discovered that the name on each of the three letters was mine! With this consensus, Mr. Kahn immediately offered me the commission. Upon receiving Mr. Kahn's invitation, I read the libretto and was deeply impressed with its powerful emotional qualities. The words seemed to "set themselves," and I accepted the commission.

The problem of writing a full-length opera while keeping up with the day-to-day administrative duties of the Eastman School was formidable. I became more than ever a midnight composer. Most of *Merry Mount* was written between the hours of eleven in the evening and two in the morning. But I was entranced with the beauty of the libretto and the dramatic qualities of the story, and writing the score became a real labor of love.

In the meantime, I had countless conferences with the librettist and interviews with the distinguished general manager of the Metropolitan Opera Company, Maestro Gatti-Casazza. "Gatti," as everyone called him, wanted a genuinely "grand" opera. He urged on me the example of *Aida* with its choruses, its ballets, and its large orchestra. For good or ill, I complied and *Merry Mount* is in truth a "grand" opera, requiring a large cast, large chorus, large ballet, and a huge orchestra.

Maestro Gatti's choice of conductors for the premiere was between Artur Bodanzky,[1] head of the German "wing" of the Met, and Tullio Serafin,[2] head of the Italian "wing." Maestro Gatti finally decided upon Tullio Serafin, a delightfully sympathetic person and a magnificent operatic conductor. The only problem was that Maestro Serafin had no contact with the English language.

I recall playing the score for him for the first time. He listened with rapt attention, but it was clear that he had no idea of what the words of the libretto meant and no conception of the story. In the middle of the first act, there is a lively chorus of the Puritan children playing games with the mountebank, Prence. As I came to the Children's Dance, he brightened visibly. At the end of the dance, he beamed upon me and said, "Ah, bambini!" ("Ah, children!").

Maestro Gatti had advised me to take *Aida* as a model. The model, intentionally or not, actually proved to be Mussorgsky's *Boris Goudonov*, my favorite opera since my student days when I first heard it with Chaliapin under the baton of Toscanini. Like *Boris*, *Merry Mount* is essentially a one-man opera with the character of Wrestling Bradford dominating the entire opera. Like *Boris* also, the chorus is an integral part, almost an individual character of the [opera].

It was probably for this reason that Earl Moore asked for the right to give a concert performance of *Merry Mount* at the 1933 Ann Arbor May Festival, preceding the Metropolitan [Opera] premiere in February 1934. The Metropolitan, somewhat to my surprise, consented, perhaps with the urging of the publishers, Harms, Inc., who had invested many thousands of dollars in the printing of the vocal score.

---

1   Artur Bodanzky (1877–1939), opera conductor. He succeeded Toscanini at the Metropolitan Opera in 1915 and was known for his fiery temperament and for his conducting of Wagner.

2   Tullio Serafin (1878–1968), Italian opera conductor. He was principal conductor at La Scala in Milan before World War I, conductor at the Metropolitan Opera 1924–34, then artistic director of Teatro Reale in Rome.

And so, *Merry Mount* had its first performance in concert form [on] May 20, 1933, with the Ann Arbor Festival Chorus and [the] Chicago Symphony Orchestra. The part of Wrestling Bradford was sung by the famous baritone, John Charles Thomas,[3] the part of Sir Gower Lackland by Frederick Jagel,[4] Lady Marigold Sandys by Leonora Corona,[5] Plentiful Tewke by Rose Bampton,[6] and Praise-God Tewke by Chase Barromeo, all of the Metropolitan Opera Company.

The concertmaster of the Chicago Symphony at that time was the late Jacques Gordon, a brilliant violinist in his own right and a superb concertmaster. In later years, he was to form his own quartet, the Gordon String Quartet, one of the finest quartets in my memory. Still later, he joined the faculty of the Eastman School, where he remained until his death.

The first performance was an unqualified success with both audience and critics. The soloists were superb, the chorus eloquent, and the Chicago Symphony its usual brilliant self. The Associated Press reported that a sellout audience of five thousand gave the work a "rousing reception," and that the composer received a "personal ovation." The *Detroit Times* headlined "Merry Mount wildly acclaimed." The critic from the *New York Times*, referring to the choral episodes, wrote "the effect is overwhelming." Even Julian Seaman[7] of the *New York Mirror* was convinced, writing, "Having sampled several flavors concocted by Dr. Hanson of late, I came not exactly to scoff, but at least to doubt; I remained to applaud most vigorously."

With such a reception for the first performance, the future of *Merry Mount* seemed assured. Perhaps I had written the "great American opera" for which, we have been assured, the world has been breathlessly waiting. But Ann Arbor is not New York, and a concert performance was not a Metropolitan stage performance. The good ship *Merry Mount* was to sail much rougher and less friendly seas. Even today, its place in the operatic repertory is still vigorously debated by equally fervent friends and enemies.

---

3   John Charles Thomas (1891–1960), popular American baritone. He was first known for his roles in Broadway musicals later for his opera and concert appearances.

4   Frederick Jagel (1897–1982), American tenor. He sang twenty-three seasons at the Metropolitan Opera following his debut in 1927.

5   Leonora Corona (1900– ?), American soprano. She was born Lenore Cohron and sang eight seasons at the Metropolitan Opera, principally Italian roles.

6   Rose Bampton (1907–2007), American mezzo-soprano. She sang eighteen seasons with the Metropolitan Opera; she was also a noted recitalist; especially known for her singing of Berg, Schoenberg, and Samuel Barber.

7   Julian Seaman (1896–1982), American author, critic, freelance writer. He wrote for the *New York World* for several years, then the *New York Mirror* 1932–39.

Chapter Twenty-Four

THE METROPOLITAN OPERA PRODUCTION OF *MERRY MOUNT*

Early in 1934, *Merry Mount* moved into its final rehearsal. There had been numerous piano rehearsals, chorus rehearsals, and ballet rehearsals, all under the watchful eye of Maestro Serafin. The ballet was under the personal direction of Madame Rosina Galli, the wife of Tullio Gatti-Casazza. The chorus was prepared by the extraordinary chorus master, Giulio Setti.[1]

The cast selected for the first performance included the famous baritone, Lawrence Tibbett, in the principal role of Wrestling Bradford. Edward Johnson, the Canadian tenor later to become manager of the Metropolitan Opera Company, was chosen for the part of Sir Gower Lackland, and the superb basso, Louis d'Angelo,[2] for the part of Praise-God Tewke. The Swedish Wagnerian soprano, Goeta Ljungberg,[3] was assigned the role of Lady Marigold, and the part of Plentiful Tewke was given to the brilliant American contralto, Gladys Swarthout.[4]

Tibbett, d'Angelo, and Gladys Swarthout were beautifully cast for their respective parts. The swash-buckling role of Sir Gower, at best a none-too-graceful part, hardly suited Edward Johnson, who was much more at home in less strenuous characterizations. Goeta Ljungberg, in spite of her opulent voice, was miscast as the sophisticated English noblewoman. One of Miss Ljungberg's problems was the English language, which she sang with a Swedish accent. The same problems confronted certain singers taking minor parts. It was somewhat disconcerting to hear some Puritans and Cavaliers projecting their lines with a strong Italian or German accent!

---

1 Giulio Setti (1869–1938), chorus master and later conductor at the Metropolitan Opera.
2 Louis d'Angelo (1888–1958).
3 Goeta [Göta] Ljungberg (1893–1958), Swedish soprano. She sang with the Stockholm Opera 1918–26, the Berlin State Opera 1926–32, and the Metropolitan Opera 1932–35.
4 Gladys Swarthart (1900–99), American mezzo-soprano and movie actress. She sang with the Chicago Civic Opera and the Ravinia Opera; she had sixteen seasons with the Metropolitan Opera following her debut in 1929 and appeared in five motion pictures.

As far as Tullio Serafin was concerned, he solved his linguistic problems very simply. When I saw the orchestral score after he had conducted it, I noticed that every word of the text and every stage direction had been meticulously translated into Italian.

The day for the final dress rehearsal finally arrived. As I sat alone in the vast auditorium of the Metropolitan, I remembered the words of Eugene Goossens, "There is no more thrilling sound in the world than a minor third played by two clarinets in the pit of a darkened theater." I quite agree. I shall never forget that dress rehearsal. The tuning of the orchestra suddenly stopped as Maestro Serafin raised his baton. There is a complete silence as the lights slowly dim, a soft roll in the tympani, and the trombones intone a solemn chorale (the motif of the Puritans) over a soft background of clarinets and bassoons. This is a thrill worth the hundreds of hours of composition, scoring, and copying. Whether the opera will be a success no longer seems important. The thrill of the moment is enough!

The first performance of the opera was scheduled for Saturday afternoon, February 10, in order that the premiere might be broadcast nationally over the radio network of the National Broadcasting Company. The day was, as I recall, bitterly cold with the mercury at or below the zero mark. The weather did not, however, discourage the intrepid opera-lovers of New York City and the surrounding territory (including a loyal contingent from Rochester), for the auditorium of the Metropolitan was jammed to capacity, including hundreds who stood patiently through the four acts of the opera. The audience was enthusiastic beyond all my hope. The role of Wrestling Bradford, which called for tremendous acting as well as singing ability, suited Lawrence Tibbett perfectly, and his performance could be described only by the adjective "tremendous." The orchestra and chorus were superb, and Maestro Serafin's conducting left nothing to be desired.

After the performance, we waited impatiently for the newspapers. How would the critics react to this new attempt of an American librettist and composer in the new field of opera? As I recall, we sat up all night waiting for the first reviews. The first [was] the *New York Times*, under the by-line of Olin Downes. The headlines were most encouraging, "Merry Mount Gets a Stirring Ovation." The article of the veteran critic, Lawrence Gilman, in the *New York Herald Tribune* was headed, "50 Curtain Calls Cap Opening of Merry Mount."

Most of the critics agreed upon the effectiveness of the choral scenes and the enthusiasm of the audience. The taciturn Maestro Gatti-Casazza, a powerfully impressive man of few words, was quoted by the press as saying, "It was fine. A grand performance. A fine work." Even the critic,

Harold Strickland, who had given me such a bad time over *Pan and the Priest*, wrote, "After fourteen tries the General Manager yesterday made his fifteenth attempt at producing a native American opera, and succeeded."

Maesto Gatti apparently agreed. Although the short season of the Metropolitan was already half over, he scheduled six more performances during the few weeks remaining in the New York season. He scheduled four performances in other cities, including Brooklyn, Philadelphia, Boston, and Rochester. The Boston performance, however, was destined not to take place.

The management which brought the Metropolitan to Boston had two objections to the opera. There were a few lines in Richard Stokes's libretto which were a bit spicy, especially in the confrontation of Wrestling Bradford with the woman taken in adultery. It would, in this day and age, pass unnoticed, but it had caused some concern to the broadcasters at the initial performance. The second concern of the Bostonians was much more important. In using Wrestling Bradford as the name of the psychologically unbalanced minister, Mr. Stokes had used (I am certain without malice) a surname of great historical importance to all of New England, the honored name of "Bradford." This was too much, and *Merry Mount* was refused. At least we acquired the privilege of saying that we had been "banned in Boston."

In later performances, there were occasional changes in cast. Both Leonora Corona and Margaret Halstead[5] replaced Miss Ljungberg. Rose Bampton sang several beautiful performances as Plentiful Tewke. Richard Bonelli[6] was an excellent Bradford, and Frederic Jagel was superb as Sir Gower Lackland. Tullio Serafin, however, remained on the podium for all of the performances.

The season had been a good one for American opera. Pitts Sanborn[7] wrote in the *New York World Telegram*:

Completing its shortest season since 1901–02 . . .the Metropolitan Opera House in the last fourteen weeks has made history. These fourteen weeks might well be termed the "American season." Not only were three American works in the active repertory, but an American work had

---

5   Margaret Halstead [dates?], American soprano. She made her Metropolitan Opera debut in 1932.

6   Richard Bonelli (1889–1980), American baritone. He was born Richard Bunn; sang with Chicago Opera 1925–31 and Metropolitan Opera 1932–45; taught at Curtis.

7   Pitts Sanborn (1879–1941), important American music critic. He worked for the New York Globe and later for the New York World Telegram.

the honor of opening the season, and an American work has tonight the honor of closing it.

Deems Taylor's *Peter Ibbetson* opened the season; Howard Hanson's *Merry Mount* closes it. Three representations go to the credit of the former, six to the credit of the latter. There are also three to the credit of Gruenberg's *Emperor Jones*.

Merry Mount, a world premiere on February 10, attained the extraordinary number of six performances at the Metropolitan alone in the course of seven weeks, besides one each on the company's visits to Brooklyn and Philadelphia. Only a single other work on the season's list did as well numerically, and at the Metropolitan [only] one [did] better—*Salome* of Richard Strauss.

At long last, we seemed to be seeing the beginning of an American operatic repertory. In the last four years of his regime, Maestro Gatti had produced at least five American operas, of which three had been successful with the operatic public. Deems Taylor's *Peter Ibbetson* was a work of great charm and sensitivity. Gruenberg's *Emperor Jones*, based on the Eugene O'Neill play, was an opera of great power, and the genius of Lawrence Tibbett as actor and singer gave the story and the music maximum impact.

Maestro Gatti was delighted with his experiment. He told me that the next year he planned a "piccola stagione" [i.e. small season] of American opera in which he would repeat Deems Taylor's *The King's Henchman* and *Peter Ibbetson*, Gruenberg's *Emperor Jones*, and *Merry Mount*. But fate was not in favor of Gatti's "piccola stagione." A few weeks later, following what was reported as a disagreement with his board of directors, he suddenly and unexpectedly resigned and returned to Italy.

The great American basso, Herbert Witherspoon,[8] was then appointed general manager to succeed Maestro Gatti. Herbert, a good friend of mine, was enthusiastic about a season of American opera at the Met. During the summer before taking over his Metropolitan duties, he was in charge of music for the Chicago World's Fair. I was a member of his advisory music committee, and he discussed with me at length his plans for making the Metropolitan an American opera house. These plans included not only the continuation of Gatti's proposal for a season of American opera but also the commissioning of new operas by American composers. He wished to offer increased opportunities for American singers. He intended to

---

8   Herbert Witherspoon (1873–1935), American bass and opera manager. He made his Metropolitan Opera debut in 1908 and retired from singing in 1914; president of Chicago Musical College and later Cincinnati Conservatory.

experiment with opera in English and to attempt a general revitalization of the old opera house.

His enthusiasm was infectious, and we were all convinced that a new era in opera in the United States had arrived. Again, the fates ruled differently. Herbert Witherspoon had barely seated himself behind his desk in the Metropolitan Opera House when he was seized with a heart attack. The hope of a "golden age" of American opera died with him.

He was succeeded by the Canadian tenor, Edward Johnson,[9] but this golden moment had passed. The country was feeling the effects of the Depression. Mr. Johnson's task was to keep the Met alive and reasonably solvent. The new American operas, regardless of their success, were stricken from the repertory. *Traviata* and *Il Trovatore*, *Pagliacci* and *Cavalleria*, and their colleagues once again galloped to the rescue. The Establishment had won again. Opera was saved but the Americans died. The Metropolitan was to see fewer American operas produced in the next thirty years than in the last four years of Gatti's regime.

Merry Mount, *The King's Henchman*, and *Emperor Jones*, which had been so successful were never done again at the Metropolitan. The popularity of *Merry Mount* with the public continued in many performances of the orchestral suite, the choruses, and some of the arias in concert form.

A few years ago, *Merry Mount* was revived in a full stage production in San Antonio, Texas, undertaken by the dynamic young conductor of the San Antonio Symphony, Victor Allesandro.[10] The orchestra, chorus, ballet, and the stage direction of Leonard Treash were all superb. The principals, including the magnificent American baritone, Chester Ludgin,[11] and the brilliant American soprano, Beverly Sills[12] (from the New York City Center Opera), Brian Sullivan[13] (tenor from the Metropolitan Opera Company), the gifted young American contralto, Joyce Castle,[14] and the fine singer-

---

9   Edward Johnson (1879–1959), Canadian tenor. He sang with the Metropolitan Opera for thirteen years; he was general manager 1935–50.

10   Victor Allesandro (1915–76), American conductor. He was educated at the Eastman School of Music; conducted the San Antonio Symphony 1950–76.

11   Chester Ludgin (1925–2003), American baritone. He was a leading singer at New York City Opera 1957–91.

12   Beverly Sills (1929–2007), American soprano particularly famed for her coloratura roles. She became manager of New York City Opera in 1980, chair of Lincoln Center in 1994, and chair of the Metropolitan Opera in 2002.

13   Brian Sullivan (1917–69), American tenor. He had an uneven career with many professional and personal crises.

14   Joyce Castle, American mezzo-soprano. She studied at the University of Kansas, where she is currently professor of voice, and at the Eastman School of Music.

actor, Val Patacchi.[15] The minor roles were also in the hands of talented young American singers.

So perfect was their diction that every word could be heard by the audience which filled the huge auditorium. The performance was aided by cuts which shortened certain scenes, speeded up the action, and gave greater impact to the dramatic scenes. The audience again received the work with the greatest enthusiasm, the morning paper carrying the headline, "Merry Mount Smash Hit."

And so I felt that in San Antonio, Texas, about thirty years after its premiere, *Merry Mount* was finally properly presented and heard. Perhaps the future of American opera, at least for the present, lies not in the Metropolitan Opera House, but in the New York City Center Opera and the opera centers in Chicago, San Antonio, San Francisco, and Los Angeles.

At the time of this writing, there is not, as far as I know, a single "grand" opera by an American composer in the permanent repertoire of the Metropolitan. This seems strange. American composers have been unusually successful in the field of light opera and musical comedy. Many Broadway musicals continue to hold the stage.

The reasons for the comparative lack of success of the Americans in "serious" opera are complex, but some problems are worth mentioning. In the first place, opera in the United States has always been an imported art. Although every European country with an operatic tradition insists on the performance of opera in its own language, the United States for the most part insists on the performance of all operas in the original language. The Italian opera singer, in most instances, sings his operas in Italian. The American singer, on the other hand, must sing Verdi in Italian, Wagner in German, and Gounod in French. In other words, although opera in Europe is a popular art form, in the United States it is an art for the elite.

I recall with wry amusement a conversation with Edward Ziegler who was, in Gatti-Casazza's regime, the Metropolitan Opera's business manager. I was arguing that opera would never become a widespread, popular art in the United States until we presented opera in our own language. He responded, rather loftily, that the Metropolitan would always present opera in the original language. I asked him why we in the United States, with no operatic tradition, should go against the experience of all of the great operatic countries of Europe, where all operas were presented in the vernacular. He responded again with the dictum that at the Metropolitan we always present operas in the original language. "That," I said, is

---

15 Val Patacchi (d.1996), American singer. He taught for thirty-years at Stephens College in Columbia, Missouri, and was for ten years director of the Brevard Music Center in North Carolina.

undoubtedly the reason that you are presenting *Boris Goudonov* in Italian." He gave me a withering look and replied, "That is an exception!"[16]

A second problem is the scarcity of opera houses in the United States. The Metropolitan Opera House has always been essentially a European opera house transported to the United States. I would say that there is really only one American opera house, City Center Opera in New York City. There are, it is true, short operatic seasons in other cities, but they are for the most part extensions of the two opera companies in New York. With so few opportunities for the American composer in the field of opera, it is not surprising that most composers choose other forms in which to write.

There is another problem which, though technical in nature, is of enormous importance to the composer. A musical show intended for Broadway generally has its "try-out," its first performance in the "provinces." After the rehearsals and the first performance, the composer, librettist, and producer have the chance to make changes, to "tighten up" the action, to delete or to add, until they feel that the production is ready for its crucial test on the New York stage.

In grand opera, on the contrary, it is a one-shot project. The costs of operatic production are too great to allow for experimentation and alteration. When the opera is finally mounted, that is it! The performance of *Merry Mount* in San Antonio was a better performance than the performance at the Metropolitan, first because the singers could all sing English, and second because there had been an opportunity in the ensuing years to make desirable changes, to eliminate static elements in the dramatic action, and in general to "tighten up" the entire production.

If opera is ever to become a viable art form in the United States, the entire philosophy of operatic production, in my opinion, must be drastically changed. Perhaps, in the twenty-first century this may come about.

---

16   Hanson wrote these comments before the development of technological advances that provide supertitles with translations. Prior to this development, members of the audience only had access to printed translations of the libretto, which were difficult, if not impossible, to follow during the performance.

Figure 15. Howard Hanson playing the cello.

Figure 16. Howard Hanson at his writing desk.

Figure 17. A portrait of Howard Hanson (c.1916).

Figure 18. Howard Hanson at age twenty-one.

Figure 19. Howard Hanson with his overtone analyzer.

Figure 20. Howard Hanson with his new goatee and mustache.

Figure 21. Howard Hanson in the early 1930s.

Figure 22. Howard Hanson composing at the piano in 1934.

Figure 23. A studious Howard Hanson in 1936.

Figure 24. Howard Hanson in his office at the Eastman School of Music.

Figure 25. Howard Hanson conducting.

Chapter Twenty-Five

SERIOUS CHALLENGES AT THE EASTMAN SCHOOL

Although my trips to Rome and Germany, and my contact with the Met, constituted the more glamorous aspects of my life in the early days of the Eastman School, most of my time was spent in the routine (and sometimes not too routine) duties of school. Some of the problems—musical, educational, and personal—were difficult for a youth of limited experience.

My principal headache in those early days was the opera department. It was, at the same time, a stimulating and rewarding experience. While the department was a part of the Eastman School, it had obligations to the Eastman Theatre. The members of the department were at the same time both students and professionals. When they were in the classroom, they were students. When they were on the stage of the theater, they were professionals.

The faculty, assembled to direct the department, was certainly one of the most distinguished ever assembled in any music school. Its director was the gifted Russian opera singer and producer Vladimir Rosing.[1] He was assisted by a brilliant young man, later to achieve fame in Hollywood as producer and director, Rouben Mamoulian.[2] For a short time, the dancer who was in charge of ballet training was none other than the famous Martha Graham.[3] Presiding over the musical ensemble was the distinguished Eugene Goossens, also one of the conductors of the Rochester Philharmonic.

---

1   Vladimir Rosing (1890–1963) Russian-born tenor and opera director. He was appointed director of the opera department at Eastman in 1923; later served as artistic director of the Southern California Opera Association.

2   Rouben Mamoulian (1898–1987), famed producer and director. He was later associated with the production of George Gershwin's *Porgy and Bess* and with *Oklahoma* and *Carousel* by Rogers and Hammerstein; he directed many notable Hollywood films in a career spanning more than a quarter century.

3   Martha Graham (1894–1991), famous American dancer. Following her departure from Rochester, Graham went on to become the first lady of American modern dance.

The young faculty of the opera department were all men of unusual talent, and all became distinguished in their professions—Ernst Bacon[4] and Otto Luening[5] as composers and educators, Bernard Kaun[6] as a composer for films, Paul Horgan[7] as a writer, and Nicolas Slonimsky as a historian, writer, and lexicographer.

I recall one of my most delightful memories of Nicolas. I dropped into a rehearsal of, I think it was, *Faust*. It was a "piano rehearsal," and Nicolas was presiding at the piano. As he was accompanying the singers, I stepped behind him to look at the score. As I looked over his shoulder, I was amazed and delighted to see that the vocal score was covered over by the morning Rochester newspaper, the *Democrat and Chronicle*, which Nicolas was reading while playing the score from memory!

The students came from all parts of the country. They were all, as I recall, on generous scholarships. Many of them were already young professionals. The other students of the school were, for the most part, much younger and less experienced both in art and in life. Trying to weld a unified student body out of such disparate elements was an impossibility and led to innumerable problems.

Vladimir Rosing, the director of the department, was an unusual person. A Russian singer and actor who had enjoyed considerable success in England, Rosing was devoted to opera as the highest of musical art forms. He believed passionately in the equal importance of music and dramatic action in the production of all operas. He believed with equal firmness in opera in the vernacular and argued constantly that opera could never become indigenous to the American soil until all opera in the United States was sung in English. I must say that his productions—even of some of the old, standard repertory [such as] *Faust, I Pagliacci*, and the like— were both exciting and dramatically convincing. I still recall a striking performance of *Carmen* with Mary Garden[8] as guest artist in the title role, the

---

4   Ernst Bacon (1898–1990), American composer. He studied with Ernest Bloch in San Francisco and Karl Weigl in Vienna and served on the faculty at Converse College and Syracuse University.

5   Otto Luening (1903–96), American flutist, conductor, and composer. He taught at various schools such as Barnard College, Columbia University and Juilliard; he was co-director of the Columbia-Princeton Electronic Music Studio 1959–80.

6   Bernard [Bernhard] Kaun (1899–1980), American composer and orchestrator. He had a long and highly successful career in Hollywood.

7   Paul Horgan (1903–95), American novelist and writer. He was awarded the Harper Prize in 1933 and was a two-time recipient of the Pulitzer Prize for History.

8   Mary Garden (1874–1967), Scottish-born American soprano. She sang Mélisande in the premiere of Debussy's opera, sang several seasons with Opéra

remaining parts [being] taken by students. Eugene Goossens was in the pit with a professional orchestra drawn from the Rochester Philharmonic, and the performance moved with a fluency that I had admired in some of the finest small opera houses of Germany.

Mr. Rosing's faults, if they were faults, were that his creative genius was accompanied by an almost complete lack of organization. A rehearsal scheduled for eight o'clock in the evening might begin an hour or more late and end at some undefined hour after midnight. A stage action, previously set and rehearsed, might be scrapped in the middle of a dress rehearsal, the orchestra of union musicians (at so many dollars per hour) sitting around while the director went through an agonizing reappraisal of his intentions.

A more serious fault, from my standpoint, was the basic lack of interest in the needs of the individual student. The students served the needs of the department. The department was less concerned with the needs of the students. I am sure that we all fall into this trap. It is very easy for any of us, concentrated on the achievement of an artistic goal, to convince ourselves that what is best for us must, therefore, be good for everyone else. At least Mr. Rosing was frank about his aims. He intended to produce a professional opera company, and all other considerations were subordinated to this supreme purpose. The road might be bloody, but the goal must be achieved.

Another problem which worried me was the question of student discipline, about which educators were more concerned in the 1920s than in the 1960s. The undergraduates were no problem. They were all of college age and accommodated themselves without difficulty to the usual regulations of student life. The students of the opera department were, as a rule, considerably older. A few were teenagers, but many were already young professionals, well past undergraduate age. It was impossible to ask them to abide by rules suitable for an eighteen-year-old.

At the same time, the undergraduates of the school resented the fact that opera students did not have to observe the same hours, dormitory regulations, and the like. The philosophy of the heads of the department compounded the difficulties. At least some of them preached the ancient and convenient gospel that it was impossible for a young artist to portray convincingly the part, for example, of Mimi in *La Bohème*, or of the courtesan Violetta in *La Traviata*, unless she herself had "lived" the part. This was a philosophy warmly endorsed by at least a few amorous gentlemen, and, as a result, the opera department was denounced from at least one pulpit as a den of iniquity. To add to my troubles, our dean of students at

---

Comique, and then made her Metropolitan debut in 1907.

the time was Miss Marion Weed, a charming lady who had herself been a member of the Metropolitan Opera Company and viewed the problems of the opera department with alternating shock and sympathy!

The day finally came when the opera department was ready for its formal debut. The New York Theatre Guild had shown its interest in sponsoring the New York appearance of the group, to be known as the American Opera Company. Artistically, the company was ready, but we had run out of money. Mr. Eastman called me in to discuss the problem. Being accustomed to a smoothly run and efficient business organization, he was, I am afraid, somewhat fed up with the vagaries of an opera company. He was not sure that he wished to invest any more money in a precarious operatic enterprise. I persuaded him that we had already spent many thousands of dollars on the experiment, and that, if we did not follow through on this final test, we would never know whether we had created a success or failure. Mr. Eastman agreed, and the company was on its way to New York.

The New York debut was an unqualified success. The students were beautifully prepared. The costumes and scenery were of the finest quality, and Eugene Goossens personally assumed the musical direction of all of the performances. The operas were all a part of the standard repertory, but the imaginative approach of Vladimir Rosing to the drama of opera, the fresh young voices of the singers, and the combination of action and music captivated both the audience and the critics.

The following season, the American Opera Company embarked upon its first tour. Judging by its New York success, it seemed that the United States was to have its first native opera company, a company of talented young Americans presenting opera in our own language. But it was not to be. Perhaps Mr. Rosing was ahead of his time. Perhaps the country was not yet ready for opera in English. (I sometimes wonder if it ever will be.) Artistically, the tour was a success. Financially, it was a disaster. The Depression was already upon us, and opera in English was not the country's first requirement.

The demise of the American Opera Company, to which we had all devoted so much time, so much energy, and so many aspirations, also lost me a friend and created my only (so far as I know) really devoted enemy in Rochester. When I first came to Rochester, Andrew Jackson Warner was the music critic on the Rochester *Times Union*, flagship of the Frank Gannett newspapers. He was most generous in his praise of my talents, both as a composer and conductor, and his support was most helpful. He was also a great friend of Eugene Goossens and devoted to Vladimir Rosing and his experiments in operatic production. For some reason, which I never understood, he blamed me for the fate of the American Opera Company. Perhaps he felt that we should have started over and tried again, although

I doubt very much if I could have persuaded George Eastman to take another flier in this unpredictable field.[9]

In any case, he became my implacable enemy. Whereas, when I first appeared on the Rochester scene, he had hailed me as an extraordinary talent, from this point on I became a plodding pedestrian. Nothing which I did could possibly be right. He became dedicated to my total destruction. At first, I objected to this strange [turnaround]. How was it possible that I could be a great talent one day and a plodding mediocrity the next? I soon discovered, however, the power of the critic embarked on a personal vendetta, and the impotence of managing editors where critics are concerned. I had to learn to live with it, which I did for three long decades.

As though the problems of the opera company were not enough, I was plagued with another problem which I was afraid might bring me into direct confrontation with George Eastman himself. In our effort to admit to the Eastman School only students with high possibilities of development, we were making extensive use of various tests, chief of which were the "Seashore Tests of Musical Talent," devised by Carl Emil Seashore, dean of the graduate school of the University of Iowa. All students in both the preparatory and collegiate departments were required to take these tests. On the basis of the results of the tests, students were classified by our psychology department as "safe," "probable," "possible," and "discourage."

Dr. Hazel Stanton, at that time in charge of the department, kept detailed and meticulous records of these tests together with a history of the correlation of the test results with the students' actual accomplishments. I must admit that she made an excellent case for the validity of the tests. Mr. Eastman was impressed with the high degree of correlation between the results of the Seashore tests and the success of the student. I, too, was impressed and supported the use of the tests as a part of the criteria to be used for admission. President Rhees was somewhat less impressed and told me that, when a test was devised which could accurately measure industry, determination, and dedication to a purpose, he would go along with the validity of psychological tests!

All went well until Dr. Stanton insisted that the Seashore tests become the final criterion in the admission of a student to the Eastman School. Melville Smith, the chairman of our theory department, agreed. Eventually, as was bound to happen, a student appeared from the Pacific Coast.

---

9 Andrew Jackson Warner came from one of Rochester's most socially prominent families. His grandfather, Andrew J. Warner, and his father, J. Foster Warner, were among the area's most successful architects. His brother, John Adams Warner, was a brilliant pianist and organist, but abandoned a career in music to become the fourth man to join the newly formed New York State Police. Ten years later, he married the daughter of Governor Al Smith.

He had been tentatively admitted on the basis of excellent recommendations from responsible teachers. He had credibly passed his auditions in performance. But he had failed his Seashore test.

The recommendation of the psychology department was that he be shipped back to his native habitat. I objected. He had passed his auditions, he had come from across the continent, and (it seemed to me) should be given a fighting chance to prove himself. In spite of the fact that I had faith in the testing procedure, I did not believe that the tests should be the *sole* criterion for the acceptance of a student. On the basis of his audition, I admitted the student.

The fat was most definitely in the fire. The psychology department felt that its decision should be final. I insisted that the tests were only one part of the entrance requirements and must be considered in combination with other data, the high school record of the student, his recommendations, the results of his auditions, and any other available information.

A final confrontation was inevitable. It came when the psychology department refused to allow the admissions committee access to the test scores of candidates for admission. It seemed to me that the students were being used for the tests, and not the tests for the students. In the meantime, Mr. Eastman had become quite convinced of the validity of the tests, largely through my own support of their usefulness. It was quite apparent that either the psychology department or I had to go. I presented the case as objectively as I could to Mr. Eastman. I need not have worried. His answer was one that I had heard many times before, "You're the expert. You decide."[10]

I had one more problem, a very personal one, which no one could decide for me. I was a very young man, only a very few years older than many of my students, and a very romantic young fellow. Many of the young ladies were most attractive. I even "dated" some of them, to the joy of the student body, who were delighted to find that their young director was human. Marriage seemed the logical solution, but I was taking care of my mother and father, the latter a hopeless invalid, to whom I was completely devoted. I had not yet recovered from my infatuation with the lovely young lady from Scotland, and, between the school and my composition, I was working eighteen-hour days. Romance had to wait.

---

10 The school psychologist, Hazel Stanton, left the Eastman School of Music in 1932. The Seashore Tests continued to be administered, although their usefulness in the process of admitting students to the school soon became negligible.

Chapter Twenty-Six

THE DEATH OF GEORGE EASTMAN AND RUSH RHEES'S RETIREMENT

The final performance of *Merry Mount* on the tour of the Metropolitan, [which took place] in the Eastman Theatre in Rochester, was a social as well as a musical event, and Rochesterians crowded into the large Eastman Theatre to hear "their own" opera. There was, however, one sad note. As I stood on the stage following the performance and looked out into the audience, there was one conspicuously empty seat, the seat on the end of the first row of the mezzanine, the seat always occupied by George Eastman. The opera was dedicated to him, and it had been my fervent hope that he would live long enough to hear it performed. But he died on March 14, 1932.

Even today, over three and a half decades later, I find it difficult to write about him. My attitude toward him was, I supposed, an equal mixture of affection, gratitude, admiration, and hero worship. He was a strong man, yet shy. He had a tremendous love for his city and for the community of which he was a part, but he was also a lonely man. I am sure that, to the general public, he seemed aloof, but to the few who knew him well, he was kind, sympathetic, and understanding.

His death at his own hand was a tragedy from which some of us have never recovered, and yet his action was understandable. He was not only a bachelor, but a proud and sensitive individual separated from the world by the very power and wealth which he had created. The approach of an illness which might have left him helpless was, I am sure, something which he could not and would not face. I recall so well his sense of physical independence. He would never, until his last days, allow anyone to help him with his heavy fur coat. He could always "manage" by himself. At the end, there seemed to be in him a sense of finality, of conclusion. He had accomplished much of what he had set out to do. He seemed to want to write the *finis* to the book in his own hand. His final note, "My work is done, why wait?" told the story.

His death left a cloud of gloom over the city which is difficult to describe. Even those who knew him only from a distance could not help but realize the tremendous loss which the community had suffered. His departure left a void which no one else could fill. Whether in business, in education, or in philanthropy, his name led all the rest. Rochester had come to rely on him with a completeness which it did not itself realize. At his death, it appeared that the life of the entire city might stop.

To the sense of loss, to those of us who knew him best, was added the fear that we had let him down; that perhaps, if we had been more thoughtful, more considerate, the tragedy might not have happened. His home was presided over by a devoted housekeeper and administered by a coterie of equally devoted servants. Perhaps they were too devoted.

I recall going one day to Mr. Eastman's palatial home on East Avenue, being admitted by the butler, and told by the housekeeper that my visit should not last over five minutes. At the end of five minutes, I dutifully rose to leave. Mr. Eastman said, rather sadly I thought, "Do you have to go so soon? No one comes to see me anymore." So I defied the housekeeper and stayed on. We discussed for the first time in my experience the question of immortality. With my youthful enthusiasm, I argued that it seemed impossible that the soul of man should not continue on to higher development. His response, as I recall, was rather resigned. "I don't know. How can you know?" This was, I believe, our last conversation.

My first concern after the shock of Mr. Eastman's death was the fate of the Eastman School. Some of the items in the school's budget had been personally authorized by Mr. Eastman and paid by him. I did not know how these activities could possibly be carried on without Mr. Eastman's help. I need not have worried. A few weeks later, Mr. Thomas Hargrave, the head of Rochester's most important legal firm, advised me, "Don't worry. Mr. Eastman has taken care of everything. He was so pleased with the development of the School of Music that he had left in his will many more millions for the school's endowment." Our immediate worries were over, but nothing could compensate us for the death of "G.E."

As though the death of George Eastman was not enough, we were soon faced with another calamity, the retirement of Rush Rhees, for thirty-five years president of the University of Rochester. Rush Rhees was another remarkable man. Under his guidance, the University of Rochester had added the Eastman School of Music and a distinguished School of Medicine and Dentistry, both with the help of George Eastman.

The relationship of George Eastman and Rush Rhees was one of those things that happen very rarely. Each had great respect for the other, but Dr. Rhees would never solicit money from Mr. Eastman. He would simply present the problems to G.E. and let Mr. Eastman decide what (if anything) he wished to do.

This worked most definitely to the advantage of the university. I recall a visit to Rochester from the distinguished Dr. Abraham Flexner of the General Education Board. Dr. Rhees had arranged for Dr. Flexner to meet with Mr. Eastman and discuss the possibility of adding a medical school to the University of Rochester. According to a report in the *New York Times*, "Dr. Flexner proposed a $6,000,000 medical school for Rochester. After several conferences, Mr. Eastman turned solicitor. Convinced that the school could not be adequately financed for $6,000,000, he offered to give $4,000,000 if the General Education Board would give $5,000,000. The board agreed, and the school was established." I remember meeting Dr. Flexner at Mr. Eastman's home after this incident. "I have to get out of here," said Dr. Flexner, "before we lose all of our money!"

[Another] example of George Eastman's generosity involved Rush Rhees's $10,000,000 campaign for the university's endowment. After Dr. Rhees's campaign, [Eastman] called and said that, in thinking over his $2,500,000 pledge to the general endowment, he had worked out a plan to distribute $30,000,000 worth of property to four institutions: the University of Rochester, the Massachusetts Institute of Technology, Hampton Institute, and Tuskegee Institute. Rochester's participation in the $30,000,000 gift was 58 percent.[1]

The retirement of Rush Rhees following the death of George Eastman seemed more than I could stand. President Rhees treated me more like a son than a university dean. Every summer, he and Mrs. Rhees would invite me to the Rhees summer place on Cranberry Isle, off the Maine coast. Here I learned a great deal about the art of administration. I also learned a great deal about avocational art, for Dr. Rhees was an expert woodworker in his spare time, and the house was filled with excellent examples of his art. From him I learned the very important fact that man does not live by his vocation alone!

President Rhees, like George Eastman, could never be replaced. The university, however, was fortunate in securing as his successor a brilliant young man from Yale University, Alan Valentine. Unlike many university

---

1   Hanson's narrative breaks off rather abruptly at this point. It should be added that George Eastman subsequently named the University of Rochester, Cornell University, Massachusetts Institute of Technology, and the Young Women's Christian Association (YWCA) as beneficiaries in his will. The day before his death, however, he drew up new codicils to the will that made a few personal bequests (most notably to his niece Ellen Dryden and her children), but left the bulk of his estate to the University of Rochester, thus excluding Cornell University, Massachusetts Institute of Technology, and the YWCA.

presidents, who regard the arts as more or less frills on the educational garment, Valentine was a firm friend of both the arts and the humanities. During the fifteen years of his administration, the Eastman School continued to grow in strength and fame.

I have always been grateful that both George Eastman and Rush Rhees lived long enough to see [the] Eastman School of Music take its place among the great music schools of the world. By the time of Mr. Eastman's death, the school had quadrupled in size. The curricula had been expanded to include a graduate division offering [the master of music and master of arts] degrees and culminating in the doctor of philosophy degree in music. The Eastman School student orchestra had grown from an embryonic symphony of thirty-five players to a full-fledged symphony of over a hundred student players. [It was] an orchestra so proficient that it presented weekly symphony concerts over the nationwide network of the National Broadcasting Company. The day was soon to come when there would be no major symphony orchestra in the United States which did not number Eastman graduates among its members.

In the meantime, the fame of the American Composers' Concerts and the annual festivals of American music had made the Eastman School the virtual center of American music. Not only did composers come from all parts of the country to hear their music, but talented young composers came in large numbers to the school to study the techniques of musical composition and to live and work in a creative atmosphere. As I have already said, many Eastman graduates are now numbered among the country's most distinguished young composers. Within one decade, for example, three of the ten composers awarded the Pulitzer Prize were Eastman graduates: Gail Kubik,[2] Robert Ward,[3] and John LaMontaine.[4]

At the same time, the school was assuming a position of educational leadership as the outstanding university music school, sending teachers of music to virtually every music school in the United States. By the time that the school had reached its third decade, almost one-third of the schools and departments of music admitted to the National Association of Schools

---

2   Gail Kubik (1914–84), American composer. He served as staff composer at NBC and was music director of the Motion Picture Bureau at the Office of War Information during World War II. He won the 1952 Pulitzer Prize for his *Symphony Concertante*.

3   Robert Ward (1917–), American composer. He taught at Juilliard 1946–56, later was chancellor of the North Carolina School of the Arts. He won the 1962 Pulitzer Prize for his opera, *The Crucible*, based on Arthur Miller's play.

4   John LaMontaine (1920–), American composer. He won the 1959 Pulitzer Prize for Piano Concerto No.1 ("In Time of War").

of Music had Eastman School graduates as deans, directors, or chairmen of their music departments.

It has always been my contention that, in the educational climate of the United States, the arts can develop most effectively within the framework of the American university. This is, of course, a far cry from the typical foreign conservatory of music, an institution devoted almost exclusively to the development of musical techniques, with little if any attention paid to the general education of the student.

It is also a far cry from the classical American conception of the place of the arts in an American university, the philosophy perhaps best exemplified by Harvard University. This philosophy, as I understand it, is that the theory, history, and philosophy of the creative arts is the proper concern of the university, but that the university should not concern itself with the practical techniques of the art. This meant, for example, that the university (or the college) could properly undertake courses in music theory, history, aesthetics, and the like, but should not be concerned with performance. In this philosophy, composition occupied a kind of no-man's land between the field of theory and the practical technique of musical composition.

The battle between the academic musician and the practical composer or performer was not finally joined until many years later when the Eastman School pioneered in the setting up of a professional doctorate in music.[5] The reasons for the setting up of this degree were quite simple. In most American universities, the only available doctorate in music was the PhD with a major in musicology. Many musicians teaching in academic institutions needed the doctor's degree for very practical purposes, but unless their major interest was musicology, there was no appropriate doctoral program open to them. Since many college presidents insisted that any musician in a responsible position must hold a doctor's degree, graduate schools throughout the country began fitting all musicians into a Procrustean bed. By doing so, they merely succeeded in making mediocre musicologists out of gifted performers and composers.

The effort to set up a professional doctorate which would attempt to combine musical scholarship with creation and performance met violent opposition from the more academic-minded musical scholars.

---

5   It is a little difficult to understand why, in a chapter concerned with the death of George Eastman and the retirement of Rush Rhees, Hanson decided to expound on the reasons behind the establishment of the doctor of musical arts degree, which was not conferred until the 1950s. Nonetheless, his advocacy for a professional doctorate in music was one of his major achievements as a leader in musical education, and his thoughts on the subject are important.

I particularly recall my friend at Columbia University, the musicologist Paul Henry Lang,[6] accusing us of setting up a doctor's degree in piccolo playing.

Curiously enough, my greatest support in this venture came from another distinguished musicologist, the late Otto Kinkeldey.[7] Dr. Kinkeldey was unalterably opposed to the granting of the doctor of philosophy degree in any field other than that of musical scholarship. He was, however, equally convinced that there should be a professional doctorate in music granted for achievement in the practical fields of creation, performance, and education.

I have never been very much concerned personally with academic degrees or titles. Many of [the] most distinguished musicians whom I engaged for the faculty of the Eastman School were graduates of foreign conservatories and had no degrees whatsoever. At the same time, it was quite obvious that, in the developing plan of education in the United States, degrees had become essential as a part of a musician's professional equipment. For this reason, I pressed for the establishment of a professional doctorate, [in addition to the] bachelor's and master's degree in the field of music. My efforts finally bore fruit, and in the 1953–54 [school year] the doctor of musical arts [degree] was established in the University of Rochester. Since that time, many universities have adopted the same pattern, and the professional doctorate in music now seems to be firmly established. But it was a hard fight.

---

6   Paul Henry Lang (1901–91), highly influential professor of musicology at Columbia University.

7   Otto Kinkeldey (1878–1966), faculty member at Cornell University and the first person to be appointed a professor of musicology in an American university.

Chapter Twenty-Seven

CHAUTAUQUA MEMORIES

Although our traveling "Chautauqua Circuits" of the second decade made an important contribution to my development as a musician, it was not until many years later, after my return from the American Academy in Rome, that I made the acquaintance of the venerable Chautauqua Institution itself. The Chautauqua Institution, situated on beautiful Lake Chautauqua in the southwestern part of New York State, was founded in the nineteenth century as a religious institution. As far as I have been able to discover, there was never any relation between the institution and the traveling Chautauquans of the West and Middle West, although it is logical to assume that the latter received their inspiration from the former.[1]

I am told that the original Chautauqua of the nineteenth century was also a tent city, and this may have been the origin of the famous "traveling" Chautauqua tents of the early twentieth century. The original Chautauqua, although basically religious in its purpose and founded by the noted [Methodist minister, John Heyl] Vincent, soon expanded its interest into the field of education, music, and the arts.

Today, although the institution offers lectures by statesmen, poets, artists, writers in almost every conceivable field, orchestral programs, plays, operas, ballets, and credit courses in college subjects, the emphasis on religion is still very strong, and one can hear in the Sunday morning services in the great amphitheater some of the most inspiring congregational singing in the world.

In the 1920s and 1930s, the musical director of the Chautauqua Institution was the American conductor and composer, Albert Stoessel. Mr. Stoessel was a superb musician and an accomplished conductor, serving during the winter season as the head of the Opera Department of the Juilliard School of Music in New York City. He had conducted in New York a performance of my early *Concerto da Camera*, and when he read of the

---

1   The first Chautauqua was organized in 1874 on the shores of Lake Chautauqua in New York State. Within a short time, other Chautauqua assemblies were organized. Independent Chautauquans had permanent facilities, while Circuit (or Tent) Chautauquans were an itinerant operation. See chapter 4 for Hanson's experiences as a teenager with the Circuit Chautauquans.

success of *Pan and the Priest*, performed by the New York Philharmonic under Mengelberg, he immediately invited me to conduct a performance of the work with his Chautauqua Orchestra.

The Chautauqua Symphony proved to be no other than a part of the New York Symphony which I had previously conducted in the ballroom of the old Athenaeum Hotel at the un-Christian hour of 8:30 in the morning! The ballroom had, or I should say has, a low ceiling, and the sounds of the orchestra were quite deafening. I felt for the hotel patrons, especially since both Pan and the Priest were rather noisy individuals. The orchestra was of first-rate quality, but as I look back, I realize the enormous progress that has been made over the years in the technique of instrumental performance.

At the end of the composition, Pan gives a triumphant out-cry in which the trumpet leaps to a high C and finally to a D above high C. I still remember, with some feeling of guilt, the red face of the solo trumpeter as he realized the high D, apparently by brute force. With the modern development of the embouchure, today's trumpeters can take such a note without raising an eyebrow. In those days, it was something of a feat.

My youthful musical offering was well-received by the Chautauqua audience, and in future years I was frequently invited to return for guest performances. Some years later, when Mr. Stoessel was involved in completing his opera, *Garrick*, he asked [me] to relieve him by taking over the major responsibility of the entire summer session, which I was happy to do.

As I look back to those early days, I realize more than ever how indebted I am to the conductors who gave such opportunities to a fledgling composer: to Serge Koussevitzky, Frederick Stock, Walter Damrosch, Rudolph Ganz, Willem Mengelberg, Albert Coates, Eugene Goossens, Fritz Reiner, Arturo Toscanini, José Iturbi,[2] and not least Albert Stoessel. He not only presented many of my early works at Chautauqua, but he also presented some of my major choral works at the Worcester Festival, of which he was also musical director.

It was, therefore, with great sadness that I received word of his sudden death from a heart attack. He was a comparatively young man, greatly loved both by his orchestra and his public, and his death threw the institution into a panic. The later Arthur Bestor, president of Chautauqua, asked me if I would take over the baton for the six-week season. I appreciated the invitation but suggested that I take the first two weeks, and that we search for two other conductors to complete the remaining weeks.

---

2   José Iturbi (1895–1980), Spanish pianist and conductor. He was the director of the Rochester Philharmonic 1936–44 and later appeared in a number of Hollywood films.

He agreed, and I shared the season with Vladimir Golschman,[3] music director of the St. Louis Symphony, and Willem Willeke,[4] the cellist of the Kneisel Quarter and conductor of the Juilliard Orchestra. The death of Mr. Stoessel saddened us all, and the season was in this sense depressing. Musically, however, it proved rewarding.

Chautauqua was rapidly becoming a summer musical center, and many distinguished artists were with us as guest soloists and teachers. I recall especially Olga Samaroff-Stokowski,[5] certainly one of the great pianists and teachers of her day and the mentor of some of America's most brilliant young artists. It fell to my lot to present one of her young students as soloist with the orchestra. The young man proved to be an extraordinary talent. He played, as I recall, the second Rachmaninoff piano concerto. He was splendid in rehearsal, and at the evening concert he played so brilliantly that I turned to the audience after the enthusiastic applause had finally subsided and said, "I think that we have all seen musical history made this evening." And indeed, we had. The young man was William Kapell.[6]

My colleagues included James Friskin of the Juilliard faculty, who had been my teacher at the Institute of Musical Art, and his wife, Rebecca Clarke Friskin, violist and one of England's most accomplished composers. The director of the piano department was the noted president of Juilliard, Ernest Hutcheson,[7] and the orchestra included such famous instrumentalists as that greatest of flutists, Georges Barrère,[8] and the eminent cellist Georges Miquelle, later to become a member of the Eastman School's artist faculty. The concertmaster was Mischa Mischakoff,[9] concertmaster

---

3   Vladimir Golschman (1893–1972), French conductor. He led the St. Louis orchestra 1931–58.

4   Willem Willeke (1880–1950), cellist and teacher. He was also a medical doctor, but became the principal cello teacher at the Institute of Musical Art in New York.

5   Olga Samaroff (1880–1948), distinguished American pianist and teacher. Born Lucy Hickenlooper, she studied in Paris and made her Carnegie Hall debut in 1905; married Leopold Stokowski in 1911, and they divorced in 1923/ She taught at Juilliard and the Philadelphia Conservatory.

6   William Kapell (1922–53), gifted American pianist. He studied with Samaroff and already had a major career when he died in a plane crash while returning from a concert tour of Australia.

7   Ernest Hutcheson (1871–1951), Australian pianist and teacher. He studied with Carl Reinecke and Berhard Stavenhagen (both students of Liszt); member of the Juilliard faculty, then dean 1926–37, and then president 1937–45.

8   Georges Barrère (1876–1944), flutist and teacher. He was an important soloist and recitalist and taught for thirty-nine years at Juilliard.

9   Mischa Mischakoff (1885–1995), Ukrainian born violinist. He was perhaps the most successful concertmaster in the United States, serving in

of the Chicago Symphony and later concertmaster of the NBC Symphony under Arturo Toscanini.

The most important influence on my life also had to do with music, if indirectly. Rehearsing in the large amphitheater, I noted a charming young lady obviously deeply interested in the music. She seemed very young, but her concern with the music was most serious. I did not meet her until one evening [when] she came backstage after the concert. I have a powerful tendency to talk to the audience, especially when there is music which might be helped by some explanation, a tendency which some of my friends applaud and some deplore. On this occasion, I spoke of the contemporary composers who seem to delight in "obfuscation."

The young lady asked me to explain why I had used the word "obfuscation." I explained that the literal translation was "to darken the glass," that some composers did not want the audience to be able to "look into" their music too easily and, therefore, resorted to "obfuscation." The young lady's name [was] Margaret Elizabeth Nelson. She came from Pittsburgh, and her parents, Mr. and Mrs. John Evon Nelson, had a charming summer home on Lake Chautauqua. I met them both and found them to be dedicated Chautauquans. Mrs. Nelson was a regular attendant and sponsor of all the good things that Chautauqua offered. No musician, opera singer, or lecturer was completely happy if they did not see the lady with the beautiful red hair in the audience, for she was always there.

Her husband was a man of keen intellect, a leader in the world of business, and a man with whom I greatly enjoyed talking about politics and the state of the nation. I believe that he was at first a little concerned about having a musician become too interested in his daughter. However, when he discovered that I was able to discuss budgets, income from endowment, and the rising costs of maintenance of standards in education, he was less apprehensive.

My courtship of Margaret Elizabeth, or Peggie as her friends called her, encountered many obstacles. My father, an invalid for many years, had died. In the meantime, my mother had developed Parkinson's disease. Being an only child, my duty to look after her was quite clear. At the same time, it hardly seemed fair to confront a young lady, twenty years my junior, with such a problem.

I suppose that, in the life of a composer, almost everything which concerns him also has something to do with his music. I have never been a very faithful letter writer and, concerned with my responsibilities at the

---

this capacity for the New York Symphony 1924–27, the Philadelphia Orchestra 1927–30, the Chicago Symphony 1930–37, the NBC Symphony Orchestra 1937–52, and the Detroit Symphony 1952–68.

Eastman School and at home, my correspondence with Peggie was somewhat desultory. There came a time when I realized that I had not written [to] her for weeks. The tone of her letters was understandably slightly frigid. Christmas was approaching, and I realized that something must be done. I sent her, post-haste, dozens of "sweetheart" roses and set to work on something which I hoped would be very personal. The result was a *Serenade for Flute, Harp, and Strings*, dedicated to her.

As soon as it was finished, we recorded it and sent her the score and the recording as a Christmas present. The composition apparently was a success. We were married the following summer in Chautauqua. Our Chautauqua courtship was hectic. We would sit up half the night to be followed by an 8:30 a.m. rehearsal with the symphony. We both seemed to survive without difficulty, but we almost lost a French horn soloist.

I had scheduled for performance one of my favorite works, the enchanting incidental music to the *Midsummer Night's Dream* by Mendelssohn. The night before the concert, Peggie had accepted my proposal of marriage, and I was in an exalted state of mind. When, in the concert, we arrived at the Nocturne with its haunting French horn solo, I lingered lovingly over every phrase, played beautifully by Edward Murphy. The demands on the breath control of the long phrases of the Nocturne are formidable, even when taken at a reasonable tempo. Edward's masterly technique survived the ordeal brilliantly, and the performance admirably reflected my emotions. Afterwards, however, he approached me with the remark, "Please, let's never do *that* again!" I am afraid that I have not kept my promise, for whenever I conduct this music the nostalgia is overpowering, and I linger over each note in spite of the agonized look of the horn player.

[Peggie's] parents and mine are now gone, but she still has the summer home on beautiful Lake Chautauqua. She "invites" me to Chautauqua for a portion of each summer, and I "invite" her to Bold Island for the remainder of the summer. The rest of the time we spend in Rochester or traveling. It is a very happy situation. With her tremendous love for music, she is both my most appreciative and also my most exacting critic. Incidentally, the *Serenade* remains one of my most popular and best-known compositions.

The *Serenade* has been performed by many famous flutists with many famous orchestras. Its first performance, as I recall, was not in concert but over radio station WHAM, with Joseph Mariano as solo flutist and Eileen Malone[10] [as] harpist. This version has been recorded by Mercury Records.

---

10   Eileen Malone (1906–99) taught harp at the Eastman School of Music 1931–89, the longest tenure of any faculty member at the school at the time of her retirement.

It was later performed in Philadelphia and on tour with William Kincaid as soloist and Eugene Ormandy conducting, and recorded by Columbia [Records]. Some years later it was performed by Georges Laurent[11] and the Boston Symphony under Serge Koussevitzky and recorded by RCA Victor. There is also a recording by the Cleveland Symphony under [the direction] of Louis Lane, and a television recording by members of the Minneapolis Symphony.

The Boston Symphony performance was the occasion for one of the few errors in program notes by Harold Burke, the scholarly annotator for the Boston Symphony programs. In describing the work, he indicated that it had been written as a Christmas present to my wife "who had been a flute student at the Eastman School." This involved two slight errors. Peggie has never been a student of the Eastman School and, furthermore, has never played the flute. Nevertheless, so famous was Mr. Burke for the accuracy of his program notes that young flutists who are studying the *Serenade* regularly approach Peggie and insist that she give them a lesson in the proper interpretation of the composition.

[For] the second season following the death of Albert Stoessel, the position of musical director of the Chautauqua Symphony was given to Franco Autori,[12] who had been conductor of the Buffalo Philharmonic Orchestra. Maestro Autori proved to be a highly sensitive musician and highly regarded by the members of the orchestra. The Chautauqua Symphony under his direction maintained a high standard of performance, and we worked together on many occasions.

I recall the performance of one composition with some amazement, and I must say, some gratification. The Maestro and Mrs. Autori were sitting with Peggie and me one evening in their home, drinking some rare and delicious wine which Franco had brought back during his tour of Spain. As we were enjoying its bouquet, he asked me if I would be willing the following season to be the soloist in my piano concerto, which had recently received its premiere by Rudolf Firkusny[13] and the Boston Symphony. I replied that I never practiced the piano and would be totally unprepared to appear as a soloist.

---

11   Georges Laurent was principal flutist with the Boston Symphony from 1918 until 1952.

12   Franco Autori (1903–90), Italian-born American conductor. He was conductor of the Buffalo Philharmonic 1936–45, associate conductor of the New York Philharmonic 1949–59, and conductor of the Tulsa Philharmonic 1961–71.

13   Rudolph Firkusny (1912–94), famous Czech pianist. He studied with Cortot and Schnabel and gave many performances of new music; he taught at Juilliard, Aspen, and Tanglewood.

He pressed the invitation. After a few more glasses of wine, I felt that my piano technique had improved remarkably and agreed to perform [the concerto] with him. When the time drew near, I begged to be excused, but he was adamant. I have never since my early days at the Institute of Musical Art practiced so diligently. My respect for the responsibilities of a concert pianist increased enormously.

At the rehearsal, I was petrified. However, Franco Autori, Mischa Mischakoff, and other members of the orchestra assured me that I was an excellent pianist, and the performance went off smoothly to the delight of the large audience, which was intrigued to see me in this unexpected role. I must admit that I did not play the work from memory but had the score on the piano. This occasioned some surprise. Certainly, a composer would know his own music. Why then did I bother with the printed score?

This is a misconception on the part of an audience. Many, perhaps most, composers who perform or conduct their own works (except in the cases of established concert performers such as Rachmaninoff) insist on having the score before them. I think that the reason lies in the fact that a composer writes slowly at a tempo many times below the speed of performance. Also, he frequently writes several versions of the same phrase until he arrives at the one which seems "right." When the actual performance arrives, it is easy to become confused, to suddenly remember three or four versions of the same phrase. Which one did he finally decide to use? By the time he has decided, it may be too late!

Franco Autori resigned to take over the directorship of the Tulsa Philharmonic,[14] and was succeeded by Walter Hendl, music director of the Dallas Symphony.[15] He is twenty years my junior, but our paths have crossed on many occasions. Many years ago, I was conducting Loeffler's *Pagan Poem* with the New York Philharmonic. The composition has a very important and difficult solo piano obbligato, and I was delighted to find as the soloist a brilliant young pianist, Walter Hendl, who was also the assistant conductor of the New York Philharmonic.

Since those days, he has conducted works of mine, including an excellent performance of the *Nordic* symphony, and at my retirement followed me as director of the Eastman School [while] continuing his direction of the Chautauqua Symphony.

---

14   Hanson's chronology is not accurate. Autori did not take over direction of the Tulsa orchestra until 1961, but he left Chautauqua after the 1952 season.

15   Walter Hendl (1917–2007), American conductor. A student of Fritz Reiner at Curis, he was assistant conductor of the New York Philharmonic 1945–49, conductor of the Dallas Symphony Orchestra (1949–58), associate conductor of the Chicago Symphony (1958–63), and director of the Eastman School of Music (1964–72).

Chapter Twenty-Eight

THOUGHTS ON ORCHESTRAL CONDUCTING

I remember one winter when I was paying a brief visit to the winter home of my dear friends, the McKays of Lake Alfred, Florida, I was taken to visit Mrs. Curtis Bok,[1] the patron of music and founder of the Curtis Institute in Philadelphia. We were discussing the training of conductors at Curtis and at Eastman, and she expressed surprise that conducting could be "taught." She remarked that it had always been her contention that conductors were born. I jokingly answered that it did help for them to be born.

Seriously, I think that Mrs. Bok was right. he art of conducting cannot be "taught" any more than the art of composition can be "learned." It is true that an experienced conductor can show the novice the rudiments of the art. He can warn him about pitfalls to be avoided. He can even show him the "tricks of the trade." In the final analysis, however, he must find his own way. I doubt very much that Serge Koussevitzky, Arturo Toscanini, or Willem Mengelberg were ever taught conducting, although I am sure each of them had their own models from [whom] they learned a great deal consciously or subconsciously. I am sure, for example, that Serge Koussevitzky learned much from the great Artur Nikisch, for whom he had great admiration. I doubt if he ever "studied" with him.

In my own case, I know that I owe a great deal to all of the great conductors with whom I have worked as a composer. This is particularly true of my relationship with Dr. Koussevitzky. Observing how he was able to draw a certain kind of sound out of the orchestra, I found myself trying for the same kind of sound in my own way. He told me, at one time, that he considered me his best "pupil," although I had never studied with him.

I remember Eugene Ormandy objecting to the phrase, the "Philadelphia sound." He said, quite properly, that it is the "Ormandy sound," and he is entirely correct, for no one I have heard gets the same kind of sound from that orchestra. Before him, there was the equally famous "Stokowski sound," which no one else has ever successfully emulated.

---

1   Mary Louise Curtis Bok (1876–1970), American philanthropist. She established the Curtis Institute in 1924, naming it in honor of her father who was the founder of Curtis Publishing Company.

Thoughts on Orchestral Conducting

Whether he conducts with a baton or without a baton, whether he conducts with broad generous movements or with small precise beats, whether he presides over the orchestra like an expert swordsman about to deliver the fatal *coup* or with the dignity of a high priest, none of these things is especially important. What is important is whether or not he is able to communicate his wishes to the orchestra, and (most important) whether he is truly in command. Even an encyclopedic knowledge of the orchestra, [combined] with the wisdom of the most distinguished musical scholar, will avail him nothing if this quality of communication and command are absent.

It is, therefore, easy to understand the fascination of the conducting profession and the reason that so many musicians have been bitten by the conducting bug. During my first decade at the Eastman School, I almost succumbed, but not quite. By the end of the 1930s, I had conducted most of this country's major orchestras and a number of the famous orchestras of Europe. It is true that much of my conducting was concerned with my own music and the music of other American composers. However, I conducted many conventional programs, not only in Rochester and Interlochen, but [also] as a guest [conductor] of orchestras such as the NBC Symphony, the New York Philharmonic, Los Angeles Philharmonic, and others.

On a number of occasions, the critical views of my conducting were so favorable, even when the critic did not like the music, that I must admit [to having had] some temptation to enter the profession seriously. My repertory was, of course, limited. I had devoted so much time to American music that there were large areas of musical literature that I had hardly touched. It is also true that I had conducted more Sibelius than Bach, but even this did not seem to be a fatal defect because, after all, all music is music, and as José Iturbi once remarked, "The baton is always in the key of C."

I had also the tremendous advantage of youth, for with youth much is forgiven. I recall one harrowing experience with the Los Angeles Philharmonic Orchestra in the Hollywood Bowl. It was in the "Scherzo" from William Grant Still's *Afro-American Symphony*. There is a concluding passage where the phrase is truncated, with the result that what the musicians call the "harmonic rhythm" does not coincide with the meter. I had conducted the first performance of the symphony in Rochester and knew it so well (or thought I knew it so well) that I became careless. At the end of the movement, I forgot the rhythmic irregularity and reached the end of the piece two beats before the orchestra! The orchestra finished the last two beats successfully without me. (You would be surprised what an orchestra can do without the conductor.) I am sure that few in the audience, with the exception of the composer, knew that anything untoward had occurred. One critic remarked that the orchestra apparently had not had sufficient time to rehearse one composition!

I was chagrined and mortified by my carelessness and spent a number of restless nights haunted by the two missing beats. Sometime later, my wound was at least partially healed when a senior member of the orchestra told me that he had been a member of the orchestra when the great Toscanini himself came out "one beat short." My pain was also somewhat lessened when one of the most gifted young conductors that I know came off stage after a performance, with the remark, "Good God! What happened? I almost lost them!"

Conducting clearly is both an exciting and a nerve-wracking profession, but I do not believe that it was its difficulty which turned me away. I know, too, that some of my Rochester colleagues were convinced that I wished to become musical director of the Rochester Philharmonic as well as the director of the Eastman School, a kind of czar of music for the City of Rochester, or (as the Germans put it so aptly) a General-Musikdirektor. I did, perhaps, have to some degree the latter ambition. I remember a New York critic referring to me (I think not unkindly) as "Rochester's one-man musical monopoly."

The truth was that I have always been opposed to the merging of the philharmonic and the school for reasons which I think should be obvious. It would be impossible to fill both positions successfully. I [also] found, after serious reflection, that I really did not want to become a symphony conductor. What interested me was not the conducting over and over again of the Beethoven Fifth or the Brahms Fourth, but the conducting of new music, including my own—the fascination of reading a new score and seeing what I could find (as Dr. Koussevitzky put it) "behind the notes."

Finally, I believed then, and I believe now, that the most important thing in building a musical culture is education, that the educator together with the composer has the greater opportunity of achieving a kind of immortality which, I suppose, is one of man's most basic instincts. The work [and] the influence of the educator lives on long after his work is done, even to the generations far beyond.

I suppose that it was this philosophy which has prompted me, even after retirement, to undertake each year a strenuous series of eight double concerts with the Los Angeles Philharmonic for the school children of that city and its environs. The invitation to conduct these concerts came from my dear friend, William Hartshorn, head of the Music Department of the Los Angeles Public Schools. He had actually been a member of a class in theory and composition, which I had given one summer as a visiting professor, holding the Alchin chair of musical theory at the University of Southern California.

One half of the concerts were given for very young students of grammar school age, and the other half were concerned with high school students. The programs were carefully planned for the different age groups, and Mr. Hartshorn's teachers prepared the students admirably in order that they might receive the maximum amount of benefit. In addition, the Los Angeles Philharmonic, certainly one of the great orchestras of the United States, took these educational concerts most seriously, and it was a joy to work with them.

The young students were also most responsive and delightful. It was my job not only to conduct the programs but [also] to comment in a way which hopefully would be helpful to the young people. I tried in my comments to avoid unrelated factual material (such as the number of Bach's children) but to try to concentrate on what the composer was trying to say and the technique which he used in saying it.

After the concerts, I received hundreds of letters from my young listeners, telling me what they liked most about the programs. Some of the letters, particularly from the little ones, were both charming and illuminating. I recall one letter with great satisfaction. It went something like this:

I have never heard a symphony before. I like it very much. I didn't hear hardly no mistakes.

I remarked to my wife, "Ten years old, and already a music critic!"

I hope that these concerts have opened the beautiful world of music to at least a few more youngsters. After all, at least in my philosophy, music is not for the performer, for the conductor, or even for the composer. Music is for people.

Chapter Twenty-Nine

WORKING FOR UNESCO

As far as music and government is concerned, I believe that my most frustrating experience was as a member of the United States National Commission for UNESCO.[1] My membership on the commission came in a somewhat roundabout way. A number of leaders in the musical world were concerned over the fact that there was no forum where organizations representing the various facets of music, education, composition, publication, recording, concert performance, music industries, and the like could come together to discuss mutual problems.

As a result of the labors and devotion of men such as Edwin Hughes, the American concert pianist; Harold Spivacke, chief of the music division of the Library of Congress; Franklin Dunham of the broadcasting industry; Julia Ober, president of the National Federation of Music Clubs; and others, the National Music Council was formed in order that music might, when the occasion demanded it, "speak with one voice."

Dr. Hughes served as the council's first president and also as its executive secretary. With Dr. Hughes, the guidance of the council was a labor of love. He sacrificed countless hours and indefatigable energy to making it an important part of America's musical life, bringing into the council such diverse groups as the Musicians' Union, the Association of Piano Manufacturers, the Music Teachers' National Association, the Music Educators' National Conference, the National Association of Schools of Music, the American Musicological Society, and dozens of others.

With the growth of the council, the task of filling both the offices of president and executive secretary became too arduous, and Dr. Hughes asked me to become a candidate for the presidency. I accepted the position and continued as president for a number of years, although Dr. Hughes continued to be the motivating force of the council until his death.

After a number of years, the council had made such an impression on the development of music in the country that it was formally recognized by the Congress of the United States and granted a congressional charter. It was probably for this reason that, when the National Commission for

---

[1] United Nations Educational, Scientific, and Cultural Organization.

UNESCO was set up by our government, I was the first (and for some time the only) musician to be appointed to the commission.

The reasons for my frustration came from many sources. In the first place, UNESCO is an international organization, a subsidiary of the United Nations. In the second place, the order of letters in the title of the organization was all too prophetic. The "E" for education easily occupied first place in importance, "S" for scientific was a reasonably close second, and "C" for culture a very poor third. And since music is certainly not all of culture, it occupied a small rung on a very small ladder.

Third, and I think unfortunately, much of the very limited program in music was assigned to the International Music Council, located in Paris (which was also the headquarters of the parent UNESCO organization). Paris was inclined to go its own way without consultation with the United States Commission, and the coordination of our very limited musical program was extremely difficult.

Finally, and probably most important, the whole of UNESCO was operated on a pitifully small budget. The small amount which finally filtered down to the music program made any really important program impossible. We published many documents about what we would *like* to do, but seldom if ever had the chance to *do* anything. We did, however, turn out what seemed to be tons of mimeographed material until, in despair, I accused the commission of "trying to save the world by mimeography."[2]

There was still another problem. The commission was, much of the time, dominated by educators and scholars, and the routine sometimes became rather academic. The commission might, for example, embark on a "major project" for the year. The project might be of prime interest to the educator and of some interest to the scientist. It might prove to be a project toward which the artist could make little if any contribution. Yet we were all supposed to work as a "team." I argued for years against this completely "horizontal" approach, winning a number of battles but always losing the war!

Then too, we might admit that the artist is perhaps not as good a team-worker as the educator. Of all the laborers in the arts, the musician has probably the greatest sympathy for the team approach. In the realization of a piece of music, there must be teamwork between the composer and the conductor, the conductor and the orchestra, the soloist and the conductor.

---

2   In an era previous to the development of photo-copying technology (such as xerography), mimeography was for many years the favored low-cost printing option.

In this sense, the painter seems to have the least "team discipline." I recall vividly one of the earliest conferences of the arts in UNESCO. The congregation consisted of musicians, writers, painters, sculptors, and architects. The presiding officer was a very able woman, a professor of English. She conducted the conference like a department chairman presiding over a meeting of instructors.

Her technique as a chairman was impeccable, but she was no match for the painters. One artist, a man of some renown, asked for the floor and presented a long and impassioned speech about government and the arts. "Why doesn't the government support the living artist? Why doesn't the government do something for the visual arts?" He didn't want conferences. He wanted to paint! The patient chairman tried to explain that this was, indeed, the purpose of the meeting. The artist, however, having delivered his diatribe, was not interested in further discussion but stalked out of the meeting to the applause of his colleagues.

Once in a while, the arts did have a chance to be heard and to fill some place in the program. For the national conference of UNESCO in Cleveland, I was invited to arrange a *Symphony of Freedom*, which was to express in words and music some of the spiritual aims of UNESCO. With the composers' permission, I was able to incorporate parts of Randel Thompson's inspiring *Testament of Freedom* and Aaron Copland's *A Lincoln Portrait*. [I used] portions of my Third Symphony as background for narration and concluded with the grand old hymn *Faith of our Fathers*. We were fortunate in having the aid of the superb Cleveland Symphony Orchestra, a splendid Welsh male chorus, and Leonard Treash as narrator. The address of the occasion was given by Eleanor Roosevelt, and I felt that for once at least music had made some contribution.

In spite of the frustrations of the National Commission, there were also great opportunities, [the] chief of which was the privilege of working with a great many distinguished individuals. Many of the members of the commission were men and women of eminence in their professions, and it was an education to come to know them and to participate in the discussions. This was especially true when, in 1949, I was appointed a member of the United States delegation to the International Conference of UNESCO in Paris. I do not remember the names of every member of the delegation, but I do recall many of them vividly. They represented virtually every facet of education, science, the arts, and government.

The chairman of the delegation was Milton Eisenhower,[3] brother of the president and later president of Johns Hopkins. I have never known a more able or fairer presiding officer. Watching him preside over meetings

---

3   Milton Eisenhower (1899–1985), American educational and civic leader. He was the younger brother of President Dwight D. Eisenhower;

of a group of such varying interest was itself an education. The delegation included such members as Senator Mike Mansfield,[4] then (I believe) a freshman member of the Congress), the theologian Reinhold Niebuhr,[5] motion picture actress Myrna Loy,[6] Ambassador George Allen,[7] political scientist Frederick Dunn,[8] Stanley Ruttenbergh[9] of the CIO, and Oscar Hild, who was president of the musicians' union of Cincinnati and rumored to be the probable successor to James Caesar Petrillo as head of the American Federation of Musicians.[10]

Mr. Hild supplied me with my favorite story of the conference. Once evening he [and] Mrs. Hild decided to attend the Paris Opera, where a ballet in which they were especially interested was scheduled for performance. Arriving at the opera house, Mr. Hild discovered that the performance had been canceled because of a strike of union orchestral players. His remark to us on returning to the hotel was brief and succinct. Said Mr. Hild, "That damn musicians' union!"

The meetings were long and sometimes tiring but interesting. I was, as I always am, amazed by the "simultaneous translations" of the expert reporters assigned to such conferences. This was notably true in the address of Dr. Niebuhr, a philosophical presentation of great subtlety, yet which the reporter translated into French, including the impromptu remarks with apparently the greatest of ease.

---

president of Kansas State University 1943–50, Pennsylvania State University 1950–56, Johns Hopkins University 1956–67 and 1971–72.

4   Michael (Mike) Mansfield (1903–2001), Democratic politician. He served in the House of Representatives 1943–63, United States Senate 1953–77, and was Senate Majority Leader 1961–77.

5   Reinhold Niebuhr (1892–1971), American Protestant theologian. He was professor at Union Theological Seminary 1928–60.

6   Myrna Loy (1905–93), American actress. She enjoyed a long and successful Hollywood career, extending from her first film in 1925 and her last in 1980.

7   George Allen (1903–70), American government official. He served in the State Department and as ambassador to various countries.

8   Frederick Sherwood Dunn (1893–1962), American political scientist. He served as director of the Yale Institute of International Studies and later taught at Princeton University, where he was the first director of the Center for International Studies.

9   Stanley Ruttenberg (1917–2001), important figure in the American labor movement. He was an economist for the AFL-CIO, and later served as Secretary of Labor in the Johnson administration.

10   It is perhaps amusing that Hanson mentions Petrillo's middle name ("Caesar"). Petrillo successfully brought an end to the Eastman School's regular broadcasting of concerts, and he most certainly would not have been among Hanson's favorites.

The conference, however, was not all work, for both French officialdom and the American Embassy were magnificent hosts. One unique event was a dinner given for us in the Louvre. I am told this [was] the first time this famous museum had been used for such an event. It almost proved my diplomatic undoing. It was a rainy evening, and as my wife and I walked between the lines of the *Garde Republicaine* into the Louvre, we were both primarily concerned about getting rid of our raincoats and rubbers. Neither of us could see a *garderobe*, but we did see in the distance a group of people apparently waiting to help us.

One man held out his hand, and I was just about to present him with my rubbers when some instinct (or perhaps my wife's elbow) stopped me. I looked down and realized that the man to whom I was about to give my rubbers was Georges Bidault,[11] the premier of France! I never did discover where to put my rubbers.

We were entertained at the Quai d'Orsay and at the American Embassy by Ambassador and Mrs. David Bruce,[12] but the most charming of all was an evening after an especially grueling day at the home of Kenneth Holland, who was serving as liaison officer between the American Embassy and UNESCO. Mr. Holland, who is now president of the International Institute for Education, and Mrs. Holland are both musicians, Mrs. Holland being an excellent pianist and her husband an accomplished clarinetist. Ambassador Allen proved himself to be the possessor of an excellent voice and a man who loved to sing, as they say, "around the piano."

Mary Holland and I improvised at the piano some stirring accompaniments to such classics as "Juanita," "Annie Laurie," and "By the Old Mill Stream," with Ambassador Allen in the solo role. We also improvised some variations on Chopin whose centennial was being observed by UNESCO. Before the evening was over, someone with a statistical mind suggested that [we] concoct a UNESCO cocktail by mixing the favorite drink of each member country in direct proportion to its contribution to the UNESCO budget. The favorite drink of the United States was declared to be whiskey, and since the contribution of the United States to UNESCO was approximately half of the entire budget, I can report that the evening ended happily.

---

11   Georges-Augustin Bidault (1899–1983), French politician. He served his country both as foreign minister and prime minister in a number of governments following the end of World War II; he was exiled to Brazil in 1962 for alleged antigovernment activity and returned to France in 1967.

12   David Bruce (1898–19 ?), American civil servant. He served as ambassador to France 1949–52, ambassador to Germany 1957–59, and ambassador to Great Britain 1961–69.

The Chopin tribute, which Mary and I contributed, was entirely appropriate. Since it was the year of the Chopin centennial, UNESCO had invited a group of composers from member countries to compose special works in his honor. The composers included Florent Schmitt and Jacques Ibert from France, Andrzej Panufnik from Poland, Carlos Chavez from Mexico, Francesco Malipiero from Italy, Lennox Berkeley from England, and me.

The commemorative concert was given in the Salle Gaveau and broadcast over the national radio. My own composition was a *Pastorale for oboe, harp and strings*, performed by a splendid solo oboist. I had begun it just before we embarked for France on the Queen Mary, and actually finished it on the boat. I think that it sounded more French than Polish, which is probably why the French audience liked it. Its first American performance was by the famous French oboist, Marcel Tabuteau,[13] with Eugene Ormandy and the Philadelphia Orchestra.

This was not, however, my only experience with the Chopin centennial. I had been appointed chairman of the Chopin Centennial Committee in the United States, a committee sponsored by the Kosciusko Foundation.[14] The principal event was a gala Chopin concert by Arthur Rubinstein[15] at the old Metropolitan Opera House. My duties were simple, to greet the audience and to thank Mr. Rubinstein for his graciousness in giving the program for the benefit of the foundation.

When it came time to begin the concert, I walked out on the stage and made my short speech. I then went to Mr. Rubinstein's dressing room to tell him that we were ready. He said to me, "I thought you were going to speak." "I already have," I replied. "I'm sorry," said Mr. Rubinstein, "I wanted to hear your tribute to Chopin." Then he thought a moment and said, "Perhaps it is just as well. When I go on stage and see those white teeth of the piano glaring up at me, I get frightened." This, coming from the great Rubinstein, should comfort the young concert pianist.

---

13 Marcel Tabuteau (1887–1966), eminent French-born American oboist. He served as principal oboe of the Philadelphia Orchestra 1915–54 and teacher of oboe at Curtis 1924–53.

14 The Kosciusko Foundation was founded in 1925 and serves as an American center for Polish culture, sponsoring exhibits, publications, festivals, concerts, etc.

15 Arthur Rubinstein (1887–1982), Polish-born American pianist. He was widely regarded as one of the greatest pianists of the twentieth century, especially noted for his playing of the music of Chopin.

Chapter Thirty

WORKING WITH UNIVERSITY OF ROCHESTER PRESIDENTS

The regime of Rush Rhees as president of the University of Rochester saw not only great strides in the growth and prestige of the Eastman School as an educational institution of international importance, but [also] its physical development as well. The original building included the studios, classrooms, and offices of the school, a large theater seating approximately 3,200 people, and a beautiful chamber music hall seating about 500, named Kilbourn Hall in honor of George Eastman's mother, [Maria Kilbourn Eastman].

In the six years following the opening of the school, Mr. Eastman added an annex to the Eastman Theatre, which included facilities for building and painting scenery, a wardrobe department for designing and making costumes, quarters for the ballet, a large rehearsal hall, and [a] garage. He also had constructed three [adjoining] dormitories on the Prince Street campus for women students of the Eastman School, and an eleven-story annex primarily for practice rooms, the top floor being devoted to something rather unusual for a music school in those days: a gymnasium.

As I have already indicated, my years with President Rhees were happy ones. The governance of the Eastman School as set up by George Eastman was rather unusual in the history of American universities. The deed of the gift stipulated that the Eastman School should be governed by a board of managers responsible to the board of trustees of the University of Rochester, of which the Eastman School was a part.

There was always the legalistic question as to what would happen if the actions of Mr. Eastman's board of managers were not approved by the trustees of the university, but so far as I can remember no such disagreement ever occurred. The original board, as I have already [related], consisted of only four of us, so that the red tape, which is an inescapable part of most organizations, was virtually nonexistent. In 1933, four new members were added to the board: M. Herbert Eisenhart, then president of the optical firm of Bausch and Lomb; Charles F. Hutchison, superintendent of Eastman Kodak; W. Roy McCanne, president of Stromberg-Carlson; and Raymond K. Thompson, treasurer of the university. The board, therefore, remained comparatively small in size, and, as the new members were all close personal friends of mine, the halcyon days continued.

In 1935, President Rhees insisted on retiring, having served the university brilliantly for thirty-five years. We were all worried about the appointment of his successor. For the Eastman School, this was of special concern. Today we frequently speak of the "arts and the humanities" in one breath. It has been my experience, however, that many university presidents who will defend the humanities to the death frequently have little interest in the arts or in music, except at the nonprofessional level.

Fortunately for all of us, the trustees made a very wise choice in the appointment of Alan Valentine of Yale University as the new president of the University of Rochester. I admired him greatly. He was reputed to be the youngest man ever to become president of a university, and I found myself for the first time in my career serving under a younger man.

President Valentine's first action was to examine in considerable detail the organization and structure of the university of which he was the new head. At the Eastman School, he studied the details of our admission procedure, our scholarship program, and other administrative procedures. I recall his going over, one by one, hundreds of applications in the registrar's office to see their disposition and the reason for our judgments. He was apparently fully satisfied with our decisions and permitted us to carry on in our usual manner.

One of his first acts as president was to assist us in building a library to house the famous Sibley Music Library. This valuable collection of books and manuscripts had been given to the university by the late Hiram W. Sibley and housed in the Eastman School of Music.[1] Under the direction of its librarian, Barbara Duncan, and with funds from Mr. Sibley and Mr. Eastman, the library had become one of the great music libraries in the world. President Valentine saw that the housing of the library was woefully inadequate and authorized the [construction] of a special library building, probably the first university building in history to be devoted entirely to a music collection. It is a tribute to the present librarian, Dr. Ruth Watanabe, that the growth and use of the library has increased until [the time arises when] the present building is again "woefully inadequate."

President Rhees had bequeathed to his successor a university of growing importance and prestige, well-organized, and heavily endowed. It consisted at the time of his retirement of three campuses: the College of Arts and Science, the School of Medicine and Dentistry, and Strong Memorial

---

[1] The original collection of books and manuscripts was donated to the University of Rochester in 1904. It was transferred to the Eastman School of Music in 1921.

Hospital on the River Campus; the Women's College and the Memorial Art Gallery (a gift of Mr. and Mrs. James Sibley Watson) on the Prince Street Campus; and the Eastman School and [Eastman] Theatre in downtown Rochester.

The River Campus had been completed only a short time before Dr. Rhees's retirement. It was the result of a fund drive, the purpose of which was to remove the Men's College [from Prince Street] to the new campus on the Genesee River. The Women's College remained on the old campus. Dr. Rhees, a graduate of Amherst [College], was never (as I recall) a believer in coeducation at the undergraduate level. Even in the old campus, the College for Men and the College for Women each had its own separate identity. With the removal of the men to the River Campus, the two colleges became separated in fact as well as in theory, although the women were allowed to infiltrate the River Campus for graduate courses.

President Valentine and his charming wife, Lucia, brought a new cosmopolitanism to the university. He was an English scholar and writer with previous experience in administration as master of Pearson Hall at Yale University. Mrs. Valentine had a sophisticated appreciation of the arts and literature and was a warm supporter of the university's program in music.

The new president's educational philosophy, as I saw it, was quite clear. Like Dr. Rhees, he was not interested in size. He wished to create a university of distinction and national importance. He was particularly proud of the School of Medicine and the School of Music, both of which had acquired international reputations. On a number of occasions, he referred to the schools of medicine and music as the "bright stars in the crown of the university," which probably did not endear him particularly to the faculty and loyal alumni of the men's college, who were a bit smug about their beautiful new campus.

Although he had won his "colors" in rugby as a Rhodes Scholar, he was not greatly interested in the athletic prowess of the college. He did not greatly care whether Rochester beat its traditional rival, Hobart College, at football, even to the extent of saying publicly that he did not think that "who won" was very important. This did not increase his popularity with the football-conscious alumni. His search for distinction in the faculty and for superior teaching in the classroom was generally recognized and applauded.

His administration of the university was also simple and direct. He appointed strong deans of the colleges: Lee DuBridge (later president of the California Institute of Technology) as dean of the Men's College; and the distinguished biochemist, Janet Clark, to the Women's College. The dean of the medical school was the pathologist, Dr. George Whipple, a winner of the Nobel Prize and a man for whom he had great admiration and affection.

Having placed his confidence in us, he allowed us to run our own show, with a minimum of interference from the central administration. He did expect us to produce. He did expect us to spend money wisely and to be conscious of budget limitations. As far as the music school was concerned, he gave its board of managers every cooperation, and the affairs of the school were conducted smoothly and efficiently.

After fifteen years in the president's office, Dr. Valentine retired to devote his time to writing and lecturing. I have always guessed that, in spite of his efficiency, he never really enjoyed administration, that his real interest lay in [creativity]. Also, I think that he was depressed that so much of the interest of the "old grads" was still concerned with the development of a winning football team. Perhaps he simply felt that he had done as much as he could for the university. In any case, he retired somewhat abruptly. M. Herbert Eisenhart, chairman of the board of trustees of the university (and also chairman of the board of managers of the Eastman School), did his best to urge him to reconsider, but he remained adamant in his decision. In any case, he brought much to the university and left it a more distinguished institution.

Provost Donald Gilbert served as acting president for a year. The following year, Cornelis Willem deKiewiet, formerly dean of the faculty of Cornell University and acting president of that institution, was appointed president of the University of Rochester. The coming of President deKiewiet changed the entire complexion of the university. He proved to be a rather remarkable man, possessing both great courage and initiative. His first major act was to unite the men's and women's colleges on the new River Campus. The moving of the Women's College to the River Campus seemed to me highly justifiable. The buildings occupied by the women students were becoming obsolete. Library, classroom, and laboratory facilities could not compare with those on the new campus. They were likely to remain inferior unless the university undertook the building of new and comparable facilities on the old campus.

The difficulties of moving were equally great. There must be a new drive for funds to build dormitories and classrooms for the women. Equally important and difficult was the task of persuading the alumni of both colleges of the wisdom of the change. The Men's College had always been proud of its all-male tradition. The alumnae of the Women's College were equally jealous of their autonomy. In spite of difficulties, President deKiewiet insisted on the change and accomplished it brilliantly over all objections. His friends called it "courage," and his enemies bull-headed "Dutch stubbornness." In my opinion, it was not only a courageous but a necessary step if the university (and especially the Arts College) was to continue to develop.

Other parts of his educational philosophy filled some of us with dismay. The policy of the previous administrations, as I have said, was to appoint strong deans and let them assume responsibility for their colleges. If the dean could not handle his assignment, he could easily be replaced, since deans do not have tenure. The new president's policy, on the contrary, called for a strong centralization of authority in the university administration, the final authority resting with the president and filtering down to the deans through a series of vice-presidents, provosts, and other university officers. Coupled with this was his insistence that the central core of the university should be the College of Arts and Sciences.

Under this policy, the College of Arts and Sciences itself became the university, the rest of us being adjuncts of the main body. For the medical school and the music school, this was hard to take, since these two colleges had already achieved world fame. The college did not completely escape. It was fragmented into colleges of liberal arts, education, engineering, and business administration, the first two years of the Liberal Arts College constituting the "core" for the other River Campus colleges.

Fortunately for us, the Eastman School was located in downtown Rochester, four miles from the River Campus, and our physical separation kept us from being entirely absorbed and drowned in the Genesee River. We were able to escape the "core curriculum" of the first two years, although it was suggested [for the Eastman School] by one of the vice-presidents. We were also able to control our own admissions and scholarship programs, a necessity for a professional music school. We were even able to keep our semi-autonomous academic faculty, which had been so valuable to our students and which I was greatly afraid of losing.

I do not mean to imply that the deans were not consulted in this all-university organization. We were all members of the president's "cabinet," but even this inclusion did not always make us happy. I can recall being present at a number of meetings when the principal item on the agenda was the problem of parking on the River Campus and the best plan for circumventing the desire of the state highway commission to construct a thruway feeder at a very disadvantageous point. I could add little to the discussion of either subject, important as I know they were. I could not help thinking of all the work lying on my desk and of all the students and faculty whom I wanted to see and who wanted to talk with me.

Another problem was more serious. Under the regime of Rush Rhees and Alan Valentine, the arts, humanities, and sciences seemed to be given equal consideration and importance. Now the emphasis seemed to be changing quite definitely in the direction of the sciences. As long as the Eastman School could live on the income from its own specified endowment, we had no problems. However, if we needed to draw on the income from the "general" endowment funds—that is, funds assigned to the university as a whole and not to any specific school—we were in trouble.

This situation was further complicated by the fact that, when the Women's College was moved to the River Campus, the beautiful Gothic student union, Cutler Union, and the newest of the dormitories on the Women's Campus were sold to the Eastman School.[2] The payment from our capital for these buildings, plus the cost of maintenance, deprived us of the interest on about one-sixth of our entire Eastman endowment. This situation has since been considerably ameliorated, but at the time it produced real hardships, particularly in the matter of faculty salaries.[3]

One last problem was the schism between the president and the board of managers set up by Mr. Eastman to govern the school. The president did not approve of the arrangement in Mr. Eastman's Deed of Gift and insisted that the authority was vested in the board of trustees of the university. The board of managers, some of whom had been personal friends of Mr. Eastman, declined[4] to retire. The impasse was not resolved until President deKiewiet's retirement in 1961. With the coming of the new president, W. Allen Wallis, the board of managers was reconstituted.

In spite of the difficulties of the deKiewiet regime, I must admit great admiration for his singleness of purpose and his courage in carrying it out. If he had accomplished nothing more than the merger of the College for Men and the College for Women, his labors for the university would be justified. I also realize that the present pattern of the university, with its abundance of vice-presidents, provosts, and deans, is the normal pattern of the modern university. Perhaps it is the best (perhaps the only) pattern possible. Perhaps someday we can return to a pattern which is smaller, simpler, more direct, and more personal.

I must also say that the problems of those difficult days of transition were considerably lightened by the presence of Lucea deKiewiet, the president's lovely wife. Both Peggie and I were (and are) very fond of her. Although she was by nature retiring, her sympathetic personality touched and illumined all whom she met.

---

2   The Eastman School of Music paid $931,000 for the dormitory and for Cutler Union, plus an additional $105,000 for furnishings and redecoration. This amount was transferred from the school's reserve funds to the university's College of Arts and Science building fund.

3   This is a very illuminating comment, since faculty salaries at Eastman were a great source of concern, especially in the latter years of Hanson's tenure as director. There was much faculty activism in the years immediately following his retirement, including the organization of a faculty association primarily charged with seeking improved salaries.

4   Hanson originally wrote, "refused to retire," perhaps indicating a more strenuous opposition to President deKiewiet.

Chapter Thirty-One

THE AMERICAN SOCIETY OF COMPOSERS, AUTHORS, AND PUBLISHERS

I have referred to the importance to American culture of the radio networks in the 1930s, an importance which today has almost entirely disappeared. Nothing illustrates this better than the decision of the Columbia Broadcasting System [CBS] in 1936 to commission a group of six American composers to write works for the Columbia network. The six commissioned [composers] included Aaron Copland, Roy Harris, Louis Gruenberg, Walter Piston, William Grant Still, and me, the project being under the direction of Deems Taylor, at that time musical advisor to the Columbia Broadcasting System.

The Swedes in the United States were planning to celebrate the 300th anniversary of the settlement of New Sweden in Delaware, and it was suggested that I might write a work in celebration of the tercentenary. I decided to write a symphony, my third, for the occasion. The first three movements had their first performance by the C.B.S. Symphony under the direction of Howard Barlow.[1] I do not remember whether I originally intended the symphony to be in three movements, like the *Romantic*, but I doubt it. In any case, it was obvious that the work demanded a fourth movement.

The first movement was long and stormy, the second an extended lyrical slow movement, and the third a short dynamic rhythmic form, with the motive announced in the solo timpani. A finale was essential, and I began to work on it at once. When it was completed, Dr. Koussevitzky offered to give the entire symphony its first concert performance in Boston. However, when he saw the fourth movement, he was not satisfied. He argued that the work was long and powerful and that the climax was too short, the ending too abrupt.

I must admit that he was right, but having once completed a score, it is difficult to change. I was not, however, in the least chagrined by Dr.

---

1   Howard Barlow (1892–1972), American conductor. He was music director at C.B.S. 1927–43, then conductor at N.B.C. of the "Voice of Firestone Orchestra" 1943–59.

Koussevitzky's insistence. He obviously had the success of the work very much at heart and was convinced that the ending must be expanded. Finally, the solution came to me, and Dr. Koussevitzky was completely satisfied. He studied the score so thoroughly that he said to me on one occasion, "I know this score much better than you." In any case, the performance was magnificent, and "our" new finale took the audience by storm.

The reception by the critics of Boston and New York was, as usual, mixed. Several considered it the best of my three symphonies and a strong and mature work. Others felt that it leaned too heavily on Sibelius. This critical charge of "Sibelian" influence has followed me almost from the beginning. Some reviewers have found the influence of the Finnish master in my first symphony, the *Nordic*, although I doubt very much that I had heard a single Sibelius symphony at the time of writing it. I can also find no influence of Sibelius in my second symphony.

The third is, however, a different matter. I had in the meantime conducted most of his symphonies and some of his shorter works and was influenced by them. It is actually difficult for me to assess the degree of influence. Sibelius was of Swedish and Finnish descent and was himself undoubtedly influenced by the folk-music of both countries. I was brought up as a child on Swedish folksongs and folk dances. It is very likely that we have both drawn inspiration from the same sources.

Dr. Koussevitzky had no doubts about the symphony. He [conducted] it again at least four times that season in Boston and again in Cambridge. Then he performed it in New York City and on tour. The tour included Rochester, where Dr. Koussevitzky again performed the symphony over the objections, I am told, of the Rochester management which considered it "too modern" for Rochester ears. In an interview, Dr. Koussevitzky defended his choice of program, describing the symphony as "the equal to any of the great symphonies," certainly the ultimate encomium.

Dr. Koussevitzky's insistence on changing the end of the finale reminds me of a similar confrontation with another great conductor, Pierre Monteux.[2] Mr. Monteux had written me that he planned to perform *Lux Aeterna* with the Concertgebouw Orchestra in Amsterdam. A short time later, he wrote me concerning a certain place in the score where I had written the French horns *above* the trumpets. He felt that this was illogical,

---

2 Pierre Monteux (1875–1964), distinguished French conductor. He became conductor of Diaghilev's ballet in 1911, conducting the premieres of *Petrushka* and *The Rite of Spring*; conductor Boston Symphony 1919–24, then associated with Concertgebouw Orchestra 1924–29; founded and conducted the Orchestre Symphonique de Paris 1929–35, then conductor of the San Francisco Orchestra 1935–52; later conducted London Symphony 1961–64.

that the horn and trumpet parts should be reversed. I replied by letter that the reason for the unusual placement was that I wanted the peculiar quality of the four horns in their high register straining and "crying out" above the heavy brasses. He did not reply, but sometime later, looking at the orchestral [score] which he had used, I observed that he placed the trumpets above the horns!

The end of the [1930s] brought [new] emphasis on American music. Dr. Koussevitzky presented in Carnegie Hall two concerts with the Boston Symphony Orchestra, devoted entirely to American music, including the first New York performance of my Piano Concerto with Rudolf Firkusny as soloist.

The American Society of Composers, Authors, and Publishers (ASCAP) was also active in promoting the performance of American music, both popular and serious. There was an all-American concert of symphonic music in Carnegie Hall, with the composers conducting their own music, a concert of American symphonic works at the New York World's Fair of 1939, and a huge festival of American music (both popular and serious) at the Golden Gate International Exposition in San Francisco.

The Rochester Philharmonic Orchestra and I were invited to present the program in connection with the New York World's Fair. It was suggested that we invite Mayor Fiorello LaGuardia[3] to open the concert by conducting our national anthem. I was delighted with the idea. The mayor's father was, I believe, a bandmaster,[4] and the mayor was an enthusiastic music lover. The mayor was happy to accept and appeared punctually at the beginning of the concert. He raised his baton and brought it down in two-four meter. The "Star Spangled Banner" is, of course, in three-four meter and begins with an upbeat, not a downbeat. The orchestra was staggered but kept doggedly on. I noticed that the musicians were all careful not to watch the conductor!

The ASCAP Festival at the Golden Gate International Exposition was something that happens once in a lifetime. The symphonic program was presented by the San Francisco Symphony in a huge outdoor amphitheater. I conducted my third symphony, the other conductors being Edwin

---

3   Fiorello LaGuardia (1882–1947) colorful mayor of New York. He served three terms 1934–45.

4   Hanson's recollection is correct. Fiorello LaGuardia's father, Achille LaGuardia, served as a bandmaster in the United States Army, being discharged in 1898.

McArthur[5] and Richard Hageman.[6] The final program was devoted to music by the famous composers of popular music. It seemed to me that everyone was there: W.H. Handy, composer of the "St. Louis Blues;" Irving Berlin; George M. Cohan of "It's a Grand Old Flag;" Judy Garland singing Harold Arlen's "Somewhere Over the Rainbow" with the composer conducting; and even the composer of "Sweet Adeline."[7]

I had no part in the program, but the master of ceremonies asked me if I would conduct the orchestra while Irving Berlin sang his "God Bless America." And so Irving Berlin, singing in his small, high voice, climaxed the festival with his most famous song. I have conducted for many distinguished soloists, but never with greater pleasure.

The purpose of the great ASCAP Festival of American Music at the San Francisco [Exposition] was, quite frankly, to show the importance of the organization—the American Society of Composers, Authors, and Publishers—in the nation's music. The society had been formed in the early part of the century, largely through the efforts of Victor Herbert and John Philip Sousa.

Up to this time, neither the composer, the author, or the publisher had adequate protection in the rights of his work. It is true that a composition could be copyrighted to protect it from piracy or plagiarism. There was, however, little if any protection of the rights of performance for profit.

The story of ASCAP's creation is interesting. According to the legend, Victor Herbert was enjoying dinner with friends in a famous New York restaurant. During the evening, the café restaurant delighted the diners with Herbert's music. The composer pondered the fact that, if this had been a performance of his music on Broadway, he would be receiving compensation for his music. Since it was being performed in a restaurant, he received no compensation. And yet, he reasoned, this was definitely a "performance for profit." The chefs were paid, the waiters were paid, the members of the café orchestra were paid. Everyone was paid except the composer and his colleagues, the author and the publisher. From this modest beginning, ASCAP was born.

---

5   Edwin McArthur (1907–87), American accompanist, conductor, pianist. He was especially known for his collaborative work with Kirsten Flagstad; later taught at the Eastman School of Music 1967–72.

6   Richard Hageman (1881–1956), Dutch-born American composer, conductor, pianist. He conducted at the Metropolitan Opera 1914–32; head of the Curtis Institute 1932–36; later music director of Chicago Civic Orchestra and Ravinia Park Opera; also conducted six seasons at the Hollywood Bowl.

7   "Sweet Adeline" was written in 1903 by Henry Armstrong, with lyrics by Richard Gerard.

In the early days, both the prestige and the income from "performance rights" were indeed modest. With the advent of radio, and particularly national radio networks, the situation changed radically. Much of the [programming] of radio networks consisted of music, and especially popular music. Since most of the famous composers and songwriters were members of ASCAP, it was necessary for the networks to sign contracts with ASCAP for the right to broadcast this music.

For a time, all went smoothly. The ASCAP fees were modest, and the networks signed contracts which gave them the privilege of performing any works in the huge ASCAP catalogue. However, Gene Buck,[8] the president of ASCAP, realizing the tremendous profits of the broadcasting industry, insisted on a substantial increase in performance fees. Buck, himself a songwriter and a man of tremendous energy and courage, was adamant in his demands, and the networks rebelled.

The was the beginning of the famous music strike of 1941.[9] All of the music in the ASCAP catalogue was banned. The only music generally available was music "in the public domain," which meant either music which had not been copyrighted or music on which the term of copyright had expired. The result on radio programs was catastrophic, since almost all of the favorite popular music of the day was under ASCAP control. It was possible to play the music of Stephen Foster, but not that of Irving Berlin, Jerome Kern, George M. Cohan, William Handy, or the other popular writers of the time. The popular quip was that Stephen Foster's "Jeannie with the Light Brown Hair" had been played so much that it had grown gray!

The difficulties between ASCAP and the networks were eventually compromised. Today, under the expert guidance of men like Stanley Adams and Herman Finkelstein, the composer, author, and publisher live together in comparative peace and equity [with] the radio and television stations.

In recent years, ASCAP has taken great interest not only in the popular composer and author but also in the composers of serious music. Many ASCAP composers of symphonies, operas, and choral works can live today with some degree of comfort on their ASCAP royalties, something which would have been quite impossible in the early part of the century. And so ASCAP, beginning as a protection for the "popular" composer, has become over the years the greatest friend of the serious composer, and has exerted a highly beneficent influence on musical creation in the United States.

---

8   Gene Buck (1885–1957) served as president of ASCAP 1924–41.

9   ASCAP demanded a 100% increase in royalties. The strike began on January 1, 1941.

Chapter Thirty-Two

EXPERIENCES WITH SEVERAL AMERICAN PRESIDENTS

The degree and the quality of interest of the presidents of the United States in music and the arts, and the effect of that interest on the development of the arts in our country, is an interesting study. I never met President Roosevelt and have no personal knowledge of his concern with the arts. It has seemed to me that his support, for example, of the Federal Music Project in the depths of the Depression sprang from his humanitarian concern for the difficult economic position of the artist in Depression times rather than from a personal involvement in the arts. My friend, Eugene List,[1] the American concert pianist, who has played at the White House many times, has told me that both President Roosevelt and President Truman enjoyed music, the latter being himself an amateur pianist.

My first involvement with the White House was during the first term of President Eisenhower. It was, however, more political than cultural. W. Robert Rogers, executive director of the Washington National Symphony Orchestra, had organized an "Artists for Eisenhower-Nixon" committee and asked me to be chairman of a sub-committee of musicians for the campaign. I soon found that most musicians—both composers and performers—were apparently Democrats! I did manage, however, to form a small but distinguished committee which at least proved that *all* musicians were not Democrats. We were able, I think, to convince some voters that the selection of a Republican president and vice-president would not take away what little support the arts already had [from] our government.

As a matter of fact, President Eisenhower's tenure actually marked a greater recognition of the arts in government than in any previous regime.[2] This recognition was, however, not "social," as in the presiden-

---

    1   Eugene List (1918–85), American pianist and teacher. He studied with Olga Samaroff and achieved wide attention when he played for Churchill, Truman, and Stalin at the Potsdam Conference in June 1945; he taught at the Eastman School 1964–75.

    2   Hanson omits reference to the extensive federal program in music under the WPA (Works Progress Administration) during the Great Depression.

cies of John F. Kennedy and Lyndon B. Johnson. It had to do rather with the *use* of music in government. President Eisenhower's taste in music was primarily of the semi-popular variety. He was an ardent fan of Fred Waring,[3] and on our first meeting we spent most of our time talking about Fred. This was quite alright with me, as I am also a Waring fan and a great admirer of what he can do with a group of singers.

Howard Mitchell,[4] music director of the Washington National Symphony, has told me that President and Mrs. Eisenhower both gave encouragement to the orchestra, and it is interesting to note that the important Cultural Exchange Program was initiated during his presidency. My first interview with the president was the occasion for a sartorial predicament which still amuses my friends. My wife and I attended the inauguration, but I had never had the opportunity of speaking with [President Eisenhower]. It was in the following summer that, as we were sitting on the porch of our cottage on Bold Island, we observed a small outboard [motorboat] coming toward the island at top speed. A young man leaped from the boat and rushed up the hill to the cottage.

Breathlessly, he handed me a message scribbled hastily on a piece of wrapping paper. It was from the mayor of the small fishing village of Stonington and read, "President Eisenhower would like to see you Monday morning at ten o'clock." I was delighted, but the invitation presented difficulties. On our island, our wardrobes are strictly limited, mostly blue jeans and dungarees. I had one suit (pretty well "beat up" from the automobile trip from Rochester), one clean blue shirt, no tie or cuff links, and a pair of heavy rubber "platform" shoes (highly suitable for the Bold Island rocks but not exactly what is indicated for the White House). To compound the difficulty, it was Saturday afternoon, and stores were closed.

I borrowed a tie and cufflinks from our friend, Dr. Eugene Selhorst (associate dean of graduate studies at Eastman), who was visiting us, packed my one blue shirt, and wearing a knitted shirt which I hoped would pass, set out for Washington. There was nothing that I could do about the shoes. I arrived in Washington Sunday evening and was met by a White House aide, who appeared somewhat shocked at my unconventional appearance. He asked me if I had a "conventional" shirt. I told him that I had *one*, and that I was saving it for the morning. He seemed relieved.

---

    3   Fred Waring (1900–84), popular bandleader, radio and television personality. He was especially influential through his establishment of choral workshops that attracted many aspiring conductors.

    4   Howard Mitchell (1910–88), American cellist and conductor. He was the leader of the National Symphony 1950–69.

Checking in at the Hilton, I told the bellman of my problems and asked him to bribe someone to press my one and only suit, even if it was Sunday. Locking myself in my room, I waited in no little suspense, wondering what I would do if my suit were not returned. But the bellman was a man of honor and initiative, and I went to bed with my freshly pressed suit hanging triumphantly in the clothes closet.

The next morning, I presented myself promptly at the White House gate. The guard asked my name, looked at the president's list of appointments, and told me that the president was expecting me. "Do you have any identification?" he asked politely. I looked in my wallet, but I had left so hastily that I had nothing with me except a Gulf credit card in my wife's name. The guard fortunately had a sense of humor. He said, "Since you are obviously not Mrs. Howard Hanson, I assume that you must be Dr. Howard Hanson." On being ushered into the reception room, I was greeted by Sherman Adams and Jim Haggerty[5] with the question, "Where in the world is that island of yours. We want to go there!"

The president greeted me most graciously. We talked a bit and were joined by Arthur Fiedler,[6] who had come to present to the president a new album of recordings of the Boston Pops Orchestra. I have a picture of the three of us, with the president obviously in very good humor. My principal remembrance of the interview was, "How blue his eyes are."

Some years later, he came to Rochester to attend the ceremonies in connection with the inauguration of W. Allen Wallis as president of the University of Rochester. One event was a concert in the Eastman Theatre by the Eastman Philharmonia Orchestra, the student orchestra which was to achieve fame for its tour of Europe, the Middle East, and Russia on the Cultural Exchange Program of the Department of State.

President Eisenhower attended the concert and stayed to the last encore. The Secret Service men, anxious to get him away before the large audience poured out of the theater, escorted him backstage toward the stage entrance. The final encore was Sousa's famous march, "The Stars and Stripes Forever," and as the president heard what we were playing, he left his escort and came out on the stage (standing inside the concert-set) until the march ended. At its conclusion, I went quickly to greet him. His

---

5   Sherman Adams and James (Jim) Haggerty were members of the Eisenhower administration, the former serving as chief of staff and the latter as press secretary.
6   Arthur Fiedler (1894–1979), American conductor. He was famous throughout the United States as the long-time conductor of the Boston Pops 1930–79.

remark was, "I've marched hundreds of miles to that music, but I never heard it played so beautifully!"

The next morning, at Mr. Wallis's inauguration, we met again, and he asked me if we had recorded the Sousa march. When I told him that we had, he said, "I want a copy." Bob Sattler, our manager, immediately procured a copy which we presented to him. "But," said President Eisenhower, "I want you to autograph it." Later, we walked through the corridors of the Eastman School, the president waving gaily to the secretaries who greeted him. Afterwards, a group of them told me that they had gotten his autograph. To which I loftily replied, "The president asked for *my* autograph!" President Eisenhower [was] a great president and a great human being. We may never see his like again.

Music at the White House in President Kennedy's time was something different. Although dedicated Republicans, Peggie and I were fortunate in being invited to the White House for the famous Casals[7] recital and the formal dinner which followed. This proved to be a social-cultural *tour de force*. The famous cellist, at the age of eighty, played magnificently with a verve which completely belied the catalogue of years.

Then, too, his political credentials as a liberal were impeccable. His self-imposed exile from Spain and his long battle with the Franco dictatorship would have ensured his welcome, even if he had not played at all. The audience constituted a "Who's Who" of musicians and patrons of music. The great figures of the composition world of the United States—Samuel Barber, Aaron Copland, Roy Harris, Walter Piston, Virgil Thomson, and many others—were there. And the conductors—Leopold Stokowski, Eugene Ormandy, Leonard Bernstein, Erich Leinsdorf, George Szell—all were there, [the men] immaculate in white tie and tails, the ladies in a dazzling assortment of gorgeous gowns.

The attitude of the Kennedys toward the arts has always puzzled me. They were the most lavish of hosts, and I doubt if the glamour of the Casals dinner will ever be surpassed. However, I have always had the uncomfortable feeling that, like so much of "society's" interest in the arts, art itself played the minor role.

The atmosphere of the dinners of President and Mrs. Johnson, to which we were invited, seemed to be much simpler, less formal, more relaxed, and—perhaps for [these reasons]—more genuine. I recall

---

7   Pablo Casals (1876–1973). Spanish/Catalan cellist. He was an ardent supporter of the Spanish Republican Government, which fell to Francisco Franco and his supporters, and he vowed not to return to Spain until democracy had been restored.

especially the dinner in honor of another veteran artist, Mischa Elman.[8] It was a "black tie" rather than "white tie" buffet rather than a formal dinner. For those guests whose acquaintance with the [music of] Bach was limited, the program added a segment by the famous Swingle Singers,[9] newly arrived from Paris, whose vocal adaptations of Bach were completely delightful.

I had been asked to say a few words of introduction and tribute to Mischa Elman, but I was not sure that I could arrive in time for the occasion. I had already promised to give the commencement address at Gustavus Adolphus College in St. Peter, Minnesota, the day before. Samuel Adler,[10] who was in charge of the evening at the White House, assured me that he would have a White House limousine at the airport to get us there in time.

Arriving at Dulles International Airport, we went immediately to claim our baggage but could not see anyone who looked like a White House chauffeur. Suddenly, there came over the public address system the words, "Calling Mr. Eastman! Calling Mr. Eastman!" My wife said, "You had better answer it." She was right. It was for us. Some of my kind friends have said that over the years my name and that of the Eastman School have become synonymous. However, this was the first time that it had been officially recognized.

We arrived in plenty of time. I made my introduction of Mr. Elman, who played brilliantly. After the performance, President Johnson put his arm around my shoulder and said, "That was a fine introduction. I wish you would introduce me sometime!" Mrs. Johnson proved to be an extraordinarily gracious and thoughtful hostess, talking with many of us and discussing some of the problems of music in a democracy. Her interest seemed both genuine and informed, and I was greatly impressed both by her charm and her understanding.

Peggie and I were tired after our strenuous trip and left somewhat before the rest of the guests. As we were going down the steps, we heard someone calling to us. It was Mrs. Johnson wishing us a good night and thanking us for our contribution to the evening's success, a truly generous and gracious lady.

---

8   Mischa Elman (1891–1967), Ukrainian-born violinist. He studied with Leopold Auer in St. Petersburg and became one of the most famous and successful violinists of his generation.

9   The Swingle Singers was a highly popular vocal group, founded in Paris. The original group flourished 1962–73.

10   Samuel Adler (b.1928) taught at the Eastman School of Music 1966–94.

Among the various state dinners, I recall with pleasure a dinner given by the late Secretary of State John Foster Dulles,[11] in honor of Prime Minister Nehru of India. At the conclusion of the dinner, an aide came to inform me that Madame Gandhi wished to speak with me. After being presented to her, she told me that she wanted to discuss with me the general problem of the financial support of the arts. I probably looked somewhat puzzled, whereupon she explained that, with the decline of the personal wealth of certain of the Maharajahs who had supported the arts in the past, it was difficult to find substitute sources of income. She wished to know how we in the United States solved the economic problems of the arts. I replied that I was flattered to be asked such a question by so distinguished a representative of a country whose culture was infinitely older than ours, but that I had no answer. Indeed, I was about to ask her the same question!

---

11   John Foster Dulles (1888–1959), American statesman. He served as Eisenhower's secretary of state 1953–59.

Chapter Thirty-Three

HONORARY DOCTORATES AND OTHER HONORS

I recall sitting on one of those omnipresent panels called by Washington to discuss the plight of the arts. I don't remember much about it, except that most of the members seemed to be writers. I was sitting next to John Steinbeck,[1] who seemed more interested in discussing the bordellos of San Francisco. At one point, the discussion turned, as it always does eventually, to government's relation to the arts. I raised the point that our government has no way of recognizing the creative artist, or, for that matter, the performing artist. Britain has its knighthoods, France its many decorations, and other European countries their various "orders" which can be used to indicate the country's appreciation of its distinguished citizens, including artists.

Such an order might or might not be important to the individual, but is in my opinion important to the art, indicating as it does that the country concerned respects the arts and considers them important in the life of the country. This was, of course, long before the establishment by President Kennedy in 1963 of the Presidential Medal of Freedom awards.

My suggestion was met with lofty disdain by all of the "intellectuals" present. They were not interested in baubles, whether in the form of pieces of metal, colored ribbons, or lapel buttons. I felt that I had committed a *gaucherie* of the worst type, particularly when I admitted some pride in having a modest decoration from the king of Sweden, although I had never worn it. I felt somewhat less embarrassed by my naivete when I observed that at least two members of the panel were sporting the little lapel button indicating their membership in the French Legion d'honneur. I gathered that French decorations were acceptable.

In spite of the haughtiness of some of my colleagues toward honorary degrees and other forms of "decoration"—although I have seldom seen them refuse such an honor—I think honors are very nice things. They give

---

1   John Steinbeck (1902–68), noted American writer. He wrote a total of twenty-seven books, including *The Grapes of Wrath* for which he received the Pulitzer Prize in 1940; received the Nobel Prize for Literature in 1962.

you the warm and friendly feeling that somebody knows you have been doing [something] and think it worthwhile. It also frequently reminds one of pleasant occasions in the past and important events in one's career. I remarked to my friend Hamilton Allen that, when I received my thirty-third doctorate, I felt as though I had achieved the highest degree in Masonry! I suppose, however, that the degree which I appreciated the most was the first one, an honorary doctorate of music from Northwestern University. I had just been appointed to the directorship of the Eastman School. Perhaps I would be a great success, or perhaps I would fall on my face. There was no way of knowing. The honorary doctorate from my alma mater seemed to indicate that they were betting on me!

There is one degree which I remember with particular affection. It was awarded by a very good friend of mine, a man for whom I had the great respect, the late Howard Lowrie,[2] president of the College of Wooster. The president wrote me expressing his desire to award an honorary doctorate at the next commencement. He knew that I had already received a number of Mus. Doc. degrees, the doctor of letters, doctor of humane letters, doctor of fine arts, doctor of literature, and a few others, and very generously asked me if I would let him know which honorary degree I would prefer.

I wrote [to] him immediately telling him that I had been practicing medicine without a license for many years and that I would appreciate an honorary doctor of medicine degree! He replied with a long, beautifully tongue-in-cheek letter in which he expressed his regret that he could not comply with my request. In the first place, there was no honorary medical degree; second, there were strict laws on the granting of medical degrees; third, Wooster had no medical school. I received, as I recall, the degree doctor of humane letters. I wish that I had asked for a doctor of divinity degree!

Another degree which I also remember with affection was from the University of Arizona in Tucson, presided over by my friend Richard Harvill.[3] I remember giving the commencement address to a large graduating class in the evening in the great football stadium under the light of a beautiful Arizona moon. I also remember telling the graduates that I was not going to give them one of those speeches which ends, "Our generation has erred. To you of the new generation we pass the torch. You will succeed

---

2   Howard Lowry was the seventh president of the College of Wooster and was responsible for establishing the school's well-regarded independent study program, begun in 1947.

3   Richard A. Harvill served as president of the University of Arizona from 1951 to 1971.

where we failed." Then I went on to say, "I am sure that your generation can be just as stupid as ours, perhaps stupider!" I was greeted with howls of applause.

I remember also some off-beat degrees which were not part of a conventional college or university ceremony. One was an honorary degree from the City of Philadelphia, presented in the Academy of Music after a symphony concert. I do not know of any other cities which are empowered to award honorary degrees. Another was an honorary degree awarded by the State of New York through its board of Regents. I recall with pleasure that one of my colleague recipients on that occasion was a fellow Scandinavian, Dr. Glen Seaborg,[4] the atomic physicist.

Commencements are always dignified affairs, but funny things can happen. As a Nebraskan, I appreciated the award of honorary degrees both from the University of Nebraska and from Nebraska Wesleyan University. The commencement ceremonies at the University of Nebraska were conducted by the chancellor of the university, the distinguished scientist Reuben Gustafson.[5] The chancellor, deans, the various dignitaries and honorary degree recipients marked in solemn procession to the stage of the convocation hall. When all of the graduates were in the hall, the signal to be seated was given. We all sat down, except the Catholic archbishop for whom no chair was available. We all rose from our chairs, offering the prelate our seats. This resulted in complete confusion, until some bright undergraduate solved the problem by bringing on the stage an extra chair!

Of all of the awards, I suppose the one which I value the highest is probably the Pulitzer Prize. I was the second composer to receive this prize, the first being my friend William Schuman, for many years president of the Juilliard School of Music. Whether or not one agrees with the Pulitzer awards on every occasion, it must be said that the award is made after the most careful deliberation by juries of the greatest probity and in the strictest secrecy, I was a member of the award committee in 1947, the year after I had received the Pulitzer Prize. I can, therefore, testify to the hours of discussion and debate which went into the determination of this award.

Incidentally, in my day the award had comparatively slight monetary value. The "prize" was for the magnificent sum of $500, which was at that time taxable! I am glad to say that since that time, the Internal Revenue Bureau [Service] has declared the Pulitzer Prize tax exempt. In spite of its slight monetary value, the prestige of the Pulitzer Prize is still enormous.

---

4   Glenn T. Seaborg (1912–99), American scientist. He received the Nobel Prize in Chemistry in 1951.

5   Reuben G. Gustavson served as chancellor of the University of Nebraska from 1946 to 1953.

The appellation Pulitzer Prize-winning composer, poet, journalist, or whatever still carries great prestige.

The Huntington Hartford Award, which I received in 1959 was financially most rewarding. It carried an award of $5,000 tax exempt, which in those days of high taxes increased its value considerably. The Ditson Award, sponsored by Columbia University, which I received in 1945, was valuable primarily because it was an award by one's peers. It was an award to musicians by musicians and, for this reason, had more than a sentimental value.[6]

I have already said that, of all the groups to which I have been elected, the American Philosophical Society is probably the most important. In 1935 I was elected a member of the National Institute of Arts and Letters, at that time probably the most prestigious society in the creative arts. Since that time, it seems to me that the National Institute has been increasingly dominated by political forces. I question whether today any "conservative" could be elected to the institute. One must be an "intellectual-liberal," whatever that means.

I was pleased by my election to the Royal Academy of Music of Sweden, because it provided some link with the land of my parents. Such an election probably means less to Swedes than to other nationalities. The Swedes have a way of being absorbed by the land to which they migrate. The French seem always to be French, although they may have come here many years ago. The Hungarian seems to remain a Hungarian, the Pole seems to remain a Pole. Perhaps the Swedes should be complimented.

---

6   Howard Hanson was the first recipient of the Ditson Conductor's Award, which is presented annually to honor conductors for their commitment to the performance of American music.

Chapter Thirty-Four

EASTMAN SCHOOL STUDENTS

I have often been asked the question, who have been my most interesting and most gifted students. It is difficult to answer, because in my forty years as teacher and administrator at Eastman, in addition to the five years at the College of the Pacific, I have had the privilege of working with hundreds of gifted young musicians. Even if I limit my answer to those students who have studied with me personally, the number is very large. There is, in addition, the besetting difficulty that I may, in mentioning many, forget the names of some who might be the most outstanding in talent and achievement.

I have always been a little vain about my ability to remember both the names and the faces of former students. Frequently, I have met graduates of the Class of 1926, whom I had not seen for many years and have been able to recall not only their names but even incidents in their student careers, even the concerto they performed on graduation. But memory is a fickle thing. It sometimes fails one at crucial moments.

I recall to my chagrin such a happening which occurred only a short time ago. I had been commissioned to write a work for chorus and orchestra, *Streams in the Desert*, by the Texas Technological College in Lubbock, Texas, for its International Arid Lands Conference. The premiere took place under my direction, and I was greatly pleased with the splendid cooperation of the student chorus and the orchestra. At the conclusion of the performance, in reply to the generous applause of the audience, I complimented the performers on their splendid work and proceeded to mention, quite blithely, the individual names of a number of Eastman graduates on the faculty who had been of great assistance.

As a result of the excitement, however, I neglected to mention the name of one of Eastman's gifted graduates on the Technological faculty, Mary Jeanne van Appledorn.[1] The omission was completely un-understandable. Mary Jeanne had been the organizing genius of the entire festival. It was she

---

1 Mary Jeanne van Appledorn (b.1927), American composer. She served on the faculty at Texas Technological University 1950–2008.

who, more than anyone else, was responsible for the festival's success. And yet, by a curious quirk of the human memory, hers was the name I forgot.

Probably the student who has most closely followed my own pattern of activity is the American composer and president of the Juilliard School of Music, Dr. Peter Mennin[2]. He is, I am sure, like me a compulsive composer. He writes because he must. As a matter of fact, his compositions in my class developed so rapidly that I was sometimes not sure whether I was listening to the final movement of his first symphony or the first movement of his second symphony. Again, as in my own case, he began as a composer and teacher, turning later to administration first as the director of the Peabody Conservatory in Baltimore and later as president of the Juilliard School of Music, but never giving up his primary interest in composition.

He had received his undergraduate degree from Oberlin Conservatory and came to Eastman with an excellent background. In spite of this, he ran into difficulties with our admissions office, then presided over by Arthur H. Larson. Peter was in every way eligible for admission to graduate study. I do not know to this day what there was about his application which worried our registrar and admissions office. Perhaps it was nothing more than a clash of personalities. In any case, Peter came to see me. Both his talent and technical knowledge were readily apparent, and my insistence that he be immediately admitted to the graduate division overcame whatever red tape was involved. He eventually emerged as one of the most brilliant PhD composition graduates who ever came out of Eastman. Considering his career, we would have been very embarrassed if he had been denied admission. Many years later, he followed me as president of the National Music Council, presiding over that organization of presidents with ability and imagination.

Another of our most gifted composer graduates had entrance difficulties of a somewhat different kind. I first met William Bergsma[3] when he was an undergraduate at Leland Stanford University. I was giving summer courses at the University of Southern California and conducting some Hollywood Bowl concerts. Bill came down from Stanford to attend my classes. It was again readily apparent that here was a great composition talent, and when he indicated that he would like to transfer to Eastman, I readily agreed. However, on arriving in Rochester, Bill also ran into formidable red tape. He was an undergraduate, and my classes were limited to graduate students.

I must admit that this problem had never occurred to me. My theory was the very first direct one, that any student who was ready for graduate

---

2   Peter Mennin (1923–83).
3   William Bergsma (1921–94).

classes should be admitted. William Bergsma's philosophy was even more direct. He had come to study with me. If he was denied admission to my class, he would return to California. Once again, I was wound up in the red tape of my own institution. As diplomatically as I could, I argued that, in unusual cases such as this, rules were made to be broken. My reasoning again prevailed.

William Bergsma began his professional career as a member of the Juilliard faculty, later leaving to accept the deanship of the School of Music of the University of Washington in Seattle. I am very fond of him and of his music. I believe that I am the only composer with whom he has ever "studied" composition, and I wish that I could claim credit for his sensitive and beautifully constructed scores. As in the case of Peter Mennin and other gifted graduates, I wonder if it is really possible to "teach" composition. It is, of course, possible to advise on technical matters, particularly in the fields of form and orchestration, but this is about all.

A third case of red-tape cutting was the most difficult, but the one which I handled the most expeditiously. It concerned the very talented Alec Wilder,[4] whose music is on the border frontier which lies between "serious" music and sophisticated jazz. Alec was completely uninterested in academic degrees and did not wish to register for any formal course. My only solution to this problem was to invite him to become a member of my class without telling anyone about it. It was strictly un-academic, irregular, and possibly educationally illegal. Pragmatically, however, it was a beautiful [idea] and probably the only solution. Although our backgrounds and interests were quite different, I do think that I was able to be of some help in purely practical musical matters, including the preparation of legible manuscripts!

In contrast, I remember one composer-student who nearly drove me out of my mind. He was talented but insisted on writing his music on long rolls of wrapping paper with the lines drawn in. As a teacher, I always liked to play the scores of my students at the piano, as I distrust the completely visual approach to an orchestral score. Score-reading of new works is a challenge under the most advantageous conditions. If you have ever tried to read at the piano an orchestra score written on rolls of wrapping paper, you have achieved the ultimate!

Many of my students, without deserting the field of composition, expanded their interests into adjacent areas, [including conducting]. I remember with pleasure two composers, Victor Allesandro (now

---

4   Alec Wilder (1907–80).

conductor of the San Antonio Symphony) and Richard Horner Bales[5] (conductor of the Orchestra of the National Gallery in Washington, DC).

I have never taught conducting, but it seemed to me imperative that the conducting talents of these two young men should be given some opportunity. Conducting courses in those days consisted primarily of classes in baton technique, given by the excellent American maestro, Paul White. Opportunities to work with a professional orchestra were hard to come by. The most practical solution seemed to be to invite my two young friends to attend my rehearsals with the Eastman-Rochester Orchestra, a professional orchestra which we used primarily for concerto concerts, American composer concerts, broadcasting, and recordings. At unexpected moments, I would "throw the baton" at one of them and ask them to rehearse so that I might go out in the hall and listen. It was a rough-and-ready educational technique, but it worked astonishingly well, as their eventual success proved quite conclusively.

Musical composition is tangent to so many other fields of musical scholarship and experimentation that it is not strange that some of our composers have expanded into these fields. For example, Gardner Read (who won the New York Philharmonic competition) has written what is probably the definitive book on the problems of musical notation.[6] Vladimir Ussachevsky[7] is one of the most prominent experimenters in the field of electronic music, and Paul Oncley[8] is making valuable contributions to the field of acoustics. Composers such as Leon Dallin[9] have written extensively on the problems of music theory, and Bernal Flores has followed my own research into a new theory of tone relations. Because of their interest in the education of the professional musician, many have been drawn into the academic field of music as deans, directors, and heads of music departments too numerous to list here.

---

5   Richard Bales (1915–98), American composer and conductor. He led the National Gallery Orchestra 1943–85.

6   *Music Notation: A Manual of Modern Practice*, first published in 1964.

7   Vladimir Ussachevsky (1911–90), Russian-born American composer. He graduated from the Eastman School of Music and then pursued additional studies with Otto Luening; member of the faculty at Columbia University 1964–80 and the University of Utah 1980–85.

8   Paul Oncley, a 1932 graduate of the Eastman School of Music, worked as a military acoustician and later as a research scientist at the Bell Telephone Laboratories.

9   Leon Dallin is perhaps best remembered for his *Techniques of Twentieth Century Composition: A Guide to the Materials of Modern Music*, first published in 1957, and then revised in 1964 and 1974.

Chapter Thirty-Five

AN AUTHOR AND A LECTURER

As a music theorist, I have always contended that the historical approach to music theory is not enough. The modern theorist should, of course, be able to analyze the music of the masters, to explain (as much as possible) the sources of their musical language. They should also, however, be able to suggest new paths, new theories, including those that break with creative and scholarly tradition.

This attitude has puzzled some of my academic colleagues, since I am in my own composition essentially a traditionalist. I do not believe that this is a contradiction or an inconsistency. A composer may, in his writing, look both experimentally forward toward the future and backward with appreciation and understanding to the past. The theorist, in my opinion, should do the same.

On this assumption, I began as long as forty years ago an intensive study of the resources of the twelve-note chromatic scale. This resulted in the publication in 1960 of a rather complex volume, with the title *The Harmonic Materials of Modern Music*, and the subtitle "Resources of the Tempered Scale."

The purpose of the book [was] to analyze *every* possible combination of tones in the twelve-tone equally tempered scale, the scale which has served music from the time of Johann Sebastian Bach up to the present time. Much of this material has, of course, been used in the music of the seventeenth, eighteenth, nineteenth, and twentieth centuries. Curiously enough, however, much of the theoretically available material has <u>not</u> been used, primarily because it did not fit into the musical-aesthetic pattern of any particular period of musical composition. By examining <u>all</u> of the material available, it [was] my hope to expand the young composer's musical vocabulary and yet, at the same time, build his musical communication firmly on logical principles.

The entire theory is, obviously, too complex to be presented with any completeness in a short space of time. Nevertheless, the basic plan is, I believe, quite understandable, even to the layman. The theory equates the twelve-tone scale with its geometric counterpart, the dodecahedron, and delving into the relationship between the twelve "points" of that figure. A simpler explanation might be the division of a circle into twelve equal parts.

Examining such a circle, it will be readily apparent that there are six basic relationships. These will be the clockwise relationship of *1* to *2, 1* to *3, 1* to *4, 1* to *5, 1* to *6,* [and *1* to *7*]. Each of these six relationships has its complementary counterclockwise relationship, that is *1* to *11, 1* to *10, 1* to *9, 1* to *8, 1* to *7,* and the duplicate relationship *1* to *6.*

Reduced to musical terms, this gives us fundamentally six "galaxies" of tonal relationships. Within these galaxies there are, of course, a multitude [of] different possibilities, <u>not</u> an infinite number. Each galaxy has its own characteristics, and by mixing the different ingredients of any one, or combining one with another, the tonal palette offers an enormous range of expression.

It is fascinating to observe by studying the music of both the past and present, that composers can quite easily be "classified" according to the predilection of the individual composer. A composer such as Palestrina writes almost exclusively in the fifth category. Mozart and Beethoven cling for the most part to the same relationship, but expand frequently into the second, and even the third category. Wagner, on the other hand, makes extended use of the sixth and third categories, and it is not until the more dissonant of the contemporary composers that the first category is extensively used, frequently in combination with the sixth.

This theory, therefore, seemed to me to offer the young composer not only signposts to the future but also a more accurate understanding of the past. I have always objected to the subjective categories which music critics and writers on music are inclined to use so freely: for example the terms "classical" and "romantic." Brahms was certainly in the form of his symphonies a classicist. In their emotional connotations, however, he was an undeniable "romantic." The same thing may be said of Beethoven, and even of Mozart and Bach. For this reason, a factual description of the composer in terms of his personal musical vocabulary (which can be studied and analyzed) seems to have more meaning, both to the musician and to the layman.

New theories of this kind are bound to encounter opposition both from the right and the left. The conservatives are quite willing to stay with the theories of the past, either for reasons of loyalty or apathy. The radicals are somewhat inclined to resent the imposition of order on what seems to them to be a completely "free" art. Yet, in all art there is an order which cannot be contravened. A dissonance is what it is and leaves its own impression upon the ear and mind of the listener. A combination of this consonance with that dissonance produces its own effect, differing from every dissimilar combination. The Beethoven Ninth could not exist without the fifth category of sound. *Tristan and Isolde* could not exist without the sixth category.

On the other hand, the indiscriminate mixing of categories without control can very easily become a jumble, comparable with what might happen if one put together a sentence consisting of a series of words, each of which was the first word on successive pages of the dictionary, without regard to its "meaning." An example might be, "A abandon abatized aberuncate."

Although my philosophy of music theory is still far from general acceptance, there is evidence that its influence is steadily growing. Its study at the present time seems to be limited to graduate divisions of music schools, but it does seem to be filtering down to undergraduate levels.

About the time of my retirement from Eastman, I accepted [the position] of editor-in-chief of the Scribner Music Library, which after many years [was] being completely revised and reedited. In connection with this library, Nicholas Slonimsky and I are writing a volume on music history and theory, of which he is undertaking the historical aspect and I the theoretical.[1] The theoretical section will include both the classic and the "revolutionary" approach, the latter in a much simplified and more easily understood form.

In addition to my theoretical writings, I have presented innumerable papers, many of which have been presented as lectures in various colleges and universities. The forum for these presentations [has] included commencement speeches, papers before the National Association of Schools of Music, the Music Teachers' National Association, the Music Educators' National Conference, the National Music Council, and even the American Acoustical Society. The subjects have varied from historical, theoretical, and pedagogical [issues], to lectures which were quite frankly propaganda for American music.

These have from time to time subjected me to attacks from "liberals" as a chauvinist. Perhaps these criticisms have some validity, but I have always believed that, as the French saying goes, "It is necessary for everyone to cultivate his own garden." In other words, American music will never be developed in Italy, Germany, or France. If the young American composer is not given an opportunity for growth in his own country, there can never be a creative American art. Koussevitzky expressed it in more general, more eloquent terms, when he remarked that each musical

---

1   Hanson's manuscript speaks of this project in the present tense, suggesting that he was currently working on it.

generation must pay its debt to the past by developing the music of the present and the future.

It is a philosophy which seems to me to be completely logical. It has, quite obviously, undertones of nationalism, but it is this very nationalism which has been responsible for the development of the great periods of musical composition in Italy, Austria, Germany, France, Spain, and most recently Russia. Other countries, for example Sweden, which has always been essentially international in its artistic viewpoint, have never become more than museums for the art of other countries. Of recent years, even Sweden is showing increasing concern for its own composers through subsidies for the performance, publication, recording, and dissemination of their music. I have never been able to see how this can be equated with political (and especially military) nationalism. It is, to the contrary, simply cultivating one's own garden, making one's own contribution to the world's store of music.

The reason for this prejudice against any form of Americanism in art can be explained by the historic fact that the United States has never declared its artistic independence. In the early days of our musical development, we were under almost complete domination of the Germans and Austrians in instrumental music, and of the Italians in opera. Later we came under strong French influence, and more recently under Russian and Hungarian domination. We have never had much of a chance to develop our own indigenous approach, except in the field of popular music.

I have always been a little amused and perhaps also slightly bitter about the double standard of nationalism. A Frenchman who works with devotion for the propagation of French music is considered a patriot and a man of good taste. If he is sufficiently devoted, he will probably receive from the grateful French government some version of the *Légion d'honneur*. An American who does the same things for his own country will probably be condemned as a chauvinist, a nationalist (a bad word when applied to Americans), and perhaps even a fascist!

Two lectures given [at] Harvard[2] recall this predicament. I had been invited, to my great surprise, to inaugurate the Louis Elson[3] lectures in Harvard College in memory of that pioneer in musical theory and scholarship. Harvard, with its (at that time) one-sided approach to the study of

---

2   Hanson wished to give the date but left it blank.
3   Louis Elson (1848–1920), American music historian, writer, and editor. He was music editor of the *Boston Advertiser* 1886–1920, and a lecturer at New England Conservatory.

music [and] with its complete devotion to musical scholarship as opposed to performance, had never been my favorite university.

I was, therefore, greatly surprised and also pleased at the invitation. I carefully prepared two lectures. The first had to do with what seemed to me to be the problems which were delaying the development of a creative approach to music in the United States. I suggested that, if we were ever to make our own contribution to the world's music, it was high time that these conditions be remedied. My second lecture was a detailed historical account of the development of composition in the United States, from the beginning of the Republic up to the present time.

In the audience was the distinguished musicologist and librarian, Otto Kinkeldey, who was at the time a visiting professor at Harvard. At the conclusion of the lectures, he told me with a frankness which I valued that he felt that my first lecture was "pure propaganda." "Your second lecture, on the other hand," he said, "was a splendid historic document."

A quite different but most exciting experience was the opportunity of speaking on the subject of music appreciation to an audience of twenty thousand school administrators at their convention in Atlantic City. I was invited to bring with me (at the expense of the convention) the entire Eastman Symphony Orchestra so that I might illustrate the lecture with live musical examples.

The demonstration was a complete success. I have always objected to the fact that most musicians spend their lives lecturing to other musicians about the importance of music! Here was an opportunity to speak to the men who were superintendents and principals of American high schools from every part of the country on the place of music in the high school curriculum. It was an unforgettable experience.

The lecture upon which I probably spent the most care was in Philadelphia.[4] I had just been elected a member of the American Philosophical Society, certainly the most important society of its kind in the United States, with its membership going back to Benjamin Franklin. In addition to its enormous prestige, I was conscious of the fact that there had been, in its history of two centuries, only two musicians who had ever been elected to membership.

As I have said before, I have always enjoyed speaking and have never been subject to stage fright, which is common among public speakers. On this occasion, I must admit [that] I was worried. My listeners were, for the most part, scientists and [others who were] eminent in their various fields. My paper was on the "galaxies of sound," to which I have already referred,

---

[4] Again, Hanson wished to include the date but did not supply the information.

and I prepared it with the greatest care. The reception of the paper was fascinating. I found this most distinguished audience very much interested in the presentation of an essentially "scientific" paper on musical creation. The question-and-answer period which followed was most stimulating, and it gave me new stimulus for continuing my rather unorthodox studies.

I recall a similar experience in speaking on the same subject [to] the Association for the Advancement of Science in Atlanta, Georgia. My paper was scheduled for the mathematics division of the conference. I was somewhat perturbed, since I can lay no claim to professional competence in this field. My fears, however, were considerably abated by the remarks of the speaker before me. He was a theoretical mathematician, a professor from Columbia University. His remarks, as I recall them, were something like this: "The common conception of a theoretical mathematician is someone who proceeds from a to b, then from b to c, and finally from y to z. As a matter of fact, what we really do is to take the inductive leap and say to ourselves, Let's go back and see if we can prove it." Perhaps art and science are, after all, not too far apart.

Chapter Thirty-Six

AN INVITATION FROM THE STATE DEPARTMENT

The year 1961–62 provided me with the most fantastic opportunity of testing some of my favorite theories, theories having to do not only with music education in the United States and its practical results "under fire," but equally important, basic philosophies about music itself and its importance as a means of communication across language barriers.

I had been for some years a member of the advisory music panel of the Department of State, concerned with the sending abroad of musical organizations of the United States on the Cultural Exchange Program. These ensembles had included many of the great symphony orchestras of the country (including Philadelphia, Boston, New York, and Cleveland), string quartets, other chamber music organizations, vocal groups, popular music groups, in fact a rather complete cross-section of our musical activities.

Many of the ensembles met with great success, but it did not seem to me that the effect of the tours was all that it might be. After all, the Philadelphia Orchestra and Eugene Ormandy, the Cleveland Orchestra and George Szell, the New York Philharmonic and Leonard Bernstein were hardly unknown to European audiences. The reputations of [the] conductors and orchestras were well-established, and their appearance on State Department–sponsored tours did not really prove anything which was not already known. We had heard too often the cynical remark that the United States was proving that it had the money with which to "buy" the best orchestras in the world.

If a part of the program was for the purpose of showing our foreign friends (and enemies) that the United States was not exclusively a nation of bathtub manufacturers, it seemed to me that we had to present something different, something that was indigenous, home-grown in the strictest sense. I argued without success for the sending abroad of the National High School Orchestra of Interlochen. It seemed to me that European audiences could not fail but be impressed with such a talented group of American teenagers, although I could see that the logistic problems would be formidable.

The idea, however, was beginning to take hold, and in the summer of 1960 a number of music schools in the United States received invitations from the Brussels Exposition to present their student orchestras in concerts. This was not the type of thing I had in mind, and on behalf of the Eastman School I declined the invitation. William Schuman,[1] the distinguished American composer and president of the Juilliard School of Music, did accept, and the Juilliard School Orchestra represented the United States most acceptably, not only at the Brussels Fair but [also] in concerts in England and Scandinavia.

The following winter, the department extended an invitation to the University of Michigan to send its famous concert band under the direction of William Revelli[2] for a long tour of Europe. This also proved highly successful and paved the way for the invitation from the State Department to the Eastman School to present its student orchestra in a tour under the department's sponsorship.

There were several unique points about this proposal. It would be the first student symphony to present an extended tour of three months in the winter concert season, following to a considerable extent the same path traveled by our country's famous professional orchestras. Furthermore, the concerts would include not only [Western] Europe but also the Middle East, Poland, and Russia. The tour would not be limited to appearances in academic centers, but would include sophisticated music centers such as Berlin, Moscow, and Leningrad.

We had already organized at Eastman an orchestra, [the Eastman Philharmonia], which I hoped could undertake successfully such a challenge. It was an orchestra composed of the most talented orchestral performers in the school. The players were selected strictly by audition, with no regard for academic seniority. In other words, if the best oboist was a freshman, he would receive the solo oboe position. Furthermore, all members selected for the tour were made to understand that they were undertaking a highly important personal as well as musical [responsibility], that they would be in a very real sense "musical ambassadors." It seemed to me that this combination of musical talent and personality was essential.

The logistics of getting a student orchestra of symphonic proportions ready for an extended tour of foreign countries presented tremendous problems. They included not only the tasks of preparing suitable programs which would be acceptable to both concert managers and audiences, but

---

1   William Schuman (1910–92), American composer and music administrator. He won the 1943 Pulitzer Prize for his cantata, *A Free Song*.

2   William Revelli (1902–94), famed conductor of bands at the University of Michigan 1935–71.

[also] the seemingly endless problems concerned with harp trunks, cello trunks, huge trunks for double basses, music, music stands, wardrobe trunks, and the like. Added to these were the problems involving the personnel. These included not only the familiar involvement with such matters as passports and immunizations, but also legal permission from parents, since many of the players were under eighteen years of age.[3]

There was one particular problem: the problem of cost. In spite of the fact that no one, including the conductors received more than the usual per diem expense, the cost of transporting a large orchestra to Europe and touring vast expanses of territory was formidable, and the budget of the State Department for the Cultural Exchange Program was limited. I was under considerable pressure from the Assistant Secretary of State for Cultural Affairs, to take abroad only a chamber symphony. However, I insisted that, if we attempted the tour at all, it must be with a full symphony complement, capable of playing not only the standard repertoire, but [also] the large scores of contemporary music.

It was a long battle involving many conferences, but our judgment finally prevailed. We even received permission to include additional associate solo players, so that we would be protected in case of illness. The personnel finally included twenty-six violins, eight violas, eight cellos, six double basses, four flutes and piccolo, four oboes and English horn, six French horns, four trumpets, four trombones, tuba, timpani, four percussion, two harps, and piano, certainly not the largest orchestra possible, but large enough to perform a varied repertoire.

In preparing for the tour, the orchestra made a number of appearances both in and outside Rochester, the most important being a concert at the Second Inter-American Festival, held under the auspices of the Pan-American Union. The other orchestras invited to participated included the National Symphony of Washington, the Orquesta Nacional of Mexico, and the Canadian Broadcasting Orchestra of Toronto. The Eastman Philharmonic [also] appeared before the Music Educators' National Conference in Buffalo and presented a program before an audience of some twenty thousand school administrators in Atlantic City.

On November 24, [1961], we left Rochester by plane for New York, cheered on our way by a huge congregation of well-wishers who came to wish us success and safety on our musical safari. This was especially gratifying to me because our decision to embark on this mission had not met with unanimous approval. Although it was generally agreed that the City

---

3   This is certainly untrue, and it is unclear why Hanson would make such a statement. Few, if any, members of the orchestra were under the age of eighteen.

of Rochester was greatly honored by the State Department's invitation, there were those who frowned on the necessity to remove students from their classes for a three-month period.

The most amusing objection came from a few officers of the Rochester Civic Music Association, the organization which sponsors the Rochester Philharmonic Orchestra. For years, they had bemoaned the "necessity" of having students in the Rochester Philharmonic, although there had been a large contingent of advanced students in the orchestra ever since its inception. Now suddenly the tune remained the same, but the words had changed. "How could the Rochester Philharmonic exist without the presence of these advanced student performers, most of whom would go with the Eastman Philharmonic on its tour?"[4]

The group which left New York City the night of November 24 consisted of the members of the orchestra and its two conductors (Dr. Frederick Fennell and I); concert manager Robert Sattler, on whose shoulders fell the heavy burden of supervising the entire operation; librarian Donald Jones; stage manager Arthur Achock; property manager Gino DePalma; Dr. Jacques Lipson, our physician, and Mrs. Lipson; and finally our two charming chaperones, Peggie Hanson and Virginia (Mrs. Robert) Sattler.

We left New York by Iberia Airlines in a storm and arrived in Lisbon early the next morning, after a not-too-restful night.[5] To complicate matters further, our two harps had been sent on to Madrid by mistake, and the evening's program included Repighi's *Fountains of Rome*, [which] demanded two harps. Contrary to our fears, everything went smoothly. The two harps arrived in time, the orchestra had apparently recovered from its all-night flight, the audience was both cordial and enthusiastic, and the critics warm in their praise the next morning. We were apparently off to a good start.

---

4   Although Hanson seems to belittle the concerns of the Rochester Philharmonic, the orchestra did stand to lose about twenty of its players during the three-month tour.

5   Hanson's memory does not serve him well. The departure from New York was delayed for more than three hours, and the arrival in Lisbon was at around noon.

Figure 26. Howard Hanson with his father.

Figure 27. Howard Hanson with his mother in front of Cutler Union in Rochester, New York.

Figure 28. Howard Hanson and Margaret Nelson at their wedding.

Figure 29. Howard Hanson.

Figure 30. Howard Hanson with his mother.

Figure 31. Howard and Margaret (Peggie) Hanson.

Figure 32. Howard Hanson.

Figure 33. Howard Hanson.

Figure 34. Howard Hanson conducting the Eastman Rochester Symphony in a recording session.

Figure 35. Howard Hanson conducting.

Figure 36. Howard Hanson studying a score.

Chapter Thirty-Seven

THE EASTMAN PHILHARMONIA TOUR (I)

We were scheduled for concerts in Spain the next ten days, including the cities of Madrid, Seville, Valencia, and Barcelona. It was at the first of these concerts in Madrid that an incident occurred which, in a strange way, ensured the success of the entire tour. Our European manager, Anatole Heller of Paris, met us in Madrid, and I had the impression that he was not overly pleased at having the job of presenting a tour by a student orchestra. Although he was both friendly and courteous, I could tell that he was also a bit apprehensive, even though he had received good reports on our initial Lisbon appearance.

A mechanical deficiency changed everything. We were in the middle of a movement of the *Firebird Suite* of Stravinsky when the lights suddenly went out. Both the stage and the audience were in darkness. I knew that we had rehearsed the work many times, and I decided to try to carry on in the darkness. The orchestra accepted the challenge and responded brilliantly. We stopped at the end of the movement, and the lights came on.

The audience was ecstatic in its applause. Indeed, here was a phenomenon, an orchestra so well-trained that it could play from memory in the dark. The critics were equally impressed. Luis Gomez, writing in the *Hoja del Lunes*, expressed the general opinion when he wrote, "We expected to hear a student orchestra, with its appeal and also its defects. What an agreeable surprise to find that the Eastman orchestra is equal to professional orchestras."

The story of the orchestra's triumph was widely disseminated by the press both in Europe and in the United States. Mr. Heller was convinced that he had no ordinary student orchestra on his hands. The orchestra's reputation spread rapidly, and we [no] longer felt that in each concert we were "on trial."

The students proved to be excellent ambassadors as well as musicians. In Madrid, the members of the orchestra were the guests of the students of the University of Madrid. It was known that some of the Spanish students held anti-American sentiments, blaming the United States for its "support" of General Franco.[1] Our students refused to be drawn into any political confrontation, saying that they were here on a musical mission. The meeting ended in a spirit of friendship with felicitations on both sides. Only in Barcelona did we encounter any hostility. At a dinner given by the United States consul, several Catalans present as guests of the consul were unbelievably rude, acting as though we were individually and personally responsible for Generalissimo Franco![2] This was, however, most unusual. For almost the entire tour, we were received with the greatest courtesy.

When we arrived in Seville, we found a great part of the city under water following severe floods. The theater in which we were scheduled to perform was flooded, and we were forced to move to a smaller theater which could not accommodate the entire audience. As a result, many of the audience stood during the entire concert. With the permission of the US authorities, we were able to donate the entire proceeds of the concert to the relief of those who had suffered from the flood. Quite apart from the material help involved, the gesture did no harm to our standing as "friendly ambassadors."

We left Spain and Portugal with happy memories of their friendly audiences and departed for Fribourg, Switzerland, to give a concert in the ancient University of Fribourg. The atmosphere of the university was quite different from that of our Spanish audiences, but equally fascinating. The concert was in the great convocation hall of the university, a hall with unexpectedly good acoustics. We were greeted with great dignity by the chancellor, the welcoming speeches being (as I recall) in French and Latin. I would have given a great deal to have been able to respond with classic tongue. I could have made it in Italian, but my high school Latin was too far behind me. The entire experience, including the town of Fribourg itself, had a kind of a medieval atmosphere which lingers pleasantly in my memory.

One part of the experience was memorable but not so pleasant. I should have explained that transportation of the orchestra through Europe was by planes, three altogether, of which two were passenger planes and one a cargo plane for instruments and baggage. They were old but sturdy "prop" planes, chartered from the British Air Lines. Since, however, there was no adequate airport in Fribourg, it was necessary to land in

---

1   Francisco Franco (1892–1975), military general and ruler of Spain 1936–75.

2   The people of Catalonia, with a distinct language and culture, were particularly resentful of the Franco regime.

Geneva and proceed to Fribourg by automobile.[3] The scenery was magnificent, with the Alps above and the lake below, but transportation in the hands of a virtuoso chauffeur was at a speed that was literally breathtaking. It was bad enough going up, but much worse coming down! We did miraculously arrive back in Geneva in one piece to find our three planes patiently waiting. (What a heady feeling it is to know that the plane will not leave until you are ready.)

Our next concert was in the delightful city of Rennes, France. We debarked in Paris and then [went] by [automobile] through the lovely countryside to Rennes. According to some quaint but charming custom of the [Rochester] Chamber of Commerce, Rennes had been designated as a "twin" city of Rochester.[4] Perhaps for this reason, we were received with special pomp and ceremony, including a formal "state banquet" with speeches by the mayor, the chancellor of the University of Rennes, and (it seemed) a multitude of other dignitaries, including officialdom from Paris. By this time, I had acquired the technique of responding (appropriately but certainly briefly) to the ceremonial felicitations.

I do not remember very much about the concert, but I do recall the city itself. The hotel accommodations left something to be desired. I recall that the floor of the bathroom sloped at about a five-degree angle. The town itself was beautiful, with an architectural atmosphere [reflecting] pre-Republic days. We were also fortunately allowed time to do some exploring of the neighboring country, [including] historic Saint Michel, which we all swarmed over like children on a holiday.

Rennes was followed by, of all things, a whole free day and night in Paris. Many of the students took the opportunity to see and hear the Paris Opera. I must confess that Peggie and I used the evening for the less cultural experience of the Café de Paris. Fortunately, on a long tour such as this, comedy occasionally shows its charming face, banishing (at least for a time) the tension of concert performances. Luxembourg was such an occasion. We were supposed to leave by plane for that city the following morning, but the weather was impossible. We finally got as far as Brussels, but here the weather closed in on us completely.

Our Luxembourg concert was unfortunately a matinee, and the problem of arriving on time was acute.[5] After a number of telephone calls, it was decided to charter buses for the orchestra and trucks for the baggage

---

3   Hanson speaks here and elsewhere of the discomfort of travel by car. The orchestra members, however, made such journeys by bus, a far less comfortable experience.
4   The correct phrase is "sister city."
5   In fact, the concert was at 5:00 p.m.

[to] get there as soon as was physically possible. We arrived, as I recall, about an hour late, but found a large audience patiently awaiting us. To our dismay, we discovered that, although we had arrived, the truck which contained our wardrobe trunks had not.

The stage was, of course, bare, since the men handling those very important duties had not arrived. We all set about moving chairs and, when necessary, improvising music stands. The stage was soon in order, but dressing for the concert was another problem. Since the important thing was to give some kind of a concert for the patient audience, we decided to improvise our dress to the best of our ability. I recall conducting the performance in striped trousers, with brown shoes, a blue shirt, and a red tie. The members of the orchestra appeared in equally casual costumes. I explained to the delighted audience that we did not usually dress in this manner for a concert performance.

The concert was a huge success and, I must say, the orchestra played beautifully, although everyone was tired and hungry. When we arrived at the intermission and went off stage, we found to our delight that the kind [people of] Luxembourg had quickly assembled a buffet for the entire orchestra. We happily munched on sandwiches until it was time to go back and finish the concert. Just a short time ago, my wife met a couple who had attended our Luxembourg concert. They said that the people of Luxembourg, were still talking about it with affection eight years later.

We had a little time the next day to see something of the charming little country and to stand with awe in the American cemetery, where thousands of white crosses mark the graves of the American war dead. The memorial erected in their honor is simple and most impressive. I can never lose the memory of those seemingly infinite rows of white crosses.

The great American hero to the natives of Luxembourg is, of course, General Patton,[6] whose army saved the tiny duchy from being overrun by German soldiers. One story, which was unknown to me, illustrates the grim humor of those war days.[7] It seems that a division of American troops was surrounded by the Germans. The story goes that the German general demanded their surrender. Receiving no satisfactory reply, the German

---

　　6　George Patton (1885–1945), American general and commander of the US Third Army during the final stages of World War II. His career was marred by controversy, resulting from his notorious independence and outspoken nature, but he was one of the most distinguished and effective military leaders of his generation.

　　7　Hanson here relates the story of Bastogne during the famous Battle of the Bulge, the last major German counter-offensive of the war.

general sent a captured American soldier to the officer commanding the surrounded American troops.

When the emissary returned, the German general demanded, "Was hat er gesagt?" ["What did he have to say?] To which the American prisoner replied, "The American general said, "Nuts!" The German general did not understand. "Was ist das Nutz? Ist positiv oder negativ?" ["What is this nuts? Is it positive or negative?] To which the American soldier replied, "It is positively negative!"

Before leaving Luxembourg, we were invited to a farewell luncheon at which the native wine of the duchy was served. My wife always followed the diplomatic axiom that, if you can find something nice to say about the country you are visiting, by all means say it. [Therefore, she] remarked on the excellence of the local wine. "Is it possible to buy this wine in the United States?" she asked. Her host said that he thought it could be bought only at one shop in Chicago. When Peggie asked why they could not secure wider distribution, her host replied sadly, "I guess it is because we drink the rest of it ourselves."

Chapter Thirty-Eight

THE EASTMAN PHILHARMONIA TOUR (II)

Our short stay in Belgium, where we gave concerts in Louvain and Brussels, was pleasant but uneventful. The performance in Louvain took place in the famous old Catholic university of that name, where the atmosphere reminded us somewhat of the University of Fribourg. Since Louvain is only a short distance from Brussels, it was possible for us to stay at an excellent hotel overlooking a beautiful park in Brussels and commute by car to Louvain, a pleasant change from some of our previous "one-night stands."

The most memorable event about our Brussels concert was the [pleasure] of meeting the late Herbert Hoover Jr., [who was] at that time US ambassador to Belgium. I had always been a great admirer of his father, although I had never met him. The ambassador proved to be most gracious and quite enthusiastic about the success of our tour. There were a good many students from the University of Brussels at the concert, which resulted in one mildly amusing incident. We had used Sousa's "Stars and Stripes Forever" as our final encore at most of our concerts, which was invariably received with great enthusiasm. When we played it in Brussels, the reception was more than enthusiastic. It was positively boisterous, or perhaps I should say "rowdyish." We learned later that the tune [from] the trio of the march had been used for a student song of a very lewd character. The students were delighted—we considerably less so.

Of the entire tour, my only real disappointment came in our brief visit to Sweden. Perhaps I had expected too much. As I have said, both of my parents were born in Sweden. I had been honored many years before by election to membership in the Royal Academy of Music and had received a minor decoration from the king for my participation in the celebration of the tercentenary of the founding of the Swedish settlement in Delaware.

I suppose that, at least subconsciously, I expected some kind of special red-carpet treatment. This we did not get. We played only two concerts, one in the beautiful new concert hall in Gothenburg [i.e., Göteborg] on the west coast, the other in the medieval University of Uppsala. The weather was bitterly cold, the audience small and apathetic. We had no opportunity of playing in Stockholm, even though we stayed in the spacious Grand Hotel of that city overlooking the canal, commuting to

Uppsala. I must say that Stockholm's leading newspaper did send its principal critic to review the Gothenburg concert, for which he wrote a most complimentary review.

I must also admit that our lukewarm reception was not entirely the fault of the Swedes. For example, we found that, although our Gothenburg concert was sponsored by the University of Gothenburg, our State Department officials had scheduled the concert during the Christmas vacation period. For the Swedes, the Christmas season is a period of extensive celebration and certainly the worst possible time for the visit of a foreign orchestra.

Our visit to the University of Uppsala was equally dispiriting. Arriving at the University by car from Stockholm, we found no one to greet us, and the convocation hall where we were to play [was] securely locked. After wandering about for some time, we finally found someone to let us in and eventually were met by the chancellor of the university, who sat with my wife during the concert.

The convocation hall proved to be a great room with a high-domed ceiling and the worst acoustics imaginable. I have always preferred "live" halls, but this was too much! A loud chord in the brass would ascend to the dome and echo back and forth for about five seconds. I recall that we opened the program with my own arrangement of the Purcell *Dioclesian Suite* for woodwinds, brass, and strings (much of it antiphonal). At the end of each section, we stopped to allow the sound above us to disperse before going on to the next, a disconcerting experience.

Again, as in Gothenburg, the university was in its vacation period, and the students for whom the concert was supposed to be given were not there to hear it. Then, too, the atmosphere of the university, unlike the universities of Fribourg and Louvain, was quite "stuffy" and not particularly cordial. I remarked to some of my Swedish friends in the United States that I imagined that all good Swedes had migrated to the United States. We did enjoy our short stay in Stockholm, certainly one of the world's loveliest cities. With its canals and waterways, it lives up to its title of the "Venice of the North," just as beautiful and much cleaner! We were glad, however, to leave the not-too-hospitable shores of my mother and father's homeland for the far-away shores of Greece.

The flight from Stockholm to Athens, even in our propeller-driven planes was delightful, and the view of the Alps from above was breathtaking and a bit "scary." As we approached Greece, our first view was of the fabled Mount Parnassus. It seemed hard to realize that there really was such a mountain, that it was not just a legend. I am sure that it also brought back to some of us our early days of piano practice on a pretty deadly set of exercises titled "Gradus ad Parnassum."[1] The mountain was much prettier with its peak partially veiled in the clouds below us.

Our concerts in Athens were in happy contrast to our Swedish experience. The audiences were receptive and enthusiastic, and once again we were running out of encores. The concerts marked also the first appearance with the orchestra of our very gifted associate director, Frederick Fennell. When we began the tour, it was my understanding that we would move more slowly, playing at least two concerts in all major cities. It was my thought, therefore, that Dr. Fennell and I might alternate the conducting chores. I reckoned without the local concert manager, forgetting that he also had something to say about the concerts. As a result, when it was discovered that there would be, for example, only one concert in Madrid rather than two (a condition which existed until we came to Athens), the local manager would insist that the principal conductor conduct [the one] concert. I hasten to add that this had nothing to do with the quality of the conductors. If Mr. Black were the conductor and Mr. Blue the associate conductor, the concert [manager] would insist on Mr. Black.

In Athens, for the first time we gave more than one concert, and I was delighted to turn over the baton to my gifted associate. Dr. Fennell's success with the Athens audience was tremendous. I am sure that the Philharmonia, having played a dozen successive concerts under me, was glad to have a change. In any case, he made a profound impression on the Athenians, who gave him a rousing ovation.[2]

The cultural affairs office, now in charge of the music division of the USIA[3] in Washington, offered us every courtesy. The members of the orchestra had a chance to see some of the historic scenes of modern and ancient Greece. The Sattlers, my wife and I, however, had too many diplomatic housekeeping chores to attend to and saw little of the surrounding country. Peggie and I did have one unexpected sightseeing experience which we shall never forget. We were staying in a hotel across from the principal square of the city. The morning after our arrival, we ordered breakfast in our room. Before sitting down to the table, I raised the

---

1   Hanson is referring to the technical studies composed by Muzio Clementi (1752–1832).

2   Hanson was subjected to much criticism, especially from members of the orchestra, for not allowing Fennell to conduct more concerts on the tour. Fennell only conducted nine of the forty-nine concerts presented by the orchestra, also sharing the conducting responsibilities for three others. Perhaps Hanson is being slightly disingenuous in claiming his all-too-frequent appearances on the podium were due to circumstances beyond his control.

3   United States Information Agency.

window shade. There, framed directly in the center of the window, stood the Acropolis. No artist could have framed a picture so effectively. What a way to be introduced to one of the world's masterpieces of architecture!

Christmas was almost upon us, and the State Department had very generously scheduled two concerts and three days of vacation [on] the fabulous island of Cyprus, in the pastoral city of Nicosia. We were housed in a rambling but very comfortable hotel, from which we made many excursions into the countryside.

I doubt that the small city had heard many (if any) symphony concerts, and the audiences were quite ecstatic. They wanted us to perform the Gershwin *Rhapsody in Blue*, but the theater where we played had no piano. As a matter of fact, there was only one grand piano on the island, and the owner would not let it out of his hands, even for one concert. Therefore, there was no Gershwin.

We were royally entertained by the representative of the Eastman Kodak Company, incidentally the only representative of the [company] whom we met on the entire tour. We also had a grand Christmas party with all of its trimmings, presented to us by a member of our own foreign staff. We were quite overwhelmed by his generosity, until some weeks later when we received a letter from the hotel, enclosing the bill for the party—quite a bill!

For Peggie and me, the most exciting excursions were the climb to the ruins of the medieval castle of St. Hilary (reputed to have been built by Richard the Lion-Hearted returning from the Crusades) and a visit to the ancient fortress on the coast. The great personal experience was the opportunity of meeting Prime Minister Makarios.[4] On Christmas Eve, we had made pilgrimages to two orphanages, one Turkish and one Greek, bringing with us presents for the youngsters there. When we approached the Greek orphanage, we found the entrance guarded by soldiers and discovered that the prime minister was inside the orphanage on a similar mission.

When we told the guards the purpose of our visit, we were very quickly permitted to enter. On meeting Prime Minister Makarios, he graciously suggested that we present our presents to the youngsters at the same time. Among other presents, Robert Sattler was handing out bags of candy, including "tootsie rolls." When the prime minister asked what they were, Bob offered him a tootsie roll, which he manfully accepted and ate on the spot.

---

4   Archbishop Makarios (1913–77), archbishop and primate of the Cypriote Orthodox Church. Born Mihail Christodolou Mouskos, he became the first president of Cyprus in 1959, serving three terms in that position.

Later we were invited to the palace of the prime minister, who personally showed us about the grounds and presented Peggie, Ginnie Sattler, and Dorothy Fennell with roses which he picked from his garden. Peggie told him that we were going to concertize in Russia in February and invited him to come along as our spiritual advisor! He took her gentle ribbing in very good part, and we enjoyed a most interesting conversation.

Sometime later, talking with an American diplomat, I commented on the remarkable charm and personality of Prime Minister Makarios. He agreed completely but added that anyone who stood in the way of his ambitions for the Greeks in Cyprus would be—and he made a slashing gesture to the throat. I suppose that this is to some degree true of any man in public life charged with both great power and great responsibility. It is difficult for us to think of Prime Minister Makarios except as a most charming host.

Chapter Thirty-Nine

THE EASTMAN PHILHARMONIA TOUR (III)

Our idyllic holiday in Nicosia was followed by a strenuous two weeks in Syria, Egypt, Lebanon, and Turkey. Our concert in Aleppo, Syria, was the scene of a rather touching experience. While we were in Nicosia, I received a letter from the American Embassy in Damascus. The ambassador informed me that, as far as he knew, the citizens of Aleppo had never heard their national anthem played by a symphony orchestra. As a matter of fact, he did not know whether there was a symphonic arrangement of the Syrian national anthem in existence. Could I possibly orchestrate and perform it in Aleppo.

My first reaction was that the time was so limited as to make it impossible. On second thought, however, the idea was so intriguing that I called in our orchestral librarian, Don Jones, and told him that I would be willing to sit up all night and make an arrangement of the piano score (which the ambassador had sent me) if he would be willing to copy the parts. He readily agreed, and a day or two later we opened our concert with the Syrian national anthem. I was later told that our performance of my arrangement of the Syrian national anthem was recorded, and that it was used to begin and end each day's broadcasts from Damascus. It would be interesting to know whether, in these tense days in the Middle East, an American's orchestration of the Syrian anthem is still being used. Incidentally, it proved to be one of the more attractive of the world's national anthems.

In other respects, the atmosphere of the Aleppo concert was somewhat tense. The town and the audience seemed to be pretty well divided between pro-Nasser and anti-Nasser sentiments.[1] At the beginning of the concert, I was introduced by the mayor of the city, who used the occasion for what was apparently a political harangue. This was received with applause and hisses by the audience, and during the intermission one party or the other exploded a bomb in the courtyard of the theater. Apparently, no one was injured, and the concert proceeded in comparative calm.

---

1   For three years (1958–61) Syria had joined with Egypt to form the United Arab Republic under the leadership of Egyptian President Gamal Abdal Nasser. The decision to secede from this union of the two countries was controversial, dividing many Syrians into pro-Nasser and anti-Nasser positions.

The morning following the concert, we left for the small and rather dismal airport which served Aleppo. There we found communications awaiting us from the American embassy indicating that our upcoming concerts in Egypt were in deep trouble. There was some kind of diplomatic stalemate between the French and Egyptian governments. France, according to one report, had excluded certain Egyptian citizens, and Egypt was reciprocating by barring French citizens. This did not, of course, affect the members of our orchestra. Unfortunately, however, the associate manager of our European representatives, Carlotta Flatow, who was with us at the time representing Anatole Heller, was a French citizen. Even more important from a practical standpoint, the man in charge of all of our instruments and baggage, Edouard Ebner, although born in Egypt, was also a French citizen. The Cairo authorities were quite adamant in their decision that the two could not be admitted.

The logistics of an orchestra's musical baggage are exacting. The trucking and handling of hundreds of thousands of dollars' worth of musical instruments cannot be entrusted to any baggage man who happens to be assigned to the job. Therefore, I wired that it would be utterly impossible for us to give the concerts scheduled in Cairo and Alexandria without our usual staff. The impasse was complete.

Since there was no reason for our sitting in the Aleppo airport waiting for a final decision, it was decided that we would proceed with our three planes to the Cairo Airport. If the Egyptian authorities would not admit us, we would turn back to Beirut, Lebanon, our next stop after Egypt. In order not to provoke further antagonism, only the planes carrying the orchestral personnel (all of whom had the properly validated passports) landed. The third plane circled above Cairo, ready to head to Beirut if the problem could not be resolved.

We were met at the Cairo airport by members of the Cairo Symphony, carrying welcoming wreaths of flowers, but also by some very determined-looking members of the constabulary. I stated that we wanted very much to have the privilege of concertizing in Egypt, but that we obviously could not play without our instruments, whereupon Mr. Sattler (a very persuasive gentleman) took over. I was later told that the arguments were presented to no less an authority than Colonel Nasser,[2] who ruled that the restrictions on our French baggage man might be waived in this instance. In any case, we did play a series of successful concerts in Cairo and afterward in Alexandria.

---

2   Gamal Abdel Nasser (1918–70), Egyptian leader. He led the revolution that removed King Farouk I and then served as the country's second president 1956–70.

Our stay in Egypt left us with a strange mixture of impressions. We reacted with typical tourist enthusiasm to the grandeur of the pyramids, the atmosphere of the bazaars, and the sounds of the streets. The audiences were warm and friendly in their response. At the same time, we felt that we were being watched as foreign and perhaps suspicious characters. The super-nationalism of the Egyptians seemed quite apparent, coupled with (I am sure) some distrust of the West. One of the music critics reflected this nationalism in a rather amusing way. Our first concert was given in the magnificent ballroom concert hall of the new Cairo Hilton. The acoustics of the hall proved opulent, and it was a pleasure to play in those surroundings. The write-up of the principal critic was, however, quite reserved—certainly not ecstatic.

The next night we presented a program in the local opera/cinema. The stage was very wide and shallow, the acoustical backdrop inadequate, and the auditorium itself a haze of tobacco smoke, hardly ideal circumstances. The acoustics were execrable. The next morning, the same critic wrote something to the effect that he had not been too greatly impressed by our concert in the auditorium of the new Cairo Hilton. but that, when he heard us in their own magnificent auditorium with its superior acoustics, he discovered that the orchestra was, indeed, most excellent!

We were sorry that we could not have played in the famous Cairo Opera House, which was being renovated. The opera house made famous by the premiere of Verdi's *Aida*, though badly in need of repair, proved to have great charm. I had always imagined it as a huge opera house. Instead, it proved to be small and intimate, seating as I recall less than a thousand people. It was, however, suitable even for so great a production as *Aida*, since the stage was huge, at least as big as the auditorium.

Cairo was the scene of perhaps the funniest incident of the tour, an incident which might have had international repercussions. It was our custom to begin each concert with the national anthem of the country in which we were playing, followed by the "*Star-Spangled Banner.*"[3] (It is, incidentally, amazing how beautiful our national anthem sounded to us.) Before leaving the United States, we had assembled most of these anthems in our library. Those we did not have, we borrowed from the Philadelphia Orchestra through the kind offices of Eugene Ormandy. One of these borrowed anthems was that of Egypt. At the morning rehearsal before the first Cairo concert, I asked Dr. Fennell if he would mind rehearsing the Egyptian national anthem, which was new to us.

---

3   This statement, supported by other documentation, seems at odds with the apparent lack of a suitable anthem when arriving in Syria.

As he raised his baton and the first bars of the anthem sounded through the hall, employees of the hotel rushed [in], apparently (to quote Dr. Fennell), "appearing from the woodwork" and yelling "Farouk is back! Farouk is back!"[4] We were playing the wrong anthem! I hesitate to think what would have happened if we had opened our concert with it.

After our concerts in Cairo, we journeyed by train to Alexandria,[5] where we played one concert and also celebrated New Year's Eve. "Celebrated" turned out to be the wrong verb because Alexandria, in spite of the beauty both of the city itself and its location on the Mediterranean, proved to be a pretty dismal place. Most, if not all, businesses owned by foreigners had been "sequestered," a term with which I was not familiar. Under this arrangement, the foreign business or industry was taken over by the state. The original owner-manager was allowed to continue to run the business, but under the supervision of an official of the state. The result was hardly inspiring, and we were glad to be out of that environment.

Beirut was another matter. We were lodged in a brand-new hotel, put up (I believe) by Pan Am. The rooms were beautiful, with balconies overlooking the blue Mediterranean—and it was really blue, a gorgeous blue. Not the least of the attractions was the fact that we could get real American hot dogs, hamburgers, and milkshakes, of which opportunity the members of the orchestra took full advantage.

In spite of the beauty of the city, the atmosphere was tense. We had already experienced the tension between the Greeks and Turks in Nicosia, and between the pro- and anti-Nasser forces in Aleppo. The situation in Beirut was even more serious. There had been an abortive "putsch" by antigovernment forces, and we entered the concert hall between lines of soldiers armed with machine guns, hardly the best conditions for a symphony concert. Fortunately, everything went well, and we had no trouble. As a matter of fact, Beirut is one of the places which we would dearly love to revisit.

The concerts in Beirut were followed by concerts in Ankara, Izmir, and Istanbul. The Turks proved most hospitable, and we made many friends there. I recall especially a touching reception by the students and faculty of the national conservatory in Ankara, where they told me that they were trying to create an "Eastman School" in the nation's capital. The weather was cold, but the warmth of the people was an effective antidote.

---

4   They were referring to the deposed king, Farouk I.
5   It is entirely possible that Hanson traveled by train to Alexandria, but the members of the orchestra made the four-hour journey across the desert by bus.

We enjoyed the city of Izmir,[6] with its biblical associations and, again, the warmest hospitality. We almost failed to arrive, because the runways of the Izmir airport were considered too short for the safety of our planes. We finally made it, through the courtesy of the Turkish government, which transported us as I recall by military planes.

I have not stressed as much as I should have the debt which we owe to the dozens of dedicated members of the US embassies and consulates, and especially to the public affairs officers and cultural attaches. There were a few who apparently could not care less. I recall that the responsible US officer in Cairo did not even bother coming to attend any of our concerts. This was, however, the rare exception.

For this reason, I cannot refrain from mentioning the officer in charge of our performances in Istanbul. He called upon us in our suite in the Istanbul Hilton Hotel, bearing a box of my favorite American cigars and followed by a waiter bearing a tray of genuine American martinis.[7] As we talked with him and his charming wife, we discovered a number of common interests. In the first place, we discovered [his] name to be Hanson, Arnold Hanson, even spelled with an "o" like ours!

In talking about the United States, with considerable nostalgia Arnold mentioned that they would love to be able to get back in the summer. They had an island off the coast of Maine, Harbor Island. I replied that we also had an island off the coast of Maine. "Where is your island?" he asked. "Two and a half miles due east of Stonington," I replied. "Where is your island?" You guessed the answer, "Two miles due east of Stonington." We had neighboring islands off the Maine coast, so we had been summer neighbors without knowing it.

We were scheduled to leave for concerts in Zagreb, Yugoslavia, but the day before we were to leave, we were told that the trip to Zagreb had to be canceled because of severe snowstorms. We strongly suspect that the reasons were diplomatic rather than barometric. However, there was no place where we were happier to be grounded than in the city of Istanbul, overlooking the picturesque Bosphorus and in the company of our newfound friends, the Arnold Hansons. We remember Istanbul with great joy. To be able to visit the gorgeous Blue Mosque and other exciting places in the company of such friends was a privilege far beyond our expectations.[8]

---

6   Izmir is the city long known outside Turkey as Smyrna.
7   Hanson and his wife were known to be fond of martinis.
8   It is interesting to note that, here and elsewhere in his narrative, Hanson speaks very little about the members of the orchestra. One might have expected mention of Karen Philips, who had to be left behind in Istanbul

There is still another "small world" story connected with Istanbul. As we were sitting in the dining room of the Istanbul Hilton, we heard voices that sounded very familiar. One of them could not be mistaken. I leaped to my feet and sought out the voice. It was, indeed, the voice of my friend and colleague, Professor Dexter Perkins, the distinguished historian and chairman of the History Department of the University of Rochester. With him was his charming wife, Wilma, who has always been one of my favorite persons. Dexter had been lecturing in India, and they were returning to the States.

---

because of an attack of appendicitis. After recuperating from her operation, she later rejoined the orchestra in Warsaw.

Chapter Forty

THE EASTMAN PHILHARMONIA TOUR (IV)

[Our] stay [in Istanbul contrasted greatly with the five strenuous weeks which were before us. There was, however, one more charming and humorous interlude. As we proceeded from Istanbul to Hannover, where we were to spend the night before entering the "corridor" for Berlin,[1] we were informed by our pilot that we would have to set down in Bari for refueling. I suggested, since the distance was not much greater, that we refuel in Rome, to which he agreed.

Neither Peggie nor Virginia Sattler had been to Rome. Bob [Sattler] had experienced Rome as a relief from the bloody days of Anzio,[2] and I had, of course, lived in Rome during my academy days. The pilot informed us that we should be on the ground [in] about an hour and a half, and we determined to try the unusual experiment of "seeing Rome" in one hour.

We left the plane and the airport through an exit marked EMPLOYEES ONLY, found a lone taxi waiting and embarked for the city.[3] We explained to the sympathetic driver that we had fifteen minutes to get to the city, fifteen minutes for return, and one hour to sightsee. The driver was "molto simpatico" [very sympathetic, cooperative] and entered into the spirit of the expedition with gusto. In the period of sixty minutes, we visited the Colosseum, the square of San Pietro ([i.e., St. Peter's)], the Trevi Fountain, the Arch of Constantine, the Forum, [the Basilica of] Santa Maria Maggiore, and a few other of my favorite haunts, returning to the airport over the Appian Way. I doubt if there has ever been a more efficient tour.

On the way to the airport, I discussed with Bob what we should pay our host-driver. He had been most cooperative, and we had bounded in

---

    1   Berlin was located in Soviet-controlled East Germany, and access to the city was limited to a specific air corridor leading from the west.

    2   Sattler had been a member of the US armed forces that had fought the Germans in Anzio prior to the liberation of Rome.

    3   Hanson offers no explanation as to how he and his party cleared Italian customs and legally entered the country. Perhaps by leaving through the employee exit, he avoided the delay that a legal entry into Italy would have entailed. But this does not explain how he could have later re-entered the airport and resumed his journey to Germany.

and out of the taxi like actors in an old Mack Sennett comedy to his obvious delight. We agreed that five thousand lire would be right. I asked the driver in Italian how much we owed him, to which he responded, "I think five thousand Lire would be right!"

After a restful night in Hannover, West Germany, we departed for West Berlin. We had heard a good bit about the "corridor" into Berlin, some of which was not reassuring. Our trip, however, proved uneventful, and we arrived without interruption or delay.

The contrast between West Berlin and East Berlin was startling.[4] West Berlin appeared prosperous, bustling with activity and almost completely rebuilt after the war. There were a few places where some rubble was still in evidence, testifying to the terrible devastation of the bombing raids, but these patches were boarded up and away from casual view. Across the [Berlin] Wall, however, East Berlin seemed extremely drab and desolate. As one looked across the city at night, the outlines of the separation of the two cities were marked by the difference between light and darkness. The west was brilliantly lighted, but the east seemed a pall of gloom. The effect of *chiaroscuro* seemed spiritual as well as physical, and I was interested to see its effect upon members of the orchestra.

The concert itself, in the beautiful new concert hall of Radio Free Berlin, was an enormous success. The critical reaction was especially interesting. One critic, on the *Telegraf*, wrote, "The first concert of the Eastman Philharmonia was virtually a sensation. No one would have expected such a perfect and exemplary performance of a student orchestra. Under the compelling conducting of Howard Hanson the orchestra played with electrifying vitality. . . . After the concert, a comparison with the standards of our schools of music is depressing."

Even the conductor of the student orchestra of the famous Hochschule told me that his orchestra could not have performed a program of such difficulty. It was in strange contrast to my experience in Berlin three decades before, when I had been asked the question, "Wissen Sie Brahms in Amerika?"[5]

Our concerts in Berlin were followed by one more concert in West Germany, in the charming city of Münster. Here we visited the famous town hall of the fourteenth century, where in 1648 in the Friedens-Saal was

---

4   Berlin was divided at the time between the western zone, controlled by the US and its allies, and the eastern zone, controlled by the Soviet Union.

5   In chapter 22 Hanson mentioned the incident but gave the question as, "Kennen Sie Brahms in Amerika?"

signed the Treaty of Westphalia, ending the Seven Years' War.[6] We were toasted by the dignitaries of the city, and I responded in my not impeccable German. How I wished I had worked harder at my foreign languages years ago.

From Münster, we went on to our long-anticipated tour of Poland and Russia, our first experience behind the Iron Curtain. Arriving in Poznán, the first problem which developed was that of transportation. Our three British planes were not allowed beyond Poznán. From that point on, our travel had to be by bus, transportation of not exactly deluxe character. We regretfully said farewell to the crews of our planes, for whom we had developed a sincere friendship, and went on our way.

We played in Poznán, Kraków, Lodz, and Warsaw, and were delighted with the audiences, although not always with the accommodations. The Poles impressed [us] as being a wonderful people, rich and spirit but economically poor, and not happy with their Russian alliance. My wife and I recall especially the hotel in Lodz. We were ushered into a suite hung with rich tapestries and beautifully furnished, but bitterly cold. We were informed that this was the suite reserved for visiting dignitaries. "Ignace Paderewski stayed here when he was president of Poland."[7] "It is beautiful," I replied, "but it is very cold." "Oh," said the maid blithely, "it's always cold here."

She was, however, solicitous for our comfort and quickly secured two rather beat-up electric heaters which we connected. Here our troubles began. For when we turned on the heaters, the fuses blew, and the lights went out. We could have heat without light, or light without heat. What a subject for a sermon!

If we could be somewhat critical about accommodations and the quality of the roads over which our busses traveled, we had only praise for the halls in which we played. Most of them were old. Only one, as I recall, was new, but they were uniformly excellent so far as acoustics was concerned. All of them were constructed on a similar pattern, a large room of rectangular construction, with apparently a fixed relation of height to length and width, and the stage at one end fully open to the room itself. Considering some of the acoustical atrocities that have been constructed in this country [i.e., the United States] at enormous expense, it might be wise for the architects to visit the concert halls of Poland.

---

6   Hanson is referring to the Peace of Westphalia, involving the two peace treaties (May 15, 1648, and October 24, 1648) that ended the Thirty Years' War, not the Seven Years' War.

7   Ignace Jan Paderewski (1860–1941), famous Polish pianist. He became president of Poland in 1939.

The Poles who talked to us seemed only slightly less bitter toward the Russians than they were toward the Germans at whose hands they had suffered so grievously. One slightly acidic story which we heard a number of times had to do with the Palace of Culture, which had been built by the Russian government and presented to the people of Warsaw. It is a massive building and towers high above the ground. The story goes this way: "The finest view of Warsaw is from the top of the Palace of Culture. Do you know why the finest view of Warsaw is from the top of the Palace of Culture?" The answer comes, "Because, from the top of the Palace of Culture you cannot see the Palace of Culture!" In spite of their sufferings, the Polish people have not lost their typical sense of humor.

A grimmer story came also from Warsaw. An attaché of the American embassy, Mr. Alpert by name, had been most helpful during our visit to Warsaw. During one of their tours, our students visited the scene of the terrible Jewish pogroms. Apparently one of the local guides made some remark which indicated that he did not consider that our American friend was sufficiently impressed by the seriousness of the Jewish slaughter. To which [Mr. Alpert] replied, very quietly, "Oh, I do take it very seriously. You see, my mother and father were both killed here." The argument ended in a kind of stunned silence.

I have probably painted my account of our visit to Poland in darker colors than necessary. We were impressed with the gaiety of the people under difficult circumstances, with the chic appearance of the women and the gallantry and courtesy of the men. We were also impressed with the fact that, [despite] the ban on religion, the church we visited on Sunday [was] thronged with worshippers. The history of the Poles has been filled with conquest and tribulation, but the spirit of the Polish people seems to rise above it.

Chapter Forty-One

THE EASTMAN PHILHARMONIA TOUR (V)

As we toured over Poland, our minds went forward with both anticipation and some trepidation to our coming four weeks in Russia. We realized that this was the crucial test. If we could succeed here, the entire tour would be a triumph. If we failed, then our tour would have been a failure, regardless of our success in the countries which we had previously visited. Considering the vast expanse of that gigantic country, our tour covered a representative group of cities, south from Odessa on the shores of the Black Sea to Leningrad in the north, and including the cities of Moscow, Kishinev, Chernovtsky, Lvov, and Kiev.

Our opening concert was in the famous Tchaikovsky Hall in Moscow, the home of the excellent Moscow orchestras and the Moscow Conservatory, from which many of the great Russian composers and artists have graduated. Not since Berlin had we felt so keenly the importance of a concert. Everything went well. Our program was essentially romantic and included my own Second, or *Romantic*, Symphony. We discovered very quickly that our choice of an opening program was a wise one. The Russian public, certainly the audience for which we played, loved the romantics, and my symphony was greeted with warmest applause. The critic in *Tass* [wrote], "The audience warmly applauded Hanson's Second Symphony, performed in Moscow for the first time. Resting on broad vocal themes and distinguished by a high degree of professionalism, this work is regarded by Moscow critics as one of the most striking manifestations of American romanticism of the 20th century."

Another critic mentioned specifically the reaction of the audience, writing, "The concert made a tremendous hit. After the concert, the audience applauded the conductor and orchestra for over fifteen minutes. The orchestra encored Piston's piece (*The Incredible Flutist*), fragments from Stravinsky's ballet *The Firebird*, and Sousa's march, which earned an ovation."

I was considerably relieved by the enthusiastic reception of the Sousa march, which we played as our fourth or fifth encore. We were accompanied throughout our Russian tour by a representative from the State Department, and I had been advised to remove the "*Stars and Stripes*

Forever" from the list of encores. The theory was, I suppose, that the Russians might be offended by the title and charge us with making musical propaganda. My argument was that the title was unimportant, that (to misquote Shakespeare) "music was the thing."

In any case, I decided on my own to go ahead and use the march throughout Russia. To my relief, it was received with the greatest enthusiasm everywhere. Indeed, the fame of the march preceded us from city to city, and if, by the fourth or fifth encore, we had not played it, we would hear calls from the audience which sounded something like "Amerikanski March."

The applause of a Russian audience when it is pleased and wants "more" is the most demanding that I have ever heard. It begins rhythmically with slow but loud handclaps, the claps spaced almost a full second apart and then increasing in tempo until it breaks into a cloudburst of sound. It is a thrilling sound to a performer, and I can recommend its adoption by our more conservative symphony audiences.

From Moscow, we went to Odessa, the orchestra by train and Peggie and I by plane so that I might accept an invitation to meet with the Union of Composers in Moscow.[1] The meeting with the Russian composers was both pleasant and rewarding, although I could feel some tension. I had the impression that the Russians felt that it was proper to be friendly, but not too friendly. My colleague, Walter Hendl, who has recently conducted a series of concerts with Russian orchestras, tells me that this feeling seems to be rapidly disappearing, and that on his visit to Russia he was invited into the homes of the composers without any fear on their part that they might be accused of being "too friendly." I suppose that the barometer goes up and down in tune with the political climate.

While in Moscow, we had little time for sightseeing, though we did visit Red Square and its fascinating museum. We visited a number of the famous old churches but found most of them to have been converted to historical museums. As I remember, we found only one active church where a service was being conducted. Most of the worshippers seemed to be elderly men and women, although we did see some young soldiers in the congregation.

We were looking forward expectantly to a few days in Odessa and bright, sunny days on the shores of the Black Sea. Alas, we arrived in a

---

[1] While Hanson enjoyed the luxury of traveling by plane to Odessa, the members of the orchestra had to endure a thirty-hour train ride. They were so upset that they took a vote to voice their disapproval of the pending travel arrangements.

blizzard so heavy that it was almost impossible to see anything. The Black Sea proved to be very black.

Musically, however, things were most pleasant. The audiences again were friendly and approving, and we had our full share of encores. We heard a performance of *Faust* at the Opera, complete with the scene in Purgatory, generally omitted in our productions. We were not greatly impressed with the performance, particularly by the orchestra. Many of the instruments themselves seemed inferior (something apparently quite common in the provincial cities), and the tone quality and intonation [left] much to be desired.

We were, however, enormously impressed by the vitality of the musical schedule. As I recall, four or five new works were scheduled within a six-week period, something inconceivable in our opera houses, where anything after 1900 is considered a "novelty."

Physically, we were not very comfortable. It is difficult to understand how a country which could launch a "Sputnik"[2] could have such superannuated plumbing. It seemed to me that I was spending half of my time climbing up the walls of the bathtub fixing the old-fashioned flush toilet. As a matter of fact, I became quite proficient.

From Odessa, we went on to Kishinev, Chernovtsky, and Lvov. It was, I believe, outside Chernovtsky that we had the opportunity of visiting a communal farm. We were allowed to visit one farmhouse, which we suspected had been specially "set up" for the occasion. At least it was equipped with radio and even a tape recorder. We were greeted most hospitably by the farmer, who took us into his wine cellar and treated us proudly to some wine. "This wine," he said, "is my own wine." Later we were given supper in the cooperative dining room, with many speeches and much wine. The wine was quite "green," unaged and treacherous. In a speech acknowledging their hospitality, I said pointedly that the wine was the native wine of the country and should be savored *slowly*. I hoped that our students were listening. Apparently, they were, for we all came out of the supper in reasonably good condition.

Later we were treated to a speech by the gentleman in charge of the collective farms, much of it pure communist propaganda. When the students were invited to ask questions, one of our number asked if it would be possible for an individual farmer to own his own land if he did not wish to be part of the collective enterprise. The speaker did not understand the question. Our young student pressed the question further. "What should a farmer do if he wished to be responsible for his own land in a

---

2   Sputnik was the first satellite launched into earth orbit.

free-enterprise system?" The speaker hesitated and then responded that such a farmer would have the privilege of writing to the government in Moscow and petition for the privilege. I am afraid that there was a titter which ran through the members of our group!

Of these three cities, Lvov proved the most interesting. The city has had a politically checkered career, as the capital of Austrian Galicia, later as a part of Poland, and again after the Second World War taken over by the Russians. Perhaps for this reason, it seemed to be a more cosmopolitan city than some of the other cities we had visited. Perhaps the Polish complexion of the city explains one curious experience. I had heard of a new piano concerto by a Russian resident of Lvov which I wanted to hear. The composer heard of my wish and gladly offered to meet me to discuss his new work. I was advised by our embassy that it would be better for everyone if we went through the regular "channels" which, in this case, would be the Lvov Union of Composers. This I agreed to do.

Arriving at the Union, I was greeted by the composer, but was immediately taken over by a young lady who apparently was the secretary of the Union. I told her that I wished to hear a tape of the composer's new piano concerto. "Certainly," said she, "but first I would like to have you hear some other works. Here, for example, is a choral work in which the farmers give thanks to the Russian Fatherland for their liberation." I listened dutifully for about twenty minutes (which seemed longer) and then asked if I might hear the piano concerto. "Of course," said my mentor, "but first I would like you to hear another choral work. This is a song of praise by the workers to the great Russian army." Another twenty minutes went by.

To shorten a very long story, I never did hear the concerto which I had come to hear. I did, however, hear a piano concerto by a Polish composer! All this time, the composer, whose work I had asked for, was with me. What the answer was I do not know. Perhaps the composer was being disciplined, although he was the president of the Union. In any case, I never heard the work which I came to hear!

We heard the local symphony, a surprisingly good one, and paid a delightful visit to the conservatory where we were handsomely entertained. On a free evening, we attended a professional ballet performance at the opera, conducted by an advanced student of the conservatory. It seemed to be the custom to place a visiting musical dignitary in the first row, immediately behind the conductor. I was so close that I could read the orchestral score over his shoulder. I am sure that the young conductor was nervous having me literally at his elbow. I was almost as nervous myself. Sitting so close and following the score, I felt almost responsible for the performance. "Watch out! Don't bring the brass in yet! Give them a cue for the next measure!"

Whenever we went to listen to a local performance, we were invariably accompanied by someone assigned to the job. I had the feeling that we were being helped, but also that we were under observation. After the performance that I have been discussing, our guide said to me, "You did not enjoy the performance." I replied that I had enjoyed it. "You looked worried," he said. I explained that the young conductor was talented but obviously not experienced, and this is why I might have appeared "worried." He did not seem happy about my explanation.

Whatever my feeling about the performance, I heartily applauded the idea of allowing a talented young student to have the experience of conducting professional performances under professional conditions. Perhaps if there were such opportunities in the United States for gifted young Americans, our orchestras, ballet, and opera companies would not have to be directed almost exclusively by foreign-born and foreign-trained conductors.

The happiest experience of all came as we were all sitting in the dining room of our hotel after the evening meal. As I recall, I was at the piano playing, when a familiar voice echoed through the room: "Is there anyone here from Rochester?" It was our very good friend, Hamilton Allen, theater editor for the Rochester *Times-Union*. The Gannett newspapers had sent him to Russia to see how we were getting along and to cover our story. It was a welcome breath from home. We had been away a long time. He stayed with us for several days before going back to Rochester and was a most welcome companion. My only regret was that his charming wife Mary could not accompany him.

Chapter Forty-Two

THE EASTMAN PHILHARMONIA TOUR (VI)

Kiev, in the Ukraine, proved to be another of our most pleasant memories. We were staying in a new hotel, which was most comfortable and in walking distance from the magnificent concert hall. I remember that our hotel suite even had a piano for my use, and our Ukrainian hosts could not have been nicer.

We had the additional pleasure of sharing the concerts of the week with the splendid Leningrad Orchestra, which was on tour. They would play one night and we the next, until we had each played, as I recall, three concerts. The members of the Leningrad Orchestra were highly complimentary about the performance of our students, and we made many professional friendships. When, the following winter, the Leningrad Orchestra toured the United States and played in Rochester, it was like renewing acquaintance with old friends.

The weather in Kiev was severe, with a series of heavy snowstorms, but in spite of the hazards to navigation the audiences could not be kept away until we played to capacity audiences. We also did some sightseeing. On one occasion, we asked to see the great gates of Kiev, immortalized in Mussorgsky's *Pictures from an Exhibition*. The taxi driver told us that he, a native of Kiev, had never heard of the great gates until he had been introduced to them by American tourists, admirers of Mussorgsky's music!

After hearing the magnificent musical picture of the great gates, especially in Ravel's orchestral transcription, I must admit that we were disappointed. The "great gates" proved to be rather small, not (I think) over twelve feet in height and not particularly massive in design. I almost wish that I had not seen them. My imagination of the great gates, based on Mussorgsky's music, was so much better than the real thing. Perhaps, after all, that is what art is for.[1]

We heard at the opera an excellent performance of Verdi's *Aida*, sung, of course, in Russian. (When will we in the United States learn the trick

---

1 It is rather surprising that Hanson was ignorant of the fact that Mussorgsky was inspired by Victor Hartmann's drawing of a proposed "great gate," a drawing he submitted when the city was considering the erection of such a structure. However, no such great gate was ever constructed.

which every operatic nation abroad has learned many years ago, that we must have adequate English translations and opera in our own tongue?) The managing director of the opera proved to be Premier Khrushchev's son-in-law, and we were shown every consideration, including the director's box. During intermission, I was taken downstairs to the orchestra room to meet the members of the excellent opera orchestra, and, in spite of the language barrier, we managed very well with speeches of congratulation and felicitation.

Incidentally, one of the strangest conversations of my experience was, I believe, in Lvov, where a member of the Lvov Symphony and I had an animated conversation. He, a native Russian, spoke to me in Spanish, and I responded in Italian, each helping the other over tough spots and, of course, using that indispensable aid to foreign conversation, gesticulation of the two hands!

We left hospitable Kiev with regret and proceeded by train on the long trip to Leningrad. The Russian trains are not [un]comfortable, particularly if one is lucky enough to secure a "soft" compartment (i.e., with padded seats), and they move along with reasonable speed and comfort. In Leningrad, we had three concerts, all in the exquisite Hall of the Nobles. All through Poland and Russia, Dr. Fennell and I divided the concerts between us, with the result that Peggie and I were able to do much more sightseeing than in the earlier part of the tour. Our visits included the beautiful city, the famous museum [i.e., the Hermitage], reminiscences of Peter the Great, and not least the famous circus.

Some of the comical sketches at the circus indicated that the regime might be becoming a little less self-conscious and able to laugh (at least a little) at itself. One sketch had to do with state medicine and the doctors. It seemed that a man had just been pulled out of the Volga River, barely alive. An ambulance was sent for, and a doctor arrived bearing a huge hypodermic needle, about a foot long. He administered it quickly to the drowning man, who immediately came to life and showed signs of a quick recovery. When he was well enough to talk, the doctor asked for the identification card which would entitle him to medical service. The man produced the necessary document from his dripping clothes. The doctor took one look. "You are from the wrong district," said the doctor, whereupon his assistants threw the man back into the river!

The Hall of the Nobles proved to be the most beautiful concert hall I have ever seen. Apparently, it had been exactly what its name implies, a hall of the nobles, a grand ballroom with a great stage for the orchestra at one end. The acoustics were so sensitive that one felt as though one were playing on a giant Stradivarius violin. The slightest *pianissimo* had a velvety sheen, which I have experienced only once before, in the Academy of Music in Philadelphia.

The final concert was a nostalgic experience. We were at last at the end of our strenuous three months, but now that it was over, we were relieved but a little sad. The audience jammed the hall. I would say that at least 300 stood through the entire concert. At the end, the audience would not let us go. We played one encore after another. When we had completed our sixth encore, the audience still showed no signs of willingness to leave. [Therefore,] we played the "*Stars and Stripes Forever.*" This simply brought more applause. We played it again, until we thought that we [might] indeed be playing the "*Stars and Stripes*" forever!

Even the repetition of the march did not satisfy the audience, and so we played for them the moving little elegy of Edvard Grieg, *The Last Spring*. It ends, as you know, with a nostalgic whisper. This, I was sure, would end the program of encores. Not at all. The applause continued. I looked at my watch and realized that we had an hour remaining to change our clothes and catch the midnight train for Moscow. I left the stage and motioned for the concertmaster to follow me.[2] Several minutes later, in my dressing room, I could still hear sounds from the auditorium.

I slipped on an overcoat and went backstage. Looking out, I saw the entire audience on its feet, applauding an empty stage. I rushed to find Dr. Fennell, and we both went on the stage for a final bow. A part of the audience pressed forward to the stage apron, the men holding out their hands and many of the women showering us with flowers, which seemed to appear from nowhere. My wife says that I am sometimes too sentimental, but I swear that I heard one elderly lady cry in English, "God bless America." Maybe I just imagined it.

Arriving in Moscow, we spent two whole days resting and saying goodbye to our Russian and American friends. As we prepared to board the Russian plane for Amsterdam, our translators and guides bade us a tearful goodbye, one remarking, "Goodbye. You have taught me the joy to live." It was the most touching compliment she could have paid us.

The plane trip was followed by a day and night in Amsterdam. Anatole Heller had arranged for us a beautiful suite of rooms in Amsterdam's finest hotel. The tapestry was all in gold, and the warm sun came through the windows thawing our hearts and [bodies] after the black Russian winter. The next night, we arrived safely at the air base at Niagara Falls, and then at a late hour back to Rochester.[3]

---

2   Presumably, the exit of the conductor and concertmaster signaled the rest of the orchestra to follow.

3   The flight from Amsterdam was to Montreal, where Hanson and the others changed planes for Niagara Falls. They all then returned to Rochester

Our safari was over, but not quite. Our success as "musical ambassadors" had spread across the United States, and we were invited to present concerts in our own country. We accepted very few because they were, after all, students and had to get back to school. We did play a concert in the Academy of Music in Philadelphia under the auspices of my good friend, Louis Wersen, director of music for the Philadelphia public schools.[4] In the beautiful acoustics of the Academy of Music, I think we were able to reproduce some of that silken sound which we had experienced in Leningrad. Eugene Ormandy, in a statement to the press, gave us the accolade of which we are the most proud, when he declared, "This is not a great student orchestra. This is a great orchestra!"

The University of Rochester, through its alumni, sponsored a gala concert in Carnegie Hall.[5] I must admit that I was frightened. Suppose that, after a triumphal tour of Europe, the Middle East, and Russia, we should fall on our faces on our own doorstep. Perhaps the critics [would] simply say, "Why the trip?" I need not have worried. The orchestra played a difficult program of contemporary American music magnificently. We opened the papers the next day to read four "rave" criticisms from four of New York's best-known critics, a unanimous verdict.

A short time later, we gave our "final concert" in the Eastman Theatre.[6] We had played dozens of concerts there before, many in preparation for the tour. The audiences had seldom exceeded 500 in an auditorium seating over 3,200 people. This time it was different. Even Rochester had heard of us, and the theater was packed with enthusiastic listeners. In addition to the concert, we had a grand banquet in the Rochester Club, attended by many notables including Lucius Battle, assistant secretary of state for cultural affairs, who extended his warmest thanks for the orchestra's contribution to the country's cultural exchange program. Dr. Fennell and I both received the gold cards of life membership in the American Federation of Musicians as an expression of the union's appreciation. It was a festive experience which we all appreciated. The Eastman Philharmonia had been recognized in its own town. At the next concert of the Philharmonia, the Eastman Theatre audience was again back to its usual five hundred!

---

via buses, arriving in town well after midnight.
4   This concert took place on April 7, 1962.
5   The Carnegie Hall concert took place on November 16, 1962. Since this was during the first semester of the 1962–63 school year, the personnel of the Eastman Philharmonia was no longer identical to the personnel that had toured Europe, the Middle East, and Russia during the previous school year.
6   Hanson's chronology is a bit puzzling here. If this concert actually took place after the Carnegie Hall appearance, then it occurred about eight months after the Philharmonia had returned from its tour. His description of the event as the "final concert" does not seem to support this timeframe.

Chapter Forty-Three

ENCOUNTERS WITH VARIOUS MUSICIANS

I suppose that all performers by the nature of their profession are to a considerable extent troubadours and nomads. Much of the time, [the performer] is working with other performers, with orchestras, ensembles. The composer's work is, for the most part, confined to his workroom, where he works by himself in the creation of his compositions. And yet, the most interesting part of a composer's life frequently concerns his relationship with performers, whether they be conductors, soloists, or ensembles.

Many of these contacts with great performers may be quite casual and in passing, and yet [they may] be invaluable. I still recall happily a short visit backstage at the Eastman Theatre with Fritz Kreisler.[1] Even more than his magnificent playing, I recall his human warmth, his interest in what I was attempting to accomplish at the Eastman School, and his concern that the musical verities be preserved.

I remember talking to the great pianist, Josef Hofmann[2] during an intermission in one of his Rochester recitals. After paying my respects, I apologized for intruding on the intermission period. It was, as I recall, his fiftieth year as a concert artist, having begun his career as a child prodigy. I remarked that, after such a career, I supposed that walking out on the stage meant nothing, involved no tension whatsoever. "Not at all," he replied. "Even after fifty years, the tension of walking on the stage has never left me."

The next morning, prior to his departure, he paid me the greatest courtesy of visiting me in my office. He was at that time director of the Curtis Institute and was interested in discussing some of the current problems in music school administration. Josef Hofmann, in addition to his preeminence as a pianist, was a genius in mechanics, with a number of inventions to his credit. As we were talking, I noticed that he had focused

---

1 Fritz Kreisler (1875–1962), Austrian-born violinist and composer. He made his American debut in 1888 and became one of the world's most famous and beloved concert artists.

2 Josef Hofmann (1876–1957), Polish-born American pianist. One of the greatest pianists of his generation; became head of the piano department at Curtis in 1924, director 1927–38.

his attention on the light on my desk. He then proceeded to give me a short lecture on the reflection of light and its effect on the eyes. He did not approve at all of the particular light fixture on my desk. The reflection angle was wrong. It was not good for my eyes to work in such a light.

I was intrigued by the forcefulness of his comments, but after his departure proceeded to forget about it. About three weeks later, a huge package arrived in my office. On opening it, [I] discovered that it was [a] newly designed set of desk lights, courtesy of Josef Hofmann.

A regular artist in our concert series was the brilliant violinist, Jascha Heifetz.[3] One evening following his recital, I met him backstage. He told me that he had heard some of my recent works and wished that I should write a violin concerto for him. I was very pleased at his interest and told him that I would be interested in writing such a work. A year or two later, Mr. Heifetz returned for another concert. He asked me what progress I had made with the violin concerto. I confessed that I had been busy with other works. He made no comment, but a year later he asked me the same question and received the same answer.

The next time he came to Rochester, I went back to greet him. He looked at me and, with a twinkle in his eye said, "Go to hell!" I never did write a violin concerto, and it is one of my great regrets. To hear Heifetz play my concerto would have been an unforgettable experience.

In the case of all composers who regard music as a form of emotional and spiritual communication, the temperament of the man and the character of his music must be inextricably intertwined. Haydn must have been a cheerful man. Beethoven must have been disturbed and rebellious. Their music identified them.

On the other hand, the outward personality of the composer does not always reflect his creative spirit. It is frequently said that the clown is basically the saddest of men. The quietest man sometimes writes the most bombastic music. I remember particularly my only meeting with Dmitri Shostakovitch.[4] A group of composers from the USSR were invited to visit the United States as guests of the Department of State. A few of us,

---

3   Jascha Heifetz (1901–87), violinist born in Vilnius, Lithuania. He studied with Leopold Auer, made his American debut in 1917, and was one of the greatest violin virtuosi in history.

4   Dmitri Shostakovich (1906–75), eminent Russian pianist and composer.

including (as I recall) Aaron Copland[5] and Roy Harris,[6] took part in the national radio panel discussing the problems of the living composer in a scientific age. Shostakovitch proved to be a man of small stature, delicate features, and intensely nervous. In talking with him, it was difficult to believe that this man had written the *Stalingrad Symphony*, with all its noise and furor.

A similar example might be Sergei Rachmaninoff.[7] Certainly no one's music is more emotional, more personal, more involved with the composer's innermost feelings. And yet, meeting him socially for the first time, one might think that he was a foreign diplomat—correct, proper, with his white gloves and his impenetrable facade.

On the other hand, I vividly remember my one and only meeting with that superb French pianist, Alfred Cortot.[8] In my opinion, he was the most sensitive of all pianists, the complete opposite of so many of today's pianists who seem to regard the piano as a percussive instrument, a giant xylophone.

He liked my music and told me that he wanted to conduct it in France. Later, friends told me that they had heard him conduct an orchestral work of mine in Paris, but I never saw him again. When I learned of his death, it was as though I had lost a close friend, although I had met him only for a matter of minutes, another case of friendly ships that pass in the night.

I did not meet Ernst Dohnanyi[9] until late in his life, when he was a member of the artist faculty of Florida State University in Tallahassee. I had been invited by my friend Karl Kursteiner, dean of the School of Music, to speak at the university and was delighted to find the eminent Hungarian pianist-composer in residence.

---

5   Aaron Copland (1900–90), distinguished American composer. He was head of the composition department at the Berkshire Music Center at Tanglewood 1940–65 and was the recipient of many awards.
6   Roy (Leroy Ellsworth) Harris (1898–1979), American composer. He held teaching positions at numerous American colleges and universities.
7   Sergei Rachmaninoff (1873–1943), famous Russian-born composer, pianist and conductor. He left Russia following the Bolshevik Revolution, spent much of his time in the United States, and became a naturalized US citizen several weeks before his death.
8   Alfred Cortot (1877–1962), Swiss-born French pianist and teacher. He enjoyed a major career as a concert and recording artist; taught at the Paris Conservatory 1907–17, founded in 1919 the École Normale de Musique.
9   Ernst (Ernö) von Dohnanyi (1877–1960), Hungarian pianist, composer, and teacher. He was the leading teacher of piano at the Academy of Music in Budapest for many years and served as conductor of the Budapest Philharmonic Orchestra 1928–44.

Mr. Dohnanyi was, as I recall, in his eighties, a statistical fact which had nothing to do with his remarkable vitality. I recall vividly his performance [with faculty colleagues] of his own piano quintette and the Brahms Quintet. His playing had a breadth and a passion characteristic of the "grand manner" of the past generation, a manner which unfortunately has passed.

My wife and I had a delightful dinner with Dohnanyi and his charming wife. Our conversation turned to the effects of the Second World War on both the arts and the artists. He himself had suffered greatly. If my memory is correct, one of his sons had been killed by the Russians and another by the Germans.[10] He, like so many nonpolitical artists, was caught in the ebb and flow of the passions of the war. Like a number of non-Jewish artists (including Richard Strauss) who tried to keep the arts alive during those difficult days, he took no part in the political activities of his fellow artists. As a result, he found himself after the war more or less ostracized by his colleagues. In spite of this, he exhibited no bitterness. I still remember his remark, "What was an old man to do? I was an artist, not a politician."[11]

---

10   One son was killed in combat against the Russian army; the other was executed by the Germans for his role in the plot to assassinate Hitler.

11   Hanson's manuscript for this chapter is incomplete, breaking off at this point after including some unrelated comments concerning recordings of some of his compositions.

Chapter Forty-Four

COMPOSING DURING THE 1950s

The decade of the fifties was creatively one of the happiest for me and one of the most productive. From it came a variety of works which gave me particular personal satisfaction. I was not happy about the increased centralization of the university and its effect on the Eastman School, and perhaps for this very reason composition offered a happy escape from an increasingly bureaucratic world.

My alma mater, Northwestern University, celebrated its hundredth anniversary in 1951, and I was invited to write a work for the occasion. As a student at Northwestern, I had written one movement of a piano concerto, which I had converted in Rome to a *Concerto da Camera* for piano and strings. I had always been fond of the opening episode of this early work, and the idea occurred to me to use this introductory theme as a basis for a set of variations for solo piano and strings. It proved to be a happy thought. The theme lent itself beautifully to the variation form, sometimes embodying a youthful solemnity, at times stormy and at times nostalgic. It seemed appropriate to call it *Fantasy Variations on a Theme of Youth*.

It is dangerous to put new wine in old bottles, and to put oneself back thirty-six years into the state of mind and emotion of youth was a challenge. Fortunately, the recapture of my youthful fantasy seemed perfectly natural, and the composition almost "wrote itself." It is a modest work, not overly long, overly intellectual, or pretentious, but it was a satisfying experience. Some years later, it was recorded by the brilliant young pianist, David Burge, who by coincidence was also a graduate of Northwestern.[1]

To this period also belongs my first venture into original composition for band. Up to this time, several of my compositions had been arranged for band, including the second movement of the *Nordic* Symphony, arranged by Dr. Maddy, and a piano composition, *March Carillon*, arranged by the gifted composer and arranger, Erik Leidzen.[2] I had never written a composition specifically for band or wind ensemble.

---

1   David Burge also earned his doctorate at the Eastman School of Music.
2   Erik Leidzen (1894–1962), noted band arranger and composer for the Salvation Army.

Early in the decade, Colonel Santelman, conductor of the United States Marine Band, called on me. The National Association of Band Masters had asked him to persuade me to compose an original work for the medium. As a boy in the Midwest, I had grown up on the music of the great bandmasters of that era—Sousa, Conway, Creatore, and Bohumir Kryl. I had even played trombone in the local park band, and it seems strange that I was never tempted to write a piece for band.

Perhaps the reason was that the bands of the early days varied greatly in instrumentation. Arrangements were habitually loaded with "cues," which meant that a melody originally scored for oboe might actually appear in a clarinet, a flute, or even a cornet or trumpet. With the advent of the more highly sophisticated wind ensemble, pioneered by conductors like Frederick Fennell, what we might call the "promiscuity" of the old band arrangements was gradually disappearing, replaced by a better balance of instrumentation.

Colonel Santelman was a powerful persuader, and I began at once to plan my first work for winds, brass, and percussion. The result was the *Chorale and Alleluia*, consisting of three major sections: a solemn chorale primarily for brass, followed by the rhythmic chanting of the alleluias principally [for woodwinds], and the finale in which the chorale and alleluia episodes are combined. It proved unusually successful, and I was delighted with my first experience in this, to me, new idiom.

This new work was followed the next year by two sacred works, [the first being] a setting of the psalm *How Excellent Thy Name* for women"s voices, written for the Phi Mu Alpha Sorority[3] of which Kathleen Davison was at that time national president. [It was] first presented at the national convention of the sorority in Chicago. Later, I made a second arrangement for mixed choir.

The other work was my Fifth Symphony, with the subtitle *Sinfonia Sacra*, commissioned by Eugene Ormandy and the Philadelphia Orchestra. It is a programmatic work based on the story of Mary Magdalene at the tomb of Christ on the Day of Resurrection, an attempt to picture in music some of the anguish, fear, turmoil, and final transfiguration when she realized that her Savior was risen from the dead. It is a relatively short work for a symphony, the material being presented in one movement, in contrast to my Sixth Symphony, which is in six movements. Mr. Ormandy's performances of the work, both in Philadelphia and New York, were as might be expected magnificent, giving the symphony the best possible introduction

---

3   Hanson confuses the fraternity Phi Mu Alpha, of which he was a member, with the sorority Sigma Alpha Iota. It was the sorority that commissioned his work.

to the public. Later he repeated it on the European tour of the Philadelphians, including a presentation in Vienna.

The decade brought forth three additional orchestral works, the *Elegy for my Friend, Serge Koussevitzky*, commissioned jointly by the Boston Symphony and the Koussevitzky Foundation; the *Summer Seascape*, commissioned by Edward Benjamin and first performed under my direction by the New Orleans Symphony; and the *Mosaics*, commissioned for the anniversary of the Cleveland Orchestra by George Szell.

These three works, although written within a three-year period, are quite different in character, but they are all among my favorites of my own works. The *Elegy* is a highly subjective work, reflecting my affection for that great conductor and friend [Serge Koussevitzky]. The *Summer Seascape* is perhaps the most pastoral of all my works, a sunny day on the sea off our beautiful Bold Island.

Mosaics is another experiment in the variation form. It is also programmatic, based on the different moods induced by the reflection of light on the mosaics in the Cathedral of Palermo, Sicily, reflections at dawn, in the bright light of noon, and finally the faint mysterious glow of the evening.[4] *Mosaics* received its first performance in Cleveland and later on tour and in New York City, under George Szell, certainly [one] of the world's greatest symphony conductors. It represents to me one of [the] most complete realizations of my musical career. Again, under George Szell, it could not have had a more propitious christening.

The final work on the list of the fifties was the *Song of Democracy* for chorus and orchestra, set to the words of Walt Whitman. The genesis of this work is, I believe, of some interest. The National Education Association was about to celebrate its hundredth anniversary, and the Music Educators' National Conference (a division of the NEA) was to celebrate its fiftieth birthday. Vanett Lawler, the executive secretary of the MENC, was charged with the responsibility of providing a suitable commissioned work for this double educational anniversary.

Vanett asked me if I would undertake the assignment. I was delighted to do so, because of my long association with MENC, providing we could find [a] poem suitable for the occasion. I suggested the Whitman poem, "*Sail! Sail thy best, Ship of Democracy, Of value is thy freight.*" She suggested an even more appropriate poem, "*An Old Man's Thoughts of School.*" We decided to begin [with] the latter: "An old man's thoughts of school / An old man gathering youthful memories / That youth itself cannot," and

---

4   Hanson apparently is referring to the world-famous mosaics at the Cathedral of Monreale, rather than the rather undistinguished Cathedral of Palermo.

then proceed to the poem: "Sail! Sail thy best / Ship of Democracy / Of value is thy freight / 'Tis not the present only / the past is also bound in Thee."

I set the poems in the manner which would make them suitable for a chorus of young voices and added an accompaniment for either piano or orchestra. The work had three "premieres": a private audition by the Howard University Chorus conducted by Werner Lawson, at which President Eisenhower was the honored guest; a performance with the same chorus and the National Symphony of Washington in Constitution Hall; and finally a performance at the NEA national conference by the Philadelphia All-High School Chorus and the Philadelphia Orchestra.

The *Song of Democracy* apparently filled a genuine need in the choral-orchestral repertory, [having] had hundreds of performances, so many that even the publishers have happily lost track of the number. It was even transcribed for male chorus by Lieutenant Ford and given by the Air Force Glee Club in an arrangement for orchestra and band at the Air Force Academy under Saul Caston.

Its most recent major performance, a particularly brilliant one, was presented by the Mormon Tabernacle Choir, prepared by its conductor Dr. Condie,[5] and the National Symphony under the direction of my good friend Howard Mitchell. It had been selected as the final number of the Inaugural Concert, preceding the inauguration of President Nixon. The audience, which filled Constitution Hall, was exceptionally distinguished, including President and Mrs. Nixon, Vice-President Spiro Agnew and Mrs. Agnew, members of the cabinet, the diplomatic corps, and official Washington in general.

At the conclusion of the concert, the president left the presidential box and came on stage to congratulate all of us personally. It was a generous and gracious gesture, which we all appreciated. I am not sure that his Secret Service escort was equally happy!

The beginning of the 1960s was a somewhat less successful time [for composition, compared with the 1950s.] Happy with the effectiveness of the *Summer Seascape*, I decided to expand it to a three-movement suite and call it the *Bold Island Suite*, using the *Summer Seascape* as the middle movement and adding an opening and a closing movement. Again, the suite had the distinction of first performances in Cleveland and New York, with the Cleveland Orchestra under George Szell. The critical response in both cities was favorable. I did not hear either performance, as we were at that time on tour in Russia with the Eastman Philharmonic. I did, however,

---

5   Richard P. Condie (1898–1985), conductor of the Mormon Tabernacle Choir 1957–74.

conduct it at our own May Festival and felt that it did not "come off" as I had hoped. Perhaps if I had heard Dr. Szell conduct it with his magnificent orchestra, I might have felt differently. In any case, I quickly lost interest in the work, and, as far as I know, it has not been played since.

The following year, I had a somewhat similar experience. I had been commissioned by the Department of State to compose a work in celebration of the anniversary of the Declaration of Human Rights. I called it the *Song of Human Rights*, embracing excerpts from that document and quotations from the late President Kennedy. The work had its first performance with the National Symphony Orchestra and the Howard University chorus before another brilliant audience, including the late Adlai Stevenson.[6]

I had hoped, if possible, to duplicate the *Song of Democracy*, but the legalistic phrases of the Bill of Rights were hardly the poetry of Walt Whitman, and the task of setting it to music was both more difficult and, to me, less satisfying. Because of the greater problems of the setting of prose, the speech-like patterns also place a greater technical burden on the singers. In spite of these difficulties, it has had many performances by choruses which have met its challenges successfully.

The 1960s also saw the completion of a number of sacred works: the *Four Psalms* for baritone, solo cello, and string quintette, already mentioned; a setting of the 121st and 150th psalms for soloist, chorus, and orchestra—the latter written at the request of Ward Woodbury for his University of Rochester Glee Club, and the former for Dean Robert Hargreaves of the School of Music of Ball State University of Muncie, Indiana. I also made a setting for chorus and orchestra of the thirty-fifth chapter of Isaiah, under rather interesting circumstances.

A conference on arid and semi-arid lands was to be held at Texas Technological College in Lubbock, Texas. One sector, under the direction of Professor Mary Jeanne Van Appledorn, was devoted to a project called "Focus on the Arts." On behalf of the conference committee, she asked me to accept the commission for a choral work for the occasion. I could not imagine what musical subject would be appropriate for a conference on arid lands, until I suddenly remembered the words of the prophet Isaiah, "And the desert shall blossom as the rose." What could be more appropriate? I started to work with enthusiasm. There are few passages in the Bible more beautiful than Isaiah 35.

Peggie had recently undergone an eye operation, blessedly successful, and the passage, "Then shall the eyes of the blind be opened," had for me

---

6 Adlai Stevenson (1900–65), American politician. He was a one-term governor of Illinois and then unsuccessfully ran for president in 1952 and 1956.

a very personal poignancy. With the words, "and the parched land became a pool," the chorus shouts in excitement, and from the orchestra comes the sound of the riotous rushing of waters. Finally, at the end [come] the words, "and sighing and sorrow shall be no more." The orchestra subsides into silence, leaving only the sound of the voices.[7]

The chorus which sang the first performance was eloquent. At the end of the performance, there was a moment of complete and frightening silence, which seemed like an eternity. Then came a bust of applause, and I turned to find the entire audience on its feet! The emotional reaction of audience is supposed to be unpredictable, but I wonder. Some months later, the work was repeated in Tulsa, Oklahoma, by the splendid chorus of Oral Roberts University and the Tulsa Philharmonic under Franco Autori. Peggie and I attended the performance, as she had not heard the Texas premiere. Here was a different orchestra, chorus, conductor, and audience, but the reaction of the audience was amazingly similar to that of the first performance—several seconds of complete silence, followed by a sudden burst of applause, and the audience on its feet as if at a signal. A strange experience.

The most nostalgic of the commissions came from the Centennial Commission of the State of Nebraska. The commission asked me to write a special symphonic work to celebrate the hundredth anniversary of the admission of my native state to the union. The work was a set of variations on the beautiful Lutheran Christmas chorale, "Thou holy, beautiful, hour," celebrating the birth of Christ, and [I] gave it the name *Dies Natalis.*

The first performance was given by the Omaha Symphony, of which Joseph Levine[8] was the music director. An experienced conductor, Mr. Levine had rehearsed the work with great care, and the performance went beautifully. In the audience were hundreds of friends from my youth, many of whom had traveled many miles to attend the concert. It was a "once-in-a-lifetime" occasion.

The following day, Peggie and I drove to my birthplace of Wahoo, Nebraska, to attend an even more nostalgic event. The Women's Club of Wahoo and the Historical Society had taken over my parents' home, the house where I was born, [and] had restored it to its original condition,

---

7 In his discussion of this choral work, Hanson neglects to mention its title. The work in question is *Streams in the Desert* (1969).

8 Joseph Levine (d.1994), American pianist and conductor. A graduate of Curtis, he was pianist for the Philadelphia Orchestra and later conductor of American Ballet Theater 1950–58; he also conducted in Omaha, Seattle, and Honolulu.

even to the extent (where possible) of the original furniture, including my old Mason and Hamlin piano.

Gathered to greet us [was] the daughter of my first piano teacher. [Also among the greeters] were Albin Peterson, the moving force in the restoration of the old home; Mrs. Swanson, the president of the women's club; my first Sunday School teacher, Ora Gilchrist (now in her nineties); and dozens of old friends, relatives, and high school classmates. As I entered the music room and saw the room with its furniture and piano as I remembered them, it seemed that I had been transported over a half century to the beginning of the 1900s.

In front of the house was a plaque, announcing Wahoo as the birthplace of its favorite sons—C.W. Beadle, Nobel Prize–winning geneticist; Hollywood producer Darryl Zanuck; "Wahoo Sam" Crawford of baseball's Hall of Fame; the painter C.W. Anderson; and Howard Hanson, designated as a "music composer." It reminded me of the famous sign which once decorated the approaches to Wahoo. The sign bore our names with the inscription, WAHOO IS PROUD OF ITS BRAVES. WE SAY THIS WITHOUT RESERVATION!

The final commission of the decade was, from a professional standpoint, the most important. The New York Philharmonic, in celebrating its 125th birthday, had commissioned twelve composers (six foreign and six American) to write works celebrating the event. My five American colleagues, invited by Music Director Leonard Bernstein and manager Carlos Mosley, were Elliott Carter, Aaron Copland, Roy Harris, Walter Piston, and Roger Sessions.

For my commission, I wrote my Sixth Symphony. It consisted of six short movements: an introduction, a scherzo, a slow melodic movement, a second scherzo, a transition movement, and a finale. The slow movement [constituted] a kind of "key" to the musical arch. I conducted the first four movements in Philharmonic Hall and was delighted with the playing of the orchestra which Mr. Bernstein had brought to such a high state of perfection. The members of the orchestra gave me their best, which was superb, the audiences were more than cordial, and the critics were unanimous in their approval. Even *Time* magazine bestowed one of its rare accolades. As I have said before, I do not trust a composer's evaluation of his own music until after the passage of several years of time. I can say, however, that of my six symphonies, [the last] is the one which gives me the greatest happiness.

The final work of the decade was the setting of Walt Whitman's "The Mystic Trumpeter," commissioned by the trustees of the Conservatory of Music of the University of Missouri in Kansas City, through its dean emeritus, my good friend, Archie Jones. The poetry of Walt Whitman has always fascinated me. I recall setting "The Untold Want, Portals," and "Now Finale to the Shore" when I was in my teens, and since those early days I have set several of his poems for chorus and orchestra. I always wanted to write music for "The Mystic Trumpeter," but the length and complexity of the task dissuaded me.

Finally, I hit upon the idea of making the setting for narrator, chorus, and orchestra, giving the declamatory passages to the narrator and the dramatic and emotional segments to the chorus, and undergirding the whole with an orchestral accompaniment which reflected the passions of the poem. Although written [when I was] seventy-two, it is a curiously youthful work, embodying many of the characteristics of the *Songs from Drum Taps* written thirty-five years earlier.

Chapter Forty-Five

REFLECTIONS AT THE END OF A LONG CAREER

As one approaches the end of a long career devoted primarily to several aspects of one art—creation, performance, and education—one might be expected to be "filled with prophecy." However, I feel less sure of *ex cathedra* pronouncements today than I did fifty years ago. Some things seem to become clearer as the years pass. Some philosophies seem increasingly secure. Others seem more rather than less confused.

We have entered the decade of the 1970s in a schizophrenic state of mind. In the 1960s we were widely proclaiming an "explosion" of the arts, meaning I suppose a sudden flowering of the arts. But by the end of the decade, we were already deploring the "crisis" in the arts. We enter the 1970s in a state of artistic and societal anarchy. The idols of the past in musical creation and performance seem to be superseded by the Beatles, even on the list of honors of the throne of England!

We live undoubtedly in a different society. It is probably a more democratic society. It is also at the same time a less discriminating society. Even the word "discriminate" has assumed a political rather than a qualitative meaning. As a result, the old norms no longer exist, and new ones have not yet been formed.

Of one thing we can, I believe, be quite certain. The change in our social structure has radically changed the public's attitude toward the arts. Into this whirlpool of change has been poured the tremendous power of the mass communications media, radio, the press, and above all television. The new popular idol of London, Berlin, Rome, or Paris today may (and probably will) be the new idol of New York, Chicago, and Los Angeles tomorrow.

In the past, the arts in general (and this applies most of all to music) always have been the property of a small, elite "establishment." This has been true from the Renaissance through the beginning of the twentieth century. It was true in the days of kings, princes, and nobles. It has been equally true in nineteenth- and twentieth-century United States until very recently. Whether the norms established by the affluent society of aristocracy or wealth were just ones and completely healthy may be questioned.

The norms, however, did exist and were meticulously observed, perhaps at times too meticulously.

The great composers were Bach, Mozart, Beethoven, Brahms, and Wagner. The "modernists"—Schoenberg, Webern, and Stravinsky—were listened to with respect if not always with affection. The great conductors were Nikisch, Weingartner, Furtwängler, Toscanini, Koussevitzky; the great pianists were Paderewski, Rubinstein, Moszkowski, Schnabel, etc. These norms are still preserved today in the great living conductors and performers, but I think it is safe to say that, at least in the public mind, their relative importance is much less. The latest pop idol is more apt to appear on the cover of the weekly magazine than the most distinguished classicist.

This points up dramatically the most important question facing the arts, namely, "What does the new public want from its art and its artists?" In a popularity poll for baritones, I am afraid that, by present standards, Frank Sinatra would be the overwhelming victor. Robert Merrill, of the Met, might make it only if he appears more frequently on the *Johnny Carson* Show.[1]

If we examine the problem of the "musical crisis" in depth, we should probably in all honesty confess that most of us (especially those of us in the profession) speak from the somewhat prejudiced viewpoint of vested and special interests. The conductor of a major symphony orchestra, quite naturally, feels that the most important thing in music is the perpetuation of the symphony in something like its present form. The opera impresario, conductor, or singer, again quite naturally is concerned about the art form closest to his personal interest. The directors and faculties of professional music schools ask how the great professional organizations can survive if there is no adequate place where the young professional can be trained.

The contemporary composer, concerned with the performance of new music (including his own) asks what is the purpose of keeping the symphonies and the opera houses alive if music is already a dying art, and will be a dead art in another generation. And, if one reads history thoughtfully, it is not such a silly question.

The public school music supervisor asks the quite obvious question, "How can the professional music schools survive if there is no back-log of potential talent coming to them from the public schools?" It is difficult to develop a violinist sufficiently competent to enter the Philadelphia Orchestra in four years of college!

All of this reasoning is, of course, predicated upon the fact that we are (all of us) thinking of the preservation of the artistic *status quo*. We

---

1   Hanson is referring to the popular and highly successful *Tonight Show* hosted for thirty years by Johnny Carson.

want the preservation, in perpetuity if possible, of the great music of the past—music which demands the existence of great orchestras, choruses, chamber ensembles capable of its performance. The historical argument is overwhelming. Certainly, civilization cannot afford to lose its Haydn, Mozart, Beethoven Brahms, Wagner, Mahler, Sibelius. And yet, there are literally millions of young people who, at least at the present time, could not apparently care less. Give them a couple of electric guitars, a bass fiddle, and some drums, and they are happy. They have proven that they will rally by the hundreds of thousands to the support of their kind of music, although its popularity may have been assisted by the presence of other elements besides the music itself.

This is, I believe, the reason that some of our most gifted conductors are predicting the demise of the symphony orchestra, not because they do not consider it a great and important artistic asset, but because they question whether the interest of the general public is sufficient to support it.

The death of the orchestra would be mourned by thousands, perhaps hundreds of thousands, of Americans. However, in terms of the vast population, the percentage would be relatively small. I cannot believe that the dweller in the ghetto, the poor, the underprivileged, would be greatly upset. Their chances of hearing a symphony orchestra remain minimal.

This problem of what we might call "democracy in art" is further compounded by the increasing pressure for government subsidy of the arts at the local, state, and federal levels. Such subsidies obviously must come from taxes levied on the general public. This should give that general public some voice in the expenditure of such subsidies. If the general public shows no interest in the survival of the symphony orchestra, should the local council, the state legislature, or the Congress appropriate large sums of money for an organization designed to serve only the comparatively affluent and sophisticated stratum of society?

This whole argument of what we might call "social relevance" sounds quite convincing until we realize that the art of music, at its highest level, never has been democratic. The genuine appreciation of great music is both a natural and an acquired taste, natural in that there must be a basic and visceral sensitivity to sound, acquired in that there must be opportunities for hearing.

This has nothing to do with cultural snobbishness, although the appreciation of great music can be affected. It has nothing to do with social position, wealth, or (I am afraid) even education. If there is in the soul of the listener the seed of the sensitivity for such understanding, it can be developed. Otherwise, the chances of success are small.

The next question follows naturally. If great music appeals to only a small portion of the total population, is it "sociologically" worth preserving? If only a minority "appreciate" poetry, should the publishers discontinue publishing it? Beethoven is a great composer, not because he is the choice of a majority body-count of the world's population, but because he is the choice of a comparatively small number of people of both the present and past ages who know something about music. Those who would "save" the symphony by substituting rock and roll for Beethoven completely miss the point. This is not first aid. It is murder!

On the other hand, I can sympathize with those who would perform both "rock" and Beethoven on the same program. If Beethoven were "sneaked" into a rock program when no one was looking, the "rock lover" might possibly see the light and be saved! The Beethoven Fifth is, after all, pretty powerful stuff!

There are many points about the "status quo" which might, I think, be changed with profit. There is one point which we must never concede. There may be in aesthetics, or even in religion, no absolute absolutes. But some things are better than others. Some music is good, some is meretricious. Discrimination is not a dirty word. Upon our discrimination rests not only the future of the arts but [also] the future of a civilization that is worth living in.

In discussing the *status quo* of the musical establishment, certain problems come immediately to mind. I am sure that we need have no worry that music will survive in some form. The instinct for song, for rhythm, for decoration, is too deeply embedded in the consciousness of man ever to be eradicated. The question is, rather, in what form will it survive?

If we examine this problem (as news commentators say) "in depth," we come face to face with the basic question of priorities. What things are the most important in developing a healthy musical climate. We have, I am sure, all been intrigued by the continuing debate on the cost of the space program. Would it be healthier for our country if less were spent on excursions to the moon (or to Mars) and more on education, on the physical and spiritual environment, and so forth? I have no competence to pass judgment in this area, but I can attempt some judgments in my own field. Let me take a practical example.

Suppose I were to ask my listeners this question:[2] Would the death of the Metropolitan Opera Company be a national cultural disaster of

---

2 In transcribing this chapter from Hanson's draft, I was immediately struck by the fact that it read as if it were a draft for a speech rather than an

the greatest magnitude? I do not know what your answer would be. I am sure that the answers would vary greatly. My own answer would be "No!" It would not be a national cultural disaster. That is not to say that I would not be sorry to witness its passing. I would be sorry to see it go. But I would not regard it as a catastrophic event. It is a great museum for the operatic art, but its status quo is too deeply embedded for possible change. It is too irrelevant to the times. Its hull is too heavily encrusted with the barnacles of age. Its death might be followed by a rebirth of something much more significant and more vital.

Suppose I were to ask you a second question: Would the wholesale cutting off of funds for music teaching in the public schools, from their bands, orchestras, choruses, be a national cultural disaster? What would your answer be? Again, I do not know. My own answer would be an emphatic "Yes!" It would indeed be a major cultural disaster comparable to a hurricane, a tornado, or an earthquake. It might well spell the end of our entire musical culture. And yet, I know a number of music patrons (I distinguished carefully between music patrons and music lovers) who would be desolate over the demise of the Metropolitan Opera but would not even notice the deterioration of our music education program.

Again, what is the priority between the professional and amateur musical organizations? This is a more difficult question, and yet it deserves consideration. There can be no question that great orchestras such as Philadelphia, Boston, New York, Cleveland are necessary as examples and standard makers. And yet, I know some amateur or semiprofessional orchestras which are serving their communities and their art better than some of the professionals.

The value of the amateur organization is even clearer in the field of choral music. The Rockefeller Brothers Report on the Performing Arts, in speaking of choral music, refers entirely to professional groups. And yet, the choral status of the country would be one of extreme poverty if we were dependent on professional groups. The overwhelming portion of our excellent choral music is the product of amateurs. Without them, choral music would be virtually nonexistent.

The same situation applies to ballet. Most of the groups are a mixture of the professional, the student, and the amateur. Without such groups, there would be precious little ballet, and yet their importance to the culture of the United States is frequently completely ignored.

---

article or book. It is illuminating that he uses "listeners" rather than "readers" at this point in his narrative. This is followed by other references that strongly indicate that Hanson's choice of a final chapter was the text of some speech he had previously given.

Yet another priority which should be considered is that of the performer versus the creator. This age is, without doubt, the age of the performer. The almost complete neglect by our cultural policymakers of the composer (indeed of the whole creative element in music) is difficult to understand.

In this whole discussion of priorities to ensure a healthy, productive music program in the United States, much of the responsibility for an imbalance may, I believe, be justly laid at the door of the so-called establishment. By "establishment" I mean the individuals who control our most prestigious musical organizations, our symphony orchestras, and our opera houses. It consists, as a general rule, of the community's first citizens, laymen chosen because of civic interest, musical interest, social importance, money, education, or any combination of these desirable attributes.

I do not share the cynicism of many musicians toward the "establishment." Without such groups, we would probably have no symphonies at all. I have met literally hundreds of laymen and lay women [all] over the country who have given countless hours of work, dedication, and money to the support of our cultural organizations.

In spite of this, there are some problems which frequently vary from orchestra to orchestra. The principal problem seems to be that of achieving balance in direction. A few orchestras have been completely dominated by their music directors, in some cases with the happiest of results. A few are dominated by their managers, some by their presidents, others by small and tightly knit executive committees. I recall one western orchestra that was in serious trouble because the president of the board insisted on dictating the programs for the orchestral concerts. In another orchestra, the governing committee in complete contrast seemed concerned only with the budget and quite devoid of interest in the musical season itself. In yet another case, the orchestra suffered a lack of communication between an ultra-conservative president and a progressive and innovative conductor.

Some orchestras are helped (or hampered) by countless committees set up to concern themselves with every aspect of the orchestra's programs. Others depend on the judgment (or the whim) of one person. But the direction of an orchestral season requires a more balanced and more imaginative direction. Music may be too important to be left to the musicians, and yet the professional advice of competent musicians cannot be dispensed with, as it frequently is.

The box office may not be all-important but is certainly not unimportant. The impact of the orchestra on the entire community (not only on the sophisticated minority) cannot be ignored. There is no point in turning a ninety-piece ensemble into a rock and roll ensemble, or even a jazz band. (Such outfits do not require ninety men!) At the same time, the tastes of the "new young" cannot be overlooked.

What I am trying to say is that the success of the symphony orchestra depends upon the best advice of many knowledgeable people of different backgrounds, tastes, and interests. The establishment of this kind of direction is not an easy task. I do believe, however, that in these difficulties, the orchestra needs this kind of enlightened guidance.

There is a second "establishment" of importance equal to that of the governing establishment. It is the professional establishment—the conductor, the manager, the player, the composer, and (last but very far from least) the unions, particularly the American Federation of Musicians. This should be ideally a great team of dedicated professionals working for the good of mankind and the glory of music. Too frequently, however, these dedicated professionals each pursue his individual way with seemingly little thought of the art itself or its impact on the community.

Greatest in practical importance is the conductor. He should theoretically be a superman, an impeccable musician with the memory of a computer, the brain of [a] Nobel prize–winning mathematician, and the heart of a child. He should be equally at home in the music of Palestrina, Mozart, Beethoven, Brahms, Sibelius, Mahler, Gershwin, Bacharach, and Laurel and Hardy. He should make programs which please everyone. He should be charmingly autocratic; modestly egocentric; a kind, tolerant, and understanding Simon Legree with stern but permissive discipline; and a matinee idol of the first magnitude, preferably not over twenty-five.

I have worked in my time with many great conductors—Koussevitzky, Stokowski, Toscanini, Reiner, Ormandy, Szell, Stock, Serafin, Coates, Goosens, Leinsdorf, Iturbi, to name only a few. None of them attained completely the above specifications, although some approached it. The great ones, however, were all men of artistic integrity, devoted to their art, devoted to old music, to new music, to middle-age music, devoted to their orchestras. They were, in the truest sense, teachers, pioneers, musical statesmen. Some of them are fortunately still with us, but many of them are gone. They are not easily replaced, and they are sorely needed.

We need also managers, and especially managers who like music! And here we seem to be more successful. We are developing a few who actually listen to their own orchestras. I have known managers who would not enter a concert hall during a concert except in the case of a serious fire.

We need artists who do not regard music as a dead art, who understand that music did not stop in 1896. We need orchestral players who do not spend the last fifteen minutes of an orchestral rehearsal looking at their watches. Above all, we most desperately need great new composers. We need a new Mozart, a new Brahms, a new Sibelius. We should be willing to give the entire resources of the Ford Foundation for a new Beethoven who could put into music man's deepest emotions and aspirations.

It is hard to live in this arid age, an age of music for the digital computer and the tape recorder, in an age where the performer is separated from the composer, and where the composer is separated both from the performer and from his audience. But this is too sad and complicated [a] story to dwell upon here.

No account of the "professional establishment" is complete without mentioning the unions, organizations such as the American Guild of Musical Artists, the American Federation of Radio and Television Artists, and (most important) the American Federation of Musicians. Of these, the most important in the music profession, I suppose, is the AF of M, more frequently referred to as the Musicians' Union. As a member of this union for at least forty years, I am sympathetic to its basic purpose: the prevention of the exploitation of the professional performer.

At the same time, it seems clear to many of us, including a number of highly intelligent union leaders, that the time has come for a thorough re-study of the whole rationale of the union's purpose and activity. Otherwise, the very union which was designed to save (and actually did save) the life of the professional performer might prove the killer rather than the savior.

Some of the problems are important only to the extent that they tend to destroy artistic integrity, which Erich Leinsdorf has referred to as the "existing of time-clock punching" and the "bourgeois patter of work" of the professional musician. These are the regulations which reduce orchestral performance from an art to a craft.

One example may suffice to illustrate Mr. Leinsdorf's point. A normal "union" rehearsal is two and one-half hours in length, interrupted by a twenty-minute rest period. Anything beyond this is "over-time." This is quite proper. Without such regulations, some conductors would continue rehearsing indefinitely. However, the observance of such a regulation sometimes produces [results] which are frustrating and ridiculous. I recall one personal experience which illustrates Mr. Leinsdorf's "clock-punching" remark. Most conductors have timeclocks in their heads and figure their rehearsal time with the greatest accuracy. On this occasion, however, one of the players had extended his coffee break three minutes beyond the specified twenty, and we began the second half of the rehearsal three minutes late. At the end of the rehearsal, as we were completing the last movement of a symphony, we came to the end of our allotted 150 minutes approximately fifty seconds before the final cadence, whereupon the personnel manager stopped the rehearsal, as was his duty according to union rules.

Stopping a work only a few seconds before the final cadence is a devastating experience for any sensitive musician. I am sure that 90 percent (or perhaps even 100 percent) of the musicians of the orchestra would gladly have played the extra fifty seconds. But union rules are union rules.

I recall a similar experience on radio, which had nothing to do with the union. They were playing a record of my first symphony. At the end, there is a tremendous burst of sound, a short pause, and then the final chord. The engineer, whose ears were apparently only fit for treason, stratagems, and spoils, came to the pause and lifted the needle. I waited breathlessly for the final chord, which never came! The experience was devastating.

These aberrations can be dismissed as both childish and unimportant. There are other problems which are infinitely more important. The most perplexing of all is the problem of electronics in relation to the professional musician. It must be remembered that the days before television and radio were the halcyon days of many orchestral musicians. I recall that in 1924 the salaries of many members of the Eastman Theatre Orchestra were twice my salary as director of the Eastman School of Music. I don't believe that their job was that much more difficult!

The advent of talking pictures changed all that. The science of electronics, recorded sound, became the archenemy of the professional orchestral player. The musicians' union, under James Caesar Petrillo, did everything in its power to contain the monster, first by appealing to public sentiment ("Don't be satisfied with canned music!") and then by attempting to price recorded music out of the market. Neither attempt succeeded. Electricity seems to be here to stay.

Even forty years later, the same mental block seems to exist, although it may by now be subconscious. In any case, the philosophy of the 1930s seems to persist. I am not an economist, but common sense would seem to indicate that the gradual pricing of American recordings off the market is not [a] very bright idea.

The orchestras first affected were, of course, the provincial orchestras, which at current costs could not possibly find a market. With the further increase in musicians' recording fees, there are indications that even the greatest of the American orchestras are in trouble, with the large recording contracts leaving the US for Europe.

The union's recording contracts have, I am sure unintentionally, done the greatest harm to the contemporary composer, and especially to the

American composer. A recording of Tchaikovsky's "Nutcracker" by the Philadelphia Orchestra under Eugene Ormandy may still pay for itself, with perhaps a small profit. The profitable recording of a comparatively unknown work by a contemporary composer, even one who is well-known, is virtually impossible.

Union regulations concerning the presentation of symphony orchestras on television, which may well be the concert hall of the future, present similar roadblocks, even though services of the musicians already paid for may be available.

The art of music approaches the eighth decade of this twentieth century with many problems and few solutions. Those of us who are concerned with the life of music in the years ahead remain adamant in our belief in the importance of the creative and the performing arts. We believe that, in the age of materialism, the arts are more desperately needed than in any time in our history.

Those of us who have spent our lives in music education believe that student anarchists, nihilists, arsonists, murderers, are not apt to be found among the membership of our college and university choruses, bands, and orchestras. We have seen ample proof of the civilizing (which means sensitizing) power of music. What we need now is leadership.

Appendix

LETTERS FROM HOWARD HANSON TO HIS PARENTS, (1914–1922)

New York, New York, March 16, 1914

Here I am back in NY again. It seems almost natural. We had quite a time getting to Scenery Hill. We missed connections and had to drive 14 miles in a car, but it was a lovely drive thru the mountains. I felt like a lark, because it was my last "offense."

We got up at about 5 o'clock and drove about 1 1/2 [miles?] to the railroad, then took a 6:15 train for Pittsburgh, getting into Pittsburgh about 8:50.

The girls left at 9:15 for Chicago and I left at 9:40 on the "NY Day Express" for NY. I reached here about 7:30 last night. Marian was down to meet me as Carl was having a dress rehearsal at Newark. They are trying out a new play there, and Carl was asked to take part in it.

Marian and I took a taxi (very swell) up here, and we had a nice supper. The ride on the train from Pittsburgh was pretty tiresome. I had a nice dinner in the diner. It was very nice too, and it helped to pass away a couple of half hours.

I read and slept and analyzed music thru the rest of the time.

The folks here seem to be very glad to have me back again and are "crazy" to have me come here next fall as a "special student" under Prof. Rübner of Columbia.

He is <u>the</u> head of the conservatory and is a German brought direct from the conservatory of Carlsbad, Germany.

I will play my "Suite" for him tomorrow afternoon at his home at 2 o'clock. It is fine that it can be at his home, because it will be so much more private.

He seems very anxious to hear me play my compositions.

Frank Damrosch sailed for Europe last Thursday, so I just missed him. I will see Dr. Goetschius of the Institute of Musical Art on Friday, as the school doesn't open until then.

They want me to stay longer, but I intend to leave Friday night which will bring me home sometime Sunday. I am also to meet Prof. Robyn, a Swedish pianist.

But will close now and practice a little on my Suite.

Kansas City, Missouri, May 7, 1914

I am pretty peeved today. Miss Proctor told me that Mr. Horner had suggested a salary of $30 a week for me while I am here, and I am to pay my own expenses, except railroad.

I will see him before he goes home tonight and get things straightened out. It strikes me that he is getting a coach pretty cheaply at $30 a week. I certainly will talk things over with him.

I am getting rather tired of this unbusiness-like kind of dealing, and I am going to arrive at some kind of a definite agreement about all these things.

The coaching has not commenced yet and will not for quite a while. Mr. Lewens [?] arrived last night, and he will be here now for a long time, I believe.

Mr. Horner also wants me to write one piece of ragtime for the "Old Home Singers." I don't know whether I want to do it or not.

I am feeling pretty good, go to bed at nine every night, and get up quite early. I also walk to and from work, which makes it very pleasant.

I recognized Popsie's lovely letter, and was tickled to get it, alright. Am anxious to hear the particulars of the "Mother's Day" program. Well, I will close now.

May 24, 1914, Kansas City, Missouri

It is now Sunday night and I just got in. I haven't been to see Aunt Tilly yet, isn't that awful?

This morning I rehearsed the Chautauqua Quartette until eleven o'clock, then I went to church. One of the Old Home Singers, the soprano, sang a solo, and it was very nice. I enjoyed the sermon fine too.

This afternoon I went over to the studio and practiced piano for a while there. I went over and visited some of the "Cavaliers." I went to supper with Mr. and Mrs. Tregillus [?].

After supper six of us took a walk, 3 boys and 3 girls, and had a nice long walk to Westport. My companion was a girl from Macon. She is mighty nice, only 17 years old. She is with one of the orchestras with her sister, who is older than she.

I left the bunch about 10 o'clock, the other fellows are there yet, I suppose. Hard to break away!!

We are planning to work very hard this next week. Practically every evening will be filled by rehearsals.

The first program of any of my compositions will be Sunday at K. City, Kansas by the "Hornely Old Singers."

But it is about eleven o'clock, so I must go to bed.

June 13, 1914, Kansas City, Missouri

Just returned from the dress rehearsal of the "American Girls." They did very well. The Chautauqua Quartette gave theirs last night which I attended. They left today for KC, Kansas, and I heard that they made a big hit there. Of course, that is a good thing for me, as I coached them more, I believe, than anyone.

Tomorrow Lenge's [?] Symphonic Orchestra plays in Kansas City, Kansas, and I would like to go over and hear them if I have time.

I have been getting along very well lately. I have been working quite a bit with one of the ladies orchestras, and I like it very much. Have also been coaching [one] of the cellists frequently. They think I am just fine, and I don't have any trouble in getting them to do what I want.

Friday night the "Cavaliers" give their dress rehearsal, and on Saturday they give their programs in Kansas City, Kansas.

The last company from here will leave in two weeks.

The "Old House Singers" had two preludes in Kansas City, Kansas, last Saturday and came out fine. They open their season in Texas Friday or Saturday.

I will be glad to get home and take a rest. I'm tired but feeling fine.

New York City, New York, October 13, 1914

Back in little old New York again. Got back last night and started in work this afternoon. Took my first lesson in ear training and my first in piano and got along fine.

I like my teacher on piano fine. His name is Mr. Friskin, and he is very fine. I played several things for him, and he seemed to think quite favorably of my work, and made no very serious criticisms, just a few of the smaller points.

Got along very nicely in ear training. The teacher is a woman and is very pleasant and agreeable. I pushed my nose in at the beginning (as usual) and made everyone gasp by proposing some very astonishing things. They are very conservative and they certainly "sat around" when I started in. I guess they think I am an anarchist. I expect to have a fine time.

Tomorrow, I go to my friend Mr. Goetschius for my first counterpoint lesson, which I trust will go along very nicely, also will take my first lesson in harmonic ear training, another branch of ear training.

Had a fine time up at the farm but am glad to get back to the city for work again. Received Mr. Harmon's [?] check and letter. Very nice, wasn't it? Also got all of your letters, Honies, and appreciate these so much. The Democrat [newspaper from Wahoo] comes regularly, and I look forward to it. Appreciate Popsie's sending my favorite editorial section of the Bee and the "Advice to the Lovelorn." They are great.

Aunt Clara has been at home since Thursday, laid up with tonsillitis. She had a pretty bad throat but is getting better now. Ed is treating her, so she will be all right soon.

The folks at the farm are all well and will be down before the first of November, for which I am glad.

Every evening when I am here, I always go up to a little French cafe on Broadway, and I enjoy it very much. Clara is almost always with me. It is very cheering to walk along and see all the people, lights, and automobiles.

Received a letter from Lyman and Earl.

New York City, New York, October 15, 1914

How are you feeling, honies? Hope everything is going fine. I am feeling fine, and Clara is also feeling well now, too.

I took another piano lesson today, and I like my Prof. immensely. He is a splendid pianist and a very fine teacher. He has me play a few measures about 10 times until I get it just the way he wants it. He hails from jolly England and is a very pleasant man. So many good teachers are such terribly cranks, so I think I am very fortunate.

It has been raining all day, a continuous drizzle, and the river is covered with fog. The battleship is still in the river.

Uncle Ed was up again today. Aunt Clara will probably go to the theater tomorrow.

Will close, as it is about 10:30.

New York, March 10, 1915

Got Popsie's letter this morning. I have been over at the school three hours this morning. I attended ensemble class first and then took an examination from Prof. Robinson in harmonic dictation. I got along very nicely though and didn't have any trouble with it.

I have been practicing this afternoon almost all afternoon from about 1:30 to 5, which was a good long stretch.

This evening, Mrs. Frothingham [Aunt Clara's mother] and I went out to a bookstore for some shopping, so I had a nice little walk. It is lovely weather, very mild and balmy.

Marian is getting along splendidly and is up and around now. The nurse leaves in a couple of days. Carl is rehearsing to beat the band and will leave Sunday or possibly Saturday night. They seem to be getting along very splendidly and hope for a big success.

NY City, New York, April 4, 1915

It has been a lovely Easter Sunday after all. It cleared up beautifully and has been great all day. I went to church this morning to the Broadway Presbyterian Church. I didn't go to the Cathedral because they had Communion, and I don't want to take it except at my own church, and I dislike not to participate when it is being held. The services were very beautiful and the sermon quite good.

This evening, Helen Holmes, who is the "leading lady" with the "Natural Law," and her husband were up to supper and have not left yet. It is not very late yet though.

I've been getting my lessons ready for tomorrow and am already for old Prof. G tomorrow.

Tomorrow evening is our first performance. I hope it goes well, and I think that it will. The music is beautiful, and the orchestra plays splendidly.

I donned my new suit today for the first time, and it looks very nice, and with my nice little watch chain "what" you gave me, I was quite a nifty youngster.

I am still working on my double piano number, and it is not half finished yet.

NY City, May 10, 1915

Was mighty glad to get Popsie's dear letter, believe me, I have been waiting for that for about three days.

I attended one of Dr. Goetschius's classes this morning. He told me that my fugue was "stunning," which is top-notch praise from the Doctor. I guess that he was very proud of it. Many people have congratulated me on the composition, and everyone seemed to think it was such a big piece of work. I guess that my playing made quite a sensation, too.

This afternoon I attended two of Dr. Pratt's lectures on Music History. We played Beethoven's 2nd Symphony as an illustration for the second lecture. I played the first part, and it went very well, and we were quite pleased with it.

This week, our examinations begin. On Friday, I take my piano examination, on Saturday Mr. Toffer [?] gives us our questions, next Monday comes our History test, Wednesday Mr. Robinson's, and Thurs. Dr. Goetschius, quite a list, isn't it?

Tomorrow, I have another piano lesson. This evening the warships are throwing their searchlights all over, and it is a wonderful sight. Each ship has about 6 high-powered search lights, and the shafts of light cross each other. It is perfectly gorgeous.

[Evanston, Illinois,] September 19, 1915

Well, here I am in Evanston and have, with Mr. Frank, surely been making hay.

Dr. Lutkin was very much pleased with my work and took to me just like Dr. Rübner. He was really <u>tickled</u> to see me. He told Mr. Frank afterwards that he liked me very much and that there was a good chance of their being able to give me something to do here. I learned afterwards from one of the Professors that when Dr. Lutkin says that there is any possibility at all, there is likely to be a very big one. It will depend very much on the registration, which if larger than usual will require another instructor.

President Harris, head of the Uni[versity], asked Dr. Lutkin to give me a position if possible, and he would try to "loosen the trustees' money bag" a little.

I also have been granted by Dr. Lutkin a $100 scholarship which will pay my theoretical course for the entire year!!! It is just like walking into a garden of roses.

The degree bachelor of music requires 4 years theory and one year's college work. They are very careful with this degree, and it has been given to only one man in <u>15 years</u>!!! Professor Oldberg of the composition department thinks I may receive this degree in one year!!!

Evanston is a wonderful place, about 35,000 and peopled by many of the millionaires and multis [i.e. multi-millionaires] of Chicago.

The school campus faces the lake and is perfectly beautiful. This afternoon, I was over to one of the fraternity houses and played and had a splendid time.

I am staying with Mr. Frank and Dr. Laughlin, his roommate. The Dr. is an instructor in German at Evanston Academy and is a fine man. He and I are alone this evening, Sunday, as Mr. Frank went into the city for an hour or so on business.

Well, honies, I surely have missed home this last week. We had a wonderful time, didn't we?

Now you know the condition of things here. It seems wonderfully promising, and so I suppose I had better stay. It would surely be fine if I could get my BM degree this first year.

Well, I must close now. Everything has come up so quickly that it almost makes a man's head whirl.

Evanston, Ill., November 30, 1915

Got Momsie's dear letter today, and it was so cheering to get it.

I was up to the Dean's house today and showed him my "Magnificat." He was very much pleased with it and had very few suggestions to make on it.

I got my last French examination paper back today and got another A, so I am glad over that. My Trig Prof told me that I am fast walking away with it in great shape, so I guess I am pretty well fixed.

Just think, tomorrow is December 1, and I am glad. This constant work is all very fine, but it gets darn monotonous and tiresome at times.

I got back quite a bunch of papers on my examination in harmony. They seemed to get it very well. The asst. secretary made the copies of the questions for me, and she asked if there were any classes in school that could answer those questions. I said, "Oh yes, these classes can do it easily!" Piffle, so to speak.

Evanston, Ill., February 19, 1916

Got Momsie's dear letter, and it was very interesting. I bet you had quite a little trip and a nice time in Lincoln.

I received a fine letter from Dr. Seaton of the College of the Pacific saying that I am entirely satisfactory if we can arrange terms satisfactorily. He asks for from twenty to twenty-five hours a week. I wrote him that it would be satisfactory with me. He said that Oberlin and almost all the big colleges are having between twenty and thirty hour contracts, and he would like twenty-five hours.

My Symphonic Poem got through with Prof. Oldberg very nicely yesterday, in fact he was complimentary about it.

I got along pretty well in German. Did something very well and others very poorly, but it will come after time. English went very well today, we wrote about Chaucer's "Prologue," and I did quite well, I think.

Evanston, Ill., March 8, 1916

Got a very nice letter from Momsie today, which I enjoyed immensely.

I saw the Dean this morning. He told me that copyists were ready for my Symphonic Prelude anytime it is ready, so I gave it to Prof. Oldberg this afternoon to give it what the boys call the "once-over!" He also told me that Pacific College has written him about my pianistic ability. It seems that they are making at least two or more changes in the faculty, and they seem to think I may get some piano work. The Dean seems to think that I have the position. He wrote them a letter about my ability and told me to write them and give details, which I did in my letter to them this afternoon. I trust that I will get it.

The teaching progresses "apace," and I believe I am really doing good work. Most of my people seem to be able to <u>think</u>, which is very encouraging.

The completion of the Symphonic Prelude will mean quite a lot to me. I can sort of sit down and take it easy occasionally.

Hope you are both feeling just fine, Honies.

Evanston, Illinois, May 25, 1916

Just got Popsie's dear letter which I enjoyed very much.

I am awfully glad that school is about thru. I am surely ready to quit. Attended my last English and German class today, and no examinations to take in any subject.

We didn't get out of orchestra practice until about 10:30. It is getting to be quite a grind now. We are playing concertos for all the seniors almost. It surely is great stuff!

I had a session with Mr. Stulty, the vocal teacher, and Mr. Ashbaucher. After Ashbaucher's lesson, I stayed and played some accompaniments for another pupil. Mr. A thinks I am "some" accompanist.

I am going up to the laboratory this afternoon for a few hours and monkeying around a little. I am commencing to feel the reaction after the strain of the last month.

Hope you are feeling just fine, Honies.

San Jose, California, September 7, 1916

Just got Popsie's dear letter, which I enjoyed so much.

Well, today's teaching was a great success, for which I am very thankful. I had a class in Form and Analysis and Counterpoint, and the people were great. They were so interested. Miss Markley, who is sort of a private secretary for Dean Allen, said that the girls "raved" about my course.

I have some fine piano pupils. Some of them show lots of real talent. We had one interesting case. Dean Allen brought up a young boy who is poor but simply wild to compose. He played one of his compositions, which shows real talent. His folks are poor, so I told the Dean that I would give him a lesson in piano and composition once a week after school hours. The kid is really a small wonder. He may develop into something very good.

Today they had opening exercises which were very good. Dennis sang very well, too, and we had a fine address. They announced the endowment raised just in Santa Clara Valley was almost $110,000, so they are very much pleased. Dr. Seaton feels very happy over it.

I must get to work on tomorrow's lecture now.

San Jose, March 17, 1917

Was so sorry to get Popsie's note telling of Grandpa's death. I am so sorry, but I suppose that it is best. I hope that you don't feel too bad about it, Popsie dear.

I felt very badly when I heard about it, but I supposed that it would have to come soon.

I have been feeling much better physically lately. I have been keeping up the early bed idea and feel much better. Work is going just fine, and I am very much pleased with everything.

Dr. Seaton and Mrs. Seaton will leave for Hawaii tomorrow. I hope that they have a fine trip. He needs the rest.

I am feeling alright, <u>don't worry about me</u>, Honies. I am taking fine care of myself.

Must close now and go to bed.

San Jose, California, May 23, 1919

Just got through with an orchestra rehearsal for this evening and am about ready to go home and get something to eat. I have had a pretty hard day, because I have been so tired that it has been an effort to keep going. I stayed home yesterday, so I feel better today than I did then. I also had a little tiff with Allen, though that is getting to be quite natural. He is certainly getting as nasty as he can possibly be without showing it to other people. I don't know what in the world is the matter with him. The kids think it is because he is jealous. At any rate, he certainly does plenty of little things to get my goat. For example, he "canned" the Symphonic Poem of my favorite student in composition, Mr. Ishikawa, from the Senior program. He said that he did not consider it interesting enough and well enough written for the Senior recital! Can you beat that? The answer is, No!!! He can certainly do the smallest little "cat-tricks" of almost any man I know right now. It makes me mad because I have always stood up for him when other people have run him down, but I am over that now.

I finally finished my Sonata, and Jules sent the last movement east for me a couple of days ago. This is certainly a relief to have it sent. I am also trying to clean up some of my other works.

This evening we give the first performance of the Romance Rose. I certainly hope that it goes well, and I think it will as everyone is pretty well-prepared in their parts, and the orchestra is doing very well. The scenery is all up now and really looks very clever. The first act is laid in a garden, and the second is laid in the mystical "Garden of Dreams." It is all very cleverly done. We will have another performance of it tomorrow night, and then that will be off our chests.

San Jose, California, May 29, 1919

Just a few lines before running home, as I am on the program this evening. I went over to the reception last night, and we had quite a program. There were speeches from two of the students in behalf of the students, and speeches from Dean Kline and myself in behalf of the College faculty and the Conservatory faculty. I delivered a very good speech, every said, though it was pretty impromptu, as I had no time to work with it at all. Dean Allen replied, of course, and after the program we had punch.

The other numbers on the program were three songs by Dennis, which he sang very well. I played his accompaniments. The students then put on a little sketch entitled "As others see us," which was a take-off on various members of the faculty. I was represented, and the fellow who took me off did pretty well. The crowd enjoyed it a lot.

I was very much pleased at the trend of remarks. As Dennis told me afterwards, it seemed like, "We're sorry to lose Mr. Allen—but Oh! you Mr. Hanson!" They all spoke of how glad they were I was succeeding Dean Allen, and Miss Fox said in a little talk she gave that the students had decided that Mr. Hanson was to be the new Dean even before the Trustees knew about it! All of which is very encouraging and makes me feel good.

I had another practice with Jules and the boys, and they all did very well. I hope they do even better at the recital this evening. It should be a very interesting program.

This morning, Dr. Knoles repeated his address on "Bolshevism" at Chapel, and I appreciated it as much as ever the second time. He certainly understands history and political science, and is a dandy speaker.

Well, I must run along.

San Jose, December 2, 1919

Got two of your letters today and certainly appreciated them. It is certainly great to get your letters regularly, Honies.

Miss Levy of the State Board of Education called to see me today, and I had a long conference with her. She is going around the state looking over the music requirements that various schools are offering for the state certificates, and she wanted my opinion on what I considered to be essential for a student who would get a certificate to teach music in the high schools of the state. We talked for about three hours and went over a lot of work. She told me one thing that pleased me a great deal. She said that she considered our Conservatory the most professional school of music in the state of California, and coming from someone who has their fingers on every certificate and degree granting institution in the state, including the state university, it is saying a good deal and means quite a lot. It is certainly encouraging to run across something like that.

The orchestra practice last night with the soloists for the "Messiah" went excellently, too, and that pleases me a great deal. One of the students will sing the soprano part, Miss Miller will sing contralto, Mr. Dennis bass, and a man from in town, who has a lovely voice, will sing tenor. His name is Chester Herold. I think that I have spoken of him before. I have been invited down there quite often in the past years.

Who should drop in the other day—in fact, yesterday morning—but my "patroness," Mrs. Kelly of Ar-Kel Villa. She has been in the Orient for six months and just returned. She is entering her youngest son in the Academy and wants me to be sure and come out to see them. I guess that they haven't forgotten me after all. She says that her oldest son, the one who is in business in Chicago and whom I met out there over a year ago, thinks that I am quite a wonder and that he talks about me a good deal!

Will quit patting myself on the back and go to dinner.

San Jose, California, January 29, 1920

Am writing at noon today for a change of time. I got over here a little earlier from lunch.

Examinations are going full tilt, and I am very much pleased with the results. Yesterday afternoon we had our first students' solo class for the year, and it went very well. About 8 students performed, and I presided, introducing each performance. It was very interesting.

Last night we had our practice for the first time on our new oratorio, Gounod's "St. Cecilia's Mass." It is a beautiful oratorio, and at the same time not terribly difficult.

After rehearsal, I took Miss Moore and Mr. and Mrs. Dennis to see the play "Seventeen" by Booth Tarkington. If it comes to Lincoln or Omaha when you can see it, be sure and don't miss it. It was great. The others enjoyed it a great deal, and it gave me a chance to pay off some of my social debts.

Almost time for a class (or for another lesson), so must close.

San Jose, California, October 8, 1920

Got Popsies dear letter today and am so disappointed to hear that he has a bad cold again. I wish that you could get out of the cold-breeding climate and that you would be more careful than you are. It has been really lovely out here, and I am feeling fine. My work is enough lighter this year to make a great deal of difference, so I am enjoying my work very much more.

This morning, Miss Miller sang in chapel, but I did not play any solos. I will probably play Monday instead. The first faculty recital will be given a week from Monday evening. I certainly hope that everything will go fine.

We had our first chorus rehearsal Wednesday evening, and it went fine. We started right in on the "Messiah," and they did the best reading I have seen a chorus do for some time. I was very much pleased with them. We will start the orchestra Monday evening.

Did I tell you that I felt my first earthquake the other day? It was a very peculiar sensation. Something like the feeling you have on a boat when it rolls a little. There were five gentle swells and then nothing more happened. I was teaching a class, and everyone looked so surprised. Afterwards, they all laughed.

The box of magazines arrived here today, and everything looks alright. I haven't had a chance to open the box yet. I guess they did a pretty good job of nailing it up!

I think that this evening I will forget my cares and take in the movies. I certainly hope that you are both feeling swell now, Honies, and that Popsie is over his cold by this time.

Must run along now. May God bless you and keep you both, my dear Honies.

San Jose, California, November 23, 1920

Am afraid that I missed out yesterday, as it was certainly one strenuous day for me. I had some piano lessons to make up on account of the time I spent giving examinations last week, and then in the evening I had to manage the concert by Lhevinne. So the day was really a little too much to be entirely pleasant.

The concert was very good. He is a wonderful technician and does about anything to the piano that he wants to. I don't like his programs so well, though. He is very conservative and sticks quite close to Beethoven,

Schumann, etc. Of course, it was very interesting anyway. He was very pleasant personally, and I had a little talk with him. He seemed to know who I was, and when I called him at his hotel, the name "Hanson" seemed to "register" easily! Dr. Knoles was very much impressed by the concert, and the crowd was very enthusiastic.

Financially, we came out quite well, I think. Most of the seats were sold, and I think that we came out about even. I certainly hope so, as I worked pretty hard for it. The next number comes on February 7th, May Peterson. I got her alright by pulling pretty hard, and I got her at my original figure too!

Just at present, my difficulty is getting a tenor for the "Messiah." Two have gone back on me already, and I hope that I can get one to stay "put" next time. They are certainly scarce articles around here.

I was walking over to school this morning with Dr. Knoles, and he told me that the plans and estimate on moving the school over on the Alameda have already been completed and submitted. He seemed to be quite pleased with prospects. I am very glad because I did not have any idea that they had gone that far already. It must be pretty definite, I guess.

School is going very nicely, but I will be glad to get a little rest. Four of us are "motoring" to San Francisco tomorrow with a man from Sherman Clay Co., and I will spend some time looking at pianos. Then we will go over to Jessie's and spend the rest of the vacation.

It is time to eat, so I will have to run.

San Jose, California, March 2, 1921

Am feeling very happy today because I received a formal notification from the Composers' Music Corporation of New York to the effect that my "Miniatures" had been accepted for publication and that they would send my contract immediately! They also asked me for a photo for advertising purposes. It seems awfully fine to know that I am really going to have a big firm handle my music.

Last night's recital was very good, and everyone did themselves proud. Miss Howells and Jessie both played beautifully, and Miss Rogers did very well. After the program Dennis' gave us all a little party, and we had some nice refreshments and talked until quite late. I got along nicely accompanying, though I didn't have much to do.

This evening, I have another strenuous time. I have chorus practice from 6:45 to 7:45, and then have to go downtown to attend that basketball dinner, which will probably last until the "wee sma' hours" again. This is certainly a strenuous life, and I rather feel the need of more sleep just at present.

Work on the "Mass" is going nicely, and tonight we will start some intensive rehearsing for the Blossom Festival. The big chorus will meet with us next Tuesday evening, and a week from that time we will meet with my orchestra in a final rehearsal. The concert will probably be given March 19th, if the blossoms are out by that time.

Have to eat a bit early this evening to stay off hunger until dinner after the rehearsal (!), so must hurry along.

San Jose, California, June 6, 1921

Just got out of a faculty committee meeting, which was as boring as usual. College faculties seem to be especially gifted along the line of talking for hours without getting anywhere.

I have been teaching today for several periods but have spent the majority of time in the office working on various matters which always come up at this time of year. I finished the Conservatory Bulletin at about 10 o'clock last night, and this morning I had a conference with the business manager, and he wants me to have some of it done another way to save money! He did the same thing last year, and he was very "apologetic" and nice about it, but that does not save me from any work, as a lot of it has to be done all over again.

Tonight, we have one of our two final orchestra rehearsals for the final commencement concert, which will be held two weeks from tonight. We have a bunch of Concertos to work up, and I feel that we will have a good strenuous rehearsal. We are playing two organ concertos, three piano concertos, and one violin concerto!

Tomorrow night my star pupil, Richard Waring, gives his program. I will try to remember to enclose an article which I had put in the Sunday paper about him. He is a very talented young man and plays beautifully. He is also a splendid musician and will make a real artist in a short time. I wish that you were here to hear him.

I got Popsie's dear letter and am so glad that you were so pleased with the success of my piece at the Symphony concert. I certainly wished that you were here at the time, but I hope that there will be just as good a performance of something of mine next year.

San Jose, California, November 3, 1921

You have received my startling telegram by this time, and it is surely as big a surprise to me as anyone. I read of the fact that the famous Prix de Rome had not been awarded regularly for this year because the jury of critics had not found any work submitted good enough, so just on a chance I sent the scores of my "Prelude and Ballet," "Before the Dawn," and

"Exaltation," and got a telegram saying that it was unanimously awarded and that I was appointed Fellow in Musical Composition in the American Academy in Rome for three years. It is about the biggest honor which can come to a young composer, and so I did not feel that I could afford to decline it. The conditions of the award are that I do nothing but compose for the period of my appointment. I am furnished with a room and studio in the Academy itself and stay there for six months each year. The remaining six months I spend touring Europe and visiting the musical centers of the Old World and meeting composers of other lands. The salary is only a thousand dollars a year plus traveling expenses, studio and room, making an equivalent of $2000. I do not have to pay for anything except meals, not even opera and symphony concerts, so that my thousand dollars will be practically clear. Then too, a thousand dollars in Italy at the present rate of exchange is worth about $5000, and you can live like a prince on it. I talked with a boy who was sent to Italy last year by winning an essay contest on Italy, and he told me that you can buy Italy for a thousand dollars a year! He said that he had been to a reception in the Academy where my studio will be, and he said that it is about the most beautiful building in all Rome. He said that it is up on the hill overlooking Rome and right above the Vatican where the Pope lives. He said that I would be "crazy" about it.

Of course, all the students here are thrilled to think that "their" teacher was awarded the honor, and Dr. Knoles said that if I would agree to go on a leave of absence, they would keep me Dean all the time while I was gone, and when I got back they will give me a position where I will have only a little teaching to do in addition to the Deanship, so that I can go on with my composition.

Now since I am appointed definitely, everybody is so blue that you can cut the atmosphere with a knife. I am happy to know that I will be missed so much, but it has made me feel pretty blue myself. Even some of the boys in my classes cried, I am told, when they found I am leaving. But everyone agrees that only a "crazy" man would turn down such an opportunity, because it will mean that I will be one of the few "recognized" composers of America, and I ought to have no trouble in getting my pieces played and published.

I will be allowed to visit America once during the three years, but I wonder if now isn't the proper time for you two to take that European trip. It will be a much easier matter living in Europe on American money than it would even here in California, because they say that every dollar is worth about four dollars in Italian money. I do hope that we can make it at least by next summer.

I am going to leave school right after the Festival, about the 15th or 16th, and will stay home as long as I can, as I won't have to leave until after the holidays. I do hope, Honies, that you won't feel hurt because I did not wire you before accepting. I intended to, but then I knew that you would tell me to use my own judgment, and it was so hard to wire all the details that I didn't do it. However, I understand that Leo Sowerby was also awarded a Fellowship of two years outside of the regular Prix de Rome award, and the two of us will represent America in composition—and he has such a big reputation already, having had his compositions played by almost every orchestra in America, that I felt that if he could afford to spend the time, I certainly could. I also feel that if I want to cut down the time I can, because I have a list of the things which I must write in three years, and I think I can write them in one year after the experience I have had in writing "under pressure."

Must mail this, so will close. Hope that you are both feeling just fine, Honies.

Venice, July 16, 1922

Am enclosing some more postcards of Florence. Did not get [to] the church of Santa Croce or San Mininato on the Hill. Both are very beautiful. They are early Renaissance and Romanesque, almost eastern.

I also went into the museum in the Polazzo [i.e. Palazzo] Vecchio and saw some famous statues by Donatello and then went over to the Academy of Fine Arts and saw the famous "David" of Michal Angelo [Michelangelo]; then to the church of San Lorenzo where we saw the inlaid marble chapel of the Medicis and Michal Angelo statues of Evening and Dawn, Night and Day on the tombs of William and Lorenzo de Medici (called Lorenzo the Magnificent). The chapels are marvelously rich. Meyers says, "waste of good marble."

The afternoon of Friday, Dr. Anderson and I went out to Fiesola up on the mountain, the mother City of Florence. We had a beautiful view of Florence and saw ruins of the old Etruscan wall. Before we had been up to the Piazzo [Piazza] of Michal Angelo on the other side of the city.

We left Florence Saturday at 2:45 and got to Venice at 12:30, 1/2 hours late. We met Bill O'Toole, Harvard University scholarship now in architecture to whom I had wired, and we are now settled here for a couple of days at his pension.

Will write more tomorrow.

Venice is the most picturesque city imaginable.

Milan, July 19, 1922

Am here in Milan now and will try to recount my adventures in Venice before I forget them. Got in late on the night of the 15th. It was the day before a big church festival and most of the city was drunk, it seemed. We took a "Vaporetto," a little steamboat up the canal, had something to eat, and went to bed. In the morning we strolled out to see the sights and saw the famous Cathedral of St. Mark, the lion of St. Mark, the Piazza, and etc. The Cathedral is strongly oriental in influence and looks like a great Mohomedan Mosque. It was built at the time of Venetian Supremacy when she had lots to do with the Orient.

In the afternoon we looked around at some of the other churches and heard afternoon Vespers in St. Mark's. The music was not very good. Church music in Italy seems to be at a very ebb and slipshod work.

On Monday morning we went to see the Doge's Palace next to the Cathedral. It contains some very good works of art, chief of which were some early masters and a couple of Titians. Of course, the rooms were the various historic ones, such as the "Council of Three," "Council of Ten," and etc. We also went down into the prison and on to the "Bridge of Sighs" between the Doge's Palace and the prison. In the afternoon we went to Santa Maria della Salute, a big church, which one of the architects, O'Toole, is measuring up. We helped him a little and, in the process, went clear to the very top of the Dome. Saw a fine Titian painting inside. Yesterday we visited the great big International Art Exhibition held in Venice. Eight buildings by artists of 8 nations. It was very interesting comparing the works of various countries. The Moselmistic stuff looked like junk to me, nothing but lines, squares, and etc. in terrible colors. The smaller countries, Hungary and Belgium, really showed up the best. The US was not represented, nor were the Scandinavian countries. Before this we had also seen the Academia Belli Arte [Accademia di Belli Arti], which contained hundreds of fine paintings, especially "The Presentation in the Temple" by Titian, which was fine. The big masterpiece, "The Assumption," has been taken back to the church of Frari, where it came from, but we did not like it as well as the first one after we hunted up the church to see it.

The evening of our last day in Venice we hired a Gondola and took a ride on the canal, stopping to hear the music of the minstrels on the barges. It was very picturesque, romantic, and very Venetian to sit in the Gondola to hear the music float over the waters to you.

The next morning we got up at the unromantic hour of 4:30, took a Gondola to the station, and caught a six o'clock train for Milan, getting there a little after 12.

We met Mr. and Mrs. True [in Venice], and the other two, mother and daughter, who had invited us to dinner in Rome, but we had little time to spend with them. However, on Mr. True's advice, we went to the top of the Campanile and had a fine view of the city and the hundred and more islands that comprise it. It is a very unique city with waterways for streets and each island honey-combed with narrow winding streets.

I bought mother some genuine Venetian glass beads which I will send as soon as I can get something to wrap them up in.

Hope you are feeling just fine.

Munich, August 4, 1922

I hoped to have written this a couple of days sooner but have been on the jump every minute. We left Lincoln [?], where I wrote my last letter, at 6 o'clock and went direct to Munich, where we had just enough time to go up to the Travel Bureau, where I had my mail forwarded, and back to the station for a hasty lunch and a train to Oberammagau. I had 22 letters waiting for me, among which were two from you which I certainly enjoyed.

We arrived in Oberammagau late in the afternoon and went directly to the hotel where we had reservations, a very nice place with good rooms and good food. The town is a small place about like Ceresco and situated in the hilly country which you find all over Bavaria. It evidently has plenty of rain, as the hills are covered with the greenest of beautiful verdure.

The play started at 8 o'clock and lasted until 6 o'clock, with two hours off for lunch. The wonderful part about it is the spirit in which it is done, as the whole spectacle is put on entirely by the people of the village, and it must take nearly the whole population. There is a chorus of about 40, an orchestra of 50, a tremendous number in the cast, and then people for soldiers, mob scenes, etc. I am sending pictures of it and the book with the entire play in it, so you can see for yourselves how it goes. The story begins from the time of Christ's entry into Jerusalem to his resurrection, and every individual scene is given. There is not a single pause anywhere, and the whole production is timed like clockwork. First the orchestra starts, and the chorus comes on the stage from either side and stands in a long single line across the stage. The Prologue then speaks his part, followed by the chief singer and the chorus who sing of what is to come. As they are singing, they step back and to the sides, and the curtain in the middle backstage goes up revealing a tableau. Sometimes there are two, each of which is preceded and accompanied by singing in the same way. The Tableaux are scenes from the Old Testament relating to the New Testament, and they were all very fine. Then after the tableaux, the action starts. Each character, both important and unimportant, is carefully portrayed, and the acting was very fine. Each act has many scenes, which go thru without wait, as the stage is so large that the action goes on in front and on both sides of the curtained stage, while it is being prepared for the following scene. The acting was without exception very good. The part of Christ was taken by Anton Lang, who has played it now for the third time. Judas was the finest of all, as he played his part with wonderful dramatic fire. The crucifixion was gruesomely realistic,

even to the blood spurting from the spear wound in Christ's side. The weakest point in the play was the music. The chief singer flatted a great deal of the time, but when you think that the whole crowd are amateurs from a little Bavarian village, it seems wonderful to think that they can do it as well as they do.

We reported at the police station and got the necessary permission to stay in Bavaria 14 days for a $1.00 fee and left the next morning for Munich. You can't help but admire the way the Bavarian do business as compared with some other countries I know. You would expect that tourists in Oberammagau would be "gouged" to the limit, but we were not. We paid exactly what the prices were supposed to be and nothing more. Arriving in Munich, I looked up a student whom I had met in Rome, and he directed us to a Pension very centrally located, where we got room and breakfast for 200 marks a day, about 30¢. As you can get a good meal for about 125 marks, our total expenses can be kept under $1 a day.

I immediately set work to get tickets for five Wagner operas which open the Wagner festival here: "Meistersingers," "Rhinegold," "Walkyrie," "Seigfried," and "Gotterdamerung" on the 1st, 3rd, 4th, 6th, and 8th of this month. I could not get one for the first and had a hard time getting one for all of the others, but I got them at last by tipping the ticket seller 250 marks for a returned ticket. On the night of the first day, we met Elizabeth Bates and a Miss Koch, a professor in Smith College, both of whom came up for some operas. I succeeded in getting tickets for them and for Mr. Myer by the same process, for which they were very grateful. We had company with them to both "Rhinegold" and "Walkyrie," and they leave tonight for Florence.

The "Rhinegold" began at 6 o'clock and lasted three hours without pause. The conductor was our old friend Karl Muck, who "resigned" from the Boston Symphony, was sent to prison, and finally asked to leave the country as an undesirable alien during the war. The orchestra was very good, the singers quite good, and the stage effects splendid. The Festival Theatre, called Prinz-Regenten Theatre, is small, holding about 18[00] or 1900 people. There is one floor and about 5 loges so that you can see nothing of it or the conductor, carrying out Wagner's wishes. The Theatre and the arrangement of the orchestra give a fine effect. However, as to production, you would hear a better production in either Chicago or New York. You would be surprised if you could hear an American production followed by a European—ours are considerably in advance. The "Walkyrie" was last night from 4 to 9 with two intermissions. They have a fine cafe in the theatre, where you can eat in the intermissions. We had dinner checks for the second intermission and sported around with the elite of Munich and America (more Americans than Germans). The two girls and I had loge seats, very swell. I am growing a small beard again, and everyone takes me for a German, and some Americans passed in front of our box and looked at the girls and Howard with his snappy little beard, and one of the girls in the party said in English, "the German Royal family." It tickled us considerably. Miss Koch says that she thinks someone took me for a young former Prince of the Bavarian family! The "Walkyrie" was much better than the "Rhinegold," better singing and less shouting. The first night some of the artists were quite uncertain as to pitch. Last night, they were very good. The stage effects were again fine.

Will write about the museums here next installment. They are fine, and I have seen a great deal of Rubens, Rembrandt, VanDyck, etc.

Must mail this right away.

Salzburg, August 12, 1922

Here is a new heading again. Got here Wednesday afternoon from Munich. Heard "Siegfried" on the 6th and "Gotterdammerung" on the 8th and left the next day. I didn't like "Siegfried" but liked Gotterdammerung better. It is funny but I guess I am outgrowing my Wagner fancy, because a tremendous amount of the "Ring" bored me. It sounds so mock-heroic with its stories of Gods and super-men and the music seems silo-dramatic [?]. Poor old Siegfried has to stand with his hand on the magic sword and wait what seems minutes before the music exhausts itself and gets to the point where he can actually pull it out.

Saw the two big painting galleries, Alte and New Penakotek [Pinakothek], the Glyptotek [Glyptothek] (sculpture) and a couple of modern exhibitions. The modern stuff is pretty wild like some we saw in Venice but there are some very good things too.

Munich I liked very much. It is on the beautiful Istar river and is very heavily equipped with trees, gardens and so forth. Am sending some postcards which show some good views.

Salzburg is packed with tourists, come for the big festival. I got thru the customs easily though. The financial condition is so bad (4500 crowns per dollar) that many of the hotels demand payment in American or other foreign money from foreigners. I arrived for the last day of the International Chamber Music Festival, a small affair very badly managed which gave only the most modern music. Sowerby represented us with his new Sonata, and it was far too old-fashioned for them. You should have heard the other stuff! Wow! Talk about the scrapping of cats—This was of the same quality. But the small elite and enlightened audience sat there and drank it all in as the "new gospel." I met a bunch of prominent musicians and received lots of attention as American's first "Prix de Rome" man. I don't belong with this crowd, though. They live in an atmosphere of perfume, long hair, and cigarette smoke. A breath of fresh air would blow them away.

The big Mozart Festival begins on Monday, and they will give four operas, Richard Strauss conducting. I will leave the night of the last performance and spend the next day in Vienna, and then go to Berlin where I will meet my Swedish friend Holmberg. Rudolf Ganz is here, and I have been with him some. He is delighted with my work. He said that he heard my Legend in Chicago, I showed him my Symphony, and he went thru it very carefully up to the second movement, and says it is beautifully written and that I seemed to be following a "new line" different from anyone else.

I find my German gets me along quite well. I am staying at the home of a doctor, as all the hotels are full. I stayed two days at a hotel, but the room was reserved from yesterday in advance. The town is packed, and the papers contain bitter articles about the "foreign invasion" and the Festival. The people are starving, and the hotel keepers are getting rich. I don't care much about the town for that reason. Physically it is a lovely place with the wooded foothills on two sides and the beautiful Munchsberg with the famous old Fortress on top. I went up to the fortress yesterday and looked around.

It rains here almost every day which is unpleasant, though it keeps the verdure very green and nice.

Enroute to Rothenburg, September 25, 1922

At last I am where I can breathe a little again. I should have written a week ago, but I was so deep in work that I could not collect my thoughts.

I think I wrote last from Mora, Sweden, where I stayed two days and had a wonderful time. The country around Lake Seligan [Siljan] is heavily wooded with pine-forests which are so typical dress, which they still wear in Mora, Rattvik [Ranvik], and Liksand [Leksand]. After two nights, I left Mora by boat on Lake Siljen [Siljan] down to Liksand where I spent another night. Liksand is a great summer resort for the Stockholmers especially, and there are plenty of good hotels. I stayed at the big summer hotel not far from the lake, very fine. From Liksand, I went to Upsala, where I spent another night. I took in much of the city, and the next day visited the University. There I met a Prof. Ekblom, who was very fine and took me over the whole University. I liked the University very much and thought the Cathedral very fine. From the fortress, I could see over to Gamla Upsala, to the old mounds of pagan times.

From Upsala I headed straight for Stockholm, where I put in four very strenuous days sightseeing in the daytime and working at night. There is a terrific lot to see in Stockholm. I went all over the old section by the old church where Gustavus Adolphus is buried, the old market place, King's Palace, etc., and across the famous Norebro [Norrbro]. It is certainly a beautiful city; then I went thru the National Art Gallery, but was a little disappointed as I did not see much modern work that I liked, except Zorn, who is a master certainly. The Nordiska Museet which contains all kinds of relics was wonderful. They have implements from the stone age up, rooms in all periods of Swedish history, robes of Kings, the clothes which Gustavus Adolphus wore when he fell at Lutzen, and even the stuffed skin of the horse he was riding. Then there were wonderful state coaches, suits of armor, weapons, etc., in fact everything you can imagine. But the most interesting of all is Sansen [Skansen]—the outdoor museum. There they have 70 acres fitted up with old houses preserved intact from the olden times—a camp from Lapland, log cabins from Dalarna, and in fact from all over Sweden fitted out just as they were when they were in use. Then there were all kinds of animals native to Sweden, bears, deer, beavers, seals, birds, etc. The attendants all wore the national dress, and at certain times there is folk-dancing. I saw them dance on Sunday afternoon to the accompaniment of the old Spelmannen, and it was great stuff. Those old dance tunes certainly do get into your blood. It will be a shame if they ever die out.

On Sunday evening, I went to the Royal Opera—a wonderful building and very good opera. They gave "Pagliacci" and Rimsky-Korsakoff's ballet "Scherherezade." The Swedish singers were fine, but they had a guest artist, a noted Russian, who sang like the dickens, terrible! The ballet was splendid.

Attended church Sunday morning in the old Stora Kyrka [Storkyrka] and heard a great service with a fine organ and organist. On Monday night, I left for Berlin and on the way over met a young Swede who was going to Vienna to study violin, so we spent the time together very interestingly. I saw him several times in Berlin and had him out to dinner with me.

In Stockholm I received two cables asking for scores and parts which I finished and mailed before leaving Stockholm. Then in Berlin I found a letter from Lamond, asking me to come to London.

In Berlin I spent four days trying to get some of the work out of the way and am getting along quite well. I left yesterday and spent the night in the quaint old town of Nurenburg, where I saw the famous Nurenburg clock in the old Frauen Kirke, and some other interesting churches and buildings. Am now going to pay a short visit to the old medieval town of Rothenburg, which people say is almost exactly as it was in the days "when Knights were bold." Then I must get on my way down the Rhine and to London.

My experience in Sweden was wonderful, and I found out that I am a good Norsk. They are a wonderfully fine race. I don't understand why their art isn't better, but I think it is because they are undemonstrative and more introspective, and a bit self-conscious. They are just the opposite of the Italians, who are absolutely free in self-expression.

London, October 10, 1922

Have had a very busy week in Leeds. Attended the rehearsals Monday and then three programs a day from Wednesday to Saturday. The programs included many new British works which were very interesting. I was very much impressed by the Choral Ode of Gustav Holst, the same man who wrote the gigantic suite called the "Planets." I find that he is English but of Swedish origins.

The chorus sang magnificently and the orchestra, "London Symphony," was good, but the soloists were nothing to boast of. Albert Coates was the orchestral director, and I saw him several times. Sir Hugh Allen was the choral director.

I spent one night in a hotel and then was fortunate in getting into a private home with Thompson and Sowerby, where things were very homelike. As Leeds is the center of the great wool industry, I took advantage of it and had a nice Tuxedo suit tailor-made for about $40 dollars.

I am very impressed with modern British composition. A great many of the young men are doing excellent work. England is giving them a chance, too.

Leaving Leeds, which is a dirty city like Pittsburgh, Mr. Lammond and I took a car to York to see the great Cathedral. It is the third in size in the world and very impressive. We heard a short service and then walked around the old city, which is very impressive in its almost medieval character. There are many old churches there and a guild hall which dates back from the 13th century or so.

I went into the more residential part of London and spent one night in the Barkston Gordon Hotel, which is a very fine place. Then yesterday morning I found a good boarding house where I can live for 3 guineas a week, about $14.25, which is not so bad.

Yesterday we had two engagements. We were invited to lunch at the Royal College of Music with Sir Hugh Allen, the Director. We had a fine talk with the old man, who was very much interested in us. We also met two rather well-known British composers, Howells and Armstrong Giggs.

In the afternoon we had tea at the home of Percy Scholes, one of the London critics, where we met some other newspaper men and also the composer Arnold Bax, who is one of the best known of the young Britishers. He played something of his with the assistance of a young lady, Miss Cohen. It was an excellent piece of work.

I forgot to say that when I was in Leeds I met quite by chance a very wealthy patron of music, Mr. Fulford, who lives in Headingly Castle. He invited me out to his home, which is really a castle, for lunch, and I had a very pleasant time. He has invited me to visit him again when I return to England. He also introduced me to the famous Dr. A. Eaglefield Hull, one of whose text books I have used at the College. He said when I was introduced to him, "I have been noticing you. I thought you must be some distinguished man."

Coates was very pleasant and seemed interested in having me there.

At Mr. Lammond's suggestion, I wrote a letter to the Festival authorities, commending their production of native works. It made quite a hit and was published in the papers, and I heard about it yesterday here in London.

I finally saw Ernest. He came up to Leeds to see me and stayed for one concert, which was very nice of him. He also went to tea with me at Scholes yesterday, and I will see him again tomorrow.

London is big, gloomy and disagreeable. I may not stay here long but go back to Rome.

INDEX

Adams, Sherman, 217, 217n5
Adler, Clarence, 38, 38n6
Adler, Samuel, 219, 219n10
Air Force Academy, 283
Air Force Glee Club, 283
Aldrich, Richard, 65, 65n1
Allen, George, 201, 201n1
Allen, Hamilton, 222, 271
Allen, Warren, 2, 50 50n1, 55
Allesandro, Victor, 165, 165n1
Amateis, Edmund, 71, 71n18
American Academy in Rome, 3, 13, 47, 24, 65, 67–69, 67n9, 68, 69n12, 69n14, 72n24, 115, 131, 147–50, 187, 313; Villa Aurelia, 66
American Acoustical Society, 231
American Conservatory in Chicago, 38
American Federation of Musicians, 201, 275
American Federation of Radio and Television Artists, 295
American Guild of Musical Artists, 295
American Institute of Applied Musical Arts, 106
American Musicological Society, 198
American Opera Company, 103n1, 119n8, 178
American Society of Composers, Authors, and Publishers (ASCAP), 212; ASCAP Festival at Golden Gate International Exposition, 212; creation of, 213; music strike 214
Anderson, C.W., 22, 22n7, 286
Angelo, Louis d', 161, 161n2

Anglin, Margaret, 13, 13n2
Ann Arbor May Festival, 144
Appledorn, Mary Jeanne van, 225, 225n1, 284
Arlen, Harold, 213
Ashcock, Arthur, 238
Association of Piano Manufacturers, 198
Augusteo Orchestra, 4, 70, 76, 76n1, 79–80, 79n4, 149, 158
Autori, Franco, 192–93, 192n12, 285

Bacon, Ernst, 176, 176n4
Balaban, Emanuel, 129, 129n13
Bales, Richard, 228, 228n5
Ball, Raymond N., 91
Ball State University, 284
Bampton, Rose, 160, 160n6, 163
Barber, Samuel, 130, 160, 218
Barlow, Howard, 210, 210n1
Barrere, Georges, 189, 189n8
Barromeo, Chase, 160
Bauer, Harold, 38, 38n9
Bax, Arnold, 86, 322
Beach, Mrs. H.H.A., 140
Beadle, George Wells, 21, 21n4
Beecher, Carl M., 2, 45, 45n2
Bell, Archie, 144, 144n1
Benjamin, Edward, 130–31, 282
Bergsma, William, 8, 131, 226–27, 226n3
Berlin, 83, 100, 147, 154–56, 320–21. *See also* Eastman Philharmonia Tour
Berlin Hochschule für Musik, 154
Berlin Philharmonic. *See* Hanson, Howard
Berlin, Irving, 213–14

Bernsdorf, Professor von, 46
Bernstein, Leonard, 123n7, 218, 236, 286
Bestor, Arthur, 188
Bidault, Georges-Augustin, 202, 202n11
Biracree, Thelma, 129, 129n12
Bliss, Arthur, 86
Bloch, Ernest, 123, 123n12
Bodanzky, Artur, 159, 159n1
Bok, Mary Louise Curtis, 194, 194n1
Bold Island, 12–14, 16, 191, 216, 282–83
Borowski, Felix, 105
Boston Symphony Orchestra, 6–9, 19n3, 23–24, 23n12, 58, 113, 117, 121n2, 138, 144–46, 192, 192n11, 211–12, 211n2, 282, 317
Boucher, Gene, 141, 141n6
Bradley, Kenneth, 105
Brazier, Emma Jeannette, 36, 41–42
Brown, DeMarcus, 55, 51n1
Bruce, David, 202, 202n12
Brussels Exposition, 236
Bryan, William Jennings, 1, 32–34, 32n8–9
Buck, Gene, 214, 214n8
Buffalo Philharmonic, 192, 192n12
Burge, David, 280, 280n1
Burke, Harold, 192
Busch, Carl, 22, 22n9
Bush-Temple Conservatory of Chicago, 105–6
Butler, Harold, 106–7

Canadian Broadcasting Orchestra, 237
Carl Fischer Company, 62, 134
Carl Schurz Foundation, 153
Carpenter, John Alden, 65, 65n3, 129
Carter, Artie Mason, 122, 122n5
Carter, Elliot, 286
Casals, Pablo, 218, 218n7

Casella, Alfredo, 79–80, 79n7, 80n10, 119
Castle, Joyce, 165, 165n14
Castelnuovo-Tedesco, Mario, 79, 79n8
Cecere, Gaetano, 71, 71n17
Celentano, John, 129, 129n11
Centennial Commission, State of Nebraska, 285
Chadwick, George Whitefield, 57n7, 105, 128–29, 135
Chaliapin, Feodor, 42, 42n19, 159
Chautauqua; Chautauqua Institution, 188; Chautauqua Summer School, 37; Chautauqua Symphony, 188, 192–93; Circuit, Lake Chautauqua, 187, 187n1, 190–91; Redpath Chautauqua Circuit, 21, 31, 44
Chicago Musical College, 38, 60n12, 106, 164n8
Chicago Symphony Orchestra, 6, 28, 41n15, 48–50, 50n2, 143, 160
Chilman, James, 72, 72n26
Chittenden, Kate, 106
Ciampaglia, Carl, 72, 72m23
Cincinnati Conservatory, 38, 38n7, 105, 164n8
Clark, Janet, 206
Clark, William Andrews, 58, 58n9
Clarke, Rebecca, 140, 140n3, 189
Cleveland Symphony Orchestra, 23n13, 143, 192, 200
Coates, Albert, 3, 81, 81n11, 88, 91, 120, 125, 134, 188, 321
Cohan, George M., 213–14
College of the Pacific, 2, 4–5, 8, 49–52, 51n2, 54–56, 225, 305; Conservatory of Fine Arts, 52, 55
College of Wooster, 222, 222n2
Columbia Broadcasting System [CBS], 210
Columbia Records, 8, 137
Columbia School of Music of Chicago, 106

Index

Columbia University, 1, 36, 57n7, 67n9, 141n7, 176n5, 186, 186n6, 224, 228n7, 234
Concertgebouw Orchestra, 138n6, 211, 211n2
Condie, Richard P., 283, 283n5
Coolidge, Elizabeth Shurtleff [Sprague], 5, 85, 85n3, 139–41
Coolidge Festival, 85, 92. *See also* Library of Congress
Coombs, Gilbert, 106
Coombs Broadstreet Conservatory, 106
Copland, Aaron, 125–26, 130, 200, 210, 218, 278, 278n5, 286
Corona, Leonora, 160, 160n5
Cortot, Alfred, 192n13, 278, 278n8
Costello, William P., 88
Cowles, Frederick, 106
Crawford, Sam, 22, 22n6, 51, 286
Creegan, Mary Louise, 34, 34n10
Cummins, Anne Theodora, 104
Curtis Institute of Music, 30n2, 38–39, 41n18, 69n13, 106, 123n7, 163n6, 194, 194n1, 203n13, 213n6, 276, 276n2, 285n8

Dallas Symphony, 193, 193n15
Dallin, Leon, 228, 228n9
Damrosch, Frank, 36–37, 36n2, 37, 40, 42, 105, 299
Damrosch, Walter, 3, 60, 65, 65n2, 88, 106, 112, 132, 147–48, 188
deKiewiet, Cornelis Willem, 207–9, 209n4
deKiewiet, Lucea, 209
DeMille, Cecil B., 13, 13n4
Denison University, 110
Dennis, Charles M., 66
DePalma, Gino, 238
Dohnanyi, Ernst von, 278–79, 278n9
Donato, Anthony, 22, 22n8, 131
Dorais, Gene, 63
Downes, Olin, 125, 125n3, 158, 162

DuBridge, Lee, 206
Dulles, John Foster, 220, 220n11
Duncan, Barbara, 305
Dunham, Frank [Franklin], 111, 198
Dunn, Frederick Sherwood, 201, 201n8

Eastman, George, 3, 4, 44, 81, 88–21, 89n2–3, 101–3, 103n3, 108, 108n2, 114–17, 116n2, 124–25, 178–80, 182–85, 185n5, 205, 209
Eastman Philharmonia Tour; Aleppo, 257–58; Alexandria, 258, 260, 260n5; Amsterdam, 274, 274n3; Ankara, 260; Athens, 253–54; Barcelona, 247–48; Beirut, 258–60; Berlin, 263–64, 263n1, 267; Brussels, 252; Cairo, 258–61; Carnegie Hall concert, 16, 147, 189n5, 212, 275, 275n5–6; Chernovtsky, 268–69; Eastman Theatre concert, 275; Fribourg, 248–49; 252–53; Geneva, 249; Gothenburg 252–53; Hanover, 263–64; Istanbul, 260–63, 261n8; Izmir, 260–61; Kiev, 267, 272–73; Kishinev, 267, 269; Kraków, 265; Leningrad, 236, 267, 272–73, 275; Lisbon, 238, 238n5, 247; Lodz, 265; Louvain, 252–53; Luxembourg, 249–51; Lvov, 268–70, 273; Madrid, 238, 247, 254; Moscow, 236, 267–68, 270, 274; Münster, 264–65; Nicosia, 255, 257, 260; Odessa, 268–69; Paris, 247, 249; Poznán, 265; Rennes, 249; Rome, 264, 264n2; Seville, 247–48; Stockholm, 252–53; Sweden, 252; University of Uppsala, 252–53; Warsaw, 262, 265–66; Zagreb, 261
Eastman-Rochester Symphony, 35, 228

Eastman School of Music; 3–5, 7–11, 27, 27n2–3, 29, 30n4, 39n12, 56, 70n15, 84n2, 89–91, 103n3, 108, 113n8, 115, 126–29, 126–29, 126n4, 127n5, 128n6–7, 129n10–15, 132, 150n1, 165n10, 165n14, 180n10, 182, 184, 191n10, 193n15, 205, 205n1, 209n2, 213n5, 219n10, 228n7–8, 280n1, 296; academic faculty, 104, 208; American Composers' Concerts, 5, 125–28; 134–35, 184; annex, 129n12, 204; Bachelor of Music degree, 2, 4, 45n2, 56, 103; board of managers, 204, 207, 209; Cutler Union, 209, 209n2; Doctor of Musical Arts degree; 9, 185–86, 185n5; dormitories, 43, 62, 113, 204, 207, 209; Eastman Philharmonia, 9–12, 217, 236, 264, 275, 275n5; *See also* Eastman Philharmonia Tour; Eastman Quartet, 86,140; Festival of American Music, 2, 5, 10, 56–57, 128, 212–13; Kilbourn Hall, 204; Opera Department, 102–103, 108, 129n15, 175–78, 175n1, 187; preparatory department, 108, 108n1, 179; radio broadcasts, 5; recordings, 7–8, 10, 133, 137–38, 216, 228, 296; Sibley Music Library; 205

Eastman Theatre, 102–3, 108n2, 116, 116n4, 125, 129n12, 140 n3, 151, 176, 181, 204, 217, 275, 277, 296; annex, 129n12, 204; orchestra, 296

Ebner, Edouard, 258

Eckstrom, Carl Magnus, 12, 66

Eckstrom, Edward, 13

Eckstrom, Hanna, 12

Eckstrom, Hilda Amanda Christina, 12

Eckstrom, Per, 12

Eckstrom, Richard, 13

Egbert, W. Grant, 106

Eisenhart, M. Herbert, 204, 207

Eisenhower, Dwight D., 200n3, 215–18, 217n5, 220n11, 283

Eisenhower, Milton, 200, 200n3

Elgar, Edward, 65n3, 86

Elman, Mischa, 219, 219n8

Elwell, George Herbert, 70, 70n15, 130, 153

Faelton, Karl, 106

Fargo, Milford, 129, 129n10

Fennell, Frederick, 136, 238, 254, 254n2, 256, 259–60, 273–75, 281

Fiedler, Arthur, 217, 217n6

Firkusny, Rudolph, 8, 192, 192n13, 212

First Methodist Church (Cleveland), 143

Fitch, Theodore, 150, 150n1

Flagler, Henry Harkness, 121, 121n3

Flatow, Carlotta, 258

Flexner, Abraham, 183

Frank, Glenn, 32–34, 32n5, 45

Friskin, James, 1, 3, 7, 37–38, 37n5, 189, 301

Friskin, Rebecca. *See* Clarke, Rebecca

Frothingham, Marion Brooks, 13, 303

Furtwangler, Wilhelm, 48, 48n6, 138, 154, 289

Gabrilowitsch, Ossip, 112, 112n5

Galli, Rosina, 161

Ganz, Rudolph, 60, 60n12, 62, 121, 151, 188, 319

Gardner, Samuel, 41, 41n17, 131

Garfield, James A., 34n11

Garland, Judy, 213

Gatti-Cassaza, Giulio, 138, 138n8, 159, 161–62, 164–66

Genhart, Herman, 129, 129n9
George, Grace, 13, 13n1
Giddings, Thaddeus, 111, 111n5
Gilbert, Donald, 207
Gilchrist, Ora, 286
Gilman, Lawrence, 119, 119n7, 158, 164
Gleason, Harold, 90, 115, 133
Glenville High School, 143
Goetschius, Percy, 1, 37–39, 37n4, 57n7, 76, 299, 302–4
Golschman, Vladimir, 189, 189n3
Goossens, Eugene, 81, 112, 112n7, 121, 123, 162, 175, 177–79, 188
Gordon, Jacques, 41, 41n15, 160
Graham, Martha, 175, 175n3
Grainger, Percy, 62, 62n13
Graveure, Louis, 59, 59n10
Gruenberg, Louis, 130, 164, 210
Gustavson, Reuben G., 223
Gustavus Adolphus College, 219

Hafner, Victor, 74
Hageman, Richard, 213, 213n6
Haggerty, James (Jim), 217, 217n5
Hale, Philip, 144–45
Handy, W.H., 213
Hanson, Hanna, 12
Hanson, Hans, 1, 12
Hanson, Howard: advisory music panel of Department of State, 235; American Philosophical Society, 224, 233; "And the desert shall blossom as the rose," 284; "The Bell," 32; *Before the Dawn*, 2–3, 58n8, 64, 66, 312; *Bold Island Suite*, 283; chairman, Chopin Centennial Committee in the United States, 203; chairman NASM commission of curriculum, 4; chairman NASM graduate commission, 107; *Chorale and Alleluia*, 281; *Clog Dance*, 62; *Concerto da Camera*, 139, 187, 280; conducts Berlin Philharmonic, 7, 147, 153–54; conducts Gewandhaus Orchestra, 155; Ditson Award, 8, 224, 224n6; editor-in-chief Scribner Music, 231; *Elegy for my Friend, Serge Koussevitzky*, 117, 282; *Exaltation*, 56, 313; Fantasia in A Minor, 1, 19; *Fantasy Variations on a Theme of Youth*, 280; "Forest Play," 2–3, 60–62, 64; *Four Psalms for baritone, solo cello, and orchestra*, 141, 284; *The Harmonic Materials of Modern Music*, 10, 229; *Heroic Elegy*, 117, 143; Huntington-Hartford Award, 224; *How Excellent Thy Name*, 281; "Lament for Beowulf," 5, 16, 84–85, 91, 117, 143; Louis Elson lectures, 232, 232n3; *Lux Aeterna*, 84–85, 91, 120–21, 211; member of U.S. delegation to the International Conference of UNESCO, 200; *March Carillon*, 280; *Merry Mount*, 6, 43, 143, 153, 157–67, 181; *Mosaics*, 282, 282n4; *The Mystic Trumpeter*, 286–87; National Institute of Arts and Letters, 8, 130, 224; *North and West*, 3–4, 83, 87, 117, 148; *Now Finale to the Shore*, 287; overtone analyzer, 2, 16, 51; *Pan and the Priest*, 6, 117, 120–21, 163, 188; *Pastorale for oboe, harp, and strings*, 203; piano concerto (first movement), 47; Piano Concerto, 8, 212, 270; *Portals*, 287; president of United States National Commission for UNESCO, 198; Pulitzer Prize, 4, 40, 223–24; Quintet for Piano and Strings, 2, 47, 86, 139; Quintet for String Quartet and Solo Viola, 141; Royal Academy of Music of Sweden, 224, 252; *Serenade for Flute, Harp, and*

Hanson, Howard (*continued*)
Strings, 8, 191–92; setting of Psalm 121 and Psalm 150, 284; *Song of Democracy,* 9, 282–84; *Song of Human Rights,* 284; *Songs from Drum Taps,* 287; *Streams in the Desert,* 225, 285n7, String Quartet, 85–86, 91, 139; *Summer Seascape,* 282–83; Symphonic Prelude in C Minor, 48, 305–6; *Symphony of Freedom* [arr.], 200; Symphony No.1 (*Nordic*), 4, 6, 49, 68–69, 76, 83, 121, 135–36, 144–45, 193, 211, 280; Symphony No.2 (*Romantic*), 6, 10, 113, 117, 135, 145, 147, 150, 153, 210, 267; Symphony No.3, 200, 210–12; Symphony No.4, 7, 39; Symphony No.5 (*Sinfonia Sacra*), 9, 281; Symphony No.6, 10, 281, 286; *The Untold Want,* 287

Hanson, Margaret Elizabeth Nelson, 8, 190–92, 209, 218–19, 238, 249, 251, 254–56, 264, 268, 273, 284–85

Hargrave, Robert, 284

Hargrave, Thomas, 182

Harris, Roy, 126, 130, 210, 218, 278, 286

Hartshorn, William, 196

Harvard University, 27n2, 65, 65n3–4, 69, 69n13, 72, 107, 185, 232–33, 314

Harvill, Richard A., 222

Hattstaedt, John R., 106

Hawthorne, Nathaniel, 6, 157; *The Maypole of Merrymount,* 6, 157–58

Heifetz, Benar, 141, 141n5

Heifetz, Jascha, 79n8, 141, 277, 277n3

Heller, Anatole, 247, 258, 274n7

Hendel, Walter, 10, 123, 193, 193n15, 268

Henderson, William James, 38, 38n10, 65, 65n5, 87–88

Herbert, Victor, 129, 213

Hertz, Alfred, 56, 56n4, 58–60, 121

Higginson, Henry Lee, 121, 121n2

Hild, Oscar, 201

Hitler, Adolph, 69n11, 156, 279n10

Hochschule für Musik [Berlin], 100, 154, 264

Hofmann, Josef, 276, 276n2, 277

Holland, Kenneth, 202

Holland, Mary [Mrs. Kenneth], 202

Hollywood Bowl, 6, 122, 122n5, 195, 213n6, 226

Holst, Gustav, 81, 81n11, 86, 321

Hoover, Herbert (Jr.), 252

Hopkins, Mark, 34, 34n11, 200

Horgan, Paul, 176, 176n7

Horner, Charles F., 44

Howard University Chorus, 9, 283–84

Hughes, Edwin, 38, 38n8, 198

Hunsberger, Donald, 129, 129n8

Hutcheson, Ernest, 189, 189n11

Hutchison, Charles F., 204

Institute of Musical Art [New York]. *See* Juilliard School of Music

Institute of Musical Art [Rochester], 89

Interlochen, 6, 11, 109n3, 111, 113, 132, 145

Ishikawa, Giichi, 51, 309

Ithaca Conservatory, 106

Iturbi, José, 188, 188n2, 195, 294

Jacobson, Sascha, 41, 41n16

Jagel, Frederick, 160, 160n4, 163

Jones, Griffith J., 143

Johnson, Edward, 161, 165, 165n9

Johnson, Lyndon B., 201n9, 216, 218–19

Jones, Archie, 287

Jones, Donald, 257

Juilliard Quartet, 86, 140

Juilliard School of Music, 36–38, 40n14, 41n16, 139n1, 176n5,

184n3, 187, 189, 189n5, 189n7–8, 192n13, 223, 226–27, 236; Institute of Musical Art, 1, 36; Juilliard Orchestra, 189, 236

Kalas, Jan, 50, 50n2
Kahn, Otto, 157–58
Kansas City–Horner Conservatory, 22n9, 44
Kansas City Philharmonic Orchestra, 22, 45
Kapell, William, 189, 189n6
Kaun, Bernard, 176, 176n6
Kéfer, Paul, 87
Kelly, George, 50n3
Kennedy, John F., 216
Kincaid, William, 41, 41n18, 192
King Victor Emanuel, 66, 77
Kinkeldey, Otto, 186, 186n7, 233
Klingenberg, Alf, 89, 89n1–2
Kneisel Quartet, 38, 38n6, 189
Knoles, Tully, 66, 76
Konraty, Nicholas, 129, 129n14
Kosciuszko Foundation, 203, 203n14
Koussevitzky, Serge, 6–9, 19n3, 24, 49, 138, 144–49, 188, 192, 194, 196, 210–12, 231, 282, 289, 294; Koussevitzky Foundation, 9, 282
Kreisler, Fritz, 276, 276n1
Kubik, Gail, 131, 184, 184n2

Lamond, Felix, 67, 67n9, 69, 76–77, 91, 114, 321
LaGuardia, Fiorello, 212, 212n3–4
LaMontaine, John, 8, 131, 184, 184n4
Lang, Paul Henry, 186, 186n6
Larson, Arthur, 226
Lascari, Salvatore, 71, 71n21
Laurent, Georges, 8, 192, 192n11
LaViolette, Wesley, 57, 57n6, 63, 130
Lawler, Vanett, 282
Lawrence, Gilman, 119, 119n7, 158, 162

Lawson, Adele, 31
Lawson, Werner, 283
Leacock, Stephen Butler, 51, 51n4
Leichtentritt, Hugo, 153
Leinsdorf, Erich, 23, 23n12, 218, 294–95
Leoffler, Charles Martin, 129, 140, 145
Levine, Joseph, 285, 285n8
Library of Congress, 35n1, 110, 110n4, 154, 199; concerts, 5, 85, 91, 139, 141
Lieurance, Thurlow, 44, 44n1
Lipson, Jacques, 238
List, Eugene, 215, 215n1
Ljungberg, Goeta, 161, 161n
Los Angeles Philharmonic, 2, 30n3, 56–60, 56n3, 121, 122n5, 195–97
Louisville Conservatory, 106
Lowe, Liela, 31
Lowry, Howard, 222n2
Lowens, Irving, 35, 35n1
Loy, Myra, 201, 201n6
Ludgin, Chester, 165, 165n11
Luening, Otto, 130, 176, 176n5, 228n7
Luther College, 1, 21, 31
Lutkin, Peter Christian, 47–48, 47n3, 57, 76, 304

MacDonald, Dolly, 31
Maddy, Joseph E., 109, 109n3, 111–13, 280
Makarios, Archbishop, 255–56, 255n4
Malipiero, Gian Francesco, 79, 79n7, 88, 203
Malone, Eileen, 191, 191n10
Mamoulian, Rouben, 175, 175n2
Mansfield, Mike [Michael], 201, 201n4
Manship, Paul, 71, 71n20
Marceau, Henri, 72, 72n25
Mariano, Joseph, 191
McArthur, Edwin, 213, 213n5

McCanne, W. Roy, 204
McCloskey, Madame, 32
McCormack, John 141–42, 141n8
McCue, Olive, 129, 129n12
McHose, Allen Irvine, 27, 27n3, 105
McKay [family], 84, 195
McKay, George, 125
McPhail Conservatory of Music, 106, 111n5
McPhail, William, 106
Mear, Sidney, 127, 127n5
Mengelberg, Willem, 118, 138, 138n6, 188, 194
Mennin, Peter, 8, 131, 226, 226–27, 226n2
Mercury Records, 8, 137, 191
Merrill, Robert, 189
Metropolitan Opera, 6, 16, 23n12, 36n13, 138n7–8, 141, 141n6, 153, 157, 159–61, 159n1–2, 160n4–6, 161n1, 161n3–4, 163–67, 163n5–6, 164n5–6, 165n9, 165n12, 178, 203, 214n6, 291–92
Meyer, Alvin, 71–72, 71n16
Miller, Frank, 110
Miquelle, Georges, 30, 30n5, 129, 189
Mischakoff, Mischa, 189, 189n9, 193
Mitchell, Howard, 216, 216n4, 283
Molinari, Bernardino, 79–80, 79n4, 150–52
Monteux, Pierre, 211, 211n2
Montgomery, Mimi, 64
Moore, Earl, 105, 159
Mormon Tabernacle Choir, 283, 283n5
Mosley, Carlos, 286
Moullet, Jules, 69
Murphy, Edward, 191
Music Educators' National Conference, 66
Music Teachers National Association, 2, 151

Musical Art Quartet, 141
Musicians' Union, 60, 98, 201, 295–96
Mussolini, Benito, 79–80, 79n5, 91, 152

Nassar, Gamal Abdel, 257n1, 258n2
National Association of Schools of Music, 4, 105–6, 184, 199, 121
National Broadcasting Company [NBC], 65n2, 132, 162, 184
National Federation of Music Clubs, 131, 198
National High School Orchestra, 6, 109–11, 235
National Symphony Orchestra (Washington), 9, 215–16, 216n4, 237, 283–84
NBC Symphony, 8, 189–90, 189n9, 195
Nebraska Wesleyan University, 223
Nehru, Jawaharlal, 220
Nelson, Mr. and Mrs. John Evon, 190
Nelson, Margaret Elizabeth. *See* Hanson, Margaret Elizabeth Nelson
New England Conservatory of Music, 35, 105, 128, 232n3
New Orleans Symphony, 282
New York City Center Opera, 165–66
New York Herald Tribune, 67n2, 119n7, 125, 162
New York Philharmonic, 6–7, 30n3, 60n11, 121n3, 130–31, 138n6, 147, 188, 192–93, 192n12, 193n15, 195, 228, 235, 286
New York Symphony Orchestra, 3–4, 65, 65n2, 101n1, 120, 147, 188, 190n9
New York Theatre Guild, 178
New York Times, 38n10, 65, 65n4–5, 125, 125n3, 160, 162, 183
New York World's Fair, 212

Niebuhr, Reinhold, 201, 201n5
Nikisch, Arthur, 78, 78n2, 81n11, 155, 195, 289
Nixon, Richard, 283
Northwestern University, 2, 22, 22n8, 32–34, 32n5, 38, 45, 47, 47n3–4, 49, 51, 62–63, 66, 80, 100, 121–22, 222, 280

Ober, Julia, 198
Oberhoffer, Emma, 22, 22n10
Oberlin College, 70n15, 110, 226, 305
Oberlander Trust, 7, 153
O'Connell, Charles, 135–37, 137n4
Oldberg, Arne, 47–48, 47n4, 57, 304–5
Omaha Symphony, 285
Oncley, Paul, 228, 228n8
Ormandy, Eugene, 9, 23, 23n11, 133, 192, 194, 203, 218, 235, 259, 275, 281, 294, 297
Orquesta Nacional of Mexico, 237

Paderewski, Ignace Jan, 265, 265n7, 289
Page, Willis, 128
Palmgren, Selim, 102
Pan American Union; Second Inter-American Festival, 237
Paris, 22n10, 69–70, 69n12, 70, 79n6, 100, 190, 199, 200–201, 211n2, 219, 219n9, 278, 278n8. *See also* Eastman Philharmonia Tour
Patacchi, Val, 166, 166n15
Peabody Conservatory, 35n1, 38, 105, 226
Penny, George Barlow, 102
Perkins, Dexter, 262
Perkins, Francis D., 125
Persinger Quartet, 86, 139
Peterson, Albin, 21, 286
Petrillo, James Caesar, 201, 201n10, 296

Peyser, Herbert, 153, 153n1
Philadelphia [City of], 106, 118–19, 163–64, 192, 195, 223, 233, 274–75
Philadelphia All-High School Chorus, 283
Philadelphia Orchestra, 7–9, 23–24, 23n11, 41, 41n18, 133, 141n5, 189n9, 203, 203n13, 236, 259, 282–83, 285n8, 289, 292, 297
Piastro, Mishel, 60, 60n11
Piatigorsky, Gregor, 30, 30n2
Piston, Walter, 130, 210, 218, 267, 286
Pittsburgh Institute of Music, 106
Pratt, Waldo Selden, 22, 38, 38n11, 303
Prix de Rome, 3, 64–65, 68, 102, 130, 147–48, 312, 314, 319
Pulitzer Prize, 8, 39, 68n10, 127, 130–31, 176n7, 184, 184n2–4, 221n1, 223–24, 236n1

Rachmaninoff, Sergei, 73, 189, 193, 278, 278n7
Randolph Harold, 105
Ravel, Maurice, 80, 272
Read, Gardner, 131, 228
Read, Opie, 32–34, 32n6; *A Kentucky Colonel*, 33; *The New Mr. Howerson*, 33
Reiner, Fritz, 123, 123n7, 146, 188, 193n15
Respighi, Ottorino, 3, 66–67, 78–79, 78n3, 86, 147, 150, 152
Revelli, William, 236, 236n2
Rhees, Rush, 3–12, 89–91, 89n3, 102, 104, 108n2, 114–15, 124, 179, 181, 183–85, 185n6, 204–6, 208
Rhinehart, Mary Roberts, 13, 13n3
Richards, Don, 60
Riegger, Wallingford, 127, 130
Riker, Charles Cook, 104, 133

Robinson, Franklin W., 40–41, 40n13, 47, 302, 304
Rochester American Opera Company. *See* American Opera Company
Rochester Civic Music Association, 117, 238
Rochester Philharmonic Orchestra, 4, 7, 23n12, 81, 88–89, 112n7, 121, 125, 141, 151, 175, 177, 188n2, 196, 212, 238, 238n4
Rockefeller Brothers Report on the Performing Arts, 292
Rogers, W. Robert, 216
Roller, A. Clyde, 128, 128n7
Roosevelt, Franklin Delano, 45, 216
Rosenbery, Earl, 106
Rosenfeld, Paul, 65–66
Rosing, Vladimir, 102, 103n3, 175–78, 175n1
Rothwell, Walter Henry, 56–57, 56n3, 121, 123
Rome, 3–5, 47, 64–66, 68, 70–72, 72n27, 79–80, 79n6, 79n9, 84–86, 88, 91, 117, 120, 139, 148, 150–52, 157, 159n2, 175, 281, 288, 313, 316–17, 322. *See also* Eastman Philharmonia Tour
Rubinstein, Arthur, 203, 203n15, 289
Russell, Dallmyer, 106
Ruttenberg, Stanley, 201, 201n9
Rybner, Cornelius [Peter Martin Cornelius Rübner], 36, 36n12

Sabin, Stewart, 88
Saint Louis Symphony, 60n12, 121, 189
Samaroff, Olga, 189, 189n5–6, 215n1
San Antonio Symphony, 165, 165n10, 228
Sanborn, Pitts, 163, 163n7
San Francisco Symphony, 56, 56n4, 212

Santoliquido, Francesco, 79, 79n9
Sattler, Robert, 218, 238, 254–56
Schwarz, Frank, 72, 72n22
Schuman, William, 130, 223, 236, 236n1
Seaborg, Glenn T., 223, 223n4
Seaman, Julian, 160, 160n7
Searson, C.W., 35, 37
Seashore, Carl, 179; Seashore tests, 179–80, 180n10
Seaton, James Lawrence, 49, 54, 54n5, 56, 66, 305, 307
See, Arthur M., 117
Selhorst, Eugene, 216
Serafin, Tullio, 159, 159n2, 162
Sessions, Roger, 127, 286
Setti, Giulio, 161, 161n1
Shepherd, Artur, 128–29, 143
Shostakovich, Dmitri, 277, 277n4
Sibelius, Jean, 80, 86, 101, 101n2, 150, 195, 211, 290, 294–95
Sibley, Hiram W., 205
Silber, Sidney, 28
Sills, Beverly, 165, 165n12
Sinatra, Frank, 289
Sinding, Christian, 101
Skinner, Jack, 72–74
Slonimsky, Nicholas, 86, 119, 119n8, 176, 231
Smith, James Kellun, 172, 172n24
Smith, Melville, 27, 27n2, 105, 130, 179
Snell, Mabel, 34
Sokoloff, Nicolai, 121, 121n1
Sokoloff, Vladimir, 143
Sonneck, Oscar, 110, 110n4
Sousa, John Philip, 130, 213, 217–18, 252, 267, 281
Sowerby, Leo, 57, 68–69, 68n10, 76–77, 130, 135, 153, 314, 319, 321
Spaulding, Walter, 65
Spivacke, Harold, 141, 154–55, 198
Spofford, Grace, 106
Stagg, Alonzo, 49, 49n7

Stanford University [Leland Stanford University], 2, 50n2, 54–55, 59, 226
Stanton, Hazel, 179, 180n10
Steckleberg, William, 28
Stevens, Gorham P., 69, 69n12
Stevens, Lawrence, 71, 71n19, 75
Stevenson, Adlai, 284, 284n6
Still, William Grant, 130, 134–35, 153, 195, 210
Stillman-Kelly, Edgar, 128, 130
Stoessel, Albert, 130, 130n1, 187–89, 192
Stock, Frederick, 48–49, 48n5, 60, 109, 112, 121, 139, 143, 148, 188, 294
Stockholm, 320–21. *See also* Eastman Philharmonia Tour
Stokes, Richard, 6, 153, 157–58, 163
Stokowski, Leopold, 8, 189n5, 218, 294
Stone, Clement, 113, 113n9
Strauss, Richard, 36, 80–81, 102, 138, 144, 164, 279, 319
Street, William, 126, 126n4
Strickland, Harold A., 119, 163
Sturkow-Ryder, Madame, 62
Swarthart, Gladys, 162, 162n4
Sweden, 3, 12, 68, 83, 221, 224, 232, 319–21. *See also* Eastman Philharmonia Tour
Swingle Singers, 219, 219n9
Syracuse University, 106–7, 176
Szell, George, 23, 23n13, 218, 235, 282–84

Tabuteau, Marcel, 203, 203n13
Texas Technological College, 225, 225n1, 284
Thomas, John Charles, 160, 160n3
Thomas, Theodore, 48, 48n5
Thompson, Randall, 69, 69n13, 76, 91, 130, 153
Thompson, Raymond K., 204

Thomson, Virgil, 126, 130, 218
Tibbett, Lawrence, 138, 138n7, 162, 164
Tibbs, Ruth Northup, 27, 27n4
Tinlot, Gustav, 87
Todd, George, 115
Toscanini, Arturo, 6, 26, 26n1, 30n3, 42–43, 102, 118, 120, 146–47, 159, 159n1, 188, 190, 194, 196, 289, 294
Tovey, Donald Francis, 140, 140n2
Trampler, Walter, 141, 141n4
Trapper, Thomas, 38
Treash, Leonard, 129, 129n15, 165, 200
Tremaine, Charles Milton, 111–12
Truman, Harry S., 215, 215n
Tryon, Winthrop P., 125
Tulsa Philharmonic, 192–93, 192n12, 193n14, 285
Tuthill, Burnet Corwin, 106–7, 130

UNESCO, 198–200, 198n1, 202–3; International Music Council, 199
University of Arizona, 222, 222n3
University of Kansas City, 22n9, 45
University of Michigan, 6, 107, 109n3, 144, 236, 236n2
University of Missouri, 286
University of Nebraska, 28
University of Rochester, 3, 10, 12, 49, 88–89, 104n4, 115, 182–83, 183n1, 186, 204–5, 204n1, 207, 217, 262, 275; College of Arts and Science, 103, 205, 208, 209n2; endowment, 183; Glee Club, 284; Men's College, 104, 104n4, 206–7; School of Medicine and Dentistry, 183; River Campus, 206–9; Strong Memorial Hospital, 205; Women's College, 104, 206–7, 209

University of Southern California, 30n2, 66, 107, 197, 226
University of Washington, 227
University School of Music (Lincoln, Nebraska), 2, 25, 28–29
Ussachevsky, Vladimir, 228, 228n7

Valentine, Alan, 183–84, 205–8
Vardell, Charles, 39, 39n12, 135
Victor Company [RCA Victor], 135–37
Vincent, [Rev.] John Heyl, 187

Wahoo, Nebraska, 1, 12, 16–17, 21, 23, 26, 31, 36–37, 42, 45, 63, 74, 77, 83, 85, 87–88, 102, 285–86, 302
Wallenstein, Alfred, 30, 30n3
Waller, Judith, 111
Wallis, W. Allen, 109, 217–18
Walton, William, 86
Ward, Robert, 131, 184, 184n3
Waring, Fred, 216, 216n3, 312
Warner, Andrew Jackson, 88, 178, 179n9
Watson, James Sibley, 206
Watts, Wintter, 69–70, 69, n14
Wedge, George, 40, 40n14
Weed, Marion, 178
Weinrich, Carl, 141, 141n7
Wessel, Mark Ernest, 45n2
Westervelt, Louise, 106
WHAM, 5, 132, 191
Whipple, George, 206
White, Donald, 105
White, Paul, 128, 128n6, 130, 228
Wilder, Alec, 227, 227n4
Willard, John, 13n3
Willeke, Willem, 189, 189n4
Wilson, Raymond, 89, 108
Wister, Owen, 65, 65n6
Witherspoon, Herbert, 164–65, 164n8
Woodbury, Ward, 284
Worcester Festival, 143, 188

Yegudkin, Arcady, 87

Zanuck, Darryl, 22, 22n5, 286

www.ingramcontent.com/pod-product-compliance
Lightning Source LLC
Chambersburg PA
CBHW060940230426
43665CB00015B/2015